Principles for a Free Society

PRINCIPLES FOR A FREE SOCIETY

❖ ❖ ❖

Reconciling Individual Liberty
with the Common Good

WITHDRAWN

RICHARD A. EPSTEIN

PERSEUS BOOKS
Reading, Massachusetts

BMH 9484 - 3/1

ISBN 0-7382-0041-7

Library of Congress Catalog Card Number: 98-86404

Perseus Books is a member of the Perseus Books Group

Jacket design by Suzanne Heiser
Set in 11-point Minion by Vicki L. Hochstedler

123456789 -MA- 0201009998
First printing, July 1998

❖ ❖ ❖

For Eileen,
Again

CONTENTS

❖ ❖ ❖

PREFACE

❖ ❖ ❖

Over the past twenty years I have worked in the area of legal theory and have written a long set of essays that have sought to reconcile my instincts for liberty in the political realm with those toward utility in the theoretical realm. The essays involved followed a more or less systematic pattern, and I decided that it would be appropriate to bring them together within the framework of a single volume. As I began the process of compilation, however, the ambition for the project expanded. As a result, much—perhaps most—of the material in this volume is new. The discussion on social norms is largely original, as is the chapter on boundaries, and the chapter on common carriers is completely new. I have added large blocks of new material to all the other chapters, and have also extensively reorganized and revised the original material that remains. The appendix sets forth the list of essays from which material for these chapters has been drawn. The title, *Principles for a Free Society: Reconciling Individual Liberty with the Common Good*, suggests a systematic treatment, and it is a systematic treatment I have sought to provide.

Principles bears the heavy influence of the many people who have helped me with my work, both on this volume and before: Randy Barnett, Richard Craswell, David Currie, Robert Ellickson, Richard Helmholz, Daniel Klerman, Andrew Koppelman, Andrew Kull, Saul Levmore, Loren Lomasky, Ellen Paul, Randal Picker, Richard Posner, Stephen Schulhofer, Cass Sunstein, and Lloyd Weinrib have commented on my work; and while their spirited criticisms have not always persuaded me to mend my errant ways, they have forced me to rethink and refocus my arguments. I am also indebted to a set of capable research assistants who have helped me along the way: Chris Bowers, Jeffrey Greenblatt, Deborah Healy, Todd Molz, David Sommers, and L. Rex Sears (who reviewed the entire manuscript twice). As might be expected, bits and pieces of this work have been presented over the years in workshops held not only at the University of Chicago, but at the American Association of Law Schools, the American Law and Economics Association, the Social Philosophy Center, the Cato Institute, the Federalist Society, and at faculty workshops at Columbia, Fordham, Harvard, Southern California, Toronto, and Yale law schools. I also have another debt of thanks to my secretary, Katheryn Kepchar, for her usual patience in dealing with the manuscript preparation. Henning Gutmann, my original editor at Addison-Wesley, provided his wise but firm guidance on the overall shape of the project. Phoebe Hoss then worried the manuscript into its final form with her careful and thorough edit of the entire text; and my agents, Lynn Chu and Glen Hartley, steered the entire transaction through the corporate minefields when the Addison-Wesley trade book division was sold to Perseus Books.

Chicago
May 1998

INTRODUCTION

❖ ❖ ❖

Reinvigorating Laissez-Faire

Laissez-faire enjoys the dubious honor of having been refuted more frequently than any other legal or political theory. Justice Holmes did it in 1905
with a decisive utterance in his famous dissent in *Lochner v. New York*: "The
Fourteenth Amendment does not enact Mr. Herbert Spencer's Social
Statics."[1] Many other distinguished writers have condemned the theory as
representing the worst in greed or possessive individualism.[2] Nineteenth-
century critics of laissez-faire wrote as though "sticklers for absolute respect
for Liberty and Property" should favor the repeal of laws designed to guard
against fraud and monopoly.[3] In this century, laissez-faire has been accused
of inviting a social free-for-all from which the rich always have their way.
The late (and great) Professor Grant Gilmore has written, only half in jest:
"I suppose that laissez-faire economic theory comes down to something like
this: If we all do exactly as we please, no doubt everything will work out for
the best."[4] And further: "It seems apparent to the twentieth century mind, as
perhaps it did not to the nineteenth century, that a system in which everybody is invited to do his own thing, at whatever cost to his neighbor, must
work ultimately to the benefit of the rich and powerful, who are in a position to look after themselves, and to act, so to say, as their own self-
insurers."[5] Laissez-faire is said to reach these dreaded consequences because
of its misplaced devotion to "a 'pure' contract doctrine [that] is blind to
details of subject matter and person. It does not ask who buys and who sells,
and what is bought and sold."[6] More recently, lawyers, economists, and
political theorists have joined in the attack on laissez-faire: Cass Sunstein
has attacked the system for the intellectual and constitutional errors it

1

makes "by assuming that existing practice was prepolitical and natural—that is, that it was not itself a function of law, or subject to challenge from the standpoint of justice."[7] Professor G.A. Cohen has purported to demonstrate the theoretical incoherence of the principles of freedom, coercion and private property.[8] Just this year, Professor Barbara Fried[9] has revived interest in the work of the lawyer/economist Robert Hale, who in the first half of this century found illusory the intuitive distinction between freedom versus coercion on which laissez-faire (and indeed civilization) depends.[10] The attack on laissez-faire has also proceeded apace in the more popular literature. For his part Robert Kuttner berates the market "zealots" who defend laissez-faire in ignorance of the proper role for government in the operation of any complex society.[11] On both the legal and the economic fronts, the constant theme is that laissez-faire treats contestable propositions as though they were necessary and deductive truths from self-evident axioms about individual self-interest and private property. Starting from these false assumptions, its monochromatic theory propels itself along a preordained, self-destructive path.

To be sure, laissez-faire has had its staunch defenders, of whom Friedrich Hayek (who disliked the term)[12] and Milton Friedman[13] have been the most influential. Their invaluable contributions were published some time ago, and their defense of limited government, which had gained much public acceptance in the early 1980s, has met with stiff resistance during the 1990s. Although President Clinton has reassured us that the "era of big government is over," his brave words have proved little more than a cloak to conceal proposal after proposal to expand the role of government in employment, education, and health care, often with scant appreciation for the negative consequences likely to flow from the adoption of his recommendations.

I have spent most of my professional academic life defending the principles of limited government which have, since the rise of the New Deal in the 1930s, been honored, at best, more in the breach than in the observance. In this book, I try once again to reinvigorate the classical view of laissez-faire by attacking the negative characterizations of both its method and its principles. On the question of method, I hope to establish that the doctrine does not command respect out of some unthinking homage to some inflexible economic logic or to some outmoded, remote, or prepolitical principles of natural law. Laissez-faire is best understood not as an effort to glorify the individual at the expense of society, but as the embodiment of principles that, when consistently applied, will work to the advantage of all (or almost all) members of society simultaneously.

So reconceived, laissez-faire loses its deductive and dogmatic character, and reinvigorates itself with the more cautious, empirical outlook characteristic of its most sophisticated defenders. Individual liberty, private property, and free contract remain centerpieces of the basic system—but not as absolutes unthinkingly defended come hell or high water. On this point at least, the basic theory joins forces with its insistent critics by consciously identifying the principled limitations on private property and freedom of contract that advance the common good. The title of this book reflects those dual concerns. *Principles for a Free Society* captures sound principles capable of ordering a just society. The subtitle, referring to the reconciliation of individual liberty with the common good, is designed to show how best to resolve the central tensions that remain once the basic commitments are made. In working through these variations, this book supplements and continues the exposition of the world view I set out three years ago in *Simple Rules for a Complex World.*[14]

More concretely, my central mission here is to explain how a concern with the common good does not eviscerate the traditional protections otherwise provided to individual liberty and private property. The task is not easy, for the mixed associations of the term *common good* should send shudders down the spine of any champion of limited government. Just this phrase shamelessly propped up the totalitarian regimes that laid waste to both Germany and the Soviet Union. All too often the "common good" becomes a figleaf whereby mad dictators impose their will on their hapless subjects. So many innocent people have been snuffed out in its name that a defender of limited government should be allowed a moment of angst before proceeding.

Consider this noble proposition: "I want everyone to keep the property he has acquired for himself according to the principle: common good takes precedence over self-interest. But the state must retain control and each property owner should consider himself an agent of the state." It sounds just fine until Hitler's punch line: "The Third Reich will always retain its right to control the owners of property."[15] But compare this proposition with Justice Harlan Fiske Stone's oft-quoted statement on the proper scope of state power: "where the public interest is involved preferment of that interest over the property interest of the individual, to the extent, even of its destruction, is one of the distinguishing characteristics of every exercise of the police power which affects property."[16]

It is easy to spot some differences between these two propositions. Making a private individual the "agent of the state" suggests the total subordination of individual welfare to collective government ends; speaking of the total destruction of some individual's property does not require the owner's active conscription into the service of the state. But both positions find it easy to subordinate private property to state control. I cannot emphasize strongly enough that this common thread between Stone's and Hitler's words cannot support any wild assertion that the state regulation of property in the United States and other Western democracies led to the atrocities of Nazi Germany, or even has some necessary tendency to move in that direction. Still that eerie correspondence in language necessitates an effort to identify the differences implicit in these two definitions of the common good or the public interest. One account treats the common good as an attribute of some premier disembodied entity that rightly tramples all individual or private interests. The second treats the common good as the summation of interests of those individuals subject to state power so as to undercut the sharp opposition between any given person and the public at large. Within that preferred second account, we must justify any statements about the collective interest solely by how it advances the individual welfare of each and every citizen, be he friend or foe, popular or despised. So understood, their happiness, their pains, their successes, and their emotions matter; what is irrelevant, and dangerous, is some distant conception of the public good that is not anchored to the utility of any human being and that disregards the separateness of persons.

The proper standard of the common good does not only authorize state action; it also hems it in. Every social rule must take into account its consequences for all the people it governs. In principle, we should strive for a rule that leaves everyone at least as well off after its implementation as before. Since the practical impediments to achieving this individual-based account of social welfare are immense, its systematic pursuit must proceed by proxy and indirection. To advance this account, it is necessary to estimate first the gains of the parties to voluntary transactions, and then determine their spillover effects, both positive and negative, on all third parties. No one can claim that this approach will yield the right results in all cases. Nor should anyone have to meet such a burden in order to defend any principle of social organization against its rivals. Oftentimes, the first goal of a legal system is negative—to advert the social disasters done in the name of the common good. The second is to strive to facilitate incremental improvements in the operation of the system.

In *Principles,* I hope to outline a program that recognizes the limitations on individual liberty and choice without throwing us into the deadly embrace of unlimited state power. In dealing with these questions, I shall examine all three levels of law: common, legislative, and constitutional. The first and third of these are judge-made. They differ in that the constitutional trumps the legislative, which in turn trumps common-law rules. Many legal theorists have claimed that either adjudication or legislation does better at reaching the ideals of the legal system. Judge Richard Posner has, for example, long trumpeted the superiority of the common-law adjudication by independent judges over the political intrigues that dominate faction-ridden legislatures.[17]

In general, I do not think that one can make any strong assumption about the relative wisdom of common-law rules and legislation. The statute books contain many intelligent legislative schemes. The common-law courts have often perpetrated the most senseless intrusions of state power into private affairs. Frequently, judicial decisions and legislative initiatives both follow the same substantive path. The activism of the 1960s, for example, was driven by a deep dissatisfaction with market processes on matters of safety and health. In 1966, on the legislative front, the National Highway Traffic and Safety Act conferred on the Department of Transportation extensive powers to regulate automobile safety.[18] Courts promptly embraced the identical substantive approach by independently imposing on automobile manufacturers a duty to make crashworthy vehicles, and sharply noted that this duty was not automatically discharged by compliance with the detailed standards of the Traffic and Safety Act.[19]

The intellectual context, then, matters as much as the practical politics, and it is to that first set of questions this book is directed. Chapter 1 lays out the methodological program by critiquing the formal conception of natural law on which so much of laissez-faire is said to rest. This chapter shows that most of the simple rules of the classical natural lawyer are justified not as self-evident or prepolitical truths, but for their desirable social consequences. In so doing, I offer a consequentialist defense for the principles of individual autonomy, private property, and freedom of contract. The classical political philosophers—notably Hobbes, Locke, Hume—all began their accounts of the just society with an account of human nature with which their conception of natural law comported. Blackstone followed their lead in his own summarization of the common law of England. Their accounts did not assume the crude position of Homo Economicus, that all individuals maximize their individual self-interest all the time. Rather, they took a less rigorous but more defensible view that most individuals, most of the time, act out of a form of self-interest whereby they place themselves (and their families) ahead of the general population, and that legal rules should take account of both the excellence self-interest can inspire and the havoc it can wreak. Starting from this mixed descriptive portrait of human beings, private property is not justified solely as some magical relationship between an individual and a thing, but by a system of reverse engineering: private property offers everyone the security of staying apart and the opportunity for coming together by contract for mutual gain: who would surrender what he owns unless he receives back something of greater value in exchange?

The second chapter deals with the interaction of law and social norms in enforcing and defining human relationships. In so doing, I pursue the theme of limited government from a second vantage point: a sound conception of their interdependence leads to the recognition that voluntary associations thrive only if allowed a needed breathing room, which is denied them when the legal system backs every social convention with public coercion. Voluntary associations and ordinary businesses frequently operate on two levels. Where formal legal contracts may allow parties to act "at will"— or in ways that seem arbitrary and capricious, and sometimes are—these are moderated through informal social conventions that guide the day-to-day operations of these same organizations. While the dual system is not perfect, I hope to show that it works far better on average than the current legal approach which seeks to convert every sensible social norm into a legal command.

Chapter 3 then examines one of the key principles of social organization—the harm principle of John Stuart Mill—and argues that it is best explicated, not as an expression of the simple relationship between two individual parties, but again as an indirect way to advance overall social welfare. Harms by aggression and harms by competition are too easily treated as parallel violations of the single prohibition against harm to others; and their profound differences are not grasped solely by reference to the fate of the immediate parties to any dispute, but by their overall social consequences. The prohibitions against force and fraud block destructive "negative-sum games" that impoverish society. In contrast, harm by competition, which so often prompts extensive state regulation, fosters positive-sum games that make maximum use of both human and natural resources. Finally, the fear of negative-sum games gives rise to an aversion to monopoly practices, and explains why a nuanced system of laissez-faire finds a limited, but secure place for antitrust laws.

Chapter 4 switches sides by moving from the harm to the benefit principle, under which I must compensate you for the benefits you confer upon me against my will. The principle is something of an anomaly: normally, by first making a gift to you, I cannot force you to make a gift to me. But the usual autonomy principle is suspended in some limited settings, chiefly those in which necessity and mistake undermine the effectiveness of voluntary agreement. When voluntary transactions are blocked, private parties may initiate forced exchanges that allow them to demand compensation tomorrow by providing assistance today. This innocuous principle of the common law finds its most potent application in "social contract" theory. Social contracts are not just convenient legal fictions that allow the state to pile endless obligations on individuals without their consent. Rather, the term *contract* presupposes that the desirable social arrangements imitate private contracts by allowing all parties to be better off through the imposition of reciprocal obligations on all citizens. The term *social* then reminds us that these arrangements are imposed from above to overcome the transactional difficulties that stand in the path of comprehensive voluntary arrangements.

In chapter 5, I turn to the question of altruism and redistribution of wealth, long considered laissez-faire's Achilles heel. By voluntary exchanges, A becomes better off only by making B better off. Charity and benevolence are simply conceived as falling outside the scope of ordinary human behavior. But once we recognize that laissez-faire is not wedded to any notion of unbridled self-interest, we can see how laissez-faire supports a social norm of voluntary redistribution from those with plenty to those in need. This social support system will always leave some individuals short, but the alternative of state-driven redistribution is likely to alter for the worse the incentives for production. The communitarian ideal too easily becomes the vehicle for redistribution of wealth—in the wrong direction. Social Security and Medicare, notwithstanding their immense political popularity, share the common characteristic of providing generous support for the affluent elderly wealthy at the expense of the younger working poor.

Chapter 6 pursues this same theme from the vantage point of those who seek legal protection or charitable assistance. The conditions whereby someone loses these benefits typically depend on that person's conduct. It is always painful to deny recovery for an individual in need; but in many cases, the alternative is worse: it is to set up a dynamic that encourages dangerous and self-destructive behavior which, from a system-wide perspective it is critical to prevent.

In the last four chapters, I examine the relationship of laissez-faire to the system of property. Chapter 7 defends the basic necessity of strong boundaries between neighbors, but then indicates those circumstances in which the boundary conditions should be relaxed for the benefit of all concerned. Chapter 8 explores the connection between the rights created by the legal system and the remedies it confers. Building on chapter 7, I conclude that the absolute conceptions of private property make sense in most social settings but must yield under limited circumstances of necessity, when an owner must yield the right to exclude, receiving in exchange the protection of a liability rule that only offers financial compensation for the property so lost. The multiple examples in these cases show both the vitality of private property, and the principled limitations on its use.

Chapters 9 and 10 ask what forms of common property can coexist with private property, and why. Common ownership of vital resources is not strictly a creature of the modern age, but is commonplace in all legal systems. The right to exclude found in private property imposes costs on those who are excluded. Normally these costs are reduced by the outsider's ability to do business with other owners of private property. But for certain resources, such as air and water, the high cost of exclusion necessitates the development of institutions of common property notwithstanding their higher administrative costs. Chapter 10 extends the analysis of common ownership to include the broad class of common carriers that include railroads, telecommunications, and public utilities, all vast network enterprises. The monopoly power of these common carriers cannot be met by the creation of competing firms, but requires the creation of a state obligation to serve all comers under reasonable terms—an obligation that it is easier to create than to define.

The problems and issues I address in *Principles* do not, and could not, touch every divisive issue of modern times. I do not in this book seek to address many bitter social disputes ranging from abortion and rape, to same-sex marriages. Instead, my focus is on the systematic explication of the strengths and weaknesses of markets and governments in economic issues to give some greater appreciation of the proper roles of both. Today there is widespread agreement on all sides of the political spectrum that some mixed solution is required. The disagreement comes in determining the proper proportions of private choice and social control. My hope is that *Principles for a Free Society* will offer a useful guide to resolving the perennial tension between individual liberty and social control.

❖ ❖ ❖

CHAPTER I

Natural Law: The Utilitarian Connection

My purpose in this volume is, after a fashion, to square a legal circle. From the earliest times, legal and political writers have worked hard to reconcile the demands for individual liberty with those for the common good. At one level, the cynical and weary among us could dismiss their project as an impossibility because scarcity precludes the simultaneous satisfaction of all desires, be they practical or conceptual. Since it is not possible to make all people happy all of the time, we should give up this misguided quest for some holy grail and settle for a less grandiose pragmatic shuffle.

The task of legal theorizing is not, however, to satisfy all those demands simultaneously. Rather, it is to highlight the forces that could lead to a reconciliation of these two divergent imperatives, and to show why the forces that link individual liberty to the common good are far stronger than those that seemingly drive them apart.

This self-appointed task flies in the face of the pervasive negativism of this postmodern age. Many writers despair that any comprehensive theory can organize the raw and resistant data of social experience. A deep strand of legal skepticism throws up its hands at principled solutions and, by default, gives the legislature free reign to define, and redefine, legal rights in accordance with the perceived demands of majority will. Yet too often this casual approach degenerates into an exercise to find ways whereby legislative powers can be used to advance the interests of one's own group, typically defined by race, sex, and ethnicity in this age of identity politics. But this type of skepticism sacrifices all hope for any systematic understanding of legal relationships. It also carries with it dangerous consequences. Once

9

there is no sound view of right and wrong, it is easy to slip into the frame of mind that elevates one's own partisan cause to the exclusion of all other interests: after all, what is sacrificed if there are no sound principles of political or social organization?

Often the same impulse toward legislative dominance comes from the opposite impulse: a strong absolutist sense of right and wrong smothers any dissent and demands that a given legal system regulate every aspect of human life. The upshot of this resurgent fundamentalism is a dogmatism that does quite well for those in power, but less well for those who are only limited partners in this new collective enterprise.

The twin impulses of skepticism and dogmatism, then, easily lead to the special pleading that is the most insistent enemy of a free society. The only way to buck that trend is to resort to a strategy that gives a very different twist to skepticism and dogmatism. The one sure dogma—that human knowledge and human plans are inevitably limited—leads to a principled skepticism about putting first our own personal and group interests. Accordingly, a sound legal order is one that responds to the fragility of knowledge by giving no one absolute control and power. It seeks the dispersion of power across individuals and social groups.

Yet even this note of caution leaves much work to be done. The celebration of individual rights and the decentralization of social power does not explain how these twin objectives should be achieved. There is still an enormous amount of work to be done to articulate and defend the best comprehensive theory that achieves these ends. Unfortunately, however, legal and political thinkers who have confronted this problem have exhibited little or no consensus about the proper form for any satisfactory legal theory. Indeed, generally speaking, contemporary thinking typically divides legal theories into two separate philosophical camps, each with its own obscure name: deontological or consequentialist.

A deontological theory stresses that the right and wrong in an individual case depends on what people did in some particular context. It seeks to isolate individual transactions from their larger social setting. It focuses on antecedents, not on consequences. This approach is closely associated with the natural law tradition, both of John Locke and Sir William Blackstone in the seventeenth and eighteenth centuries, and of modern times. The opposite trend in legal thought looks to the consequences of actions and rules, not to their antecedents. These consequentialist theories may be conveniently, if inexactly, grouped as utilitarian. The natural lawyers had a much stronger intuitive sense of the role and place of individual liberty in ordinary life and political affairs. The consequentialists are much more concerned with economic progress and social welfare than with any conception of individual freedom, which they sometimes regard as naive, simplistic or even quaint. The intellectual divide between these two schools is strong, and bodes ill for any effort at their substantive reunification.

I aim to maneuver between the alternative risks of dogmatism and skepticism. My hope is to harmonize our intuitive respect for the past with our need to shape and control our future. In this opening chapter, I take the first step in that direction by demonstrating the eerie congruence between natural law and utilitarian theories on some of the key building blocks of our own legal tradition: liberty, property, family, and custom. All of these principles seek to create separate spheres of individual control. None seeks to demand uniformity to some single conception of the good. In subsequent chapters, I will then push the connections between the individual and the common good in both private and public law settings, where the private law setting deals with legal disputes between ordinary individuals, and the public law setting with the relationship between the individual and the state.

To turn to my immediate topic, the points of opposition between natural right and utilitarian theories have been so often rehearsed that it is here necessary only to summarize the relevant differences briefly. Natural rights theories regard themselves as theories of individual entitlement, not of social good. In general they seek to articulate the permanent and immutable truths of any legal order that they believe to be good in all societies over all times. In dealing with the basic relationships between individuals, they stress the importance of individual liberty and personal autonomy and defiantly pit these against any supposed measure of social welfare. In dealing with the proper resolution of concrete legal disputes, their emphasis on the justice of the individual case, the intimate connection between the doer and the sufferer of harm, makes them overtly anti-instrumental in orientation.* They disavow the idea that the social consequences of any legal rule could justify its adoption or rejection, and thereby reject any abstract measure of social welfare. Taken to their logical extreme, these natural law theories have—or, at least, ought to have—as their central maxim, *fiat justitia ruat*

---

* "In the common-law world generally, tort law treats the two litigants as connected one with the other through an immediate personal interaction as doer and sufferer of the same harm."[1]

coelum (let justice be done though the heavens may fall). If consequences never count in deciding the rights and wrongs of individual actions, then disastrous consequences cannot count either.

Natural rights theories have long been popular in our culture. In the seventeenth century, Richard Hooker, whose work much influenced Locke, captured the matter well: "Law rational therefore, which men commonly used to call the law of nature, meaning thereby the law which human nature knoweth itself in reason universally bound unto, which also for that cause may be termed most fitly the law of reason."[2] The instinctive appeal of Lockean thought was its insistence that all individuals are free, equal, and independent in the state of nature, "wherein all the power and jurisdiction is reciprocal, no one having more than another."[3] In the eighteenth century, Jefferson appealed to "nature and nature's law" in the Declaration of Independence. Charles Murray, in his recent defense of libertarian thought, self-consciously hearkens back to that tradition: "Freedom is first of all our birthright."[4] Yet today's technical exposition of natural rights theories often avoids such simple pronouncements of faith and instead employs a terminology that, to put the matter charitably, tends to border upon the obscure or occult. Some special thing, property, quality, or attribute is all too often "immanent" or "inherent" in something else.

There is some method to this madness. Although natural lawyers recognize the difference between analytical and empirical truths, they often strive to identify a grand set of necessary empirical truths about human nature that are not made, but rather are discovered through some combination of introspection, observation, and rational discourse.[5] The synthetic *a priori* of Kant holds that certain nonlogical truths are nonetheless true by some human necessity. For lawyers in the natural law tradition that category is hardly empty. The contingent and variegated elements of human life and experience are subordinated to those elements that are perceived as permanent, general, and inescapable, if not divinely revealed.[6] These lawyers view with suspicion the study of differences in culture and laws, first made popular in 1748 by Montesquieu in his *Spirit of the Laws,*[7] because of its implicit attack on the universality of the legal order whose basic intellectual substrate spans the generations and crosses the seas.

Notwithstanding the breadth of their claims, natural lawyers—at least, academic natural lawyers today—are often defensive, almost apologetic, about what they do. While they pride themselves in a program that is abstract, ambitious, austere, and rigorous, they recognize that they are the devoted champions of a minority outlook. To them, modern legal and ethical thinking is dominated by a dreaded reliance on conceptions of social welfare, cost-benefit calculations, realism, pragmatism, instrumentalism, and central planning—all suggesting that individuals are concerned more about short-term gratification than about the illumination of the major structures of legal thought. But even with their isolation from the mainstream, natural rights thinkers persevere, stoically confident that with suitable explication their necessary truths about human and legal relations may perhaps in time become our conventional truths as well.

Utilitarianism, for its part, exudes confidence and makes light of what it regards as the exaggerated pretensions of natural law theories. Jeremy Bentham, for example, regarded himself as the mortal adversary of Blackstone,[8] so much so that in his view natural law was not only "nonsense, but nonsense on stilts"—a derisive phrase calculated to capture the ungainliness of natural law. The philosophical hostility so often expressed toward natural law begins with the obvious point that it is odd to "find" law "out there" like a rock or a stone, or even as a necessary constituent of a human relationship. Laws are something made by human beings for their own governance. The survival of past societies has depended heavily upon their choice of laws, just as our survival and prosperity is heavily dependent upon the choices, often conscious and deliberate, that we make today. Utilitarianism is thus concerned not only with general principles of right and wrong, but also with historical context and institutional arrangements. Law is more than what is written in the statute books.

Utilitarianism also rejects the intuitionism to which natural lawyers gravitate. In examining the complex of legal and social institutions that surrounds the law as such, modern consequentialist theories place heavy emphasis upon the maximization of some social good. The choice of happiness, utility, or wealth raises important controversies within the consequentialist school, but these divisions pale in comparison to the starker opposition with classical theories of natural law and natural right. If the classical philosophy of Plato, Aristotle, Aquinas, and Locke lies at the root of natural law, then utilitarianism depends on the skepticism of David Hume, the economics of Adam Smith, the indefatigable curiosity of Jeremy Bentham, or the social-cost calculations of Ronald Coase.

This thumbnail sketch deliberately ignores or downplays important differences that surface within both the natural law and the utilitarian camps. A preoccupation with these internal differences has the unfortunate tendency to obscure some of the larger truths about the relationships between these two schools in Western, and certainly Anglo-American, thought. The key point is that, however much the two schools differ in methodology and approach, they exhibit a high correlation on results. Both theories find a large place for institutions of private property; both are concerned with the control of aggression and the keeping of promises. It is an intellectual challenge to dwell on the precise differences between Locke and Hume, or between Blackstone and Bentham. But for all their differences, they are all—when compared with the Marxists, socialists, communitarians, republicans, and feminists of our time—peas from the same pod.

I believe that this correspondence in outcomes between the classical utilitarians and their natural law rivals is not simply a matter of coincidence, much less of chance. Rather, it rests on a deep, if unacknowledged, convergence between two theories that all too often spend their time making war on each other. Some sense of that convergence was fairly evident in the works of the earlier natural law writers, many of whom were happy to refer to general utilitarian arguments in the course of their writings. To the classical natural law thinker, only the will of God could give certain rules the force of law, but it was the manifest utility of those laws that certified God's wisdom on earth for ordinary men.[9] Today's more tempered time is far more suspicious of these theistic foundations. Even so, this rejection of theistic foundations of law does not require, or lead to, a rejection of the substantive rules themselves. Rather, utility is promoted from being a mere expression of God's will to being an independent, self-sufficient criterion of the soundness of particular rules.

The classical natural law writers consistently showed their willingness to rest their conclusion on both pegs simultaneously. Blackstone could first write that God "has graciously reduced the rule of obedience to one paternal precept, 'that man should pursue his own true and substantial happiness.' This is the foundation of what we call ethics, or natural law."[10] He then carried out this theme when he first referred to property "as the immediate gift of the creator," only to justify the creation of private property by a set of arguments that possess great force independent of their theistic origins. Private property serves several ends simultaneously. It is a way to establish separate domains between individuals that allows them to live side by side in peace. It is an indispensable counterweight to the concentration of sovereign power, and thus limits the reach of political orthodoxies of all stripes and persuasions. In addition, private property works as a spur to economic production by guaranteeing to workers the fruits of their own labors. People want "habitations for shelter and safety, and raiment for warmth and decency. But no man would be at the trouble to provide either, so long as he had only the usufructuary property in them, which was to cease the instant that he quitted possession; if, as soon as he walked out of his tent, or pulled off his garment, the next stranger who came by would have a right to inhabit the one, and to wear the other."[11] Blackstone wrote with a clarity that modern scholars would do well to emulate.

Easy as the convergence between classical natural law and modern utilitarianism may have seemed, it disappeared in our own time. Today natural law methodology, with its heavy overdose of intuition and revelation, has all but sunk bneneath the battering it has received from thinkers schooled in the utilitarian tradition. My basic thesis is, however, that natural law thinking developed an acute and sound appreciation of the basic rights that any utilitarian would, on reflection, want to adopt in his society.

The first step in the reconciliaton of the two traditions is to focus on some of their major battlegrounds and show how utilitarian principle, broadly conceived, supports—even dictates—many of the categorical conclusions that natural rights thinkers took for granted. I first examine the question of whether the social and legal relations between persons are permanent, depending on the common features of mankind, or changeable, turning in some decisive fashion on the peculiar features of each separate culture. Thereafter I focus on one specific problem of recurrent importance: the duty to assist strangers as it stands in opposition to the duty to provide support within families. Next I explore the implications of these two approaches for some of the fundamental building blocks of any legal system: the place of individual autonomy, the origin of property in first possession, and the role of custom as an independent source of law, relied upon by the authoritative state powers, both legislative and judicial.

PERMANENCE AND CHANGE

The natural law program holds that permanence of certain critical elements permits, and perhaps requires, the emergence of some general legal principles. In the second century, Gaius began his *Institutes* (the standard introductory treatise for students of Roman law) with a statement of the basic position.

> Every people that is governed by statutes and customs observes partly its own peculiar law and partly the common law of all mankind. The law which a people establishes for itself is peculiar to it, and is called *ius civile* (civil law) as being the special law of

that *ciuitas* (State), while the law that natural reason establishes among all mankind is followed by all peoples alike, and is called *ius gentium* (law of nations, or law of the world) as being the law observed by all mankind.[12]

In the sixth century, Justinian took the point a step further by asserting that "[t]he law of nature is that which she has taught all animals; a law not peculiar to the human race, but shared by all living creatures, whether denizens of the air, the dry land, or sea."[13] The Roman devotion to natural law was not some idle chatter, let alone an excuse for the exercise of sovereign power. Quite the opposite: indeed, many of the rules that concern us today, such as those that regulate the acquisition and transfer of property (by capture and transfer, respectively) were regarded as "natural modes" and constant across all cultures. The local variation in private institutions does not deal with the question of whether it is a good idea to have private ownership or to enforce contracts: rather the question is this: What kinds of formality—writings, seals, oaths, witnesses, ceremonies—are needed to effectuate certain kinds of transaction—such as sales, loans, and gifts—that in some form or other must take place in all societies regardless of their variations in norms and practices? Thus it is clear that those topics which lie at the heart of the Roman system under the head of natural law retain their relevance, and often their validity, in modern legal systems as well.

Why is it, then, that the obvious differences in social circumstances and local conventions do not upset the natural lawyer's claim for the universality of his preferred legal rules? Why is the word *nature* chosen to counter some perceived threat of particularization? On this recurrent theme, a small dose of literalism goes a long way. The obvious source of human needs and desires is not culture, but human nature. What is distinctively human depends not on how persons are socialized in this or that particular environment, but on the common set of biological imperatives that has shaped the evolution of all individuals—and, indeed, of entire populations—over time. It is possible to identify these natural needs, desires, and inclinations, without retreating to a high level of abstraction or to any artificial linguistic convention. All individuals must ingest the amino acids necessary to construct the proteins necessary for life. All individuals need a caloric intake above the minimum required to sustain basic life functions. Pregnant women must carry their infants to term, and parents must raise them until they reach the stage of reproductive maturity. All individuals need protection against cold and heat, and against disease and predation. Any social order that ignores these imperatives pays a high price, perhaps the ultimate price of extinction. The biological anchor weighs heavily on the degrees of freedom found in feasible social organizations.

Back of the battle for survival lies the looming threat of scarcity. There is never enough to go around, so conflict within groups and across groups is an inescapable part of human existence. It is, moreover, a condition that calls forth its own type of human personality. Hume talked about a human condition that blends individual self-interest with confined generosity: *"'tis only from the selfishness and confin'd generosity of men, along with the scanty provision nature has made for his wants, that justice derives its origin."*[14] Although Hume treated this generalization more as a wise observation, and less as the consequence of any general theory, the logic of evolution suggests otherwise. Where resources are scarce, disinterested generosity is not a viable strategy for survival. The organism that unilaterally divides its possessions with others cannot thereby force others to divide their possessions with it. Over time, greedy organisms that retain all of what they produce, and grab some of what others have produced, will fare better in competition with those more generous organisms that retain only a fraction of their output. As the process continues, the pure altruist keeps a smaller and smaller share of the world's stock, until the retained share is insufficient to allow the survival or reproduction of its own kind.

On this score, Justinian was right, before his time, to stress the common traits of man and animals. These evolutionary pressures did not surface first in human beings. Rather, they are the driving force behind the evolution for all forms of life. Whatever the manifest difference in structure, tastes, and appearances, self-interest deserves its special status as nature's universal constant. Only the most naive form of human exceptionalism could lead us to believe that forces that operate on all living creatures, from single-cell organisms to primates, cease as if by magic to exert their influence on human beings. Traits that natural selection has molded for eons do not disappear without a trace; the opposite holds true. Self-interest looks to be the nearest thing to a universal imperative, one that instructs all individuals how to manage their initial endowments, depending on variations in their external environment. Self-interest is not some abstract reason that lies behind the Darwinian theory of natural selection. Rather, it is the necessary behavioral consequence of the prolonged and remorseless operation of that mechanism. Darwin's choice of the word *natural* is no verbal happenstance. The term hints at some tight connection between natural selection and natural law, and also reminds us that no central purpose directs or informs the process of evolution in accordance with some divine, or other, plan. The whole picture is a composite mosaic in which each organism has control over only a very small piece. There is no master or central plan. There is only the conflict, coordination, and overlap of small and separate plans, each held by individual organisms. What happens to the whole is a complex aggregation of the fates of its constituent parts.

This argument is perfectly general in form, and in no way depends upon the particular manifestations of human conduct in any specific culture. It is not bound to time or to place. It satisfies the stringent conditions of universalization that natural lawyers set for their own task. But what utilitarian could reject it as the basis of his own calculations? At a descriptive level, these theories explain how individuals maximize their welfare under conditions of scarcity and uncertainty. The biology to which the natural lawyer so frequently resorts throws him thus into the deadly embrace of maximization theories that are the hallmark of utilitarian thought.

This theory of individual self-interest is not only a theory of conflict and competition; it is one of cooperation as well. The organism that goes it alone has no allies to fall back upon when things go bad, and is blocked from engaging in any projects that require the coordination of two or more actors. The logic of self-interest does not, cannot, ignore the gains from cooperation in order to maximize only those gains from competition and aggression. With any foresight into future events, self-interest encourages voluntary arrangements with some organisms, and recognizes that although the upside of conflict promises great gains, its downside also holds the possibility of devastating losses. Voluntary arrangements sidestep these perils, and therefore can be stable over the long run without external enforcement if each party to them knows (in that peculiar biological sense of "as if") that the gains from a short-term defection are dwarfed by those from a continued long-term relationship. Given this pattern of long-term relationships, many instances of "altruism" are "reciprocal altruism" (see chapter 5)—which are not altruism at all. An isolated act of generosity is sometimes better understood as self-interested behavior embedded in a large network of reciprocal interactions which gain stability precisely because they work to the long-term mutual advantage of all parties. We have here the basis of tort (preventing aggression) and contract (enforcing voluntary agreements), which both fit well within the theory of how individuals maximize their own self-interest.

At this point, however, one must be take into account the counterexamples to the theory of individual self-interest: that is, the countless parents who have sacrificed themselves for their children, and even the individuals who have acted to their own detriment in order to advance the interests of strangers. These indeed exemplify the confined generosity Hume referred to as softening the hard edges of remorseless self-interest. How does a natural law theory deal with these two cases: benevolence to strangers, and ties within the family?

BENEVOLENCE TOWARD STRANGERS

The self-interest model cannot account for cases of genuine heroism toward strangers—save by elaborate and contrived extensions about what self-interest means. In part heroic behavior seems attributable to the capacity for conscious reflection, which humans have in far greater abundance than do other organisms. Whether in the form of personal risk or charitable contributions, the willingness to forgo benefits to one's own self serves as the foundation for much good in society. The legal system, however, does not have to trouble itself unduly with actions of benevolence: if it does not prohibit them, then they will continue to occur, and thus mediate the conflicts of interest that might otherwise divide individuals or groups.

We must not, however, overestimate the frequency and importance of these benevolent events relative to the threat to social order that the prosaic forms of self-interest pose. The easy praising of benevolence has no costless obverse in respect to controlling against harms inflicted on strangers. Quite the opposite: public and private resources *do* have to be committed to such control, and social obligations have to be structured to limit the risk of unbridled self-interest threatening the welfare of all individuals. It would be a mistake, for example, to organize a tax system around a norm of voluntary compliance simply because many people make extensive charitable contributions. The natural lawyer therefore need not trouble himself unduly with these counterexamples to unremitting individual self-interest. So long as they occur with modest frequency in different societies, rules can be fashioned that allow but do not compel altruistic behavior to go forward, and these rules will tend to serve desirable utilitarian ends. If the very worst we think about all people is not always true, then there is a cushion of safety from which we all benefit.

SHARING WITHIN THE FAMILY

The postulate of individual self-interest is also unsuccessful in explaining the complex transactions within the family. Parents routinely make enormous investments in their children in the present; and their willingness to do this is not easily explained by treating that investment as though it were "really" the front end of a voluntary exchange, with return performance due from the child at some later date. The most stylized of facts about family relationships falsify so radical a redescription of a common social practice. In order for this model to work, each side would have to receive, at the time of the exchange, assets of greater value than it gave. But simultaneous exchanges are not possible in a world of intergenerational obligations. Any such return care (by implicit agreement, "if and when I reach an old age," say) can usually be provided only in the distant future, if at all. The risk of nonperformance, given imperfect enforcement, is high; and the present discounted value of any return performance is trivial, especially with children born of older parents. Investment in children is a poor form of old-age insurance. (The perfect egotist is well advised to avoid children and to set up an annuity whose income provides, on a contract basis, pension and health-care benefits for his old age.) Yet parents continue to make enormous sacrifices to have and to raise children. To make matters worse, parents often face anguished choices about allocating special care—both during life and after their death—to children with severe handicaps, sickness, disability, and retardation, making a mockery of any effort to conjure up some implicit contract of exchange across the generations. On occasion, baser commercial motives enter into family affairs, as children come of age and become partners in the family firm. So the full range of familial behavior seriously challenges the uncompromising theory of individual self-interest.

These objections to modeling the family as a market in miniature do not undermine natural law theory by showing that there are no constants of human behavior. Rather, they reinforce the model by requiring us to recognize the interdependent utility functions ("my happiness depends on yours") within families that are themselves the result of constant biological interaction. Throughout nature, the care that primates, and other animals as well, give to their youngsters cannot be explained by any theory of individual self-interest. But it can be explained by invoking the idea of inclusive fitness, whereby what is maximized is the welfare of genes, not of individuals as such.[15] By virtue of this theory, each person takes into account the welfare of others, discounted to reflect their fraction of common genes. In the normal situation, each parent treats the welfare of the child as though it were one half of its own, that of a grandchild as though it were one fourth and so on. Under this theory, what is maximized is the expected value of the total genotype, so that each parent will trade off one unit of cost to himself for two units of benefit to the offspring even if there is no prospect of return benefit under some implicit contract. In the early stages of child rearing, small inputs from the parent generate large benefits to the child, so the amount of caring behavior is great.

The same marginal tradeoffs, moreover, are applicable to both fathers and mothers, although parents of both sexes do not invest the same amount in parental care. Breast feeding is but the most conspicuous illustration of an asymmetry in cost between mother and father. The mother is often in a better position to provide effective, low-cost care for an infant, so the theory suggests that she will provide more care than the father even though their degree of genetic relatedness is the same. Given the difference in initial endowments, the unified theory of inclusive fitness predicts differential involvement for males and females. Similarly, the theory also explains why the parental care from both mothers and fathers diminishes as a child gets older. The child's benefits from parental care are reduced as the child can do more for himself, and continued care to living children also reduces their parents' opportunities to have further children.

The existence of children, moreover, increases the gains from cooperation between parents, who are, after all, unrelated. The children in effect serve as "hostages" to guard against any intrigue between the parents, because any harm that one parent inflicts upon another necessarily reduces the prospect of the offspring's flourishing in its maturity. Emotions are not outside the realm of biological influence, but are heavily dependent on it: the love and affection that binds parents together improves the long-term fitness of both, given their common stake in the future. Played out in nature, genetic egotism, coupled with reciprocal altruism, translates into an ongoing generosity that typically characterizes relations within the family.

There are, of course, variations within the overall pattern. As external environments change, the return on parental investment in children changes as well, making for different levels of family intimacy across cultures and generations. But these variations should all conform to a system in which at the margin one unit of parental expenditure yields two units of benefit to the child. This relationship is determined not solely by the basic interdependent utility function, but also by other natural individual endowments and by external factors. Whatever these differences in level of parental support, it is highly unlikely that even today parents regard other people's children as just like their own—hence, the enormous pains and cost that people are prepared to take in order to have a baby via a surrogate mother instead of through ordinary adoption.

The biological components of the model should drive the economics, rather than the other way around. The errors that can occur from ignoring these constraints are, I believe, well illustrated by Gary Becker's ingenious "rotten-kid" theorem.[16] In the Becker model, children are constrained to act altruistically toward each other not because they care for each other, but *only because* the parents care for both children and threaten to withhold benefits from children who do not act altruistically toward their siblings. In theory, these parental constraints will break down if the gains from one sibling's misbehavior toward another exceed the benefits that the parents are able to withhold from the offending sibling. Nor can the model explain why siblings often retain a distinctive closeness even after they have reached their maturity and after their parents have died. The connection here is quite strong, and the best accounts of the evolution of both the business partnership and the small-size state stress the importance of the kinship relationship even after the death of the parents.

Becker's stylized economic model also shows the limited effectiveness of threats when some, but not all, parties to a social setting are altruistic to each other. In contrast, the biological models predict stronger loyalty between siblings because each has a stake in the welfare of the other—a state that survives the absence of any parental enforcement. Conflicts of interest persist between siblings nonetheless, when the cost to the one sibling exceeds half the benefits conferred on the other sibling. Thus, if one sibling can perform an act that costs itself 5 and yields a benefit of 8 to its fellow sibling, the narrow calculus of evolution suggests that his action will go unperformed even though the increased value to the pair is 3. The one sibling, registering only half the gains conferred on the other, will not, as a rational agent, perform an act that costs it 5 and yields it only 4 in benefits. Such conflicts are in principle no different from ones between parent and child—but the effects of the latter are softened because the repeated interactions within the close-knit settings of a family offset the short-term imbalances of discrete transactions (see also the discussion of custom later in this chapter). As for the relative power of the two models, under the Becker model, killing one sibling is far more likely to produce a private gain for the other (assuming the parents have no other child to aid) than under the biological models. With Becker, the death of the sibling could increase the welfare of the survivor, but will generally decrease it under the biological models, a result in line with popular experience.

Certain biological constants, thus, lie at the root of family behavior, and demarcate the zone of voluntary market exchange from that of the nonprice, nonexchange economy of the family. Every legal system must draw some distinction between those within the family and those outsiders who deal with the family at—to use the instructive legal phrase—"arm's length." The strongest counterexample to individual self-interest only confirms the importance of common practices, albeit with different intensities across times and across cultures.

The wise utilitarian interested in some form of social welfare will not ignore these broad facts. Instead, he will try to minimize the pressures on legal enforcement in setting the rules of social organization. His rules will therefore follow the basic pattern of natural obligation as it is perceived to arise within families. To transform inclination into duty is, after a fashion, to derive an "is" from an "ought."[17] So understood, there is no Humean gap, only some good common sense of the sort congenial to Hume's own utilitarian biases. The utilitarian's major premise is that one tries to organize social arrangements to best serve the individuals that compose them. The system of parental obligations of nurture, guidance, protection, and support, championed by the natural lawyer—reduces the costs of raising the young because it takes advantage of natural inclination to provide the assistance that the law would otherwise have to compel. Taken in the aggregate, the system thus generates high levels of care at relatively low costs. Could one imagine the cost of any system that uniformly took children from their parents at birth and assigned their upbringing to a stranger? It is no accident that the attack on the family takes place in authoritarian systems that can brook no counterweight either to the greater central power of the state, or to the conception of the common good that all its citizens are obliged to accept. On matters of the family, the natural law theorist fares, then, quite well by utilitarian standards. Long after these natural law theories were propounded, we can identify good empirical reasons to believe in the set of external constants that generate the need for some constant social response.

INDIVIDUAL AUTONOMY

The congruence between natural law rules and utilitarian dictates extends beyond the family to other areas. As the focus moves from the family to the "public" realm, the assumption of individual autonomy gains in importance until it lies at the root of huge portions of legal and political theory. Stated in its most naive form, the claim for autonomy is each person's claim to both own and govern his own body or self and the labor either generates. The standard natural law argument for autonomy is intuitive: people who enjoy control of their own persons have a right to retain control of themselves when they enter into political and social arrangements. The counterargument is that the possession of natural talents is in some measure a question of individual luck, which cannot serve as the principled basis for distributing entitlements across individuals.[18] Given this concern, it is often proposed that natural talents be socialized for the benefit of all, as all persons have an equal claim to these endowments by virtue of their common humanity. The argument itself can be given not only an egalitarian, but a utilitarian, twist by the observation that two common features of all human beings (the natural law style of argument again) are, first, a diminishing marginal utility of wealth and, second, a general aversion toward risk. These two features, taken together, imply that the shift of at least some units of resources from rich to poor satisfies some utilitarian mandate.

The utilitarian argument, however, is incomplete if it looks only at the state of affairs desired in the end, independent of the large costs necessary to obtain it. When each individual is regarded (subject to the family obligations discussed above) as the owner of his own labor, there is no need for any routine coerced transaction whereby the natural talents possessed by one person are removed to a person who is, to some unspecified extent, now entitled to their use or benefit. Instead, there is a single owner of each bit of human talent, who is then in a position to use it in transactions that benefit not only himself but all others with whom he does business. The system operates in a decentralized fashion because the cost for acquiring property rights in human labor is essentially zero. In addition, there is no need to enter into any complex system of recordation of deeds (such as that used to establish title in real estate) to explain whom X must deal with in order to obtain the benefits of Y's talents. The answer is always Y.

The rule of self-ownership also commends itself on utilitarian grounds. Its great advantage lies in its tendency to preserve the total stock of natural talents which would otherwise be dissipated in the political struggle of some groups and individuals to obtain supremacy over others. Slavery represents the most obvious systemic rejection of the principle of self-ownership; and the testimony to its overall inconvenience is that it rarely, if ever, is brought about by agreement. Its origins lie in capture and conquest, both of which aid the victor but ignore the preferences of the vanquished. Individual self-ownership, subject only to obligations within the family, is surely a better mode of social organization: connections between private persons can be made by contract, which works to mutual benefit, rather than by coercion, which does not.

The only other competitor to a rule of self-ownership is a system that confers, as it were, on each person a partial interest in the labor and output of all other persons. That complex network of human cross-ownership cannot be achieved without an extensive system of redistributive taxation and regulation (that is, coercion that gives the fruit of every A's talents to B through Z). Such a system reduces the incentive to engage in productive labor, is expensive to administer, and often produces in individual cases results at cross-purposes with its ultimate objectives. The constant exhortation of the obligation to share does not, by words alone, abolish the fact of individual self-interest, suitably qualified by the principle of inclusive fitness. So this new framework of interlacing rights gives each (self-interested) person an incentive to impose a greater share of obligations upon his rivals than he bears for himself. In some worlds at least, it is far better to receive than to give.

It is risky to oversell the virtues of autonomy, for in the end it is not the only source of individual obligation. Nonetheless, even for involuntary exchanges, self-ownership serves as an indispensable baseline for measuring which exchanges are for the common good (that is, those from which all persons gain) and those that are not. The objection that the self-ownership theory is philosophically naive and incomplete holds good only against a traditional natural lawyer's philosophical argument that individual autonomy is a "necessary" truth, like those of logic or at least those of physics. That claim will have no power against the more modest functional defense, which relies only on the most general features of human conduct. So long as there are motivational and transactional barriers to an ideal world, we must learn to live in the world of the second-best. Accordingly, we should tolerate the so-called moral weaknesses of this rule, given the inability of anyone to formulate a workable alternative system of property rights in persons. When suitably fleshed out, utilitarian arguments better explain this portion of natural rights than does natural rights theory itself.

First Possession

Similar arguments carry over to the theory of first possession, the dominant rule for the acquisition of property in land for both Locke and Blackstone in the natural law tradition, and for Hume and Bentham in the utilitarian. Here, too, the natural law influence is powerful, as the rule of first possession is often described as one that gives title by way of "natural occupation."[19] The standard natural law accounts seek to justify this principle of natural occupation by reference to an idea of individual desert, which in turn rests on the labor theory of value. For Locke, the theory reads—at least, at first glance—as though it were one of desert because of his constant insistence that the great part of the value of any land taken from the commons by first occupancy is attributable to the labor invested in that land. One key passage reads as follows:

> He that is nourished by the Acorns he pickt up under an Oak, or the Apples he gathered from the Trees in the wood, has certainly appropriated them to himself. No Body can deny but the nourishment is his. I ask then, When did they begin to be his? When he digested? Or when he ate? Or when he boiled? Or when he brought them home? Or when he pickt them up? And 'tis plain, if the first gathering made them not his, nothing else could. That *labour* put a distinction between them and common. That added something to them more than Nature, the common mother of all, had done; and so they became his private right. And will anyone say he had no right to those Acorns or Apples he thus appropriated, because he had not the consent of all Mankind to make them his? Was it a Robbery thus to assume to himself what belonged to all in Common? If such a consent as that was necessary, Man had starved, notwithstanding the Plenty God had given him.[20]

One strength of this labor theory of value is that it posits that all individuals own their own labor; otherwise, how could they be entitled to mix it with some unowned thing? But the labor theory of value runs into difficulties even if that point is accepted. Thus, one recurrent criticism of Locke is that his theory at best accounts for why the first possessor or occupier should have a lien for his labor expended, but not receive outright ownership of the land or thing in question. Locke tried to duck this difficulty by choosing an example that almost made the problem disappear—ownership of the uncleared and rocky fields of his day—answering that 99 percent of the value in the land was attributable to the labor added to it.[21] This is in essence a *de minimis* answer designed to silence anyone who would dispute the title of the laborer. But it does not deal with the discovery of vast quantities of cheap oil located beneath the lands of some lucky sheik or cattle rancher. Locke's own example did not allow him to bridge rigorously the small, but theoretically significant gap that remains. Ninety-nine percent is not 100 percent: What should be done with the unearned increment, however small, that nature has supplied? The gap between 100 percent and 99 percent keeps its importance because it separates the universe of determinate solutions from that of probabilistic calculation.

Lodged against an intuitive natural rights theory, these objections have conclusive force, but not so against utilitarian rejoinders. Initially, there are strong utilitarian justifications for individual self-ownership in the original position; so the Lockean solution cannot be attacked on the ground that the first possessor has no valid claim to his own labor or talents. Similarly, there are functional explanations to justify giving a thing's first possessor outright ownership of it. To hold that the labor theory of value accounts only for a lien, but not full ownership, gives rise to the identical problem in respect to individual self-ownership: Who gets the difference between the total value of the thing, and that portion of value attributable to the labor of the first possessor? To treat that increment as a common-pool asset necessarily imposes extensive administrative costs: first, to measure the size of the increment in each case; and, then, to assign its value to all other persons, none of whom have any specific claim to the thing in question. (Locke is right that the first possessor is different from the others: they have to displace someone in possession, while he does not.) In some cases, the unearned equity of the first possessor may be large but, at the margin, will tend toward zero. Taken over the full range of cases, assessments and reassignments necessarily reduce the total value of the stock in question, and quickly undermine the willingness of individuals to incur the costs of discovery and appropriation in the first instance. It is also possible that the costs of finding the line between total value and the lien for labor exceeds the total value of the "equity" in the thing that the public is said to hold as of right.

In the end, therefore, the strongest justification for the strict rule that first possession yields complete ownership, not the lien for labor, is not one of individual desert. It is one of modest prudence. It is therefore more congenial to Hume, who defended the rule for the boost it gives the "stability of possession" over external objects.[22] In the long run, we are all better off if the surplus in things remains well defined with a single owner, than if each and every owner surrenders some of what he has acquired in exchange for the right to some portion of the surplus of lands acquired by others. The first-possession rule leaves each thing with a determinate owner, who is then capable of entering into voluntary transactions over the thing with other persons. These transactions are facilitated, as Locke rightly noted, by the existence of both money and durable goods, which render unnecessary any limitation on how much one person can acquire on his own account.[23] A simple functionalism thus explains the appeal of the rule.

In response, it might be suggested that the best way to avoid the apportionment problems is to reject flatly the proposition that any person should have the right to mix his individual labor with external things in some social commons: no person can add his labor to things that are in common ownership. At this point, the rebuttal again takes on a utilitarian cast. Locke himself was aware of the enormous bargaining problems that exist if unanimous consent should be required to determine what particular things should be used by what persons. The last sentence from paragraph 28 of the *Second Treatise*, with its pointed reference to starvation, hammers home the point. Bargaining would inevitably break down if the consent of all individuals were necessary for the consumption of any portion of the commons. A system of first possession allows all to survive, and hence makes the lot of all participants superior to the alternative of mutually assured destruction. Now the ultimate justification for Locke is no longer desert theory, but simple necessity. Blackstone himself echoed exactly the same line when he said bluntly, "Necessity begat property."[24] Consent is not required to establish property rights because the great number of parties makes it unworkable. When necessity, not consent, becomes the origin of property, then we have a melding of a utilitarian system, with a social contract theory.

Now we come to the question, what is acquired by first possession? Here, in a manner congenial with the broad claims of the natural lawyers, all systems of private law have roughly the same contours. The basic conception of property gives to its owner the exclusive right to the possession, use, and disposition of the land in perpetuity. One standard objection to the Lockean theory is that, at most, it explains the pride of place given the first possessor without explaining why that owner receives the robust bundle of rights routinely conferred upon him by well-developed legal systems (at least, in their private law guise). Yet the functional explanation for that result follows from the utilitarian considerations set out above: it is very costly for a social system to create partial bundles of rights in discrete things. If initial capture leaves some elements of value unaccounted for, then some additional method must be found to assign whatever resources the original appropriation left hanging.

Consider one alternative: Suppose that taking possession of a thing gave right to possession only so long as actual possession of the thing were maintained. It would then follow that no farmer could leave his fields untended and go to market. Blackstone saw the point clearly, as did Bentham.* The purpose of a legal rule is to allow the right to possession to continue even when the fact of possession is no longer indubitable, unless and until the owner has decided to abandon the thing. Legal protection is thus a cheap substitute for the active defense and patrol of property, which is why theories of possession from Roman law to the present have always stressed the acquisition and loss of possession without troubling to give a precise definition of the term *possession* itself.[26]

The proposition that possession is the root of title is not a necessary truth but is heavily culture bound. In nomadic hunter-gatherer cultures, the first-possession rule applies with great power to personal property, but not to land. So long as individuals make no fixed investments in particular plots of real estate, small tribes and bands will just move through open territories instead of settling them. The costs of setting and enforcing boundaries are too high relative to the benefits they generate. But agriculture requires clearing land, an investment that the farmer can recover only over many years of successful cultivation. Change the use of land, and gains from privatization increase. It is no accident that the classical maxim warned, and promised, that "you shall reap only where you sow." Any other rule creates a fatal mismatch between investment and return: what self-interested person will labor so that only strangers may profit?

The interplay between natural law and utilitarian concerns operates throughout this transformation. Thus the standard rule that possession generates ownership of an indefinite duration eliminates the awkward problem of deciding who owns the land in question after the death of the

---

* "The savage who has killed a deer may hope to keep it for himself, so long as his cave Is undiscovered; so long as he watches to defend it, and is stronger than his rivals; but that is all. How miserable and precarious is such a possession. If we suppose the least agreement among savages to respect the acquisitions of each other, we see the introduction of a principle to which no name can be given but that of law. A feeble and momentary expectation may result from time to time from circumstances purely physical, but a strong and permanent expectation can result only from law. That which, in the natural state was an almost invisible thread, in the social state becomes a cable. Property and law are born together, and die together. Before laws were made there was no property; take away laws and property ceases."[25]

original possessor. Instead of having to reopen the ownership question at his death or that of his descendants, the present owner can develop the property in full, secure in the knowledge that the gains from improvement can be captured either by sale or by consuming the proceeds thereof, if desired, during life. The longer time horizon thus allows for intelligent planning that could not take place when the labor in question created improvements whose benefit could be captured by others. The danger of taking from A and giving to B is not confined to a world in which all transfers are simultaneous; it can also arise in a world in which investments today are not protected against expropriation tomorrow.

The first-possession rule thus has powerful functional justifications that cut across societies. The basic problems of incentives, allocation, and administrative costs that it addresses are more or less constant across different cultures, so we should expect the rule to be relatively robust—as it has been. Nonetheless, certain variations have to be taken into account as well. Thus, once first possession becomes the rule of acquisition, we have a powerful need to know when each claim of possession is perfected, and thus to develop subordinate rules to implement the central rule of acquisition. At this level, we should expect a certain diversity in the customary or statutory practices. In rocky New England soil, it may be sensible to mark the edges of one's property by stones collected from it; while in heavy forests, territories can be marked by nicks in trees. In other cases, claims offices and recordation systems may be used to establish both the scope and the priority of claims, whether to land or minerals. But these subordinate conventions do not undermine the universality of a first-possession rule; they only illustrate the myriad ways of its implementation. And the uniform principle championed by the earlier natural lawyers persists: that system of identification will be used that is the clearest and whose implementation is not too costly.

The first-possession rule is also supple enough to work in tandem with the rules that govern families and business associations. If A obtains possession of an unowned tract of land, he may do so not solely on his own account but rather as head of his family, clan, or tribe. If several persons combine to take possession of some unowned property, the property taken will be divided in accordance with the terms of their joint venture. Once it has excluded outsiders, the rule of first possession therefore dovetails neatly into the more complex rules of family and business associations, becoming widely adaptable to different forms of social organization. Thus, the rule is by no means merely some ancient survival of atomistic individualism.

The origin of property, then, is rooted in social necessity, given the practical impossibility of reaching any broad compact over the distribution of natural things. But universal necessity need not dictate the internal operation of the system. The transactional difficulties are radically reduced once individual titles are established by first possession; within this changed environment, consent now becomes the appropriate method for exchange. Since only two parties need be involved in order to transfer property rights, the bargaining range will be small in light of the large number of potential suppliers of standard commodities like acorns and apples. The natural lawyers understood that the general rules for transferring title should have a consensual basis, even though the rules of acquisition do not. Accordingly, they included in their basic rules the principles for contract, especially as a mode for transferring ownership of things already reduced to ownership by first possession. Though not couched in terms of market efficiency, their rules surely facilitated and fostered market institutions, rather than catered to any protective, mercantilist, or guild mentality.

CUSTOM AS A SOURCE OF LAW

The use of custom—the implicit norms that grow up within a community—is yet another point where there is a powerful, if unappreciated, convergence between natural law theories and utilitarianism. Within the natural law tradition, custom has long been a significant source of substantive legal rules. Operationally, one could not observe the divine hand at work; and historically, there was little understanding of the biological imperatives that work in cross-cultural settings. Even so, the fact that certain legal rules or conventions were followed in large numbers of different societies made it more likely that these norms and practices had the force of law. Admittedly, the chain of inference is faulty if adherence to custom is treated as a universal imperative, without further qualification or caution. Slavery was a common practice in many ancient cultures that regarded themselves as civilized, and conquest was generally regarded as an appropriate way to acquire slaves—as an act of mercy toward those whom the conqueror could otherwise kill with impunity. It is hard to offer any normative defense of those practices today, and we should all be better off if we do not try.

A single counterexample to a general rule does not, however, necessarily lead to its rejection; principled qualification may well turn out to be the better alternative. Custom should not be regarded as dispositive with respect to those persons who are *strangers* to the group that has generated a particular norm: conquest is a norm that may appear in all cultures at the same time; but in each instance, it is a rule that prefers the inside members to the rest of the world. Nonetheless a different class of customs is entitled to far greater respect—those that operate internal to a given group or society. Here one speaks about the rules that bind all for the benefit of all. At any given time, the gaming dynamics differ totally from what they would be in the case in which the losses are external, for now each person (or subgroup) knows in general that he (or it) is equally likely to assume either of two future roles: the owner whose land is trespassed, or the owner of the animals who do the trespassing. If forced to choose a general rule of conduct to govern both the bitter and the sweet, no one can do better for himself than by choosing the social optimum.

The basic insight at work follows from John Rawls[27] with his use of the "veil of ignorance," and from Friedrich Hayek with his devotion to the spontaneous order.[28] Customs tend to emerge from a constant pattern of interaction which places individuals behind a veil of ignorance so that, in accordance with Rawls's formulation, they must choose a general rule while in ignorance of their own position in any future dispute. So constrained, they have an incentive to choose the rule that works to the long-term average advantage of all members of society: there is no way they can better their own personal position by choosing otherwise. Likewise, Hayek's idea of spontaneous order assumes that customary practices made by people so situated in practice will through trial and error lead to the sound conclusion. Once again, the reason is that all players gain from the adoption of sound social practices in their own social communities.

Disinterested decision making lies at the root of both Rawls and Hayek, but the origins of their approach go back still further. The same theme is evident in Adam Smith's preoccupation with the impartial spectator,[29] and with Hegel's reliance on the theme of *die List der Vernunft*, or the "cunning of reason." It also lies at the root of Frederic Maitland's classic discussion of the question of tenure. Here individual nobles simultaneously occupied many rungs in the feudal ladder—"Therefore it is necessary to remember that the king was the only person who was always lord and never tenant; that his greatest feudatories had one interest as lord, another as tenants"[30]—and hence were under constant pressure to adopt those customary rules efficient for the lord-vassal relationship as a whole. Therefore, when a community has large numbers of repetitive and similar transactions, all its participants have powerful incentives—not by conscious design, but by incremental development—to articulate and support general norms that work toward the long-term advantage of its members. There is, accordingly, a good utilitarian explanation of why we should place great confidence in the slow form of evolutionary growth that natural lawyers have generally praised. Yet, by the same token, we should be wary of the actions of those who are not trapped behind the Rawlsian veil, which is why the rules that dictated the relationship between king and vassals were always more troubled.

Robert C. Ellickson has recently pointed to the development of powerful customary norms of "neighborliness" that govern disputes over cattle trespass among the ranchers in Shasta County, California (see also chapter 2),[31] but in truth, the practices go farther back in Anglo-American law. Take one example: The law of cattle trespass illustrates the convergence between customary practices and efficient utilitarian outcomes. The customary rule allowed each party to hold the trespassing cattle of his neighbor until amends were paid for the damage so caused, with an allowance for the cost of interim keep.* The underlying rules of cattle trespass were strict, so that the simple fact of the animals' straying showed both parties that amends were indeed owing. The choice of amends had the effect of avoiding any complex bargaining problems that might otherwise arise if one farmer were allowed to keep another's animals until its true owner repurchased his original right of possession.

The problem is the familiar one of bilateral monopoly. Under that rights structure, the cattle owner should in principle be willing to pay an amount up to the full value of the animal to recover it, while the landowner should be satisfied with any amount greater than the damage done plus the interim costs of keeping the animal. The amends formula cuts down the size of the bargaining range, while the requirement to pay for the animal's keep encouraged the cattle owner to put in a prompt appearance so that amends could be assessed on the strength of accurate information. As most individuals owned both land and cattle in roughly equal proportions, the rule worked an overall allocative improvement without any systematic redistributive effects. The desirable features of the system were not lost on its participants, even if the utilitarian arguments were not formally articulated. Indeed, in England, when in 1953 a legal commission proposed changing the ancient rules on the ground that they did not conform to the ethical principles behind a negligence system, the farmers rose up to defeat

---

* Thus, in the *Tithe Case,* in 1506: "[I]f I have beasts damage feasant, I shall not justify my entry to chase them out unless I first tender all amends."[32]

the reform—notwithstanding the protests of academics who dismissed their customary ways as primitive.[33]

The parties need not always, however, be uncertain of their future roles in order for efficient customs to emerge within a community. Thus, in the nineteenth-century whaling trades a multitude of customs grew up to decide which of several rival ships were entitled to keep a whale. These rules usually gave pride of place to the ship that first harpooned the whale, even if it took some time to secure it or remove its oil. But some whalers went further and devised elaborate rules that split the take when the combined efforts of two or more ships were necessary to capture the whale.[34]

In some cases, the reach of custom extended to bind outsiders to the trade as well, such as residents in the community who had knowledge of whaling customs. In 1881, in *Ghen v. Rich*,[35] the plaintiff killed a finback whale which, as was common for its species, immediately disappeared below the waves, only to be found by another man several days later as it washed up on the beach. The custom of the region called for payment of a small fee to the finder to compensate him for informing the shipowner of the whale's location. But in this case the finder dispensed with the notice and sold the whale to a third party, who auctioned off the oil. The shipowner then sued him to recover the proceeds of the sale. The custom was held good as against the finder and his purchaser. Its overall efficiency could not be doubted: to allow the finder to control the oil would put an effective end to a risky but profitable trade; to require the finder to cooperate without receiving anything in exchange could result in whales left rotting on the beach for want of an owner. Here, in effect, the custom worked in harmony with both the capture rule and the labor theory of value to provide incentives for both capture and notification.

For the relevant parties, the common practice thus has much practical utility; but by the same token, the widespread adoption of efficient practices also gives rise to a dangerous irony about the global consequences of the rule. Adopting efficient rules of capture for any particular whale creates the risk of overfishing which could destroy the entire stock of whales on which the trade depends. Handling that risk is not the province of any local custom that allocates the gain from capture to the participants who assist in it: what is now needed is some limitation on the overall catch of whales—one that has to be imposed as a matter of public law, and raises serious questions of allocation for the many practitioners of the craft. Yet even when that consideration is added to the mix, it does not result in a rejection of the customary rules for the reduced number of whales that may still be captured.

That customs tend, in most cases, to be efficient within a trade does not necessarily mean that they will be efficient in all. Custom works best in stable environments—business, legal, and technological. Customs, which generally take some time to evolve, do not respond as well to rapid changes in circumstances—unless, as is the case with medicine, sudden changes become so commonplace that a special set of higher-order customs develops to deal with innovation.

As noted earlier, the first possession rules rest often rest on an implicit customary standard when other individuals respect the claims set out by the first possessor. This practice, however, tends to work best where the rate of diffusion of ownership is slow throughout the initial set of unowned territories. Only then can one claim be securely established before a rival claimant appears. That condition was satisfied, for example, in the occupation of frontier lands before the Civil War, but it worked far less well in 1889 when the Oklahoma Sooners jumped the starting line to occupy many of the choice plots just before the former Indian territories were opened to white settlers. The mad dash to secure prime homestead plots created insecurity and bitterness for years to come.[36]

One of the great frontiers of this century, the broadcast spectrum, is subject to the same analysis. The allocation of the spectrum prior to the Federal Radio Act of 1927 took place by individual occupation of frequencies—a modern adaptation of the first possession rule. But title by occupancy could not be imitated in today's assignment of the spectrum recently auctioned off for personal communications services.[37] Every PCS band could have been occupied in a twinkling by any single provider. Given the changes in technology, only a state-run auction of well-defined spectrum could create useful property rights blessed with clear boundaries (both by frequency and territory) and free transferability. The pace of modern life makes first possession far less valuable for newly allocated assets than in formative historical times.

Custom also found it difficult to adapt sensibly to rapid discontinuities in traditional business or legal environments. This problem is well illustrated by the famous 1918 case of the *International News Service v. Associated Press.*[38] A recurrent issue in the news business is the extent to which one news service can use the content of stories—the words themselves are protected by copyright—gathered by other firms to produce its own stories. Newspaper stories are obviously of no value unless they are published to their audience—but publication means that they are also revealed to any competitor willing to pay the cost of a single paper. Since extensive freeriding would create strong inhibitions against the collection of information in the first place, the concern here is to allow the information to reach customers without allowing it to be used by rivals. Yet the protection cannot be cast too broadly: a rule that gave the story itself to the first firm that happened to cover it would create a set of local monopolies in information that could severely blunt competition and curtail public coverage. In order to work its way through these conflicting demands, the custom in the newspaper trade was, and is, that reporters can look to see what issues are covered in other stories, but then have to conduct their own independent research before publishing their own accounts.

In most cases, the threat of retaliation has proved sufficient to keep recalcitrant competitors in line; but at the height of the First World War, the International News Service (INS) broke from established practice to lift Associated Press news bulletins in New York for the stories published by its West Coast members. Why the breach in the otherwise uniform practice? The answer did not lie in some perverse decision to dishonor a custom, but was driven by the decision of the British and French governments to exclude INS reporters from the front because of the pro-German sympathies of the Hearst organization that dominated INS. Only this rapid change in circumstance led to the defection from custom; and even then, INS was careful to honor the custom in all other markets, given its own interest in the long-term stability of the system. The pirating was eventually enjoined by a Supreme Court that never quite appreciated the economic pressures that led to its breach, but contented itself with relying on the old, if overbroad, maxim that no one should reap where he did not sow. Despite the momentary disruption, the customs articulated in *INS* remain in effect today within the print media, showing their practical durability. But as might be expected, they are far weaker in curbing the broadcast media's practice of piggybacking on newspaper stories, for broadcasters face far less fear of retaliation. At this point, the most we can hope for is that a broadcast outlet will identify its source and thus use advertising as an imprecise form of compensation for the property so taken.

In modern settings, however, courts have often shown a less secure grasp of custom, honoring it in cases where the claims are dubious and rejecting it when the claims are strong. One common source of tension in the law of property is the extent to which customary title should be allowed to prevail over a written inconsistent title. When deeds were difficult to draft and systems of recordation (which give notice of title to the world) were primitive or unknown, many communities were rich in customary property rights. In response to these demands, Blackstone had articulated rules that allowed for proof of local customs. But he set the initial presumption against the recognition of local customs, and allowed them to be established only by clear proof, which included a long and continuous practice done in an open and peaceful manner.[39] Additional conditions had to be satisfied as well. A custom had to be reasonable, by which Blackstone did not mean that one had to assign the reason for its adoption, but rather that one could not assign a reason against it. The two examples he used to illustrate the rule give some sense of his meaning. A custom that allows no man to bring his beasts into the common fields until October 3 is good, although one could not indicate why this day was chosen in preference to another. But a custom that insisted that no man place his beasts in the commons until the lord first placed his was bad, for the lord need not put his beasts in at all.[40] Blackstone also insisted that these customs be certain, and customary, by which he meant that it "not be left to the option of every man, whether he will use them or no."[41] So a rule that charged special assessments was good, so long as the portions were clearly established. Last, customs had to be internally consistent, so that "one custom cannot be set up in opposition to another."[42]

Blackstone's basic guidelines have been tested in setting the rules for the creation of public rights of way on or near a beach. In most cases, private ownership back from the landward side of vegetation is established, while the strip between the low tide and the mean high tide is a commons of long standing (see chapter 7). Still a point of contention is the strip of land between the vegetation line and the high tide mark.

Most nineteenth-century courts, following in the spirit of Blackstone, took a cautious view of the creation of any public right of way, and a hostile one of the creation of the so-called profits *à prendre*—that is, the right to take, for example, fish or sand or seaweed.[43] The difference in attitude toward easements and profits was not an idle piece of formalism. The easement confined its holder to some well-specified right of way, but the profit allowed its holder to roam the land unchecked to collect his preferred goods. The commentators followed Blackstone lest ambiguous customs create uncertainty about the conveyancing of land, given that public easements could not be repurchased from the present and future inhabitants of any locale.[44] But some modern courts are more willing to create new customary rights without meeting the rigor of the early Blackstone tests. Thus, in 1969, the Oregon Supreme Court created a universal public easement on the dry land without any real evidence of a general customary practice applicable across the region.[45]

More recently, in 1995, the Hawaii Supreme Court has burdened the titles to all Hawaiian land through its expansive recognition of customary rights. In *Public Access Shoreline Hawaii [PASH] v. Hawai'i County Planning Commission*, the court held that native Hawaiians were entitled to prove customary rights to profits from the gathering of plants, firewood, and thatch on otherwise private lands. Indeed, the present incarnation of these ill-defined customs was said to be strong enough to require that any development permits include "appropriate regulations," nowhere defined, for the protection of these ostensible customary rights whose content was equally undefined.[46] These newly minted or reconstituted ancient customs have placed a major impediment on all new financing and construction in Hawaii, as title insurance companies on the island often exempt such native easements and profits from their coverage; the risk is so widespread and ill defined as to be uninsurable. To date, no one knows what native rights will be asserted. It is difficult to resist the conclusion that Blackstone was correct in his initial skepticism about the creation of customs in land.[47] It is too risky to allow either courts or legislatures to recognize—or create—public rights of gathering over private property. Once again the arguments are perfectly general and apply to primitive cultures as well as modern ones.

Within tightly-knit communities, the converse situation arises with commercial customs which meet, ironically, far greater judicial hostility. The leading case on this point is Judge Learned Hand's famous 1932 decision in *The T.J. Hooper*, which refused "to make the general practice of a calling the standard of proper diligence."[48] In Hand's view, "a whole calling may have unduly lagged in the adoption of new and available devices." At issue in *The T.J. Hooper* was whether tugboat owners were negligent in failing to have a functioning ship-to-shore radio on board their craft. The case arose when two barges and their cargo had been lost off the Delaware coast because their inadequate receiving sets failed to receive navy storm warnings that would have allowed them to take refuge behind the Delaware breakwater. Even a back-of-the-envelope cost/benefit analysis casts doubt on the judgment of any captain in the late 1920s who would choose to venture out into open waters without a radio. If the custom had sanctioned this practice, then this incident would undermine the case for using custom to determine the standard for appropriate care. But it appeared that Hand misunderstood the evidence, which showed a radio was required, but held the captain, not the tug owner, responsible for its provision. Looked at thus, the negligence of the tugboat owners (who are vicariously responsible for the derelictions of its captain) follows easily from the showing that this tug "lagged" behind the industry custom, and obviates the more perilous task of having to decide whether the custom itself lagged behind some state-imposed normative standard.

In principle, of course, that examination, if carried out correctly, should show that the custom is efficient in responding to the needs of any close-knit community. But all too often the slip 'twixt cup and lip leads courts and juries to make more errors, and at greater cost, by jettisoning custom than by following it. In 1974, in the medical area, for example, the most famous judicial rejection of standard practice—not requiring glaucoma tests of individuals under age forty—was sufficiently riddled with errors in interpreting the medical and statistical evidence that the older common law rule of custom was quickly restored by statute.[49] In modern product liability cases—featuring damage actions by injured consumers against product manufacturers—Learned Hand's alternative effort to reconstruct cost/benefit arguments from the ground up has unleashed a veritable wave of lawsuits that allows product after product to be attacked on the strength of some alternative design, even if the challenged product sets the standard for excellence and durability within its industry.

The judicial license to second-guess decisions after the fact creates the kinds of expense and uncertainty that clear industry rules are able to avoid. The custom may not be perfect; but in a world of imperfect institutions, the only relevant question is whether it is better than the next-best alternative. In most cases, ordinary customs, whether as part of a trade or of a region, do a better job than ad-hoc cost/benefit tests, so long as the risks of external harms are safely put to one side. The cautious empirical approach of Hume and Hayek—observe in order that you may understand—will usually do more to advance the welfare of the community than will any conscious effort to rejigger rules with an overt, interventionist utilitarian calculus. The small-government, reactive sense of the natural lawyer again makes good sense from a sound and complete utilitarian perspective—one that takes account of the political pressures that can lead to systematic distortions in judicial and legislative behavior. Law has this much to learn from medicine: first, do no harm. And one good object lesson of how we may avoid doing harm is found in understanding the relationship between law and social norms.

CHAPTER 2

Social Norms versus Legal Commands

Behind my opening discussion of the methodological differences and the substantive convergence between natural law and utilitarian theories lies implicit acceptance of a working definition of law. By common usage, the domain of legal analysis includes constitutions, treaties, statutes, regulations, and judicial opinions. These legal materials fit comfortably under the wing of the positivist view of law that John Austin outlined in 1832 in his *Province of Jurisprudence Determined*: law, properly so called, represents a (general) command of the sovereign to its subjects, backed by state-imposed sanctions, such as imprisonment, fines, injunctions, and damages.[1] The defining characteristic of a law is therefore found not in either its substantive content or its semantic meaning, but only from its inclusion in the class of enforced commands that subjects habitually regard themselves as bound and obliged to obey. The legal system therefore includes not only direct commands, but also the various rules that specify how laws are to be made; and these procedural rules in turn allow individuals to discover which of the multitude of lawlike propositions are, in fact, part of the system of laws applicable in a given territory.[2]

This "positivist" program stands in sharp opposition to the deontological and consequentialist theories of legal justification outlined in the last chapter. The positivist's task is not the natural lawyer's enterprise of finding out which legal rules are conformable to human nature or which, by utilitarian reckoning, advance the welfare of the population at large. Rather, the positivist program deliberately confines its attention to whether a particular pronouncement constitutes a link in the chain of legal commands. As such its business is to identify the provenance and pedigree of a given rule, which is why John Austin used the term "Province," properly so called, in the title to his jurisprudential treatise. Most emphatically, the task of the positive theory of law is not to pass on the merits or demerits of laws. Accordingly, this positivist stance reveals another dimension to the traditional accounts of natural law: where previously natural law has been set in opposition to consequentialist theories, here it is set in opposition to positivist theories. The natural law theories insist that valid laws must satisfy certain minimum moral standards; positivist theories reject any such requirement. For that reason, positivism has often been styled a "pure" theory of law because it wishes to purge jurisprudence of kindred but extraneous moral, social, religious, and cultural norms, none of which need be backed by sovereign force.

One critical consequence of the positivist approach is the marginal relevance of the "definition" question—what do we mean by law, and what distinguishes legal rules from scientific rules or social practices?—to most burning issues of legal policy. In policy deliberations, the job is not to find out *who* exercises the sovereign power, but only *which* particular rights and duties that sovereign should enforce for reasons of justice or efficiency, or indeed, any other reason. From the positivist definition of law we could not learn, for example, whether slavery was a desirable or an undesirable practice. On the other hand, we could decide that it was a legally protected institution in ancient Rome or the antebellum South. Nor could we refuse to label as law the Nazi rules that required its Jewish subjects to wear yellow stars and even condemned them to the gas chambers.

Lest the positivist definition of law be criticized for conferring legitimacy on indefensible practices, it is important to note that this separation of law and morals has its progressive as well as its reactive side. The mere fact that a given proposition represents the law of a particular time and territory does nothing to insulate that law from withering criticism on moral grounds. To the positivist, the definition of law does not discharge any "expressive" function for legally sanctioned behavior; nor does it preclude criticism from those who detest that law for good reasons, or even for bad. The law may be the law, but it is also subject to contempt, ridicule, and disrespect, if not outright disobedience. Dickens was not the first, nor will he be the last, to describe the law as "an ass." It becomes therefore an independent moral question whether "massive resistance" to the desegregation command of *Brown v. Board of Education*[3] should be treated with the same respect and admiration as massive resistance to Nazi occupation and extermination. The job of definition is not to resolve these moral questions, or even to ease the pain of those who face the choice of compliance with or defiance of legal commands; rather definition and classification merely hold the modest but critical office of determining what material falls within the same analytical box. It does not even hint that all material within the box of legal commands are entitled to the same level of individual respect.

Even this key limitation does not reduce to some idle exercise inquiries into the definition of law: the power to exclude is what gives this definition of law real bite. Most obviously, Austin's definition allows—indeed, compels—us to distinguish between a bill that fails and a law that passes, even though both have identical substantive content. More controversially, it also reduces, perhaps rightly, international law to a set of customs and political conventions, given the absence of any common sovereign that rules over the nations that, routinely but not universally, abide by its dictates.[4] More ominously, his account tracks the social uneasiness that becomes unavoidable when political revolution is in the process of displacing one established legal order with another. The phrase "law and order" has punch because when no one exercises sovereign power, the danger multiplies that liberty will degenerate into license and freedom decay into anarchy. Unless one can tell who exercises sovereign power, it is not possible to tell which set of rival pretenders constitutes law—so people often pay with their lives for mistaken allegiances.

The strongest testimony to the power of Austin's definition of law lies in the fact that it receives such little attention in both the practice and the teaching of law. Judge Richard Posner has remarked that debates over the definition of the law have formed no part of his own legal education or, indeed, of his work as a distinguished appellate judge.[5] But the absence of these pointed disputes hardly shows that the definition, or the process of inclusion and exclusion that it requires, is unimportant or irrelevant, or that the task of defining law is somehow "futile." Rather, it shows that questions of political order were never burning issues in the cloistered halls of Harvard (or Oxford or Chicago) during the late 1950s and early 1960s. The absence of actual challenges to legal authority does not show that the definition is obtuse or wrong-headed. It shows only that social conditions in the United States were, and remain, far more stable than they have been at other times and in other places. There are no pretenders to legal power. It is only when power is contested that the distinctive features of a definition of law stand out in high relief.

The implicit dominance of this Austinian conception of law has long been a feature of American legal education, in both theory and practice. It is the foundation of what Robert Ellickson, in mounting an attack on this vision, has dubbed "legal centralism."[6] Starting from the Hobbesian vision, the Austinian positivist account gains urgency because it conceives that all durable social relations must be superintended by the power of some common sovereign. The basic Hobbesian insight is that self-interested individuals will not enter into any agreement that requires their future performance unless they know that their rights are backed by the power of the sword. Let A perform first on his promises, and B will keep the property transferred; yet, when the time comes, he will also refuse to perform his promise in exchange. If so, then even before the time comes for his performance, A will know that B's self-interest makes this outcome inevitable, and A will therefore prefer the status quo without trade to the losses that follow from performing first. B will take the same attitude if called on to perform first. And the problems become only more intractable as the number of contracting parties increases, and the content of their obligations becomes more complex.

Let this process run its course, and a sea of distrust will shrink the potentially vast enterprise of trade into the tiny domain of spot transactions: the simultaneous exchanges of goods and services. Even the use of money as a medium of exchange is improbable, for why should anyone assume that the paper received in payment for one transaction could be used for purchase in the next? Hobbes may have been wrong on the upshot, but he surely was clear: "Where there is no common Power, there is no Law; where no Law, no Injustice."[7] With no one to define and enforce obligations, talk of right and wrong becomes a lament, an art form, a bit of idle chatter. And it receives that fate not because of some deep skepticism of the ability to form judgments about right and wrong rules. Hobbes was not a moral skeptic, but he recognized that moral sentiments, however refined, would be stillborn in a world without some common coercive power over individuals. That power liberates them from the destructive regime in which both parties find it necessary to defect from a solution that, if faithfully followed, would work to their mutual advantage.

THE PRISONER'S DILEMMA GAME

The destructive social dynamic that led to Hobbes's call for sovereign power has been updated and formalized in the now-familiar prisoner's dilemma (PD) game. The ultimate message of that game is that all complex organizations face what is sometimes termed a "collective action problem." Unfortunately, the one solution that is ideal from the point of view of each member of a group, cannot be reached because the parties are unable to coordinate their actions in service of their uniformly desired goal. The following simple table contains all the information needed to draw the appropriate social lesson of the perils of noncooperation.

		Player Two	
		cooperates	defects
Player One	cooperates	10, 10	-2, 12
	defects	12, -2	0, 0

As diagrammed, the table sets the possible outcomes from the simplest game in which each of two players has two alternatives: cooperate or defect from some common venture. The paired numbers in the table indicate the payoffs that each player receives from each possible combination of outcomes—four in the situation given. In the box (10, 10), both players cooperate for a total gain of 20, shared equally. In the box (-2, 12), Player One (the row player) continues to cooperate, but Player Two (the column player) adopts a selfish course of action: the upshot is an individual payoff of -2 for Player One and of 12 for Player Two. Conversely, in this symmetrical world, if Player One defects, and Player Two cooperates, then the payoffs are reversed to 12 and -2, respectively. Note that the total gain from these last two scenarios equals 10, which is less than the 20 units of total gain from joint cooperation. To complete the picture, where both players choose to defect, neither gets anything, for a total payoff of 0. The total payoffs thus decline as we move from cooperation, to unilateral defection, to bilateral defection.

Viewed dispassionately, both players in the PD game stand to profit by coordinating their behaviors to remain in the upper left cell of the game. But acting individually and selfishly, both will defect. Player One will reason that Player Two will either cooperate or defect. If Player Two cooperates, then it is in the interest of Player One to defect, thereby to increase his total payoff from 10 to 12. (We must move down from the top to the bottom box in the left column.) But suppose that Player Two chooses to defect. Here Player One should defect as well in order to increase his total from −2 to 0. (Here we move from the top to the bottom box in the right column.) Player One has a *dominant strategy* to defect whether Player Two defects or cooperates. As this game is perfectly symmetrical, Player Two has that same dominant strategy. The upshot is that both players prefer to be in the upper left box. Nonetheless they end up in the lower right box, to their mutual detriment, here equal to 20 units. Sovereign power is thus justified to move the parties back to their cooperative solution even if it costs each player some portion of the 10 units privately obtainable from cooperation. The amount of resources that should be spent in keeping that sovereign in place depends on the loss in value as the players move from the top left to the bottom right cell: if the question is one of law and order, one of life and death, then very large investments make sense.

The traditional positivist definitions of law thus marry a bleak vision of self-interested human behavior to a theory of dominant sovereign power. Suitably elaborated, this basic model explains not only why individuals confess to crimes when they and their confederates should remain silent, but also why partners cheat on each other, why sellers cheat on cartels, and why individual drillers overexploit productive oil fields. No one should doubt that this simple model captures a very large portion of the truth about self-interest and individual behavior. Indeed, if human nature were unfailingly cooperative, why adopt coercive legal institutions in the first place? Or work mightily to justify the imposition of state force as a matter of political theory?

This simple parable hardly tells the whole story, however, for similar PD games or collective action problems may be overcome without the use of state power or private litigation. Bone does not always rub against bone; sometimes cartilage softens the impact. Today the study of these quieter interactions has helped shift the focus of scholarly inquiry from legal power to social norms, which, generally speaking, are any rules, implicit or explicit, that organize and discipline cooperative human behavior, whether or not they are backed by the sovereign power of the state.[8] (Indeed one linguistic caution is that the term *social norm* could be used either in *opposition* to legal norms or as a broad term that *includes* legal norms.) Study of social norms, in both its broader and narrower senses, and the spin-off interest in social roles and social meaning, serve as a vital link among the disciplines of law, economics, sociology, anthropology, and political theory. Robert Ellickson entitled his book *Order Without Law: How Neighbors Settle Disputes* as a direct attack on the Austinian view of legal centralism. "In everyday speech, for example, one commonly hears the phrase 'law and order,' which implies that governments monopolize the control of misconduct. The notion is false—so utterly false that it warrants the implicit attack that it receives in the title of this book."[9]

The current attack on legal centralism still focuses on the PD game that sparked the original investigation into the uses of sovereign power. So central is the problem of noncooperative behavior that much social science thought converges on one single question: What social institutions and strategies can overcome the deadly, if familiar, collective action problem?[10] There is in a new articulation of the basic problem, no relaxation from the austere world of Hobbes and Austin, but only in the kinds of tools stable social groups utilize to combat them. No longer is state force the only form of social glue that holds people together. Reputation is explicitly recognized for what it always has been—a powerful constraint on human behavior. In addition, other forms of sanction, ranging from simple disapproval and gossip, to ostracism and exclusion, can be directed in predictable ways at antisocial forms of conduct.

The now-fashionable inquiry into social norms, however, only pushes us down to a more fundamental level: What conditions allow for the emergence and stability of norms? This question is, in turn, plagued by further ambiguity. Norms come in all shapes and sizes; in the simplest case, a norm can result from an express agreement among group members. In some cases, norm violations count as breaches of contract for which the violator must answer in a court of law. Yet in others, its consequences are indirect. While the violation of the norm may not trigger any direct legal action by other parties, it could well excuse them from the performance of other obligations, so as to deflect the risk of their becoming the target of any law suit. Alternatively, it could justify certain limited self-help techniques that would otherwise expose the aggrieved party to legal sanctions. Indeed, the law is rife with situations where the breach of contract by one party is used chiefly to allow the other side to rid itself of its own legal obligation to perform; or to allow it to seize, for example, premises that have been let or goods that have been already delivered. And finally, there are many contracts where the parties by agreement shun the use of legal mechanisms for enforcement, by announcing their intention at the outset to rely exclusively on the sanctions of honor, reputation, or the loss of future business.[11] Express norms may be married to many different systems of sanctions.

It would be a mistake, however, to equate social norms with express contracts: such purported equivalence ignores vital social norms whose emergence cannot be traced to an agreement of any sort. Usually the discussion of social norms is steeped in the language of custom and usage, common practice, social standards, and implied rules of conduct. All of these conventions are widely shared and respected by group members but do not rest on formal or explicit agreement. Characteristically, no one can quite figure out how these norms arose, document where they came from or why they evolved, or explain why they receive the level of respect that in practice they do. Rather, their diffuse and decentralized origin becomes an advantage, suggesting that the durability of a norm is attributable to the way in which it uniformly advances the interest of group members. The norm that just "shows up" may not reflect conscious planning and deliberation found in our basic constitutional design—a minus. But, by way of offsetting that, it cannot be chalked up to the partisan manipulation of one or another interest group—a minus. It is for this reason that natural law theories properly treat custom as a test of the reasonableness and justice of a particular norm.

Lastly, any emphasis on implicit social norms should not invite us to overlook the role played by coercive legal norms that are the subject of laws properly so called. In many instances, the legal system chooses to adopt for its standards the customary practices that have evolved within groups for the interpretation of contractual language, for the delineation of property rights, and for the articulation of the appropriate standard of care in tort cases. At this point we have a convenient blend of legal centralism and social norms. The legal system uses its power to enforce a set of norms whose origins are found in common practice, thereby dulling the sharp opposition between legal rules and social practices, as suggested by Ellickson's title *Order Without Law* (but qualified in important ways throughout the book).

Any theory of norms must deal with all three variations on the common theme: private agreements, social conventions, and publicly created norms. A complete account must approach this topic from at least two angles. First, there is the descriptive question stemming from the incontrovertible fact that different norms are enforced in different ways. What accounts for the distribution of norms across these three categories? Why, historically, are some norms generated by explicit contract, others by social convention, and still others by legislation or common law adjudication? The second question, which closely dovetails with the first, is normative. Which substantive norms should be placed in which class and why? Even if we assume that *all* norms are designed to overcome PD games or other collective action problems (which I take to be almost a truism), it is necessary to select the proper enforcement mechanism to counteract the breach. Which norms *should* be enforced by private sanctions, which by custom and common usage, and which by state coercion?

The standard literature does not appear to have much to say about the process that sorts norms into different classes, either by generation or by enforcement. Too often the analysis confines itself to the question of why enforceable norms are needed, without asking which type of enforcement mechanism is appropriate for what norm or how the different layers of enforcement do, or should, interact with each other. In answering these questions, the line between the descriptive and normative tends to blur, for the customary distribution of norm enforcement often reflects a desirable distribution, perhaps for the same reason that customs are efficient guides in other contexts (as I discussed in chapter 1).

Descriptively, it seems that many social norms are just that: norms that were enforced exclusively by social sanctions. In many cases, that separation of norms from laws appears to be both stable and desirable. As a matter of principle, the appropriate legal response should be to repeal those legal rules, widely disregarded, that stand in sharp contrast to the dominant social practices within a community. Ellickson instances protective Norwegian legislation, universally ignored in practice, that limited a maid's workday to a maximum of ten hours and gave her paid holidays and other benefits.[12] Better to remove the statute from the books than to risk its erratic enforcement; the ability of maids to quit and find other work offers a sufficient measure of social control.

In theory, two other connections between law and social norms are possible. At one pole, a system that relies exclusively on social enforcement of sound social norms could be said to suffer from some kind of a gap or defect: if social enforcement is good, why isn't legal enforcement even better? The expressive power of condemnation and approval is made stronger if the entire state stands behind a norm. Individuals have been known to hold out against social pressures and sanctions: indeed, some social practices can be undone by persistent behavior that stands in opposition to norms. If there is a social norm against integration, why not institutionalize the norm with Jim Crow laws? If there is a social norm for integration, why not enforce that norm with an antidiscrimination law? If there is a social norm that calls for survival of the fittest, why not a legal norm that prohibits the giving of charity to the weak and needy? If there is a social norm that the rich must give of their wealth to assist the poor, why not a legal statute that requires compulsory contributions to a social welfare scheme? If there is a social norm against the use of tobacco, why not have the government impose heavy taxes on its sale or limitations on its distribution?

Yet, whatever the working presumption, nothing in principle *guarantees* that any social norm generated by a given group must necessarily be regarded as good. It is in principle possible to think that the group itself has been locked into a situation where everybody is forced to obey a convention that is "bad," a situation that can be escaped only by the legal adoption of the contrary. In this scenario, the social norm represents, not the solution to a collective action problem, but the collective action problem itself against which legal coercion or state education supplies the key to our collective escape.[13] Thus, we could impose a tax on alcohol or tobacco to counteract the social equilibrium in which the consumption of alcohol and tobacco is acceptable.[14]

What these two positions have in common is the reunification of legal and social norms. The legal system either backs good social norms with force or overcomes bad ones with force. In both cases, legal centralism becomes the tool to secure some needed social conformity, as the separation of law and morals should be regarded as a regrettable lapse to be overcome by prompt legislative or judicial action. The set of purely social norms is thus regarded as falling in an awkward no-man's land between the world of purely subjective preferences (vanilla against chocolate ice cream) and the law of fully enforceable legal norms. The upshot is a diminished role for "imperfect obligations"—those enforced by conscience and social pressures but not by law— which classical natural law theory believed to embody the *correct* societal response, for example, to the implementation of norms of benevolence.[15] But we should be cautious before we jettison a principled reliance on this middle category, for there is no a-priori reason to think that legal sanctions should back all social norms. The separation of law from morals is sometimes a good thing, and sometimes a bad one. How do we establish the sound relationship between law and social norms?

In order to cover these topics, I first criticize the late H. L. A. Hart's effort to distinguish between laws and social norms. Thereafter I argue in connection with aggression, theft, defamation, and promise breaking that expensive legal sanctions should be reserved for those cases where small numbers of individual defections pose a serious peril to the social order. Next I consider the use of two-tier sanctions, both legal and social, as they operate in tandem in employment settings and for product warranties, rental housing, and cattle trespass. In these situations, a dangerous paradox often emerges: efforts to use legal force to back up social norms tend to reduce their effectiveness. I conclude the chapter with an explanation of why social norms in discrete contexts critically depend on background legal norms for their enforcement. Social norms, standing alone, do not a workable society make.

HART'S FAILED DISTINCTION BETWEEN LEGAL AND SOCIAL NORMS

One notable early effort to draw the line between legal and social norms (or, as is sometimes said, between law and morals) has been offered by H. L. A.

Hart in his extraordinarily influential book, *The Concept of Law*.[16] Hart's major intellectual mission was to defend an updated version of Austin's command theory of law against the natural law theorists such as Lon Fuller who, writing in the aftermath of the Nazi reign of terror, believed that unjust laws were not, in some sense, law at all.* Hart isolated four characteristics that separated legal from moral rules: importance, immunity from legal change, the voluntary actions characteristic of legal offenses, and the form of moral pressure.

These distinctions do not carry the day, for the opposition between law and morals, between legal and social sanctions, is not strictly an either/or matter. Sometimes both systems of control will be invoked; sometimes, either one or the other. The distribution of their use does not closely track Hart's fourfold distinction.

Importance

As to Hart's first point, the fit is far from good: moral violations are frequently regarded as important, while legal ones are sometimes viewed as merely technical. Yet the most pivotal social norms—directed to the prevention of aggression and theft—are on the receiving end of both kinds of sanction. Other practices, such as promise keeping, may be enforced by both legal and social sanctions. But only social sanctions apply when someone cancels or backs out of a dinner invitation or a trip to Disney World. The simple explanation is that neither party intends to use the promise to create legal relations. Not one dinner invitation in a million comes with explicit caveats whereby either guest or host waives damages if the other side backs out; yet that is exactly the message that such an invitation does in fact carry. Who would bring suit for damages, no matter how deliberate the breach, or how transparently thin or false the justification offered for it? Still, breaches of such promises are subject to social sanctions: return invitations get scrubbed, other hosts remove offenders from their guest lists, gossips have a field day, and business opportunities may dry up. Any contract that specifically calls for damages in the event of unexcused nonattendance should, of course, be enforced *if* anyone were quixotic enough to demand, or acquiesce, in it. But

---

*   In this context, the question, what is law? does make a real difference. If the Nazi rules were law, then individuals prosecuted for serious crimes against humanity could argue that they could not be justly attacked retroactively for conduct that was lawful when committed. That line of argument is denied them under the strong natural rights theory.[17]

it never happens. The role of the legal center is to create a default rule that farms out these cases to its social norm subsidiary.

Nonetheless, the distribution of promises between the social and the legal is uncertain at the edges. The dominant expectation is not to enforce promises between spouses, precisely because we expect the couple's informal adjustments to smooth out their day-to-day differences. The law is largely irrelevant within stable families; and the most important obligations within a marriage, those of loyalty and fidelity, are typically sustained without legal enforcement. Yet the presumption of noninterference might well be reversed on some monetary issues. In 1919, one bellwether English case refused to enforce support payments of £30 per month in an informal separation agreement entered into by a husband who left his wife behind in England when he returned to his position in Ceylon.[18] That agreement should not be analogized to an invitation for drinks when—to my eyes, at least—it smacks of a business arrangement arising out of marriage. The absence of informal mechanisms of adjustment—such as those available when internal household budgets are varied by couples living together—increases the need for legal sanctions to honor the joint expectations of the parties. Indeed, nearly forty years later, Parliament overruled the decision by statute, and thus brought the English rule[19] in line with American practice on the issue: once before a judge, the obligation may not be fixed and unmovable; but the party who wishes to escape or amend it must show that changed circumstances support the proposed revision. Contrary to Hart, the key point is not some detached importance of the underlying obligation. It goes to the coordination of various remedial devices.

The reverse set of expectations applies to business promises. The ordinary contract for services or the sale of goods is legally enforced unless some good reason displaces that expectation. Why force loan or sale agreements to restate the obvious? But, once again, these expectations are presumptive and not conclusive. The point is an old one: ordinarily infer the intention to create legal relations in business, not in social contexts. But remember as well that even ordinary rules have their exceptions, so that if the parties do not wish the legal enforcement of a business arrangement, however large and complex, then so be it. More mischievously, serious commercial promises are not enforced, because they are not "supported by consideration" (that is, for nonlawyers, they are not part of a bargained transaction). A common example is a simple promise to forgive part of a valid debt; that promise could be quite important and generally unenforceable. Similarly, the traditional common law refused to allow A by promise to B to confer benefits on C for which C could sue in his own right—a dubious legal judgment, largely reversed with the passage of time.[20]

This superficial look at the wise and the foolish in legal norms leads to one conclusion. The importance of a norm has little do with whether it is backed by legal or moral sanctions, or by both. The heterogeneity within both classes of norms precludes any rank ordering that correlates importance with the preferred or actual method of enforcement. I dare say that the sentiment runs deeper than this: even if asked to organize their own perfect legal world, most people would not use importance, however defined, as the test for separation: some norms are too important, and others not important enough, to be left to the law. Rather, the key variable concerns the interaction between the legal and the social modes of enforcement. Where the latter are available, and capable of careful application, then it is better to dispense with legal enforcement. Some matters are too important, and too fragile, to be trusted to the courts.

Immunity to Legal Change

Hart's second line of distinction—the immunity to legal change of moral rules—also fails to carry the day. Hart accepts the common-sense observation that social norms are created by an accumulation of informal practices, while law is made by some distinct enactment, publicly noted. It would be odd to decree that a new custom will take effect as of January 1, 2000, however much the "norm managers" of today might wish it so. But common law (that is, judge-made law) rules also develop by accretion; and these rules Hart's account tends to slight. Only a foolhardy legal historian would venture to find one, first clear legal prohibition against aggression or against legal enforcement of (most) promises. Indeed, common law rules are *common* to the realm, as articulated by judges who were heavily influenced by customary norms. Immunity to change tracks the difference between judge-made law and legislation, not that between law and social norms.

Capacity of Avoidance

Hart's third test—that moral condemnation requires that an actor have the capacity to avoid certain forms of harm to others—also fails to demarcate the two realms. Thus the criminal law (unless altered by statute) usually adopts a moral attitude toward mental states: the inclusion of *mens rea*, the guilty mind, into the definition of most crimes surely has that character. In contrast, the tort law typically ignores mental states either when it hews to an "objective" standard of reasonable care that impaired persons cannot meet, or when it more forthrightly holds people strictly liable for the consequences of their acts. But it hardly follows that tort law ignores the dictates of morality when it insists that individuals compensate others for the pains inflicted absent some excuse or justification—itself a qualification with obvious moral overtones. Yet the moral conceptions behind strict liability do not arise from qualifications that deal with consent and self-defense. Even on its core principle, the cases have frequently stressed the injustice of allowing a defendant to internalize the gains from his actions while forcing others to lick their own wounds and bear their own costs.[21] The criminal law may have the luxury of acquitting an assailant without convicting a victim, but the tort law that exonerates the defendant leaves the injured plaintiff without compensation. Strict liability therefore has as many moral defenders as it does detractors. The variation within the class of legal and moral judgment once again undercuts this effort to find a litmus test for moral judgment that is explicitly tied to the mental states of individual actors. The voluntariness of one person's action is relevant to both moral and legal theory (as it is to tortious and criminal liability) but decisive to neither.

Appeals to Conscience

Finally, it would be mistaken to assume with Hart that moral or social sanctions appeal solely to conscience—that is, to arguments that seek to alter conduct by pointing out the error of one's ways. Social sanctions against deviant behavior, however defined, take far more concrete forms. When divorce was regarded as socially unacceptable, divorcées found it difficult to get jobs, join clubs, or run for public office. Criticism, hostility, ostracism, expulsion, ridicule, snubs, and boycotts have long been used against individuals who violate rules of dress and decorum, even when no legal sanctions are imposed. Within cohesive social groups, these sanctions not only educate the offender; they also carry out an implicit threat to punish past actions. The traditional social hostility toward illegitimacy took its toll even without legal enforcement.

SORTING SANCTIONS

Hart's initial effort to define the proper role for legal intervention then fails. The question remains, however, Which rules should be subject to which sanctions, and why? Amid the confusion, a tolerably clear pattern emerges. One constant refrain is that legal sanctions are more expensive than social ones. Legal sanctions require the use of police, lawyers, judges, and administrators, whose behavior must be coordinated and regulated. Tax revenues must be collected to keep the system operating. Given these costs, the best way to frame the inquiry is to ask whether the superior outcome, if any, from supplementing social norms with legal sanctions is large enough to justify the extra cost, given the risk of error inherent in the operation of both systems.[22] That question of marginal impact in turn depends—at least, in part—on the cost to society of the defection of a single individual from the operation of the basic norm. A few examples might illustrate the point.

Aggression and Theft

Social sanctions against the critical cases of aggression and theft should be very strong, owing to the enormous losses these practices impose on victims. These individual losses, moreover, typically map closely into social losses, in that the gains to the aggressor or the thief offset only minimally the victim's loss. In most cases, the buyer of stolen property will pay only a fraction of the item's value of property to its owner. (Where he values it more, he can do the unthinkable: buy it.) As for physical aggression, does anyone think that the rapist's momentary gratification is greater than his victim's permanent physical and psychological scars?

The social dislocations resulting from these wrongs are likely to be huge, owing to their repetitive and cumulative nature. But social sanctions alone will not stem the tide. The single individual who—assuming he is detected in the first place—is willing to bear the scorn and ostracism of his neighbors could kill (and threaten to kill) with impunity. Worse, he may well be emboldened if given the tacit or vocal support of even a few individuals within the community. The wrongdoer's ability to increase unilaterally the size of his gain is not stopped by any broad social consensus that people should behave in more civilized fashion. Individuals who wish to be free of violence cannot have their way simply by minding their own business. The social equilibrium is massively destabilized even if 99 percent of the population responds to the social sanctions first by not performing the bad conduct and then by encouraging others to do otherwise. Right now countless community groups lobby fiercely against gang violence and sexual harassment. Their ends command at least the tacit support of huge portions of the relevant communities, but widespread social consensus and high community participation are a supplement and not a savior. Sooner or later, force must be met with force, lest the behavior of the outsider set the norms for everyone else in the group. Self-defense is one option that is routinely available, but its effectiveness depends in part on protecting from legal retaliation those who exercise the right. In any event, self-defense is not an option on which the frail and fearful can depend, so that the collective public force—the police—is often necessary to deter offenders before they attack an isolated victim. While serious disputes might arise over how many resources should be directed toward the prevention of aggression, and how they should be deployed, no one will dispute the initial collective decision to subject it to legal sanctions. The attack on libertarian theory routinely comes from those who want government to have a greater role; rarely, from those who see private aggression and fraud as inappropriate targets for government action because they are already subject to broad social disapproval.

Defamation

A second area ripe for legal intervention has been defamation. In respect to words, the great temptation is to repeat the old maxim "sticks and stones may break my bones, but names will never harm me." If there were ever a case for social sanctions only, then defamation seems to be it. But history runs the other way. Defamation was a private wrong before the rise of the welfare state, and long before our heightened modern social sensibilities. Indeed, to deny its danger is to severely underestimate the power of false words, often deliberately spoken, to wreak havoc on a chosen target. A stranger tells a man that his wife has committed adultery when she has not: divorce or physical assault could follow. A political adviser tells the President that a rival has contemplated treason or murder; banishment or execution could follow. A businessman falsely states that a rival's product is contaminated with botulism: panic, bankruptcy, and criminal charges could ensue. A celebrity is falsely charged with mob affiliations, or with having stand-ins sing high notes: a loss of major contracts leaves her without work. None of these harms are trivial; and typically, their victims will lack remedy against the third persons whose behavior changes in response to bad news: who can sue the nameless persons who do not come forward to do business, or the long-time confederate who turns elsewhere for his next deal? The old saw is that a lie travels more quickly than the truth—an unfortunate imbalance that the tort of defamation helps redress.

All the while, a strong moral consensus has developed against lying about innocent people. But a uniform sentiment in favor of ostracism may not protect innocent people from defamatory words uttered by persons outside the gravitational pull of some close-knit community. When these communities possess the ability to ferret out the information needed to expose the falsity of the charges, legal redress may not be required. Often, however, social sanctions will fall far short of that ideal because of the unfortunate alignment of individual incentives. To ordinary members of a group, the loss of contact with a single individual may not have much impact on their day-to-day lives. Why should they individually spend resources to rehabilitate the reputation of a person whose name has been blackened? It is simply cheaper to be safe than sorry. That decision, if replicated by others, could have a devastating impact on the target of a campaign of defamation organized by someone outside an institution, and carried on by newspaper stories, letters, and word of mouth. The social sanctions therefore are, and should be, supplemented by a set of legal sanctions, which (alas!) many people are afraid to deploy because of the enormous expense of prosecuting a defamation suit successfully; also, such prosecution has the unfortunate effect of republishing the libel and keeping the regrettable charges squarely in the public eye. But one can decide to forgo the remedy; no one else can take it from the victim.

Promises

The enforcement of promises raises much more complicated questions, as the cloudier discussion of the applicable legal principles set out above indicates. Frequently, parties entitled to legal enforcement of promises conclude that they are better off keeping their disputes out of the courts. They may have no confidence that judges and juries will sensibly apply the correct rules governing their disputes, and prefer to rely on the informal sanctions imposed by the operation of their trade. Typically, that response comes when the parties have repeat relationships in close-knit communities: now reputational sanctions will usually be sufficient to prevent even the unscrupulous trader from taking advantage of a situation, as when until the last decade or so the diamond industry was largely the province of Hasidic Jews trading in close proximity in New York City.[23]

Yet bypassing the legal system may not depend exclusively on diffuse social norms, widely accepted within a given community. Sometimes decentralization simply means social disapproval. In other cases, as in the diamond industry, it means loss of privileges formally imposed by arbitral agencies backed by industry-wide monopoly power. The command theory of law continues to apply; only the identity of the commander changes. For example, informal systems of adjudication, such as arbitration, are typically invoked to provide at least some of the safeguards found in ordinary civil or criminal trials—the right to present evidence and confront witnesses—even if they do not incorporate all the elements of a complex code of civil or criminal procedure. Likewise, the applicable sanctions can include suspension or expulsion from a particular trading group needed to secure one's livelihood. These sanctions carry real bite when the excluded party has no other forum in which to ply his trade. To be sure, these institutional sanctions may be bolstered by reputational losses borne by individuals, commonly thought guilty, against whom legal charges cannot be proved. But the celebration of social norms should not conceal the role of command in decentralized activities.

TWO-TIER SANCTIONS

Modern regulators, typically underestimating the importance of these institutional and reputational sanctions, often insist on direct state-imposed sanctions where the parties to a transaction might have agreed otherwise. In so doing, the former think that the imposition of legal sanctions will only supplement whatever social sanctions are already in place. Yet in many cases, legal intervention weakens social sanctions that have operated well outside the glare of the law. Illustration of this basic proposition can be drawn from many diverse areas of law: employment, product warranties, rental housing, and cattle trespass.

Employment

One important illustration of this modern practice is the question of whether employees (but never employers) should—on the ground of employers' far greater economic power—be afforded legal remedies against unjust dismissal. For example, in 1980, a mischievous reading of an employee handbook led to draftsmanship about the nonenforceability of the promises contained in such handbooks.[24] A very large percentage of private contracts take the opposite tack, by allowing firing and quitting both to take place "at will"—that is, without showing any "just cause" for terminating the relationship. Within this arrangement, however, lies a second-tier social norm that indicates that some good cause, often determined by firm or industry practice, is required for the dismissal to have social legitimacy for everyone in the workplace.

Many employers and employees have good reason to adopt a two-tier arrangement that is legally precarious but socially stable. Right off the bat, any legal system starts at a major disadvantage relative to any system of informal enforcement. In law, all decisions must be resolved before a neutral party that has to make findings of fact before it can issue any binding decision. Just that extra step means that persons who know certain information are in the awkward position of having to prove it to outsiders. The point has been one of enormous frustration to everyone at one time or another, but there is literally no way to avoid that problem in cases of coercion and defamation. But within the context of an employment relationship, the parties may agree to, and the law should respect, an arrangement whereby each party secures exit rights for itself, without having first to justify its decision before some independent party.

This system, I will freely confess, is not perfect; but over a wide range of cases, it is self-correcting. Those people who know themselves to be well treated will not leave. Those ill treated have less to gain from the continuation of the relationship and therefore, being all the more willing to go, can make credible threats in that direction. To an aggrieved employee, her freedom is worth more to her than her burdens, when all the while her employer has far more to lose by the discontinuation of her employment. Let the grievances be reversed, and the threat positions are reversed as well: the hard-pressed employer is willing to let a fractious worker go to the first outside offer. So the system settles into some kind of a long-term equilibrium. Some percentage of relationships rupture; some percentage continue on even terms, and do so because of the ceaseless adjustments the parties make within the stark but intelligible legal framework. The simple point is that the legal system is perceived by both sides as less reliable and more expensive than the set of informal social sanctions that can be used in their place. So the legal rules now provide that either side can exit at will, and leave the parties to make all lesser adjustments over time as they see fit. Stated otherwise, why spend more money for a system that might prove less reliable?

Still, today many states, by both statute and common law rule, seek to regulate dismissal on the ground that these reputational sanctions and exit rights are inadequate to deter the large institutional employer from serious advantage-taking.[25] But that conclusion misunderstands the nature of market power in a competitive environment. The size of a firm is both a liability and an asset. The large firm that makes sound decisions will have a large number of grateful employees, while the large firm that makes poor decisions risks defections in droves. Accordingly, the larger shop faces a larger risk if its inopportune firing of a single worker demoralizes its entire workforce. The costs of hiring and training and socializing new workers to a firm are immense and are vividly understood on both sides of the relationship. The employer that pushes too hard in one case exposes itself to loss of confidence in other quarters, and thus faces powerful incentives to moderate its hand. In contrast, the worker who quits and leaves the employer in a lurch will typically be subject to much weaker reputational sanctions; and that immunity from action is strengthened today because an employer fears that candid employee evaluations to prospective employers will expose him to defamation actions. So keeping mum allows the undesirable worker to out-run any deserved tarnish on her reputation.

In this social setting, the cost and unreliability of the legal system could make the system of social sanctions, *standing alone,* far more efficient than the combined legal and social sanctions routinely invoked under mod-ern law. It is for that reason that most firms consciously adopt different internal and external regimes: that is, arrangements where the social norms internal to the firm differ from the legal rules appropriate to a judicial set-ting. The second generation of handbooks all contain provisions in bold print that say: NONE OF THE UNDERTAKINGS FOUND IN THIS HANDBOOK SHALL BE SUBJECT TO LEGAL ENFORCEMENT, or something equally clear. Within this bold-letter framework, social norms often supply various procedural protections and adopt an explicit "for cause" posture. The legal agreement preserves the at-will environment by explicitly denying the aggrieved worker any legal redress for breach of these internal rules. The employee handbook is one, usually accurate, guide for how the firm expects to conduct itself in relationship to its employees, and how employees are expected to deal with the firm and with fellow employ-ees. The system of sanctions arrayed against these violations could include low-level forms of social disapproval and noncooperation; or they may be ratcheted up to reassignment, fines, suspension, demotion, or dismissal. Running the employment system is never easy, which is why personnel managers would command high salaries even in completely unregulated employment markets.

So far I have claimed only that in some cases social sanctions are supe-rior to legal ones. But, oftentimes, the introduction of legal sanctions has the unintended effect of *undermining* effective social norms. The employ-ment relationship is one such area. Maintaining internal balance becomes more difficult when state power intrudes into the workplace. The external enforcement overwhelms and displaces the internal equilibrium of the workplace *even when* the substantive content of the legal norm closely tracks the applicable internal social norm. To give but one recent illustra-tion, consider the elaborate Equal Employment Opportunity Commission (EEOC) guidelines interpreting the application of the Americans with Disabilities Act (ADA) to mental conditions. At one level, the statute simply follows the informal practices that hold in many (but by no means all) workplaces. Stated abstractly, most employers respect a social norm against arbitrary dismissal; and would make some reasonable accommodation for handicapped workers at some positive cost to themselves. But informal accommodations are clearly bounded in that, once an employer decides to go no further, then, with litigation ruled out, the worker must choose whether to quit or stay. Often she will stay because she is unlikely to persuade a new employer, unfamiliar with her strengths, to make more favorable accommodations on her behalf. The practices are messy at the edges, but the system putters—not purrs—along.

Legal intervention is intended to eliminate residual worker uncertainty by forcing the accommodations that most employers are willing to make. But the legal standard lacks surgical precision, and suffers from one defect that well-constructed social norms usually overcome. Social norms have built-in mechanisms of self-correction: people sense when too much of a good thing becomes a bad thing. They can fine-tune and monitor their responses free of external constraints. They can make accommodations that work in one setting without worrying whether they can work in all. Legal commands may get the direction correct, but lack the needed speed governor.

For example, even the *New York Times* coverage of the long-awaited 1997 ADA job guidelines expressed amazement at the unrelenting and dogmatic severity (not to say, lack of common sense) of the accommodations required of employers for workers with serious mental conditions, such as schizophrenia and manic-depression (called by government officials "bipolar disorder," as part of the campaign to eliminate descriptions that the public understands).[26] Employers are told that they may have to place workers on separate shifts, or in separate locations; that coworkers may have to put up with discomfort and unease. There is some overt recognition that the accommodations required for one worker could create dislocations for others, but the employer and coworkers are left to tough it out on their own. The numerous examples of required accommodations are all one-time tickets whose conclusions depend on a skillful alignment of imaginary facts to give the illusion that general principles govern the mandated responses for "sloppy box-loaders," "reckless limousine drivers," "loud librarians," and "medicated saw operators." But what confidence can anyone have in the regulations when one implausible guideline prohibits employers from checking to see whether employees with mental conditions are taking their medications, while another guideline prohibits the employer from explaining to coworkers the apparent favoritism in some individual case?[27] The accommodations all come from one side, so that the mutuality of informal accommodations is lost in a sea of fine print.

This entire regulatory enterprise thus substitutes a set of ostensible rules for informal adjustments that reflect the local knowledge that is wholly lacking in a remote, impersonal, and result-driven government agency. Power is vested in distant functionaries who are necessarily ignorant about the particulars of any given case. Massive interventions are routinely required by government agents who are insulated by a doctrine of sovereign immunity from the consequences of their errors. Employers are driven to skirt the law, or to watch helplessly as coworkers and customers flee the EEOC's "reasonable accommodations." To curb the abuse in a few cases, the regulation mandates a more virulent form of abuse across the board. The EEOC's mistakes cannot be corrected by softening the results in this or that case or by adding a new barrage of examples to respond to the steady stream of inquiries the regulations spawn. The best response is not to work within the system but to stress the one fundamental structural flaw that calls for its abolition. In this context, sound social order requires not mutual reinforcement, but *strict separation* between legal and social norms. The legal system must give social norms the breathing room they need to survive and evolve.

The prospect of ceaseless litigation has led to strong adaptive responses. Employers know that they cannot undo unilaterally the layers of federal and state employment regulations, especially as these relate to the antidiscrimination laws. But they have achieved major successes in moving dispute resolution under these laws to the arbitration format, which is cheaper to operate and offers expertise closer to the industry itself. These clauses have generally been upheld in both the union and nonunion sectors,[28] and the movement to arbitration can easily be recast as an indirect attack on the full range of employment regulation: the change in forum will surely produce a change in results—in, at least, some cases. The system has been attacked as a return to the bad old days before the passage of the national labor statutes.[29] The objection has some force in an environment in which the soundness of the regulation is taken for granted: arbitration could operate as a circumvention of the substantive regulation. But the use of arbitration becomes much less problematic in a world that honors freedom of contract. The speed, cheapness, and accuracy of the process cannot be presumed. But where arbitration thrives in unregulated labor markets, the best explanation is that the additional security and legitimation it provides to employment decisions outweigh its costs. Paradoxically, when regulation is pervasive, it is harder to reach that sanguine conclusion. It is never quite clear whether arbitration was adopted solely as a counterweight to substantive law or is desired for its intrinsic merits.

Product Warranty

The same two-tier system often holds for long-term relationships between buyers and sellers. Stewart Macaulay's famous early study of the noncontractual norms in business concluded that the dominant social norms were: first, that "one ought to produce a good product and stand behind it"; and, second, that "commitments are to be honored in most situations."[30] Here again, the norms certainly resonate with at least one strand of common law thought: the importance of the sanctity of contract as a means to secure stable social relationships. The fact that contracts are often written so as to eliminate warranty obligations reflects both uneasiness to trust these matters to adjudication and to the power of good will and repeat business. What we have here is another version of the two-tier system found in employment relationships. The vendor is insulated from legal liability but subject to powerful social obligations. Yet, as with employment obligations, it is doubtful that this norm could survive detailed systems of public enforcement that impose more stringent warranty obligations on sellers.

Takings

The role of two tiers of norms is critical for understanding other uses of government power outside the contractual area. The 1922 decision *Pennsylvania Coal Co. v. Mahon*[31] came about because the Pennsylvania legislature passed a law, the Kohler Act, that required coal companies to support the lands and homes of the surface owners who had already explicitly waived such legal protection. Justice Oliver Wendell Holmes, in one of his most enigmatic and influential opinions, found that the coerced reassignment of the support estate constituted an uncompensated taking in violation of the Fifth Amendment prohibition against taking private property without just compensation. William Fischel's close study of the actual practices in his informative book *Regulatory Takings*[32] shows that the social practices prior to the passage of the Kohler Act were not fully captured in the formal conveyances from surface owners to coal companies.

At first glance, it looked as though the coal companies could simply ignore the interests of the surface owners. But the actual pattern of behavior proved different. The relevant coal deposits were spread out all over Scranton. The men that worked the mines lived in the houses atop the mines and had therefore, quite simply, an interest on both sides of the issue. Their employers, the mine owners, knew and understood the local social dynamic. So having secured contractual protection against liability for the repair of the surface after mining subsidence, they routinely fixed the surface premises, no questions asked, once subsidence took place: good public relations, of course. The breakdown in the relationship occurred because a single rogue company, People's Coal, reneged on all its informal undertakings and went insolvent to boot. So the Kohler Act was passed to plug the gap in the earlier social fabric. Once the Kohler Act was struck down, the situation returned to the status quo ante: armed with their victory, the coal companies continued to make routine repairs of subsidence damage just as they had before the act was passed. The social glue that kept miners and surface owners together was just too strong.

If the mine owners were resolved to repair surface damage anyhow, why did they fight the statute? We can quickly reject the obvious answer—no reason at all—since opposition to the statute cost money, but successful legal action would not save any expenditure. Rather, the answer rests on the profound difference between doing something and having to do it under legal compulsion. The creation of a legal duty enforced by public inspectors could alter the balance of power between the coal company and the surface owner in ways that could reduce the overall effectiveness of the informal system of repairs. An obligation to repair does not indicate when, where, and how those repairs have to be made; but put the law on the surface owners' side, and the actual repairs could be too costly and too precise relative to their benefits. Parties struggle to keep legal control even as they obey social norms cutting in the opposite direction. They do so to limit the extent of their risk and to control the costs of their operations. The constant pressure to convert social norms to legal norms does not serve to rectify some imperfection: rather, it gets rid of a small imperfection and replaces it with a larger one.

Rental Housing

The same pattern of legal individualism and social cooperation also takes place in rental markets for residential housing. To explain, let me resort to an anecdote of my own. When my wife and I first moved to Chicago in 1972, we rented a two-bedroom apartment at 1700 East 56th Street, a new building that was then only partly rented. As a young law professor, I did something I might not do today: I read the lease and discovered that the landlord assumed no obligation to repair damage inside the units. But the building also had a full-time maintenance staff at the beck and call of the tenants any time day or night. So I asked the rental agent to explain why the difference between the tough talk in the lease and the prompt service in the building—even though I knew it was better than the reverse.

Her answer made perfectly good sense. The building owners knew that reputation matters in attracting and keeping tenants in a building, but they drafted the lease to retain control, without judicial intervention, of any bad-apple tenant who made it past their original investigation. They did not want to risk demonstrating to an independent third party their compliance with some "for cause" norm for withholding repair services: their private knowledge about the behavior of tenants, the condition of the units, the source of the damage, and the like could easily be lost in translation, so that they would lose control over their own operations. If the good tenants left because the bad tenants stayed, the whole building could fall into disarray. So informed, my wife and I eagerly signed the lease, knowing that the landlord had the tools to protect us from neighboring tenants who might otherwise make life unpleasant. The two years we spent there repaid our confidence. The legal risk that the landlord might deny its obligation to repair never came to pass, and the building prospered as a rental operation until it was converted into a condominium over twenty years later.

As with other arrangements, the success of the landlord-tenant relationship depends on incremental fine-tuning. But that adaptive process cannot always survive regulation. Introduce rent control, and tenants have a right to remain at below-market rents. Any spirit of cooperation between landlord and tenant is shattered in a relentless struggle of landlords to disgorge tenants who dig in to protect their state-created patrimony over the long haul. In this legal environment, the informal adjustments can never offset the massive interventions into the contract brought about by state control over the price term. The bitter struggles between landlord and tenant that take place in New York City under rent control are a product of its defective legal environment, not of some unaccountable loss of civility that never made it west to Chicago.* The social norms cannot weather a harsh legal environment.

---

* The blurb to a 1997 article on the situation in New York City read: "New York's well-intentioned restrictions on housing bring out the worst in landlords and tenants—and burden everyone looking for a place to live."[33]

Cattle Trespass

The preceding cases that speak of the precarious position of social norms under an interventionist legal order should caution us against thinking that the formal law is unimportant simply because it is not followed in some particular cases. Consider again Ellickson's study of local cattle trespass norms among neighbors in Shasta County, a largely rural county in Northern California. Local citizens followed rules that required each owner of cattle to be strictly responsible for the harm that it caused, even when a state fencing law imposed on individual landowners the duty to "fence out" cattle.[34] In effect, individual cattle owners yielded to demands to pay damages even when they had valid statutory defenses under the fencing-out rules.

Could that practical equilibrium have survived, however, if the fencing law were enforced by state inspections and large fines? Most likely, this direct enforcement would have driven any informal norms from the field. By way of corroboration, Ellickson mentioned in his introduction his initial plan to investigate "how the law of lateral support influences which landowner pays to shore up an existing urban building whose foundations are threatened by an excavation of adjoining land." But that entire project "had to be abandoned when it turned out that federal regulations designed to protect the safety of workers had essentially preempted the widely varying common-law rules of lateral support."[35] If social norms can lose out to direct government enforcement in one context, then they can lose out as well in another.

THE DEPENDENCE OF SOCIAL NORMS ON LAW

It would be a mistake, however, to assume that the only consequence of legal rules is to crowd out social norms. In some contexts, strong reasons counsel us to be wary of thinking that informal mechanisms are *necessarily* sufficient in and of themselves to handle these local disputes. In particular, the various reasons Ellickson advances to explain the generic superiority of informal mechanisms do nothing to establish their practical invulnerability. Ellickson observes that these substantive norms can drive out the legal norms, as in the cattle trespass cases. But the conclusion must be sharply qualified, for these social norms are identical to legal norms that have been well established in many similar contexts. The cattle norms in Shasta County may not have followed the fencing laws; but in using the strict liability rule, and in allowing landowners to hold cattle as security for payment of claims, they followed common law rules of ancient lineage. Ellickson's claim would be far more striking if the customary norms had evolved away from both the statutory rules and the common law practices.

Likewise, we should be careful of inferring the insignificance of legal norms to social stability from the frequency of self-help enforcement, which is common in many areas of social life. In many of these cases—as with the abatement of nuisances, self-defense, and the use of other's property in times of necessity—the self-help is sanctioned by law. The same point holds true in many jurisdictions with the self-help remedy for cattle-trespass, where the strict liability rule clarifies that the landowner may hold the cattle as security for the damage they cause, a legal rule that follows customary social practices.[36] Legal backing makes it foolhardy for anyone to resist self-help if they know that civil or criminal liability could follow in the event of substantial bodily injury or property damage. It is, therefore, one thing to say that self-help is an effective sanction in a world where escalation is countered by public force; it is quite another to assert that self-help would function with equal effectiveness if the state *never* used its coercive powers after the fact to counter defiant resistance to the self-help norm. It is easy to see in social norms *partial* solutions to social interactions where legal order has been secured by positive law. It is much more doubtful that they supply *comprehensive* control of violence that could displace state force. The same communities that rely on self-help to handle cattle trespass go to court to obtain divorces (no self-enforcing customary norms here!), punish crimes, and obtain damages in automobile collision cases. Law, as a command of the sovereign, is what makes these lower-cost self-help remedies effective.

Nor is that conclusion altered because most individuals do not know the legal rules under which they operate. I don't know many recent undergraduates, or even people in business, who are aware of the doctrine of consideration, know the scope of the parol evidence rule, or can recite the multiple exceptions to the statute of frauds. But I suspect that there are few who think that anyone can simply dishonor written leases or sales. They know when legal relationships are created; the refinements can wait until actual disputes. This seat-of-the-pants knowledge suffices for their immediate purposes. Of course, in specialized contexts more is required: at this point, it is cheaper to hire a broker, an accountant, or an agent than to learn the law oneself. The pattern of ignorance in ordinary people is rational not because the coercive side of law is unimportant; but because in ordinary transactions that they know that information can be acquired later. It is highly doubtful that we would observe the identical pattern of voluntary transactions, in the absence of a well-functioning legal system.

Similarly, few drivers (indeed, few lawyers!) know the effect of contributory negligence in a highway collision case; but, again, it hardly follows that their ignorance reflects the irrelevance of law to accident cases. The likelihood that any driver will get into a collision is low; and the need to take care to avoid personal injury, property damages, or criminal fines is sufficiently apparent that it is hard to see what is gained at the margin by one's knowing how rules allocate damages in the tiny fraction of accidents that involve two or more drivers, all of whom are substantially at fault. Rational ignorance of liability rules (as opposed to the rules of the road) is surely the order of the day for the typical driver. But once an accident does occur between strangers, litigation remains the dominant background threat precisely because, in the absence of repeat dealings, social sanctions are too weak to force the appropriate redress and settlement.

The lawyers and insurance adjusters who settle cases every day are aware of these rules. To be sure, frequently they use simple rules of thumb which ask about compliance with traffic rules, even though they deviate from the formal liability rules in some cases. But magnitude matters. In truth these traffic rules correspond with ordinary negligence principles well over 95 percent of the time, and it is hardly worth anyone's time and effort in a small case to plumb the arcane exceptions that typically turn out to be of little use in any event.[37] But as the stakes get higher, the willingness to take advantage of any opening the law affords increases, just as we might expect. So only in big cases do the doctrinal refinements make it into court. But rather than dwell on these oddities, note that for repeat players, such as hospitals and manufacturers, for whom liability is a more persistent threat, expertise about the legal rules increases to a fever pitch because of the far greater risk posed by noncompliance. And here, to return to an earlier theme, customary standards of care have frequently and unwisely been driven from the lists by courts that overestimate their own ability to fashion the applicable standard of care (see chapter 1, pages 38–40).

COERCIVE SOCIAL NORMS

This assumption of the durable power of social norms can be mischievous in yet another sense. My colleague Cass Sunstein, in his recent treatment of the subject, chides Judge Richard Posner and me for our insistence that the use of state power should generally be confined to counteracting the dangers of force and fraud: "I think that both Epstein and Posner give inadequate attention to the liberty-limiting effects of norms, roles and meanings."[38] In his view, the prevalence and persistence of "bad social norms" provide yet another justification for the use of state power. In particular, extensive forms of state regulation might be used to counter practices that everyone disapproves but no one would reject unilaterally. He thus imagines that a destructive prisoner's dilemma game arises when macho sentiments prevent hockey players from wearing helmets, or conformity keeps teenagers from quitting smoking or men and women from abandoning traditional stereotypes of sex roles.

It is, of course, possible to postulate elusive social states that everyone wants but no one can achieve privately. It is for that reason that state power is justified in preventing private aggression. But just calling a social state of affairs a prisoner's dilemma game does not make it so. Once the threat of force is removed, individuals have a lot more running room than would otherwise be the case. We do not need the state to require helmets for hockey players: the question could be left to the various leagues and associations. Nothing says that the same rule, or the same type of helmet, is appropriate for both the junior leagues and the National Hockey League. Where change is desired, it should prove possible for the league to induce one of its star players to lead the shift (as indeed happened when starting goalie Jacques Plante first donned his primitive facemask in the late 1950s), or to make the transition easier by grandfathering an exemption from the rule for players already in the league, or to require increased insurance premiums from those who insist on playing without a helmet. With these options available, why use power to engineer the shift to some uniform position? Indeed, why assume that uniformity is a desired goal? We often see mixed behaviors, as with the wearing of mouth guards or in the choice of helmet type, but do not assume that some players must be acting irrationally simply because other players have chosen a different course of action. It could well be that certain people find helmets more uncomfortable or that others are more aggressive generally. Nonconformity and conformity can both exist in many social situations; there is no need to assume that either calls for correction unless there is some real impediment to individual choice, which takes us back again to force and fraud.

Sunstein is also mistaken in assuming that anyone can climb a perch that offers special insight into the desirability of particular social practices. Thus, in the absence of force and fraud, how do we know which of these supposed new norms are bad and which good? Some brave soul could say with equal probity that the current permissiveness on sexual activity is bad, and that premarital sex would, and should, cease for all individuals if we once again made fornication a crime, and that gays and lesbians need legal compulsion to avoid some deviant form of behavior. In addition, we could slow down the unwanted headlong rush of women into the workplace by taxes, regulations, requirements, and prohibitions, all of which are meant to induce them to fill their proper roles as wives and mothers to which they ache to return. Of course, we could stifle the endless anti-tobacco campaign and help smokers once again achieve their chosen form of release and self-expression.

It is all too easy for anyone to take strong private predispositions and to erect them into universal preferences to be backed by the rule of law. As such, the battle is not over the structure of the prisoner's dilemma game, but over whether revealed preferences are true preferences instead of a regrettable manifestation of false consciousness. It is really a struggle to enshrine supposedly dominant social values into law by claiming that social pressures prevent people from expressing their true selves. Yet in a free society we all have to bear the inconvenience of having other people live their lives in ways that we find simply beyond the pale. Our job is to maintain order, to provide for separate associations and places where different versions of the good can flourish side by side with their opposites. We will not reach that goal if we think that some social practices should be prohibited because they offend our social sensibilities—even if, perhaps especially when, we are right. I know of no single embracing social norm that allows one part of the population to dictate to the rest the standards of good behavior.

We should take a more modest approach to subject matter, and understand social norms as a useful glue that facilitates all manner of social interactions. They do not stand as a substitute for law, or a barrier to law, or an invitation for (corrective) law. They cannot and do not displace law, properly so called. The usefulness of social norms depends as much on the adoption of a sound set of legal rules, as a sound set of legal rules depends for its implementation on a sensible set of social norms. The chapters that follow are directed more to the choice of sound legal principles than to the informal means of their implementation. I turn next to the harm principle and, thereafter, to its apparent mirror-image: the benefit principle.

CHAPTER 3

❖ ❖ ❖

Harm: The Gateway to Liability

One of the central issues faced by all legal systems, ancient and modern, is what redress, if any, is provided for individuals who suffer harm, particularly harm inflicted by others. Indeed, in virtually all civilizations, harm operates as the gateway through which disputes enter the legal system. If it did not, we would all become a nation of busybodies, each entitled as a matter of right to oversee and challenge the actions of everyone else. Getting a handle on the harm question requires a return to the themes of both previous chapters: first, to examine the question under both natural law and utilitarian principles; and, second, to recall that social norms are by themselves unable to cope with the imposition of harm, especially large and concentrated harm.

This chapter, then, is dedicated to an exploration of the use, scope, and limits of the harm principle. First, I examine the historical interaction between the philosophical background and the common-law rules; and then chronicle the transformation of the harm principle which has led to the modern regulatory state. In this historical reversal, the harm principle—which had, during the nineteenth century, served as a bulwark of individual liberty and as a limitation on the scope of government power—came, during the twentieth century, to work as an engine to expand social control over private behavior. The harm principle, once a shield of liberty, has now become a sword against it.

Philosophically speaking, the basic presumption in favor of liberty is said to rest on the belief that each individual's actions are of no concern to anyone but himself; and, thus, that all individuals bear the risk of harm to self, just as they may capture good fortune from their own beneficial actions. The law reverses that presumption of personal independence only when it judges, in some intuitive sense, the actions of one person to cause harm to another. Once that threshold is crossed, the legal system launches a full panoply of private and public sanctions against any actor who fails to justify or excuse his conduct. The basic position is captured in two Roman maxims, both of which are as salient today: *res perit domino,* "a thing perishes for its owner," or more loosely, "losses lie where they fall." The companion principle *sic utere tuo ut alienum non laedas,* "use your own property so as not to harm another."[1] The natural law framework trumpets both these maxims as immutable principles of social organization. Both maxims have strong utilitarian roots.

HARM TO SELF

The first principle holds that all losses lie where they fall. Within the natural law tradition, that result is said to follow axiomatically from the conception of what it means to be a separate person or to own property: who else should be asked to bear a loss for which they are not responsible? There is no obvious person whom one can sue. Simply to say that I am not at fault for my own loss does not imply that someone else is at fault. Hence any contrived effort to bring an ordinary lawsuit makes no sense in the context: who should ever want to sue himself? If the loss is to be socialized, that will have to be done through other means. It is not enough to have a worthy plaintiff for a lawsuit; it helps to have a culpable defendant.

At another level, however, the traditional rule itself looks arbitrary. Accidental losses and accidental injuries are often no one's fault but come as a result of bad luck and misfortune as capable of striking one person as another. Most people fear risk and would accordingly prefer to face a large chance of a small loss than a small chance of a large one—a certain loss of $1.00 than a 1 percent chance of losing $100. If so, then the traditional legal rule ignores opportunities to spread risk throughout society to dull the arbitrary forces of nature. Luck is no better principle, the argument continues, for allocating the consequences of ill fortune than the natural lottery is for giving people exclusive use of their individual talents and abilities. If private lawsuits do not provide a suitable vehicle to spread risk, then find some other mechanism to do the job. The tempting implication is that we should use state power to equalize the consequences of ill fortune and to create an administrative structure equal to this extensive task.

No counterattack against this line of argument could credibly deny the ravages bad luck can impose on a select few. Rather, the defense of the principle that losses should lie where they fall depends on a closer examination of the social machinery to implement this interventionist program. Most critically, there are buffers between the individual and the state, so that the role of private agreements and social practices should not be ignored. Start with one simple point: any suggestion to socialize losses does not determine which individuals fall into a given insurance pool. Wholly without use of state power, the family, even the extended family, already provides some limited form of insurance through people who can assess the risk and the desirability of assistance. Does it make any sense for state power to spread the risk beyond these friendly confines?

Probably not. The standard insurance contract is a complex affair whose many provisions must be duplicated as a matter of positive law once the maxim of *res perit domino* is rejected. The first challenge is to decide who is covered. The class of strangers herded into an insurance pool is not self-defining. In principle, that risk pool could span the globe, at which point it becomes unwieldy and unworkable. Or that pool could be limited by region and thus fail to produce sufficient diversification for dealing with natural catastrophes, such as earthquakes and hurricanes, that strike with deadly fury in a limited area. Nor is it easy to explain why any individual's cost of coverage should turn on the composition of the insurance pool in which he is placed. Lump the suburbs with the inner city, and the premiums for suburbanites increase and those for city dwellers decrease; put them into two separate pools, and the same level of coverage comes at a very different price. With markets, the rate charged to any customer will depend on his individual characteristics regardless of who writes the insurance. With social insurance, the coverage may be constant, but the premiums will vary with the luck of the draw. The government agency that can define membership in designated risk pools has the arbitrary power to help or hurt every one of its members. The price of getting rid of ill luck is having to take on the systematic risks of political intrigue, as the net losers within the plan constantly search out ways to undercut it.

The issues, moreover, do not stop once membership in a given pool is determined: next, the diligent regulator must determine the premiums that conscripted pool members must pay. If coverage could be magically restricted to losses that result from "pure" cases of bad luck, then presumably each person has an equal chance of being hurt. It is as though individuals have no control over any part of their destiny. On that simple assumption, premiums could be equalized across persons. But the underlying proposition is false: levels of risk, and of its extent, are not uniform across any known population. Irreducible differences in life style, care levels, attitudes, and behavior, to which we are all prey, influence the expected losses for each person; some fraction of the risk lies within human control even if other parts fall beyond it. We might well like to distinguish between the person who tries to stay out of harm's way and the one who rushes headlong into its path. It is doubtful that we can sort out the relative influences of bad luck and ill will in the thousands of cases falling in the gray middle. But one thing is certain: a simple system of uniform premiums will generate implicit subsidies that will benefit those group members who engage in risky behavior. In addition, the level of risky behavior, and the losses it produces over time, are certain to increase as well. Why should any individual take care if those precautions inure to the benefits of others? Accident rates should rise, and with them premium levels as well, diverting resources away from other private needs. Socialization of loss is no better in insurance than it is in other areas of life. Universal coverage against risk hardly does its job if the generosity of the moment leads to future broad-scale institutional collapse.

These complications in insurance contracting (there are many more wrinkles, but let them pass) explain in back-handed fashion the social wisdom of the individualistic principle that forces everyone to bear his own risk of loss. The rule is not meant to block the sharing of risk so commonly desired; rather, it is designed to direct the process of risk sharing into private hands where insurance companies can decide *by contract* who is covered, for what premium, and on what terms and conditions. The introduction of this financial intermediary allows individual actors to spread risk without forcing them to merge into a single collective. Since all parties come together by contract, the resulting arrangements will prove stable because each person by his own subjective lights has engaged in an insurance transaction that leaves him better off than before. Since many different firms can take the role as intermediary, the price for insurance will be competitively determined. The scope for government regulation is properly limited to guaranteeing that the insurers that collect premiums today will be solvent tomorrow when the risks mature. The paradox is thus complete: only a legal rule that lets losses lie where they fall can support active insurance markets.

Having said all this, I must run up a warning banner. Insurance markets may not, and should not, cover all individuals against all forms of loss. Some risks manifest themselves before the insurance is written, as with birth defects or AIDS. Some insurance companies will not underwrite risk against certain kinds of hazard, such as hurricane or earthquake damage. In still other situations, the manufacturer of a dangerous product like asbestos will be unwilling to renew its coverage once its present policies are exhausted: who will choose voluntarily to write you insurance for losses that are certain to happen? These situations have often created enormous political pressures to form state-mandated insurance pools to cover the risks in question. Assigned risk pools for automobile or homeowners insurance are common examples.

The pressures should be resisted, for the bare identification of a gap in insurance coverage does not justify legislative nullification of the older common law maxim. Indeed, private decisions *not* to write insurance often have useful social consequences which social insurance cannot supply. Federal flood insurance, for example, has the unfortunate effect of inducing people to build homes and plant crops in high-risk locations. The subsidy thus distorts investment in this market, as in so many others. Then once the losses occur, federal disaster programs are often administered in slipshod fashion. How much comfort should we take in knowing that a Missouri farmer received $200,000 in disaster aid following the 1993 Mississippi floods for his land, house, and equipment which he purchased three weeks before for only $138,000?[2] Matters are only made worse when the governments that mandate the subsidies refuse to pay for them, chiefly by prohibiting the companies that write specialized insurance from leaving the state. The net effect is that the capital of the firm which has been acquired for national business is siphoned off into those states that impose these exit restrictions on insurance companies.[3]

The failure of voluntary insurance markets to emerge is no sign of market failure. So long as the opportunity to contract is available, the absence of insurance shows that some risks cannot be spread or reduced in intelligent fashion. The selective writing of insurance helps to weed out forms of dangerous behavior that should not occur in the first place. That done, voluntary markets can only develop under the Roman rule that prima facie allows losses to lie where they fall. That rule does not guarantee perfect protection against bad luck, but it comes in well ahead of whatever rule falls into second place. Unless and until someone can write a "pure luck" insurance policy with no negative spillovers, we are better off following the traditional rule. Social legislation that tries to solve the problem of ill luck is more likely to create ill luck of its own.

HARM TO OTHERS

This hands-off social response to harm does, and should, alter rapidly when the question is no longer loss to one's self but harm inflicted on another person. In principle, each person could be required to bear his own losses even when these are inflicted by another, and then decide whether to insure against these losses. But that legal rule offers an open invitation to malice or carelessness: Why shouldn't I harm you if I keep all the benefit while you bear all the loss? Just this dominant asymmetry provides fertile ground for the harm principle, both as a matter of ordinary social expectations and high philosophical thought. "Keep your hands to yourself" and "mind your own business" may lack the obscurity of the *sic utero* maxim referred to earlier, but their message is equally clear: each of us occupies a separate domain. In the language of the street, no one is allowed to butt in (the polite word is "intrude") to a domain properly reserved to another.[4]

On closer inspection, the natural law formulations of the principle raise serious difficulties of their own. Now the legal system must reflect collective social judgments about what types of harm should be covered and why. The easy cases may be death and personal injury, but the matter hardly ends there. Should the application of the principle be limited to physical harm? What about competitive harms? Blocking of views? Personal offense? False or insulting words? No shortcut answers all the variations on the common theme. As in other cases, the key to applying the harm principle lies in our ability to lay bare the utilitarian judgments that underlie even the simplest cases of its application. Once those core cases are understood, the trickier cases should fall into line.

The inquiry here is not directed to some arid theme of interest only to lawyers and other pedants. The stakes are much higher and should reverberate throughout the popular culture to exert profound influence over the direction of political debate about the proper sphere of government activity. It is very hard to find anyone of any political persuasion who thinks abstractly that no sanctions should be imposed on those who harm other persons. The harm conceded, the differences of opinion are all directed to the question of whether these sanctions should take the form of personal redress to the party so injured (tort liability), or whether state power should be brought to bear in the form of fines, regulations, and perhaps imprisonment. But so long as coercion counts as a proper response to the infliction of harms, the broader the definition of harm, the more extensive the justified role of government intervention. The definition of harm thus becomes, as a first approximation, the litmus test for the use of state power.

Mill's Formulation

This legal revolution doubtless has been driven in part by powerful political forces. Yet the genuine conceptual ambiguities in formulating the harm principle have also played some part in its newer expansive role. These difficulties creep in from the earliest formulation of the principle found in John Stuart Mill's "On Liberty" (1859),[5] whose most famous passage offers a stirring affirmation of the right of each individual to go his own way.

> The object of this Essay is to assert one very simple principle, as entitled to govern absolutely the dealings of society with the individual in the way of compulsion and control, whether the means used be physical force in the form of legal penalties, or the moral coercion of public opinion. The principle is, that the sole end for which mankind are warranted, individually or collectively, in interfering with the liberty of action of any of their number, is self-protection. That the only purpose for which power can be rightfully exercised over any member of a civilised community, against his will, is to prevent harm to others. His own good, either physical or moral, is not a sufficient warrant. He cannot rightfully be compelled to do or forbear because it will be better for him to do so, because it will make him happier, because in the opinions of others, to do so would be wise, or even right. These are good reasons for remonstrating with him, or reasoning with him, or persuading him, or entreating him, but not for compelling him, or visiting him with any evil in case he do otherwise.*

---

*   A more complete analysis of Mill would require a detailed account of his treatment of various issues such as marriage and polygamy, which raise questions of "morals" that are generally outside the scope of this book. I shall content myself therefore to say that these questions should in general be treated as follows. The usual rule on individual choice is that it should be allowed where it does not involve the use of force and fraud against another, no matter how offensive one might find it. Freedom of speech rests on just this principle, as does the toleration for polygamous marriage and same-sex partnerships. Other forms of conduct, such as prostitution and gambling, may appear to fall into this category, but are in reality more complex since each carries with it the risk of harm to third parties, whether through sexually transmitted diseases or impoverishment of one's family. In those cases, categorical answers are hard to come by, and the sensible approach cautiously asks whether any set of restrictions or penalties can be enforced without excessive errors of overinclusion and underinclusion. At the margins, all theories have to make peace with some hard cases. The question is, which ones? Where? And why?[6]

Elsewhere Mill hammers the point home in stating the maxims of a good society:

> The maxims are, first, that the individual is not accountable to society for his actions, in so far as these concern the interests of no person but himself. Advice, instruction, persuasion, and avoidance by other people if thought necessary by them for their own good, are the only measures by which society can justifiably express its dislike or disapprobation of his conduct. Secondly, that for such actions as are prejudicial to the interests of others, the individual is accountable, and may be subjected either to social or to legal punishment, if society is of the opinion that the one or the other is requisite for its protection.[7]

Read as a whole, Mill's essay celebrates individual excellence and individual choice. Onward and upward are its themes. The Millian ethos assumes that people know their own minds and interests better than anyone else does, and thus should be allowed—indeed, encouraged—to follow their own inclinations unless they do harm to other persons. There is little concern with the fate of those who are overwhelmed by bad fortune or left behind by the wheels of progress. Today's all too shrill complaints of victimization, marginalization, rejection, and subordination do not rise to the level of stage whispers in Mill's moral universe. Rather, he entertains a robust belief in a philosophical version of the invisible hand: those people who lead by excellence will enrich the lives of other persons and, by indirection, the overall welfare of society as well. Mill praises risk taking in the face of inevitable doubt and attacks the mediocrity bred of security, or the illusion of security. He dares individuals to make a contribution in the world, and exhorts them to use moral persuasion to improve themselves and their fellow citizens. He spends little time weaving a safety net to catch them if they fail. With that vision of heroic and high-minded human endeavor, it is no mystery that Mill took a skeptical view of government intervention. Within his world, the prevention of harm to others was the "sole justification" for restricting liberty; it would not do to construe the exception so broadly as to swallow the principle.

Yet for all his exuberance on the powers of the individual, Mill was not some hard-nosed card-carrying libertarian. Although he works to preserve a broad ground for individual action, he also reserves a place for taxation, under the benefit principle, where needed to secure the common defense and to maintain the social order (see also chapter 4).[8] But lest one quibble about the social mechanisms for securing social peace and good order, the tenor of the essay is defined by his rhetorical flourishes, not by his grudging concessions. Mill hoped to preserve a very large sphere for individual freedom, with concomitant limitations on the sphere of government action. His reformist impulse targeted for special condemnation state religion, in a nation with an established church, and government censorship, in a state known for its strict rules of defamation and long tradition of official secrecy. He was a strong defender of liberty of conscience and freedom of religious practice, and insisted on the benefits of competitive markets—and here's the rub—notwithstanding the harm that the victorious competitor necessarily causes to the disappointed rival.* In the end, his own judgment rested on a cautious brand of utilitarianism that does not exalt simple sensory pleasures and does differentiate between pushpin and poetry. Individual and social well-being are never conflated with mindless forms of individual gratification.†

A closer look, however, reveals the cracks in Mill's intuitive edifice. The first point is simple but important. Mill's classic statement asserts that self-protection is the sole justification for using either legal *or* social sanctions: but what decides which should be used, and why? Unfortunately, that critical question is left to the "opinion of society," without the slightest clue of what fundamental principles should guide its collective deliberations. Initially, it seems clearly wrong to think that legal coercion and social disapproval should occupy the same domain. Surely the good society should find a broader scope for the latter than the former: that is, there should be at least some cases that warrant social disapproval but not public force. And

---

* "Whoever succeeds in an overcrowded profession, or in a competitive examination; whoever is preferred to another in any contest for an object which both desire, reaps benefit from the loss of others, from their wasted exertion and their disappointment. But it is, by common admission, better for the general interest of mankind, that persons should pursue their objects undeterred by this sort of consequences. In other words, society admits no right, either legal or moral, in the disappointed competitors to immunity from this kind of suffering; and feels called on to interfere, only when means of success have been employed which it is contrary to the general interest to permit—namely, fraud or treachery, and force."[9]

† "I regard utility as the ultimate appeal on all ethical questions; but it must be utility in the largest sense, grounded on the permanent interests of a man as a progressive being."[10]

there should be some way to distinguish between them. If so, then narrower grounds for using force have to be articulated and defended. Although Mill's own bottom line presages modern libertarian thought—"fraud or treachery, and force" are his words—he offers us no explanation as to why the line should be drawn there. Likewise, when he tolerates competitive harm, it is only "by common admission," without any explanation as to why. If it is just a question of "him or me," then why should someone who loses a $5,000 investment to a competitor receive no compensation when someone who loses $5 to a common thief gets full compensation? A complete theory must answer the easy cases as well as the difficult ones.

The second crack in Mill's edifice comes from his misunderstanding of the use and limits of public opinion. Public opinion may—indeed, should—be divided, but the use of public force inevitably operates monolithically. One of the main attractions of a system of liberty is that it allows people to disapprove of what others do without allowing them to prohibit or alter that conduct. Informal social sanctions may be organized by distinct groups, and their success will often depend on their ability to persuade disinterested third parties to go along with them. Where there are difficult gradations of view, public opinion is able to register both the intensity and the instability of preferences, and to move more quickly and less formally than state power. It would be a sad state of affairs if public opinion could address only those forms of misconduct sufficiently severe to warrant the use of force, for there are all forms of petty, unkind, insensitive, and graceless conduct that merit social condemnation but not legal punishment.

The conceptual difficulties are still greater when Mill, and the legal theorists who follow the same line, sought to identify the scope of individual interests protected by the harm principle. The problem derives from the two different senses in which the term *interest* may be used—subjective or legal. One sense of the term simply involves a statement that the outcome of some event or process makes a difference to a person, giving this person an interest in it. A second sense implies that the person has a stake in something that is protected by law. Thus, in the first sense, I may have an interest in the success of Apple computer because I use its machines and hope that the company will survive in the marketplace. But it is quite a different thing to have a "legal" interest in the company—that is, to own shares in it and, thus, have a say in its management and a fraction of its profits. The difficult inquiry requires specification of the relationship between these two forms of interest. People are rarely indifferent to the fate of things in which they have a legal interest. But the converse hardly follows, for there are many institutions—the Lyric Opera and the Chicago Bulls—in which I have a personal interest but no legally protected one.

Mill does not attend sufficiently to these two senses of *interest* in his elaboration of the harm principle. Thus, on one level, his account of liberty appears, as if by definition, to avoid any conflict between persons. Each person is to be master over those matters that concern him alone, and not other people, as the maxim of *res perit domino* implies. But suppose that this were literally the case: if I care about act X, and everyone else is indifferent, why should anyone else want in good faith to stop me from doing X? If Mill's claim about the limits of subjective interest and concern provided an accurate description of human motivation, then organizing social life would be easy, and the principle of liberty would not require constant defense. The natural state of the world would so organize itself as to be devoid of any intractable conflicts of interest. But subjective desires are not necessarily constrained by any moral theory; being capable of easy multiplication, they generate too many inconsistent appetites and desires for any system to satisfy simultaneously. Indeed, it is precisely because everyone's subjective interests invariably exceed their legally protected ones that liberty is so difficult to preserve. Parents do wish to influence or determine whom their children marry long after they reach full age; yet today they have no legal control over these marriages. One could seek to extend legal protection to reach these vital subjective interests; but although that maneuver would solve one problem, it would create a second problem of greater magnitude: children would not have legal protection for the choice of their own mates. Of the two vital subjective interests, of necessity one must yield if any individual liberties are to receive protection.

The brute difficulty with Mill's account arises, then, precisely because so many individual actions *do* concern more persons than one, and yet one person is given the absolute and exclusive control to engage in, or refrain from, the performance of a particular act, as it were, to the prejudice of another. Even Mill's case of religious conscience and censorship falls into that category, for one man's belief is another's heresy. Similarly, allowing competitive harms[11] and blocked views[12] without redress has always created genuine anguish because a straightforward application of the harm principle appears to cry out for relief: stop the competition and block that new construction. Mill gets the right answer in both these cases by his appeal to the common admission of mankind—a sentiment that is far from being as common as he supposes. In so doing, he makes social consent the ultimate test of responsibility. But if that test works here, then he has to explain why it does not displace the harm principle as the comprehensive test for public intervention.

Confusions of this sort complicate any efforts to rely on the harm principle to organize the law of tort, whereby one individual secures redress from another for harms done. Yet just that sense of personal affront makes it impossible to distinguish between the cases of force (compensable) and competition (not compensable), even though that distinction is central to Mill's own comprehensive view. One can try to avoid this difficulty by insisting that the harm principle is really confined to cases of physical injury, so that competitive injuries are ruled out by fiat. That line is often championed in popular accounts. The philosophical defense of "Ain't nobody's business" takes just this line: "You should be allowed to do whatever you want with your own person and property, as long as you don't physically harm the person or property of another."[13] Yet this position rules out far too much on what look like a priori grounds: defamation of the person need not only lead to death; it can lead to expulsion from clubs, the breakup of a marriage, or the loss of a loan. Surely the harm principle is sufficient to cover these even though no physical injury is involved. The complaint of the plaintiff is that the defendant's false words to a third party so altered the third party's pattern of behavior that he refused to do business with the plaintiff or, in some cases, imposed physical harms on him. Defamation is a very old wrong, and is far from being the stepchild of the modern welfare state.

A Utilitarian Approach

The intuitive invocation of the harm principle thus fails to answer the simple question of which harms should be prohibited by the legal system, and which it should tolerate or, indeed, welcome. Some simple utilitarian arguments can, however, lend philosophical coherence to the harm principle. The social conversation takes on a very different appearance if one asks whether granting an action to restrain competition, or force, will better advance some social welfare function. No longer is there any effort to ignore the indirect effects one person's conduct has on the life of another. Instead, there is some systematic effort to evaluate these indirect consequences in order to decide whether others have been hurt or helped by what one person has done. The ultimate task is, then, to decide what assignment of legal rights will advance some overall conception of social utility or welfare—that is, produce on average some net social gain, taking into account the private gains and losses of all individuals. Once this approach is adopted, we can no longer pretend that, for any particular act, only one person is concerned and all others are indifferent. Instead, the revised claim for autonomy of choice and liberty of action rests on an implicit assertion—one that Mill himself was prepared to make*—that each person presumptively has a larger stake in his own person and behavior than any other and should, therefore, be allowed control of his own actions, as the principle of *res perit domino* implies. The size of the relative stakes shifts dramatically when physical injury (or defamation) to other parties is at stake. But even here a more nuanced account is needed in order to weigh the relative magnitude of the subjective interests to decide which should be accorded the status of legal rights.

In addressing this theme, it is best to start with the easy cases and then to make incremental corrections. Here the polar opposites are force and competition, and these come out very differently. The use of force at best generates gains for one that may offset the losses to the other. Assume that all people must choose between two alternatives: neither use force nor have it used against you; or take a 50-percent chance of winning or losing in a contest of force with some random stranger. So long as the all-or-nothing condition is satisfied, we know what the outcome will be: the mutual renunciation of the use of force which has been the goal of all social contract theorists since Hobbes. This knowledge is contingent in the sense that the proposition can be denied without its running into some logical contradiction. But it is not contingent in an alternative sense: namely, that we cannot find any empirical order or regularities in human behavior. There is a middle ground between logically necessary and empirically chaotic.

It is not hard to identify some of the critical empirical constants. We know enough about the constitution of human beings, their needs and their foibles, to make a good approximate judgment about the consequences of these alternative regimes, to be confident of the probable outcome. The potential gains from the use of force are small relative to the potential losses. If each person starts with an endowment of 100, and the winner ends up with 120 and the loser with 0, then the chances of winning have to be better than 5 to 1 to come out even. The odds will not be favorable to any individual over the long run. Indeed, even the most powerful individual is

---

* "He is the person most interested in his own well-being: the interest which any other person, except in cases of strong personal attachment, can have in it, is trifling, compared with that which he himself has."[14]

subject to defeat at the hands of two or more rivals. Facing these odds, one does not need extravagant faith in the power of individual self-interest to conclude that everyone would choose to abstain from force, since each plays a private negative-sum game. People are keen on a regime of force when they alone are allowed to use it. It is for that reason that the question about the use of force has to be put on an all-or-nothing basis: no one should be allowed to benefit from restrictions imposed on others while being free of those restrictions in his own life. To allow that degree of variation permits everyone to indulge in the ceaseless special pleading that never reaches a stable resting place.

But if that same all-or-nothing choice is offered for competition, then both the calculations and the outcome will differ dramatically. Again, competition will generate some payoffs that are positive and others that are negative. In any head-to-head confrontation, these payoffs are likely to be asymmetrical, so that one party will win while the disappointed competitor will lose. But if the individual struggle occurs within the context of some larger social organization, the gains over time from successful competition are likely to dwarf the losses to the individuals disappointed in any given competitive round. New technology and new forms of business increase the size of the social pie that acts of force only shrink. The competitive losers in round one are still sound in mind and limb and can re-enter the market in round two. In life-and-death struggles, the dead do not live to fight (or compete) again, and the maimed have their prospects diminished to the point where they, too, can no longer survive in struggles with younger and healthier rivals. Everyone wants some selective advantage over his rivals. But once that particularistic avenue of advancement is blocked, then individuals faced with an all-or-nothing choice will say no to force and yes to open competition. The opposition between force and competition is thus as stark as the theoretical divide between negative- and positive-sum games.

The analysis is still incomplete: we must also evaluate the effects of these two practices on third parties. By removing from the lists potential trading partners, force diminishes the opportunities third persons have for gainful exchange. The use of force also undercuts the stability of possession and the security of exchange—both classic objectives in the English utilitarian tradition.[15] In contrast, competition *expands* the opportunities of third persons by allowing them (and more of them) to buy a given market basket of goods at a lower price and, with innovation, to enjoy the prospects of more attractive goods and services over time. The global consequences of the two rules therefore differ dramatically, but these are overlooked in any truncated inquiry that focuses solely on the fact that the conduct of one party has caused harm to the other in one discrete transaction.

Although one might quibble with the results in certain particulars, the overall conclusion seems clear: the insights of the more exhaustive inquiry are well aligned with Mill's common admission of mankind on the intuitive limits of the harm principle. Allowing persons injured by the use or threat of force a private right of action brings to the fore an effective mechanism of social control: Who is in a better position to sue for a private loss that is, in the broad run of cases, well correlated with a social one? With competitive harms, the balance of social advantage shifts the other way: If the private loss correlates with a social gain, why allow any private redress? There is, after all, an explanation why the $5 theft is worse than the $5,000 loss from an investment that does not pan out. As the basic theory is so strong, a per-se rule is appropriate: no individuated inquiries are needed. A categorical rule barring relief from competitive injury is both cheaper and more reliable than any step-by-step analysis of discrete transactions. The Latin phrase *damnum absque iniuria*, "harm without legal injury," captures just this distinction by denying relief for competitive injuries while allowing it against the use of force and, as becomes quickly evident, against the threat of force as well.

A Shield of Liberty in the Late Nineteenth Century

The strength of this analysis becomes clear if we follow the career of the harm principle in the late nineteenth century. Mill wrote *On Liberty* in 1859, after the rise of the railroad but before the huge expansion of public utilities in the period that runs, roughly speaking, from the end of the Civil War to the beginning of the First World War. Like other philosophical writers, whose frame of reference often lags behind the leading technological innovations of their own time, Mill conceived of harm as being caused in individual and not institutional settings. His key example refers to competitive examinations for admission to overcrowded professions. He was not prepared to deal either with the central place that mass organizations— giant corporations, labor unions, trusts, public utilities—came to hold in the legal order; nor with the question whether the rise of these institutions could call for a revision of either the scope or the application of the harm principle. But such cases were not long in coming before the courts, and the outer limits of the harm principle were in constant litigation in both England and the United States in the fifty years following the publication of *On Liberty*.[16]

Oliver Wendell Holmes sought to make sense of these impending developments in his famous article "Privilege, Malice, and Intent," which appeared in April of 1894.[17] In this article, Holmes sought to cut through the obscurantist arguments that dominated judicial decisions in the so-called trade cases (that is, disputes between rival sellers or manufacturers) then coming before the courts in large numbers. To him, the legal analysis was part of a two-step process. First, the harm principle set the boundaries for social concern: "The law recognizes temporal damage as an evil which its object is to prevent or to redress, so far as is consistent with paramount considerations to be mentioned."[18] Those paramount considerations were issues of policy, which contain within them a necessary denunciation of the classical *sic utere* maxim for its hopeless oversimplification of the approach. Second, Holmes was keenly aware that the Millian approach swept everything within the scope of the tort law, and the language of "privilege" was his preferred tool for sweeping much of it back out again. Almost like clockwork, he reverts to the stock examples of competition on the one hand and blocked views on the other, and dispatches both within a single well-honed paragraph:

> The first [privilege for competitive injury] rests on the economic postulate that free competition is worth more to society than it costs. The next [spoiling views], upon the fact that a line must be drawn between the conflicting interests of adjoining owners, which necessarily will restrict the freedom of each; upon the unavoidable Philistinism which prefers use to beauty when considered the most profitable way of administering the land in the jurisdiction taken as one whole.[19]

Though clearly grasping for some intelligible measure of aggregate social welfare to limit the scope of the harm principle, Holmes lacked the conceptual tools to bring his venture to a successful close. The resort to the idea of privilege was not wholly new to Holmes in 1894: he relied on it to explain why certain forms of defamatory communications were entitled to a qualified privilege: "It is for the public interest that people should be free to give the best information they can under certain circumstances without fear, but there is no public benefit in having lies told at any time."[20] But the privilege to give or receive employment references is old and well understood: it was, for example, treated as a well established part of the English law by 1789.[21] If a prospective employer had to get the consent of a prospective employee in order to check references, then the entire process of vetting job candidates would grind to a halt. As inquiries open up more opportunities than they close down, "there is no class to whom it is of so much importance that characters should be freely given as honest servants."[22] Yet Holmes missed the key difference between his novel use of privilege in 1894 and the conventional use of the term in the earlier common law cases, all of which attached privilege, as in cases of necessity, to the use of force or misrepresentation only—that is, to some act which was a prima facie violation of the basic integrity of person and property.

The privileges involved in the trade cases are really very different: they involve only the economic harms inflicted on strangers by low prices or economic combination, or both. The early efforts to make sense of these cases did not seek to analyze the global consequences of allowing or forbidding certain kinds of practice, notwithstanding Holmes's quip about the social benefits of competition. Instead, they sought to collapse these cases into the traditional two-party framework of the injurer and the victim of a discrete harm. In 1889, in *Mogul v. McGregor*, the famous early predatory pricing case, Lord Charles Bowen made it appear as though these cases were in fact species of the least controversial of torts, the intentional harms: "Now, intentionally to do that which is calculated in the ordinary course of events to damage, and which does, in fact, damage another in that person's property or trade, is actionable if done without just cause or excuse."[23] Bowen then ticked off the types of tactics that are not tolerated: fraud, intimidation, obstruction, molestation, and the like. But the desire to gain as much of the market for oneself as possible is permissible, even if it is known to cause harm to other traders: any other rule "would be a strange and impossible counsel of perfection."[24] Finally, the claim of conspiracy did not work to make the conduct illegal either: "If so, one rich capitalist may innocently carry competition to a length which would become unlawful in the case of a syndicate with a joint capital no larger than his own, and one individual merchant may lawfully do that which a firm or a partnership may not."[25]

The key elements of Lord Bowen's formulation are seriously incomplete. The traditional principle of intentional harms was limited to person and property, and Bowen's attempt to equate "property and trade" missed the critical distinction between force and competition that Mill had well sensed but not fully defended. That point had been previously well defended nearly two hundred years earlier by the English jurist Sir John Holt in his analysis of the case of rival schoolmasters: force is out, but competition by lower rates and higher quality is surely in.* The effort to create some general right of trade, without stating the particular forms of conduct against which that right is protected, does not advance legal thinking but leads to unnecessary confusion and overgeneralization, as does the analogous confusion between hard bargaining in competitive markets and improper forms of duress, such as a gun to the head.[27] Nor does it help to qualify the analysis by singling out "malicious" economic harm for special treatment. Malice is not required to establish liability in ordinary cases of assault and battery, and it is not clear why it should become relevant in this context, especially when it is so hard to disentangle the desire for a competitor's failure from the desire for one's own success.[28]

The decisions on predatory pricing were only one portion of the nineteenth-century concern with the harm principle. In addition to predation, the courts had to deal throughout the century with other practices that arguably operated in restraint of trade. Chief among these was cartelization—that is, agreements among rival producers to divide territories, impose restrictions on output, or set minimum prices. In dealing with these questions, the judges had a strong set of intuitions that monopoly arrangements did carry with them the risk of higher prices and lower quality for the goods sold. Yet, however easy, we must not dismiss these cases as was sometimes done—solely on the ground that they do not fall within the narrow rubrics of force and fraud.[29] The judicial response fell, predictably and erratically, in the middle. The basic position was that "agreements in restraint of trade are against public policy and void, unless the restraint they impose is partial only, and they are made on good consideration, and are reasonable."[30] The basic prohibition against general restraints was designed to weaken cartels by denying them contractual enforcement, thereby allowing cartel members to cheat on each other to the benefit of customers. The requirement of good consideration (that is, value passing between members

---

* "One schoolmaster sets up a new school to the damage of an antient school, and thereby the scholars are allured from the old school to come to his new. (The action was held there not to lie.) But suppose Mr. Hickeringill should lie in the way with his guns and fright the boys from going to school, and their parents would not let them go thither; sure that schoolmaster might have an action for the loss of his scholars."[26]

of the cartel) was unimportant because it was always satisfied: when several businesses enter into reciprocal promises to reduce output or divide territories, each gives up something of value that is coveted by another.

The crux of the matter thus turned on the "reasonableness" of the partial restriction (defined by time, place, or occupation), which invited an open-ended inquiry into the possible adverse effects of the arrangements on third parties, most notably consumers and employees. In this corner of the law at least, these global implications of the harm principle were more clearly grasped by judges who struggled to work their way to a coherent position. As might be expected, the decisions are numerous and complex, and it is possible on balance to think that too much judicial respect was paid to these agreements, given their impact on third parties.[31]

Even under the best of circumstances, the proper treatment of these restraints is one of great delicacy. None of these private arrangements could bind other producers who did not join their ranks. Unlike state-created monopolies, they do not prevent new entrants from undercutting whatever price advantages the parties seek to secure among themselves. In addition, the arrangements in question might well produce certain cost savings that could offset the social damages wrought when the parties to the agreement used their market power to the full. Both of these points, for example, were relied on by the court in the 1829 case of *Wickens v. Evans*,[32] which sustained a division of territories among three competing boxmakers. The arrangement did not prevent new entrants from coming into the territories, and also reduced the cost each of the suppliers had in running his business by allowing him to specialize in a particular geographical market. Likewise in other cases, the restraints on trade were justified by appeals to other concerns. Thus, the courts were prepared to enforce any agreement to prevent one worker's taking a job with a rival firm if that worker had confidential information (such as customer lists) that could work to the rival's advantage.[33]

Judicial supervision intensified when individual firms operated under a legally created monopoly, be it for running a customs office or a common carrier. No longer was it possible to break up the monopoly so created, but it was possible to impose upon a monopoly the duty to take all customers for reasonable rates, instead of charging all the market would bear. The position was stated clearly long before the nineteenth century, most notably by Lord Matthew Hale, who noted that the operation of a wharf or crane under the King's franchise required its operator to charge reasonable and moderate rates on a nondiscriminatory basis, because all persons had to come to the facility in question. That principle was consistently applied throughout the nineteenth century. [34] Its elaboration is of sufficient importance both for historical questions—the growth of railroads—and modern policy issues—the restructuring of the telecommunications industry—that it deserves a separate chapter of its own (see chapter 10).

The overall judicial product may not have been ideal, but it was very strong. The cases did recognize that far greater danger was attached to government-protected monopolies than to private arrangements. And there is little evidence that the judges got matters backward by upholding private agreements that were highly dangerous to social welfare while invalidating those that held little peril to third-party interests. On their merits, these questions present delicate challenges even today. The tasks facing nineteenth-century judges were still more daunting, for they analyzed these complex transactions arrangements before economists had developed a systematic analysis of the welfare effects of monopoly and competition: Alfred Marshall published the first edition of the *Principles of Economics* in 1890. In principle, the underlying inquiry in these economic harm cases is identical to that in cases of physical injury: the systematic gains and losses of all players (and bystanders) have to be toted up under the alternative legal rules. Finding a clean line between cognizable and noncognizable harm is far more difficult here than for conduct that violates the libertarian norms against force and fraud. The want of a coherent theory worked against the conceptual unification of the law of tort. The modern efficiency-based analyses of antitrust law represent a major conceptual revolution from the earlier fitful common law approach to the subject.

A Sword against Liberty in the Twentieth Century

This first wave of expansion of the harm principle had both salutary and dangerous effects. On the positive side, it led to a restriction of the harm principle when private harms to person and property were associated with social gains—for example, the traditional cases of necessity or self-defense. But with competitive harms, the presumption is set in favor of allowing an activity to go forward. One can easily quarrel with particular efforts to distinguish competitive harms from monopoly practices, but the errors, if any, are small when measured against the modern expansion of the harm principle, which is wholly destructive of the original Millian mission of limiting the scope of government action. Too often it seems that so long as one person is made worse off by an individual action, redress of some sort is in order, wholly without regard to the long-term aggregate benefits. Four cases illustrate how the harm principle has spilled over its traditional, narrow contours: competitive harms in regulatory contexts; harms from private acts of discrimination; harms to the right for health care; and environmental harms.

Competitive Harms

Both the United States and other industrialized countries take an erratic approach to competitive harms. Under the antitrust conception noted above, these harms are seen as the sensible price for overall economic advancement. The rise and fall of IBM, General Motors, Apple Computer, or Nintendo are the stuff for feature stories in the business section, not grounds for legal intervention, even if employees lose their jobs in droves and stockholders and bondholders lose their capital. Yet simultaneously, vast systems of regulation (the Civil Aeronautics Board, the Interstate Commerce Commission, the Federal Communications Commission, the National Labor Relations Act) have operated on the protectionist premise that various forms of competitive harms are per se unfair solely because they are damaging to airlines, truckers, broadcasters, farmers, or unions, as the case may be. Agricultural price-support programs do more than allow anyone to enter the farming business: they create a perpetual lien on the public treasury that makes it more difficult for anyone else to raise the capital for other business ventures. Antidumping laws keep out needed goods at huge administrative cost, all under the banner of "fair trade."[35] Yet the present law is so internally torn that an antidumping proceeding can mandate one set of price increases while the antitrust laws prohibit further additional ones.

In comparison with the risks of government action, the dangers from private cartels look small, if only because of the inherent tendency to yield to individual members' cheating against the cartel for their short-term advantage—a prisoner's dilemma game in which they should be encouraged to defect. And even here the risk of criminal and civil antitrust suits might deter harmful behavior that has some short-term chances of success. On balance, the entire system would operate with far greater precision if the state followed only two principles: first and foremost, refrain from creating cartels of its own; and second, direct the force of the antitrust laws solely against anticompetitive arrangements, without seeking to extend the ambit of harm to other kinds of wrong.

Just that approach seems to be taking hold in the recent American antitrust cases. The present law, for example, shows a deep skepticism toward predatory pricing, granting to defendants summary judgment in them[36] and doing so on grounds that explicitly recognize the low probability that predation will succeed as a tactic to achieve monopolization.[37] By reducing sharply the price it charges for its goods, the ostensible predator sharply increases the demand for its goods. The additional units needed to meet this demand could easily cost more to produce while generating less revenue, thereby instantly inundating the predator with short-term losses. The predator has only a slim likelihood of recouping these losses in some future period: once it tries to raise its prices back to a monopoly level, new competitors can rush into the void, forcing prices back to their competitive level. It is all pain for little gain. The strength of these tendencies makes it far more likely that suits for predation will punish vigorous price competition rather than promote it. The only predation scheme with a fighting chance of success has to be engineered by a firm that operates in a specialized market against one or two competitors, who have such poor access to capital markets that they cannot weather even a short drought in revenues. It is doubtful whether it makes much sense to hold the door open for these cases, given the powerful economic reasons for thinking that most lawsuits of this sort should never be brought at all.

But by the same token, the far greater social risk of price-fixing arrangements implies that these cases should receive a full trial, where the evidence of concealed agreement could be evaluated for what it is worth, as recent appellate court decisions have held.[38] Outside cartelization agreements, however, the strong libertarian position might well prove more durable, as a general prophylactic matter, over the long run than sophisticated efforts to divide economic harms into those that promote and retard social welfare. Many of these efforts seem difficult to understand. The Supreme Court, for example, has allowed a jury to pass on the question of whether a manufacturer is in violation of the antitrust law when it ties the sale of its service to the sale of its parts.[39] The theory is that the manufacturer crowds out rival repair outfits by the tie-in arrangement. But so long as there is competition in the market for the basic equipment, commercial buyers should be able to factor in the higher costs of parts and labor when they purchase their original products. In addition, the manufacturer wholly without the tie-in arrangement should be able to price the sale of its parts at a level that captures any residual monopoly profits even if the services are supplied by others. Against that background, it seems more likely that the tie-in arrangement may well have unappreciated efficiency advantages: for example, a common supplier for parts and labor could eliminate warranty disputes when it is unclear whether a product failure should be attributed to defective parts or faulty service, or both.

The picture is equally cloudy in the so-called vertical restraint cases, whereby a manufacturer terminates a distributor in response to the price-cutting complaints of rival distributors. The Supreme Court has held that these bare allegations, without more, do not state a violation of the antitrust laws;[40] and again, the conclusion makes good sense given the wide range of reasons for dealer termination. It could well be that the lower prices charged by one dealership increase the service obligations that others have to meet; or that the decisions by one rogue distributor could upset the overall pricing strategies the manufacturer wishes to pursue in a competitive market.[41] The sheer complexity of these vertical cases may well be sufficient to differentiate them from the horizontal arrangements. If so, then the safer course of action is to follow a simpler if somewhat naive approach to antitrust law—which focuses on the not inconsiderable matters of proof in ordinary price-fixing cases, and then calls it a day.

Discrimination

The question of whether discrimination by private employers is some form of actionable wrong was not explicitly addressed by Mill or Holmes—or, for that matter, by the early common law outside the context of legal franchises or monopolies. For Mill, the area might illustrate a tension between his worries over the use of state force and his preference for social sanctions. He was an early champion of women's rights as they related to suffrage, and a strong believer in merit as the determinant of individual success. (Remember: the disappointed competitor failed an examination; he was not subject to family favoritism or class bias.) But Mill would not have regarded the decision not to hire, regardless of its motive, as unlawful given his implicit devotion to the principle of freedom of association and contract, a principle that the antidiscrimination laws necessarily abridge. But today an invidious decision not to hire someone is treated as though it were a common law tort—assault comes most quickly to mind. The law thus echoes the older predatory pricing cases by giving malice or bad motive an all-too-central place in the analysis. David Strauss advances the position as follows:

The satisfaction of the desire not to associate with members of another racial group, at least in the employment context, should not count in the social welfare function. That desire is comparable to a taste for committing an intentional tort. In determining how the legal system should respond to battery, for example, we do not consider the utility the tortfeasor gains from committing a battery against someone else. The harm to the victim of the battery is all social loss, with no countervailing gain. Discrimination from racial antipathy should be treated in the same way.[42]

The assertion of this parallel amounts to a profound misapplication of the traditional harm principle—victory for the good guys by persuasive definition alone. First, it misstates the proper methodology for the intentional torts. As I have discussed, both gains and losses *do* count. The basic prohibition against force and fraud follows empirically because we are confident that presumptively its losses dwarf its gains. This background judgment is so strong—say, in rape and murder cases—that "we would not presume collectively and objectively to value the cost of a rape to the victim against the benefit to the rapist even if economic efficiency is our sole motive."[43] Yet the balance of advantage can shift in other contexts, such as those involving self-defense; this is the reason the doctrine of privilege is part of the law of intentional torts. If both gains and losses did not count, then why would one even worry about the excuses and justifications that play so large a role in the area?

The same approach applies to discrimination laws where again there is no shortcut to the analysis: all gains and losses count, and no preferences or desires can be blithely dismissed as illegitimate just because it makes the final tally easy. In addition, we have to avoid the inverse peril: to argue that the refusal to extend an offer to someone does not count as harm is surely incorrect if the implication is that people are indifferent to getting jobs and remaining unemployed. A refusal to make offers is surely a matter that concerns more than one person; therefore, any argument that refusals to hire should not be wrongful must stem from some more systematic analysis of the global consequences that follow from adopting alternative legal regimes. It is in this larger setting that the discrimination laws fare poorly against a competitive market.

Quite simply, making it wrongful to refuse to deal is to have the harm principle explode before our very eyes. If employers can be sued for their deliberate failure to offer jobs to workers, then workers may be sued for their unwillingness to accept job offers. Interviewing two candidates would guarantee, at best, one job and one lawsuit. The entire job market would come to a grinding halt. It is to (just about) everyone's long-term advantage to allow hiring and firing to take place only on grounds of mutual consent. So no one could identify the elusive exceptions, all persons, at all times, would take the risk that their overtures would be rejected; and none could count on legal protection to ease their disappointments. But all share in the greater profits generated by opening job opportunities in the first place.

So the stress on motive in employment discrimination law is meant to cut the harm principle down to manageable size. But in this context as well, the general theory does not explain why the harm counts when borne by workers but not by employers. Nor does it take into account the fundamental features of the operation of a competitive market. The key to job creation is not a hammer to the head of a reluctant employer; it is to increase the number of employers to which employees can turn, and to reduce the costs of searching for that employer whose own program fits with a worker's aspirations.[44] Opening up new alternatives reduces the dependence that any worker has on any employer. Better it is to find a compatible employer than to coerce grudging consent from an uncooperative one.

In contrast, the person who is killed or maimed by physical acts is not in a position to accept any offers of future employment, no matter how attractive.[45] The asserted parallel between force and discrimination thus ignores the vast differences in the choice left open by hostile action: the rejected candidate seeks another job; a maimed person licks his wounds. The refusal to deal turns ominous only when an employer is the only player in town, as in the monopoly cases. Yet, predictably, the nineteenth-century judges did impose a prohibition against discrimination on common carriers (as I shall discuss in chapter 10). But whenever markets can be opened to new competitors, free entry is far preferable to any legal rule designed to force employers to ignore their subjective preferences and to hire workers with whom, for whatever reason, they prefer not to deal.

The principle of freedom of association was central to Mill—and is central to all theories of liberty insofar as they pertain to both religion and speech. Extending the harm principle to discrimination compounds the public mischief on matters of race, sex, age, and disability. This conclusion does not change even if we take into account third-party effects, most notably a widespread public distaste that stems from not having (or, worse, from repealing) an antidiscrimination law. That return to a regime of freedom of association could be said to mark, symbolically, an insensitivity to past official racial, and to present private, discrimination. As before, some indirect harms of discrimination can be identified; and in many social settings, they matter. But by the same token, these symbolic harms do not all cut in one direction. Affirmative action causes harm to qualified applicants who are passed over on the ground of race or sex; yet their losses are not thought sufficient to stop private affirmative action programs, much less government or accreditation mandates. No theory of freedom can survive the extended definition of harm that animates the antidiscrimination laws. What possible sense does it make to defend a freedom to speak only those thoughts others do not find offensive? And does anyone think that the state should decide whether the content of the speech is such as to justify, or not, the offense? The proper conclusion is to ignore, as a matter of course, *all* these second-order harms—not because they do not exist, but because the cure of limiting their impact is worse than the disease. Force, fraud, and monopoly should be the only justifications for legal intervention. The remainder of our social ills should respond to the kinds of social responses so well understood by Mill.

The Failure to Subsidize

The next of the convolution of the harm principle stems from differences in the setting of the baseline from which harm is measured, a matter discussed more fully in the next chapter. Let us suppose that A and B each desire to purchase health insurance, but A is sickly and B is healthy. In any system in which health insurance is purchased in an open market, insurers and B will seek a solution that sets the premiums proportionate to risk. If one insurer seeks to charge B some portion of A's premium, then another insurer will enter the market, offer a lower cost, and still make a profit because B will defect from any system that makes his premium equal to A's. In traditional language, the market for health insurance follows the patterns for all other forms of insurance: subsidies are bled out. Classification of potential insureds becomes the standard practice.

To Mill, this pattern of behavior fits perfectly within the harm principle because of his implicit view that each person has the right to use and dispose of his own resources as he sees fit. But that assumption has been frequently challenged under the rubric of *social insurance.* Thus Alain Enthoven, one of the pioneers of managed competition, has written that social insurance transforms the baseline so that each sickly A is now entitled as of right to some subsidy from each healthy B.[46] The ordinary system of market insurance must therefore be banned because it allows B to take care of himself without taking care of A as well: B's purchase of cheap health insurance for his own needs thus creates an external harm on A, who now must pay more for coverage or do without.*

Once this line is adopted, there is no limit to the restrictions the state can impose on what used to be regarded as ordinary contractual relations. Want to hire your own physician on a fee-for-service basis? Can't do it, given the harm to others. Only healthy people will opt for this alternative, thereby causing an increase in the costs to the remaining members of the population. Want to do without insurance altogether? Again a wrong: same reason as above—healthy people will abandon the pools, forcing up rates for those at greater risk. Want to purchase group insurance with high deductibles? Sorry, offering that policy is a way of signaling insurers that one anticipates lower utilization of the services, and thus should be charged lower rates. This new definition of externality starts from the assumption that competition is pure externality devoid of social gain, and thus allows the most massive form of regulation from the cradle to the grave. What is true for health insurance can be carried over to any other form of insurance: discrimination (already seen to be an external harm) now becomes impermissible as well, when calculated by age, by sex, by territory, or by past conduct. Let the baseline shift to one in which equal payments are supposed to yield unequal coverage, and liberty as we know it is swallowed by the harm principle.

Once again these profound and mischievous extensions of the harm principle ignore all the collateral and indirect costs of massive government intervention: the enormous political struggles to decide which Bs have to subsidize which As, and to what extent; the increased moral hazard of risky conduct (drugs, alcohol, skydiving), secure in the knowledge that others will pay the price; the heavy-handed coercion that imposes civil and criminal sanctions on efforts to seek medical care from physicians and groups that do not have the mantle of public approval. The Millian theory of harm presupposes a common law baseline that Mill did not defend as well as he

---

* Enthoven writes: "Market failure is endemic in health insurance. For example, if free to do so, competing profit-motivated insurers would seek out those having the lowest expected medical expenses and offer them low premiums to attract their business. High risk persons would face high premiums, exclusion of coverage for pre-existing conditions, and possibly the complete unavailability of coverage. To the extent that regulation inhibited these practices, insurers would seek to avoid enrolling the sick or people likely to become sick. In seeking insurance, especially with a low deductible, a person identifies himself as a probable user of services and an undesirable customer. Insurance companies only want to sell insurance to those who are not likely to use services, so the market breaks down."[47]

might. But the modern theories presuppose an alternative, totalitarian theory of harm that is indefensible: the exercise of individual choice now becomes an act of pure negative externality.

Environmental Harms

My last example is the equally regrettable extension of the harm principle in connection with the venerable tort of nuisance, with its long lineage in both the common law and the Roman law systems. The gist of this tort was harm to neighbors by conduct undertaken on one's own property: fumes, noises, waste spillage, and other forms of physical invasion easily captured in the original *sic utero* principle. As with so many good ideas, the common law of nuisance has proved far more slippery than its proponents suppose.[48] Yet the area is capable of great clarification through the rules for injuries to property and trade that I have already considered. The first point here is that the cases of *discharge* by conscious action from the land of one person to the land of a neighbor is the paradigm case of nuisance, normally remediable by damages or injunction, or both. It would be a mistake to think that the class of wrongful harms is coextensive with the class of physical invasions, but this is not the place to worry about the details and refinements with either invasive or noninvasive nuisance: I take up these theoretically interesting challenges in the discussion of boundaries in chapter 7.

The major focus of my present concern—indeed, ire—is the modern insistence that the traditional categories of nuisance law are incoherent, so that the state is entitled to prevent damage—not to a neighbor, but to the environment more generally.* In so doing, I do not question the accomplishments of modern science in detecting hidden connections between harmful consequences in one place and apparently innocent actions in another. (The identification of positive environmental externalities should be pursued with similar vigor!) But I do fear that this new sophistication will be used in only one direction—to prove obscure causal connections—and not to debunk unsound efforts to trace serious consequences to activities that did not cause them.

---

* The most influential and unfortunate statement of the sort is William L. Prosser's: "There is perhaps no more impenetrable jungle in the entire law than that which surrounds the word 'nuisance.' It has meant all things to all people, and has been applied indiscriminately to everything from an alarming advertisement to a cockroach baked in a pie."[49]

Causation has not only its factual, but its conceptual, side, making it all too easy for courts and legislatures to expand the lists of harms that are said to call for legal redress even though they pose no threat of invasion either to the public lands and waters or to the private property of other individuals. What form of harm is there when someone develops a wetland or cuts down some portion of a newly designated critical dune area? Rarely is pollution created; rarely does one party's land cave in for loss of lateral or subjacent support. Instead, there is a general social perception that more of these valuable resources are good for mankind, or good for nature, or both.[50] At this point, the law of nuisance is transformed from a law that regulates harm to neighbors (both near and far) to one that regulates harm to that most insistent of plaintiffs, nature itself. The doctrine depends on an unhappy extension of the doctrine of internal relations which guts the ability of the harm principle to place limits on government action. As stated by Professor Joseph L. Sax, no "appropriate lines [can] be drawn between uses wholly internal to one's land and those that create external harms. . . . The ecological truism that everything is connected to everything else may be the most profound challenge ever presented to established notions of property."[51]

Such mischief! It is as though any alteration in the state of nature by the owner of private property is a wrong unless and until it is proved a good. It thus becomes a tort—indeed, a crime—for a person to build a single-family house on the side of a hill; to move dirt from one part of his land onto another; to cut down a tree, add a porch, or build a bridge over the creek unless and until prior approval is obtained from the state, no matter how large one's plot of land, and no matter whether individual neighbors applaud or frown. The harm to the environment is treated as an impersonal wrong—not to mere neighbors, but to nature itself. But that preoccupation with indirect consequences from ordinary land use and development is short-sighted even in its own terms. Sharp and rigid restrictions on development in a populated area could induce unneeded development in some pristine region freed of those regulations. The background assumption that all indirect consequences are both large and negative distorts the operation of the law in the here and now. The common law of nuisance has done a good job in regulating harms between neighbors; it could continue to do so without any gratuitous expansion.

Yet it is said that we must preserve dunes and wetlands, and that we preserve critical habitat. True enough. The great flaw in the dominant thought on these subjects is that we should have them by regulation rather than by purchase. The province of state power is not limited by the harm principle: the public can also use its eminent domain power to buy land for preservation purposes or to impose restrictions on land that otherwise remains in private hands. And, of course, nothing prohibits private individuals and foundations from setting aside land for natural uses without government compulsion. No one doubts, or should doubt, that the destruction of habitat is a leading cause of the loss of species. But that proposition is not equivalent to one that says that any particular form of property development necessarily has that harmful consequence; or that if it does, the loss necessarily overshadows the correlative gain. What is needed, therefore, is a systematic assessment of the two alternative regimes, one that treats habitat loss as a type of harm that can be regulated without compensation, and one that requires needed habitat to be purchased from its owner.[52]

Initially it is easy to dismiss the facile argument that habitat purchase should not be required of the state because of the high tax burdens it necessarily imposes. The tax payments are *transfers* from the public at large to the individual owner; these transfer payments help some and hurt others, but on net do nothing to the overall health and welfare of society. The importance of the transfer payments lies in the way in which they induce government entities and private individuals to act. If the state does not have to compensate for the property taken, then public officials and other citizens can ignore the losses generated by its actions. In this context, these social losses stem from the decline in the use value of the land, relative to what it was under private ownership. Only a false opposition between the "public" and the "private" interest could support the dubious conclusion that landowner losses just don't count in the overall social calculation. All individuals are part and parcel of society. It is government entities (like corporations) that have no social interests of their own. The losses to any particular landowner belong on the social ledger along with other debits and credits generated by habitat preservation. A rule that allows regulation to limit rights of development by designation hides real costs from public scrutiny. These costs, moreover, are not strictly economic in form: rather, the level of political discourse is necessarily compromised by removing the direct consequences of government action from public view.

Requiring compensation in cases of habitat preservation also minimizes a second set of dangers. The designation of habitat does not take place in a void, but requires comprehensive administrative action. Before that action is completed, individual landowners, who know that they will not be compensated, have every incentive to destroy valuable habitat before they are prohibited from using their land altogether. They fear a system that necessarily links public gain to private loss. The alternative view that requires government purchase of suitable habitat has exactly the opposite incentive effects: it leads landowners to regard habitat preservation as an opportunity for private gain. Their incentives are to preserve it in advance of regulation so that they can sell it, if not to the government, then to any number of private environmental groups who can purchase on their own account, or enter into some more complex arrangement which allows for limited development and limited habitat preservation.

Of course, no one should say that a compensation system has no dangers. Despite generations of unwarranted payouts under various crop-support programs, it would be foolish to assume that the only form of government harm comes from direct regulation. For those programs, the only sensible response is total termination because the government expenditures are pure transfer payments. But with habitat preservation, the role of the government cannot be so quickly dismissed, given the public good aspects of the proposed program. So now the evaluation requires a weighing of alternative perils. What is the likelihood that landowners will agitate successfully for large government habitat preservation programs funded by lavish grants? Those payments will require tax appropriations that come into public view, and can bring down the wrath of those groups who think that the stated need is vastly overblown. On the other hand, regulation operates in an off-budget fashion which is harder to monitor and harder to price. Indeed, much of the rise of the modern regulatory state is attributable to the lowered political resistance from groups with limited voting power and large land holdings. Many regulations impose restrictions that cost billions. It is difficult to imagine that there would be any explicit appropriations for these ends equal to a fraction of that amount.

The power to regulate releases government officials from any financial restraint. Freed of the obligation to compensate, officials in politically sensitive positions lack any incentive to designate as habitat only properties with great value, much less make any explicit comparison of the public gain with the private loss. Working in this environment, these officials will be tempted to act until local resistance forces them to pull in their horns. But their behavior will change radically when a price term is attached to their every action. Then they will be far more likely to concentrate their efforts on that land whose value in its natural condition is high, but whose development value is relatively low. Indeed, one function of any compensation regime is to curb appetites, so the relevant parties, both public and private, exercise greater care with resources than they would if they could take or use them for free. From an overall point of view, the narrower version of the harm principle functions far better than does its modern substitutes which pay too much attention to the public gains from regulation and too little attention to the private and governmental distortions it fosters.

Looking to the Future

These extravagant applications of the harm principle lay bare the difficulties that arise from the effort to encapsulate the entitlements of individuals in the harm principle. But these difficulties do not require a blanket rejection of that principle. Any other general principle of social organization can be similarly distorted. Equality of opportunity can be transmuted into the equality of results that again justifies equal incomes for all, or into mandated proportionate representation of racial and ethnic groups in all occupations or professions. In the end, therefore, the only way to combat these political forces—if they can be combated at all—is by revitalizing the original conception of the harm principle.

Individual actions have many consequences: for the persons who undertake them, for the persons with whom they deal, and for the persons whom they affect either directly or indirectly. It would be nothing short of a major miracle if the full set of consequences of all individual actions were either positive or neutral for all people. It is far more likely that some of these consequences will be good and some bad: every act of murder, rape, or theft produces some benefit for someone. The trick is not to pretend that particular acts have only single consequences, which can be designated as either good (so that one is at liberty to do them) or bad (so that they are caught by the harm principle). Rather, it is to try to make, over the long haul, sensible comparisons of rival institutional arrangements which, while difficult in some instances, generate strong results in the cases that do matter, such as the distinction between physical harm and competitive injury.

The modern position is strangely particularistic, focusing its attention on a single tile in the entire mosaic. The current view sees externalities *everywhere* or, more concretely, *negative* externalities everywhere. In effect, it isolates one negative consequence of any action on third parties and uses that consequence to justify the prohibition of that action, no matter how large the gain for others. This skewed social accounting has a predictable, if perverse result: every action generates some harm cognizable under the expanded harm principle. The environmentalist will not allow us to alter the physical universe; the regulator will not allow private contracts; the speech theorist will not allow any (or, at least, many) forms of offensive speech; and the egalitarian will not tolerate private gain through honest commerce. The antidote is to recall Mill's optimism and to accentuate the positive and limit the negative. The full range of consequences has to be grasped and evaluated, comprehensively and not selectively, and not case by case, but by broad categories of cases.

When and if that is done, the bottom line will be pretty much as Mill himself understood it: limitations against force (including pollution) and fraud (including defamation). To that is added some close scrutiny of monopoly and contracts in restraint of trade, much like that which took place at common law. For the rest, the principle of freedom of action (of speech, religion, contract, and association) should remain as strong and as vibrant as Mill would have it. But what must change is the reason for keeping it strong: not the naive belief that actions cause no harm, but the guarded belief that their supposed rectification causes more overall mischief than it prevents.

CHAPTER 4

❖ ❖ ❖

The Benefit Principle

The legal system focuses more readily on harms than on benefits. Harm to others operates as a wake-up call, which galvanizes otherwise indifferent people into action by demanding an immediate response, be it by way of compensation, punishment, or future prevention. Benefits to others, even when of equal magnitude, are generally greeted with less fanfare and celebration, with something bordering on complacency; and their donors, known or anonymous, are not regarded as immediate objects of affection or assistance. This general attitude has worked itself into the law. The private law of tort quickly offers a wide range of remedies to redress the harms inflicted by one person on another. Large systems of public regulation, including fines and imprisonment, are directed to the prevention of diffuse social harms. And powerful social norms pick up whatever slack is left by the gaps in the legal system.

In the midst of this general clamor about harm, the topic of external benefits is never fully neglected. Nonetheless, the benefit principle—that one should receive compensation for benefits conferred on others without their consent—has never achieved parity with the harm principle. The imbalance deserves close attention, for a culture that prides itself on doing cost/benefit analyses can hardly ignore one side of the issue while doggedly pursuing the other. Similarly, the prospect of mutual benefit is, of course, the driving force behind private contracts; and the failure to provide promised benefits has been understood, after a fashion, as a harm in need of legal redress. Nonetheless, individual actions providing benefits to strangers and neighbors often go unappreciated—or, at least, relatively unrewarded by the legal system. The law of restitution, which determines when compensation is due for benefits conferred by one person on some unrelated person, is, as a matter of form, the mirror image of the law of tort. The former's cardinal principle is said to be "unjust enrichment," which requires a return of the thing received or its fair value. But this mirror does not offer a perfect reflection: the scope of restitution has been much more limited and circumscribed. In this chapter, I evaluate the use and limitations of the benefit principle, in contradistinction to, and in conjunction with, the harm principle. And I ask, how far should one person be allowed reward or compensation from another individual on whom the former has conferred a benefit without having intended to make a gift?

Baseline Users

This quick psychological tour presupposes a sharp distinction between harms inflicted and benefits contained. Whatever the intuitive appeal of that distinction, it is often subverted: to many, its allure is no greater than the question of whether a glass is half empty or half full. In *Lucas v. South Carolina Coastal Commission* (1992),[1] one of our most notable recent takings cases, the Supreme Court had to decide whether South Carolina had taken David Lucas's property when it refused to allow him to build an ordinary home on his beachfront lot, thereby rendering his land worthless. One traditional test of the government's power to regulate under its police power holds that the state need not compensate when it prevents a private owner from inflicting harm against neighbors or the public at large; pollution of a river or the emission of fumes and noises always qualifies as harm caused under this definition. In contrast, compensation must be paid when the state asks a landowner to keep or use his land in a way that confers benefits upon other individuals, a condition that is satisfied, for example, when the state takes over land and uses it as a public park. South Carolina was not so pushy as to occupy David Lucas's land; it "merely" prohibited him building even a single family home on the lot in keeping with those already built by his neighbors. Supreme Court Justice Antonin Scalia, after too much hemming and hawing, held that the compensation was indeed owing for this total loss of use (a theme to which I shall return). But in lurching toward that conclusion, he went out of his way to undermine its intellectual foundations by first rejecting the hoary line between harms caused and benefits conferred. This distinction, we were told, lies "in the eye of the beholder":

"One could say that imposing a servitude of Lucas's land is necessary in order to prevent his use from 'harming' South Carolina's ecological resources; or, instead, in order to achieve the 'benefits' of an ecological preserve."[2]* The quotation marks are a telltale sign that the constitutional analysis (see chapter 3, pages 98–102) partakes of the artificiality of the discussion of harm in connection with habitat preservation; no one identifies particular persons whom the owner harms. Nor is this the only case where the issue arises in that form, and a matter of high principle is deflated to a dispute over grammatical form.

Scalia's sally poses a neat philosophical puzzle: Do we have any principled reason to prefer one of these descriptions to the other, or shall our efforts to evaluate the good and bad in human conduct be doomed to linguistic uncertainty? The nub of the difficulty turns on our having some appropriate *baseline* against which to make our needed calculations, and our choice of baseline in turn requires us to reach closure on the correct allocation of rights in some unstated original position. One homey example should suffice to lay bare the philosophical tension lurking in Justice Scalia's problem. If X has a right to full college tuition, then awarding X half that amount inflicts harm to the extent of the half not provided: the absence of some greater benefit becomes the harm inflicted. But if X has no right to any scholarship aid at all, then the half-tuition scholarship is just what it sounds like: a benefit conferred, albeit one smaller than X wanted.

The same principle can carry over to land use disputes. If Y leaves her land intact so that her neighbor, X, can enjoy his land undisturbed, Y confers a benefit on X if he is not otherwise entitled to a lateral support easement. But if X acquires an easement of lateral support by operation of law, then the baseline shifts; now not digging out the earth no longer confers a benefit on a neighbor who should not count on such support as a matter of right. The removal of earth now counts as an inflicted harm, even in the absence of any physical invasion. In most cases, the duty of lateral support is imposed—but not because we have no conception of what counts as a

---

* Nor is he alone. In 1994 Judge Stephen Williams, in asking whether the destruction or modification of habitat harms certain endangered species, wrote: "As a matter of pure linguistic possibility one can easily recast any withholding of a benefit as an infliction of harm. In one sense of the word, we 'harm' the people of Somalia to the extent that we refrain from providing humanitarian aid, and we harm the people of Bosnia to the extent that we fail to stop 'ethnic cleansing.'"[3]

baseline. Rather, the baseline is the standard property rule that speaks of the right to exclude neighbors, but this view is qualified in ways that allow both parties to require limited deviations from it in a manner that benefits them simultaneously. The legal outcome does not rest on any sense of linguistic skepticism; rather, it turns on an appreciation of long-term average advantage between neighbors. Returning to *Lucas*, if the owner of private property has only (or at most) the right to exclude others, then construction of a single family home harms anyone who wants the land to remain undeveloped. Yet in this case the idea of reciprocal benefits rings false to the occasion—a conclusion confirmed by the origin of the rule. The South Carolina Coastal Commission imposed the restriction on local communities; it was not imposed by these communities on their own members.

Across the board, then, any conceptualization of benefits and harms is parasitic on the choice of baselines—that is, on the initial delineation of property rights. But skepticism about the benefit principle would require us also to acquiesce in Justice Scalia's mistaken truism that any choice of baselines is largely arbitrary. Before embracing so unsettling a conclusion, we should note that this philosophical attack builds its generalizations from what it perceives to be the tricky cases. As such, it clashes with the unproblematic and incremental way that most people decide, as they must decide in their daily lives, whether benefits have been conferred or harms inflicted. The unbalanced diet of philosophical examples leads to intellectual malnutrition; we can regain our lost vigor only by taking due note of the *easy* cases which are too often overlooked. No one seriously argues that restitution is owed to persons who confer benefits on others by not subjecting them to criminal assaults. Good-citizen citations (one hopes) are not issued for not murdering small children during the past calendar year. The weakness of the fashionable arguments about the inevitable slippage between harm and benefit does not come in the first step of the argument—that is, the proposition that some baseline must be established before judgments of this sort are allowed. Rather, it comes in the next stage, via the insistence that the conventional baselines are largely arbitrary—or, at least, the product of some political theory heavily freighted in favor of the status quo.[4]

To see why this last philosophical move is too pessimistic for its own good, recall for the moment the heavy dependence the legal system places on its initial demarcation of property rights. The articulation of rights between neighboring landowners supplies the key. In that context, the first-order rule prohibits the physical invasion of the person, land, or things of another. Boundaries normally may not be crossed, and those who cross them normally do so at their own risk. "It is an elementary principle, that every unauthorized, and thereby unlawful entry, into the close of another, is a trespass. From every such entry against the will of the possessor, the law infers some damage; if nothing more, the treading down the grass or the herbage, or as here, the shrubbery."[5] (For a philosophical emphasis on boundary crossings, see chapter 7, or pages 188–90.) The only exceptions require showing some clear justification for their action: abating a nuisance, finding shelter in a hurricane, or escaping a criminal attack will do nicely. The flip side of this prohibition protects those actions that landowners undertake so long as they do not amount to boundary crossings. Ownership carries with it the right to more than exclusive possession; the possession sets the framework for the rights to use and dispose of that property. Now that the baseline is set, banning the construction of a single-family home becomes suspect because it does not allow the owner to cross the boundary that marks off property owned by some other private individual or even the state itself. It was to just this position that Justice Scalia gravitated when he held that the only limitations that "inhere" in the title to the property itself are, most notably, limitations derived from the law of nuisance—a holding that explains why the case for lateral support should come out the other way. The common law rule unites three strands into one coherent bundle, which, more than its rivals, facilitates the effective use and disposition of natural resources: development normally offers a large gain, not only to the developer but to his customers, employees, and suppliers. Some major external loss should be demonstrated before the process is curtailed, especially when no compensation is offered for the owner's loss.

The intuitive appeal of this common sense position is so strong that it is often taken for granted. Still, to avoid its being undermined on conceptual grounds alone, I must address the overall subject more systematically. To begin, we should never lull ourselves into the dangerous psychological frame of mind that defines the public-at-large to include everyone *except* the individual landowner and those dependent upon him. Rather, any social evaluation should allow all benefits and all costs to flow straight to the bottom line.

One notable effort in this direction is Donald Wittman's question whether our basic institutions of property should be organized around the principle of liability for harm or one of restitution for benefit.[6] Wittman began by observing that one single objective—creating a set of optimal incentives for trade—yields insufficient information for choosing the preferred legal rule. To use his most instructive (and ludicrous) example, suppose that the opportunity cost price for an apple is $1.00. There are two ways to charge this price to A, who wants to buy an apple "owned" (quotation marks are needed because the conception of ownership quickly becomes Pickwickian) by farmer B, both of which make A worse off by $1 for each apple so purchased. The first way—A can buy the apples and pay B the price in cash—presupposes that B has sole property rights in the apple and can exclude A at will. The second is for B to pay A some sum for the apples *not* purchased. That sum owed is reduced by $1 for each apple that A purchases. Thus, if the initial sum owing from B to A is $100, when A decides to take five apples he gets only $95 from B.

The incentive effects on A, when viewed in isolation, are the same in both systems. Insofar as A is made worse off by $1 per apple purchased in both systems, his incentive to consume is the same in both. So in a zero-transaction cost world, where administrative costs don't matter, the two legal rules should result in the same level of consumption given the same levels of wealth. (A wealth effect here refers to the differences in patterns of consumption attributable to the differences in wealth of the parties. Thus if A has greater wealth than B, assigning the entitlement to him could yield a different consumption pattern than if that entitlement is assigned to B, but these differences are not systematically connected with the choice of legal rules and are likely to prove small in any event.)[7] At this point, administrative costs make a decisive difference. If B has to pay A $100 for apples not purchased, how is that $100 determined? Perhaps we should increase it, or decrease it: after all, B may have 101 apples. Unfortunately, we have no set of institutions that can definitively choose this (or any other) number, or to match the efficiency of the zero baseline, which operates as the focal point of the conventional system.

Matters always get more vexed once the system is expanded to deal with multiple persons. In the conventional world, no one is seen to confer a benefit on B by not taking his apples. But in the topsy-turvy world, if A confers this benefit on B by refusing to take the apples, then perhaps C and D do as well: as B becomes more productive, his reward is to owe more to more people, perhaps the entire world. The limiting assumption that the relevant universe contains only two trading partners makes the ploy of A's receiving payment for the apples not purchased look far more plausible than it is. But as B shells out cash to C through Z, his only comfort is that often the shoe will be on the other foot with shampoo and roof tiles. The conventional rule is capable of easy generalization to any number of people; indeed, in one sense, the more the merrier as competitive markets do better when many sellers face many buyers. In a simplified topsy-turvy world where each of *m* individuals produces exactly one distinct good (that is, a society without firms or a division of labor), all of us could collect something from *m* − *1* individuals. But each of us could lose it, and more, in the one case in which one is saddled with the obligation of being the universal payer. The chance to reap the rewards of nonownership is a wonderful recipe for idleness! In the long run, then, this novel system does more than generate high administrative costs: it also goes haywire in setting the rules of engagement in a world with more than two people. This system was still-born because it leads to perfect equality and total starvation: no one will produce anything, so that everyone will have nothing.

The improbable outcomes of these odd property systems yield an important philosophical message to which baseline skeptics should pay heed. One of the most frequent charges lodged against any consequentialist or broadly utilitarian system is that it is indeterminate in its choice of legal rules. Yet the weird consequences that follow from viewing a nontaking as conferring a benefit on those left alone falsifies that position on the matters that concern us most: the delineation of property rights in transactions for ordinary goods and services. As ever, the point has its own political and moral overtones. We should not be tempted to say that the rich and successful are not entitled to keep their wealth because others have contributed to their enterprise by not destroying it, or that each ostensible author should treat as co-authors the millions who let him work undisturbed. Because the harm principle prohibits interference by force, then no one should be paid cash on the barrelhead for observing that principle. The usual negative responses to force—private actions, fines, and taxes—are perfectly appropriate. Social appeasement is not.

Faced with these examples, only an adamant agnosticism about the choice of baseline makes it an open question whether all persons have to pay their assailants to be free of the risk of rape or murder. The transactional complications defeat all chances of social stability under such a regime. To see why, imagine an original position that allows each person to use the bodies of other people at will. The massive insecurity such a legal regime creates cries out for correction. Let us assume that individuals by contract may deviate from the initial conditions so created, and assume optimistically that these agreements are never violated. What can one person do in order to acquire bodily security? Precious little. At any moment in time, thousands of persons are entitled to use and maim everyone else. A set of private contracts between one lone person and a thousand other people does little to eliminate the risk; thousands more find that their liberty is left unrestricted by contracts they did not sign. Unless *everyone* signs on the bottom line, individual insecurity remains. Even joining or hiring a protective association leaves open the risk that some larger group will overwhelm your private position. It is only when the property rights are reversed, so that each person is given exclusive control over his or her own body that the stable situation may be reached without having to overcome insuperable transactional obstacles. Now the contracting out runs in the opposite direction: *select* individuals are allowed physical contact with a person (as in marriage) under terms and conditions that can be strictly controlled. The choice of baselines is therefore far from arbitrary: the wrong baseline locks us into a devastating social equilibrium from which private means of correction are unavailing; the right baseline does not eliminate every practical glitch in execution, but it certainly improves the odds.

This position is not refuted by the sensible observation that individual nations are usually able to remain at peace with each other even though they are not subject to a common sovereign. Stability usually prevails because a determinate sovereign is able to curb the private use of force within each determinate territory. That degree of physical separation is not obtainable when members of different ethnic groups share a common territory or space: the risk of hostile flash points is just too great. Nor can anyone supply an ironclad guarantee that everyone will find a niche within some protective organization: the case of infants and the insane are obvious illustrations; the poor not far behind. Do we let them perish for want of affiliation? In the end, no network of contracts, however formed, has sufficient sweep to duplicate the outcomes of a system that frankly starts with the protection of person and property: thus, the traditional baseline continues to dominate all practical affairs.

One neat historical example reaffirms the power of traditional baselines. In California and other Western states, the late nineteenth and early twentieth centuries were marked by constant battles between the forces of open range (whereby landowners were under a duty to "fence out" cattle from their land) and closed range (whereby cattle owners were under a duty to "fence in" their cattle to keep them from trespassing).[8] The choice between these two rules is not simply the question whether the state prefers the partisan aspirations of farmers to those of ranchers, or the reverse; rather, it has powerful systemic consequences. Kenneth Vogel has rightly observed the radical asymmetry between the two rules. A rule that requires landowners to fence out roving cattle makes it pointless for a landowner to buy off some ranchers in order to preserve his land for agricultural use:[9] all ranchers need to sign on. Yet the very prospect of others' signing away their rights will clear the field for new entrants who will undermine the contractual efforts. The alternative system allows the landowner to permit some cattle owners to use the land without his having to open it to all simultaneously.

This analysis points strongly in favor of the universal right to exclude. So why, then, did open ranges have their day? The most plausible answer is that that system works when the fraction of farmers is so small that it is cheaper for them to bear the risks of the excessive straying that comes if ranchers are to use the open range efficiently. In the limit, the open-range system works best when no farmers are about. It follows that open-range statutes will lose popularity as population increases and land-use patterns vary, which, as Robert Ellickson has demonstrated, is roughly the observed pattern.[10] In all settings, the preferred initial solution tends to minimize the number of side transactions required to reach the ideal social outcome. Generally that condition is satisfied by following the standard common-law rule of exclusion by owner. The efficient norm for property is "Buy, don't take," just as ordinary experience has it.

POSITIVE AND NEGATIVE EXTERNALITIES

This decided preference for "Buy, don't take" should quickly put us in a tort frame of mind. The basic rule is "Shame on you for taking," not "Thank you for not taking." But how does a system of restitution fit into this overall scheme? In order to understand its rightful place, it is useful to revert to the question raised in connection with the harm principle (see chapter 3, pages 71–72): to what extent do individual actions "concern" only individual actors? And to what extent do voluntary exchanges concern only the parties to them? The law of tort—or, for that matter, the law of restitution—does not much matter for actions that affect only a single person or the parties to a particular contract. *On net* these actions unambiguously make one or more persons better off than before. Since no outsider to the act or transaction is made either better or worse off, the private gain of the individual actors or contracting parties falls all the way to the bottom line. In this constrained universe, it is impossible to detect any conflict between private desire and social interest.

Unfortunately neither harms nor benefits can be so narrowly cabined to the immediate parties. Every action, every transaction has innumerable consequences—positive and negative—that spill over to other people. The grand question for the legal system is how to sort through this endless array of spillover effects. The first cut at this problem is to follow a three-part recipe as bizarre as our earlier choice of novel baselines: (1) register *all* gains and losses to *all* parties at *all* times, including *all* externalities from individual actions, positive or negative, on some grand utility scale; (2) require the individual actor to internalize all external harms by making payment to those who have lost from his conduct exercise; and (3) allow the actor to collect a fee from those who have benefited from his actions. The actions that survive in this tripartite world are only those that produce net social benefits, measured by the extent to which an actor improves his own position after making and collecting all side payments. In a Coasean world with zero transaction costs, difficulties in valuing benefits and costs, processing claims, and collecting and distributing funds quickly vanish.[11] This broad and rigorous definition of externality thus sets the perfect foundation for determining desirable social action under an extensive framework of legal entitlements.

This zero-transaction-cost universe confers an additional blessing by removing any worry about the distributional inequities that arise from a (desirable) course of action that benefits one group while hurting another. Any legal system that could endure a full assessment of harms and benefits could also iron out any surprising financial inequities. A legal system that generated 100 in net benefits, but allocated 150 in gains to group A and 50 in losses to group B, could easily and costlessly be converted into a rule of equal benefit by requiring the members of group A to pay 100 to the members of group B. The same assumptions of costless transactions that lead to efficient resource use allow a second set of adjustments that satisfy even the most rigorous of distributional concerns. We are surely in the best of all possible worlds.

Unfortunately, even this bare outline of its features exposes it for the fantasy world it is. The rub is that this proposed course of action is manifestly unworkable as a legal program when transaction costs are both large and positive, as they always are. Accordingly, it becomes necessary to tolerate some liberty of action even in the face of inevitable spillovers, both positive and negative. It is too burdensome to champion a system in which every individual action has to be justified to every other person. But it is not costless to ignore spillover effects and to proceed as though the only gains and losses that count are those that are naturally borne by the actor himself. When (net) positive spillovers are ignored, then private benefits understate social benefits; the upshot is too few desired goods and services, even if reputation and informal persuasion help fill the gaps of a tolerant legal order.

Yet when (net) negative externalities are ignored, the upshot is too much of these goods and services, even if these same reputational and informal sanctions are at work. Unfortunately, most real world actions produce both negative and positive externalities simultaneously, leaving it unclear whether the activity will be excessive or insufficient. Playing a guitar in an airport corridor, building a house on a hillside, or ringing a church bell on Sunday are pleasing activities to some people but a source of offense to others, always in varying proportions.

What, then, are the respective provinces of tort and restitution in a world of abundant externalities? The law of tort seeks to identify the class of negative externalities that are kept on the social books; the law of restitution holds the same office for positive externalities. In both cases, the decision is made against a backdrop that recognizes that an action produces *net* gain for a self-interested actor who will be tempted to ignore any substantial losses imposed on others. A unified approach seeks to work out the connections between them, and to use these insights to explain why the law of restitution, while needed to fill in the chinks, is less central to the overall operation of the private law system than is the law of tort. When one is dealing with the law of restitution, one of the first tasks is to make sure that the remedies afforded are part and parcel of a system capable of sensible administration.

One constraint is the number of potential cases. Where compensation is required for benefits conferred on strangers, the recipient class must be small enough to be manageable. At this point, the older term *quasi-contract* is suggestive if only because the law seeks to mimic the contractual outcomes—gain for both parties—where explicit voluntary arrangements cannot at low cost provide the desired outcome.[12] By implication, when voluntary transactions are available, it is best to allow them to operate without setting them in tension with legally imposed duties to pay for services rendered without prior request. It is better that you ring my doorbell for permission before cutting my lawn, instead of your cutting the lawn and then ringing the doorbell demanding compensation for the cut grass. Even if I am out of town, the intermeddling is "officious" because I could have well guarded against the prospect of an untended garden by hiring a gardener on a long-term contract to weed and water whether I am at home or not. So in general, "First do, and then pay" invites massive impositions on strangers. That is why New York's Mayor Rudolph Giuliani received so positive a response when he ordered his police force to hound the men who squeegee your front windshield when your car is stopped at a red light; it is only a short step from such fictive contracts to outright theft.

THE CATEGORIES OF RESTITUTION

These simple examples suggest why the restitution principle occupies a smaller portion of the legal turf than the harm principle. One common object of both principles is to develop a set of rules that prevents individuals from circumventing voluntary transactions (with their promise of mutual gain) when transaction costs are low. Achieving that objective requires a two-pronged strategy. First, when someone does take without paying, damages must be *awarded,* not only to compensate the original owner but also to secure the dominance of voluntary exchanges. Second, when benefits are conferred without request, damages have to be *denied* for the same reason: to force transactions back into the preferred voluntary mold. Hence, the same common end calls for opposite treatments of harm and benefit. Yet, as is always the case in law, these two rules are best prized as workable first approximations, not philosophical absolutes. Harm itself can be justified by way of self-defense. Thus, there are important cases where the relevant conditions negate the possibility of voluntary exchange so that compensation may be appropriate when benefits are conferred on another without his consent.

Here we can take our cue from Aristotle's account of voluntary action found in book V of his *Nicomachean Ethics.* Aristotle's basic position is that all actions are presumed voluntary until we can show otherwise, and that the two major reasons for revising that original estimation are necessity and mistake.[13] The source of necessity could be natural events or the actions of other individuals; so, too, with the source of mistake. But in both cases external circumstances negate either freedom or knowledge, both of which are essential for voluntary actions. The connection between this insight and the benefit principle should be clear enough: not only do the risks of necessity and mistake negate the voluntariness of individual acts; they can also block the possibility of voluntary exchange as well.

Necessity

Suppose that a homeowner faces property damage from a major storm. That necessity in and of itself does not entitle other individuals to take it upon themselves to secure the house from harm without his consent. So long as he is available to manage the situation, the necessity in question does not preclude the opportunity for voluntary transactions—at least, when multiple parties are available for contracting. The proper procedure is for would-be merchants to offer their services and take the risk that these offers will be declined. But the situation is far different when the organized effort by the *only* conceivable rescuer is necessary to save or salvage the property, when immediate necessity prevents the formation of some contract between them. Here a risk-adjusted rate of return for the activities, capped by some substantial fraction of the property saved, becomes the legal norm.[14] This result is most conspicuous in the law of salvage, where the rescuers have to bear substantial costs to keep their fleet at the ready for disasters that could strike at any moment.

Nonetheless, the same principles seem to apply in other contexts as well; for example, where immediate necessity prevents one's hiring a physician whose services could save either life or limb. The famous 1907 case of *Cotnam v. Wisdom*[15] confirmed just that instinct by allowing a restitution remedy for a physician who gave surgical treatment that failed to save an unconscious man who had been mortally injured when thrown from a streetcar. Here a remedy was allowed because there was no risk of bypassing a voluntary market, and little risk of providing services the victim would have refused if he had been competent to bargain on his own behalf. It is perhaps a somewhat closer case as to whether the fees should be allowed only in those cases where the services were successful but not otherwise. The advantage of tying the payment to outcome is that it helps guard against the provision of medical services in hopeless cases, solely to extract a fee from the helpless victim. On the other side, it is well established that in ordinary fee-for-service medicine the payment to a physician is typically conditioned on neither the soundness of the diagnosis nor the success of the treatment: it is paid for the rendering of reasonable services in good faith, irrespective of the outcome. In nonconsensual settings, the risk of worthless service is greater, but not so powerful as to justify a switch of rules to one that looks at outcomes only. Instead, it seems better to monitor this question directly within the context of a rule that allows for payment of routine fees, and thus to refuse to reward a fee only when the physician had no reasonable basis to supply services—an easy judgment only where a patient was certain to die no matter what heroic measures were adopted.

Cotnam v. Wisdom is also insightful in its method for setting the physician's fee. Fees for services rendered do not come down from heaven. Here the plaintiff set his fee only after inquiring about the net worth of the decedent, with the obvious intention of behaving like a price-discriminating monopolist. The local Arkansas court rightly held that this information had to be ignored, and that the reasonableness of fees had to be set independent of the knowledge of the defendant's wealth. In so doing, the court mirrored the outcome of a competitive market, which precludes price discrimination no matter what a purchaser's absolute or relative wealth.*

Other restitution cases dealing with necessity are closer to the line. In *Leebov v. United States Fidelity & Guaranty Co.* (1960),[17] the plaintiff insured was a builder who used his trucks to shore up a construction site in order to prevent major landslide damage to nearby properties. Leebov's trucks were destroyed in the successful operation, and the value of the property saved was far greater than the losses incurred—losses for which the defendant insurer would surely have been held liable under its insurance policy. The plaintiff's losses were in some sense voluntary: after all, he placed the trucks in a position of danger. But here the larger context shows how they occurred in a setting dominated by necessity. The insurance company was doubtless far better off paying for the lost trucks than for the property damage their destruction prevented.

What should be the outcome, however, if the trucks are lost and the neighboring property is destroyed? In this novel setting, we do not have the key advantage found in *Cotnam v. Wisdom*—namely, of a consistent pattern of voluntary transactions against which to measure the reasonableness of Leebov's behavior. But nothing in the record hints at even a whiff of opportunism by Leebov in putting his own trucks at risk; his conduct anticipated exactly what any insurer would have wanted, playing the odds. Unless something in the insurance contract precluded Leebov's recovery of expenses, the restitution approach gains in force. If a total stranger used his trucks to prevent the landslide, the builder should be held liable for restitution: What is the injustice of forcing it to pay $10 when the plaintiff has saved it $100?

The proper response is less clear when efforts at rescue fail under conditions of uncertainty. In principle, the parties should be indifferent to receiving lots of compensation in the few successful cases, or little compensation in all cases. So long as the total expected return is the same, the incentives should not be altered, because the greater risk justifies the higher return. But calibration of risk after the fact is no easy task, and is likely to be

---

* A point that was intuitively grasped by the court in *Cotnam,* which quoted with approval the following sensible passage from *Robinson v. Campbell* (1878): "There is no more reason why this charge should be enhanced on account of the ability of the defendants to pay than that the merchant should charge them more for a yard of cloth, or the druggist for filling a prescription, or a laborer for a day's work."[16]

off by a factor of 10 or more. Rewards in medical cases are based on efforts; in salvage cases, on success. The salvage cases look like the better analogy. Ironically, the key lesson is that the want of a uniform rule offers quiet testimony to the importance of voluntary transactions.

In some necessity cases, matters are still more complicated because the benefit principle intersects with the harm principle. Thus, depending on external circumstances, a given act could result in harm *or* benefit to someone else. A takes steps to protect another's goods whose safety is threatened by storms or a band of dangerous men; his intention to benefit B may backfire, leaving the absent owner worse off from A's intervention than he would have been if A had sat idly by.

In the 1506 *Tithe Case*,[18] a farmer left his corn crop in the field where it was threatened by straying beasts. The defendant then moved the farmer's crop into a barn for safekeeping, where it was destroyed from unspecified causes. The local parson brought a damage action for his tithe share of crops against the defendant whose good intentions had gone awry. The court blessed that suit because the defendant's conduct did not fit into either of the two permissible justifications: the destruction of property for the defense of king and country—the case of public necessity; or seizure of crops because the plaintiff was in arrears in his rent. This case involved only destruction caused by animals owned by another for which "the plaintiff would have his remedy against those who destroyed it. And as for his having put it into the plaintiff's barn, yet he must keep it safe against any other mischance; and so no advantage thereby comes to the plaintiff."[19] The case therefore was unlike one in which "things are in jeopardy of loss through water or fire and the like, for there the plaintiff has no remedy for the destruction against anyone."[20]

At one level, the decision looks artificial because the critical question is not the legal availability of the remedy but the dollar satisfaction it brings: a remedy that has a one-in-ten chance of success is no perfect substitute for lost crops. In addition, the reasoning is incorrect because it does not ask whether the crop owner would, if facing the same necessity, have moved the corn into the comparative safety of the barn, notwithstanding any small alternative peril it created. The *Tithe Case* mistakenly held the defendant responsible for the potential downside of his conduct without letting him enjoy the upside.

Suppose goods worth $1,000 had a 20 percent chance of survival in the fields, a chance that rose to 80 percent in the barn. The decision to move it (at a cost of anything less than $600) would, ex ante, be welcomed by any owner eager to rid himself of the larger chance of destruction even at the cost of taking on the smaller one. Holding the rescuer responsible for the loss, without giving a credit for the benefit, has the perverse effect of inducing strangers to leave the corn to the mercy of the elements. An action that produces $600 worth of net social benefits is charged as an expected $200 loss to the interloper, which hardly induces the desired response. That loss could be offset by allowing a $250 recovery for successful rescues, so as to net out the anticipated loss (80 percent of $250 equals $200). Even that concession does not give perfect incentives to the rescuer, for it denies him any profit from an action that promises a benefit to another; but, at least, that adjustment eases the burdens that otherwise would stand in the way of benevolent intervention. Yet the better approach is forthrightly to eliminate tort liability altogether: it makes a vast difference that the intermeddler was trying to help the owner at his own expense, and not himself at the owner's expense. Unfortunately, the *Tithe Case* ignored the radically different shape of the benefit function and thus adopted an inefficient rule. It is best to encourage rescues by removing the fear of tort liability, even without the dubious assist of the restitution remedy as well, which is used only infrequently.* The remaining imperfections in the legal structure are best filled by weak social sanctions.

Mistake

The second category of restitution cases turns on mistakes of fact, where once again harms and benefits become quickly commingled. Suppose A cuts and harvests B's trees, thus committing the wrongs of trespass and conversion.[22] The widely known doctrine of waiver of tort permits the plaintiff to base recovery not on his own loss but on the defendant's gain.[23] Some early cases took the line that the tort remedy could be waived only if the market value of the timber was established by sale.[24]

Although resale is the easy case, it is not the only one: if the plaintiff keeps or uses the timber, it is more difficult to monetize his gain, but hardly impossible. At this point, two cases are in issue. If A cut the timber in good faith, he should surrender his profit to B, even though A should be allowed to recover his costs. The innocent converter may be denied a prof-

---

*   The modern law of restitution shows commendable caution on this point, typically allowing the recovery of expenses only where the plaintiff can disclaim the intention of creating a gift.[21] That disclaimer is usually possible with the professional, but not the fortuitous, rescuer.

it, but should not be saddled with a loss. A simple example clarifies the point. B could harvest timber worth $1,000 at a cost of $200. A now cuts the timber and harvests it for $250. Since B's anticipated net profit was $800, he keeps that sum only if he reimburses A for the $200 B saved, not for the $250 that A expended. The harder case arises from reversing the numbers, so that A is able to cut the timber for $200, and B for $250: here keeping the reduction at $200 leaves B better off than he would have been. Nonetheless, on balance that seems to be the preferred solution as a way to induce parties to take greater care in finding out the extent of their ownership.

But if A has acted in bad faith—that is, with knowledge of B's ownership—then the situation changes radically. B recovers the full value of the property taken by A without any allowance for A's cost of labor. The legal effort is to make sure that A loses by consciously bypassing the system of voluntary exchange. In practice the recovery of full value from A operates like a ban on A's action:[25] A is out his costs, but recovers nothing for his pains: the only uncertain question is how much he will lose—which should lead him to abandon his plans before they begin.

Here, as with the case with necessity, the use of the benefit principle in cases of mistake need not be moored to the law of tort. One early mention of quasi-contract in the Roman law is a text of Gaius, which speaks of money paid over by mistake to discharge a debt that was not owed. The explanation given was that the action to recover the money so paid could not be in contract, since there was no promise to return money paid over to discharge rather than create an obligation.* The rule is needed in order to prevent the transaction from becoming de facto a gift, when the mistake negatives any donative intent. As with conversion, restitution becomes more difficult to administer when goods are delivered by mistake and then incorporated into a larger whole or consumed. Since restoration is no longer possible, the appropriate remedy calls for providing either like goods in substitute or, that failing, a payment of the reasonable price for the goods in question. The patterns are all complex, but the main function of the legal design is to make sure that no redistribution of wealth takes place by inadvertence. The basic theme is thus to make the law imitate, to the extent it

---

* "He too who receives what is not due to him from one who pays in error comes under a real obligation. . . . This sort of obligation, however, appears not to be founded on contract, because one who gives with an intent to pay means to untie rather than to tie a bond."[26] The real obligation to which Gaius had just referred was the contract of *mutuum*—that is, a loan of goods with a promise to restore like kinds and numbers.

can, the outcome of voluntary arrangements. It is a task that can be done in concrete cases, and it sets the framework for the benefit principle in its most important function: the justification for the use of state power for, and against, its individual citizens.

The Public Face of the Benefit Principle

The particular applications of the benefit principle thus far discussed have concentrated on small-number situations that, generally speaking, facilitate voluntary transactions. As these transactions are the stuff of everyday life, it is easy to see why the restitution principle has relatively limited scope and application. But the creation of external benefits, like the creation of external harms, also covers situations where large numbers of individuals may be benefited or burdened by the introduction of some grander legislative scheme. Often the size of these harms and benefits may be small for each individual, widely diffused but large over all. The distribution of harms and benefits may be such as to preclude ordinary civil litigation, which also works best with few interested parties. Yet without litigation, some other mechanism has to be found to overcome the distortions that take place if individual actors cannot garner a sufficient return for undertaking actions that create benefits for others. At this point, however, the institutional focus shifts from lawsuits to larger administrative and regulatory arrangements. It is in this rarefied context that the benefit principle assumes equal dignity with the harm principle. Indeed, as we move away from individual cases to large questions of social organization, the benefit principle survives as the best explanation for the continuing allure and attraction of modern social contract theory.

Some of these coordination issues are solved by contract. Typically this happens when individuals and groups are arrayed in a hub-and-spoke arrangement: the persons at the hub (a promoter, a landlord, an agent) can organize the activities of those parties located at the periphery. One instructive early application of this principle comes from the law of general average contribution, which evolved in British admiralty cases to respond to the peril of the seas.[27] Under this system, the captain of a boat is generally charged in time of necessity to jettison that cargo necessary to lighten the craft and thus to preserve the value of the hull and remaining cargo. If the captain owns the hull and cargo himself, he is subject to the proper set of incentives, even if he does not make the ideal decision in a particular situation of danger. But that ownership system for most purposes is highly inefficient, given that the goods are normally shipped by widely diverse persons who have no common interest at all. Common ownership would never take place in the absence of the common peril.

The system of general average contribution introduces common ownership for the occasion only, and allows the captain to jettison the cargo necessary to save the vessel, and then to charge back the cost of the loss to the parties (including the owner of the hull) in proportion to the value of the interest that has been saved by the action. In essence, the compensation system is designed to make it appear as though each person has lost the identical fraction of his own goods, so that he is indifferent to which goods are destroyed and which are retained. With the size of his slice held constant by the legal rule, he is concerned only about the value of the pie as a whole. The secret in making this system work is to get individuals to make honest evaluations of the value of the goods—an end achieved by having owners declare their value *before* the goods are stowed. This requirement also supplies the captain with the information necessary to decide which cargo should be thrown over first (of great bulk but smaller value), which can be stowed where the crew can jettison it most easily in time of crisis. It still remains necessary to value the *vessel* saved by throwing cargo overboard.*

Thus assume a cargo owner wants to value his goods to obtain some strategic advantage over his fellows. Which way should his declaration cut? Value the goods too low, then the owner runs the risk that his cargo will be jettisoned early, leaving him too little in compensation from the remaining owners. To avoid this particular peril, the owner must declare at least the cargo's true value, which when done increases the odds of its preservation. The owner could, of course, ratchet his valuation upward to save his cargo, but only by running the alternative risk of paying an unduly high assessment to preserve goods of limited value. It is possible, therefore, to institute a regime of common ownership, limited to circumstances of necessity, that induces the persons in charge to behave like a single owner, subject only to the administrative costs of making the necessary transfer payments ex post—a bearable task given the prior declarations of value.

The system of general average contribution works by consent insofar as all parties have to agree to ship their goods under standard arrangements. But the major task of political theory is to develop a system that allows one

---

* Saul Levmore has noted that the valuation problem "was overcome by requiring each master to value his vessel upon arrival and then giving the merchants the option of acquiring the vessel at the stated price or using the self-assessed valuation for the contribution calculation."[28]

to impose obligations on those who have committed no wrong (under, of course, the harm principle) when they have not given their contractual consent. Unfortunately, the tools for that ambitious task are limited. It would be nice if theories of political obligation were only extensions of theories of individual obligation, carried over to public areas. The primary maneuver in such a reductionist effort is to shoehorn political obligations into orthodox theories of contract law, with their emphasis on actual individual consent. Grounding political obligation in the consent of the governed—as immortalized in the Declaration of Independence—is one such effort. So, too, are the countless intellectual appeals, first, to express consent; thereafter, to tacit consent or implied consent. But all these simply substitute assertion for theory, and fiction for description. The consent that one demands and finds in ordinary contracts cannot be extended to justify the powers of coercion the state exerts over its individual members—period.

More generally, the nub of the issue is that the grounds for political obligation—what does a citizen owe to the state?—cannot be satisfactorily explicated solely by resort to principles of contract law, even aided by principles of property and tort. Private property explains how individual things can be reduced to private ownership and common property preserved. Tort protects labor, property, and the exchange relationship from interference by others. Contract explains how labor and property may be exchanged. Yet so ubiquitous an institution as taxation, in any of its protean forms, cannot be derived from successive applications of the principles of property, contract, and tort, either standing alone or taken together. Repeated efforts to talk about "the social contract" as though it were a simple generalization of ordinary contracts for selling property or hiring labor fail: no one believes that the requisite consent from so many disparate people—past, present, and future—could be, or has been, collected for the controversial political programs in whose name they are invoked. The social contract is not, it has been said, worth the paper it is not written on, and modern efforts to work out that theory have all emphasized the hypothetical nature of the consent that drives the underlying transaction.[29] But just because the obvious theories fall short, do we reject (in the name of the free market, no less) all forms of taxation and regulation?

For most people the answer is no: political obligation there must be— strong enough to account for a state and its power to tax, but not so strong as to leave nothing left to individual discretion and control. With that conclusion reached, the question is how to build down toward the foundations. That's where the benefit principle comes into its own, and the language of social contract gains its lasting intellectual force. The theory here is no more than a generalization of the ordinary rules of quasi-contract outlined above. In an ordinary contract, two elements are conjoined: the parties each have consented to the new package of rights and duties, and each benefits from that exchange. With complex social settings, the notion of consent is jettisoned, but the central ideal of contract—joint gains—remains. The system, therefore, is social insofar as it represents a grand construct that is imposed on individuals and is not chosen by them, but it is contractual insofar as it imitates the distribution of net gains that any system of voluntary contracts presupposes. And since the property and tort law gives us the baselines from which further calculations are made, the approach, consistently applied, yields stronger results than any of its rivals and explains why a contractarian image has proved congenial to both libertarians and utilitarians, notwithstanding the evident differences in their philosophical grounding.

The idea of the social contract thus generates the familiar (and sound) benefit theory of taxation. The state provides benefits to the individuals within its jurisdiction and meets its own payroll by collecting taxes from the parties who are so benefited. It is allowed to force the exchanges because voluntary exchange cannot yield the desired outcomes so long as anyone and everyone is allowed to hold out for more than a proportionate share of the gain from social organization. The necessity here is not that of a raging storm or an impending car crash, but rather stems from the massive desire to obtain social improvements that better all—improvements that cannot be reached by voluntary exchange. Over and over again, political writers such as Locke and Blackstone point to *necessity* as the foundation of property and hence of the political institutions organized to defend property. Thus, Locke:

> "And will anyone say, he had no right to those acorns or apples, he thus appropriated, because he had not the consent of all mankind to make them his? Was it a robbery thus to assume to himself what belonged to all in common? If such a consent as that was necessary, man had starved, notwithstanding the plenty God had given him. We see in *commons*, which remain so by compact, that it is the taking any part of what is common, and removing it out of the state nature leaves it in, which *begins the property*; without which the common is of no use. And the taking of this or that part, which does not depend on the express consent of all the commoners."[30]

Blackstone was more pithy: "Necessity begat property."[31] In so doing, both writers create a systematic theoretical tension. How can consent serve the basis of political obligations when it fails the basis of property? Locke fell into this difficulty because he lacked a systematic appreciation of the scope and role of the restitution principle when coordination problems were acute, as when the consent of *all* owners of the commons is required before any of them may eat. Blackstone skillfully sidestepped this tension by noting the split between Hugo Grotius and Samuel Pufendorf, the great Dutch thinkers, who held "that the right of occupancy is founded on the tacit and implied assent of all mankind";[32] and Locke, who rejected tacit consent and held "that the very act of occupancy, alone, being a degree of bodily labour, is from a principle of natural justice, without consent or compact, sufficient of itself to gain a title."[33] But even universal consent is implied only because of the necessity of establishing a viable social order. Hence by speaking of necessity, both Locke and Blackstone anchor their own theories to the benefit principle of the law of restitution: the state may recover the costs both of conferring benefits on its citizens and of its service by using the coercive power of taxation. Hence the benefit conferred by political bodies becomes the basis for citizen obligations of allegiance and support.

Nor should we be surprised that the idea of restitution assumes so extensive a role in political discourse. Under the private law, the principles of restitution reach their maximum power in circumstances where voluntary transactions do not function well: cases of necessity and mistake set the stage for invoking the principle. In the public context, necessity does not relate to the need in two-person situations to violate exclusive rights in order to stave off imminent peril; rather, it stems from the stalemate that can easily emerge with time when cooperative efforts of huge numbers of persons are necessary to preserve and maintain order. While competitive markets can function well when only a small fraction of the total community participates, the political order requires unanimous acquiescence of all lest the violence of one undercut the stability of expectations that is the hallmark of both private property and responsible governments. Although the source of the necessity may differ, the legal response to it is the same: the principle of compensation for benefits conferred takes over where the principle of voluntary exchange leaves off.

It is one thing to state this familiar theory and another to make sure that it operates in the most effective manner possible. The critical question often depends on identifying the before and after, which takes us back again to the baseline problem with which this chapter began. One possible approach is to ask whether one is better off with the creation of the state than he was without it, no matter what is done after the creation of the state.

So if the state of nature carries with it serious inconveniences, the movement to a political order could well improve the welfare of all individuals from—to pick numbers—a pre-state figure of 1 to a post-state figure of 10. At the second stage, it could pass a statute that reduces the welfare of one group to 5 while advancing that of another, a bare majority, to 12. The second maneuver here is not problematic for the winners, but it raises serious issues for anyone concerned with the overall social picture, given that total losses outweigh total gains by 3.

Is that second action legitimate under a theory of restitution? If the state of nature is the baseline, then the losers at round two cannot complain: they are still better off than they were in the state of nature. On that approach, the level of political discretion is enormous, for no matter what shifts in fortune are brought on by state action, all its movements are legitimate until the protection it affords any person or group sinks below the paltry security he could obtain for himself unilaterally in a state of nature. Locke sought to counter this political risk by allowing citizens to reserve for themselves a right of revolution to forestall the possibility that they would be severely prejudiced by any sovereign misdeeds.[34] But his solution offers aggrieved individuals legal assistance that is both too little and too late. The only occasions on which that right could conceivably be exercised is when individuals find it in their interest to withdraw from the state. But any asserted right of revolution would not, and could not, be exercised when the state used its power to reduce individual, or even large group, welfare from 10 to 5: Who would give up four additional units of welfare to protest the five one has already lost? Clearly, social results will be far better if the gains from the first round of state actions can never be used to offset the losses subsequent rounds impose. What additional protections should be added to the mix?

Ideally, the task of political theory is to find some way to insure that *for each government action, taken separately,* each citizen is likely to receive equal or greater benefits than the burdens imposed on him or her. The restitution principle has to apply to each action, not just to the total program. On this view, once the state moves one group from 1 to 10 by the formation of the political order, this improvement from the state of nature does not remain in political solution but becomes vested as a matter of private right, establishing a new baseline against which further action is measured. Thus, in the next round, the 10 already achieved becomes the new baseline against which further state actions are measured. On that view, the second coercive tax could not be passed; but other taxes with greater net gain and even distribution are in no sense blocked and, indeed, are actively encouraged. Thus if the winners benefited from an expenditure by more than the losers lost, the program could go forward with a transfer payment. [35]

It is thus possible to see how a powerful theory of takings with just compensation—a strong restitution theory—can become the centerpiece of a sound system of political order.[36] The first move in the game is to recognize that all reductions in the bundle of rights associated with property, whether for one individual or for many, must yield some net benefit that justifies the use of public force. Where the legislation itself provides some benefit in kind, no additional compensation is necessary for those persons who might claim themselves aggrieved: once the state is formed, the holdout problem is not allowed to shipwreck additional maneuvers that promise some overall advantage. But often state initiatives have profoundly disparate impact; then cash compensation becomes the benefit conferred on the individual to justify the imposition of state power. In principle, the way in which costs and benefits are netted out is critical to the operation of the successful system, but the public law need only follow the procedures used in dealing with situations like general average contribution.

The basic pattern is well illustrated by the system of special assessments that has long been used to fund various forms of public improvement. The new road and sewer through an established neighborhood supply benefits to all those who use them, but their numbers are too great for this infrastructure to be achieved by simple contract among the affected landowners. So a system that allows the landowners within a district to vote on whether the project should be undertaken, knowing that each will be bound to fund his proportionate part, combines the best of democratic institutions with strong property rights. Since the payment structure is tailored in ways that block redistribution among neighbors, each owner has to make the calculation whether his benefits exceed his fees. At that point, the collective decision for this new expenditure usually requires at least a majority vote. Unanimity is too stringent a condition because a single holdout could sink a project desired by many; but simple majority rule, however appropriate for ordinary decisions, does not guard against the increased possibility that any new major project will have widely disproportionate effects on the targeted population. Popular sentiment is far more likely to be divided on the construction of a new capital project than on the maintenance expenses for an established project. In order to split the difference between these two situations, a vote by a supermajority, typically between 60 percent and 75 percent, is required for new projects. The process can still shipwreck in individual cases; but over the long haul (which is what matters most in political discourse), the supermajority compromise does best by all local citizens—which is why it tends to be adopted consensually in large corporate ventures or condominium projects faced with the same future risks.

In dealing with these situations, the social contract often operates as much by barter as by purchase. In particular, compensation for the land taken (say, for roads) need not always be made in cash, because the enormous increase in value (through access to markets) of the lands retained by the original owner affords compensation *in kind*. In principle, one would like to impose the taxes and payments in ways that equalized the gains for the affected individuals in proportion to their contribution, but often the measurement problems require the use of crude proxies (assessments by front footage or assessed valuation) to reach second-best solutions.[37] But no matter what is done, and how it is done—tasks that take us too far afield here—one point should become clear. The principles of restitution are a two-edged sword. No theory of the state can do without them; by the same token, no sound theory can go beyond them. Bluntly stated, no theory of limited government is viable unless it incorporates at its heart a theory of restitution: the government must confer some benefit of equal value on the parties whom it seeks to coerce. Otherwise, its activities go beyond the ends that called it into operation in the first place.

Indeed, the decline of modern theories of taxation can be traced to their severance from private law theories of restitution. The connection is evident in nineteenth-century thought, as when Thomas Cooley summed up the issue in a single sentence: "Taxation is the equivalent for the protection which the government affords to the person and property of its citizens; and as all alike are protected, so all alike should bear the burden, in proportion to the interests secured."[38] So simple, so smart. Cooley conceives of each person as having rights relative to the government, and his insistence that the burden be in proportion to the interest secured is an effort to constrain discretion in the imposition of government burdens. Cooley's view allows for no social or common good independent of the interests of groups and individuals in society, and his principle of lockstep advancement insures that the social power of taxation cannot be used to advance the welfare of some but to prejudice others, as occurs in the second tax in the example above.

Yet the modern view of the benefit principle bores away from within at that benefit principle. Thus Justice Harlan Stone writing a half-century later misses the major risk in one of the most chilling assertions of modern constitutional law:

The only benefit to which the taxpayer is constitutionally entitled is that derived from his enjoyment of the privileges of living
in an organized society, established and safeguarded by the devotion of public purposes. Any other view would preclude the levy-
ing of taxes except as they are used to compensate for the burden
on those who pay them, and would involve the abandonment of
the most fundamental principle of government—that it exists
primarily to provide for the common good.[39]

His version of the benefit principle mistakenly holds that the *only*
baseline that matters is the state of nature, so that the losses created by the
second enactment are fully set off by the gains received from the organization of society: in his world, it is possible to drive people from 10 to 5, or
even to 2, so long as they are not driven below 1, their baseline entitlement
in the state of nature. His misleading reference to the advance of the "common good" obviates the need to determine the welfare of society by measuring the welfare of all of its members, one at a time, and then summing
the benefits over all persons—a need well understood by Cooley, who spoke
of society as a collection of individual citizens, not as some entity that floats
above humankind. For Stone, losers are not allowed to protest unless they
are willing to exit society altogether, which they will not be doing so long as
the state of nature (or migration elsewhere) is fraught with peril. The
expansion of government power consequent on the adoption of Stone's
view is enormous, for the benefit principle that lies at the heart of a theory
of restitution is corrupted from within rather than repudiated openly. It follows once again that the failure to incorporate or understand the benefit
principle has its largest payoff in the public law, where the principle is so
much in evidence, and in neglect. There is simply no shortcut that allows
the evaluation of the social worth of any legal rule or government action
apart from the consequences it has on the population as a collective whole.

There is a strong irony here, as this nation tries to sort its way through
the financial crisis that impends in Social Security. Over and over, the common argument made by those who are in favor of keeping, with tinkering,
the present system—is that it forges some powerful communitarian alliance
among its members, which overcomes the regrettable egotism that would be
encouraged by some privatization of the basic program. But, in practice, the
effect of the current policy is exactly the opposite. By conscripting the present generation of younger persons into a program that benefits their elders,
this program only increases the divisiveness in society it seeks to avoid. Only

a few minutes of conversation with anyone under thirty, or perhaps even under forty, demonstrates that they are sure that Social Security will not be there for them when they retire, and thus have, in the face of high public taxes, to make private provisions for their own future while supporting their elders who are often better off than they are. As the issue grinds its way through commission and deliberation, the impasse should remind us that the benefit principle, rigorously applied, is indispensable to the foundation of public law and to the preservation of social peace.

CHAPTER 5

❖ ❖ ❖

Altruism: Its Uses and Limits

Altruism is a topic whose strands run the length and breadth of the social sciences, reaching even into the more distant territory of the law. Altruism gains its importance through its contrast with the model of egoism, which treats each person as being wholly self-interested and wholly indifferent to the welfare both of other individuals and of the community at large. The many instances of altruistic behavior—from casual interaction in schoolroom and play yard, to the informal interaction between good neighbors, to genuine unanticipated acts of individual heroism under circumstances of great personal peril—undermine any assumption that unvarnished and untempered egoism is the sole impetus of human behavior. Indeed, quite the opposite has been asserted: that no one behaves as the standard economic model predicts. As the noted philosopher and economist Amartya Sen once said, "The *purely* economic man is indeed close to being a social moron."[1]

Accepting this assertion does not, however, end the debate over altruism and egoism. It only begins the more difficult inquiries at the theoretical, empirical, and normative levels. On the theoretical level, the critical question seems to be the extent to which ostensible forms of altruistic behavior are reducible to self-interest, which gives a tidier and more rigorous set of explanations. Thus, reciprocal altruism—or what the biologists now more accurately call mutualism—may be regarded as a form of self-interested behavior; albeit one that takes into account the close biological ties between one's self and one's immediate family.

The point here, I hasten to add, is not simply one of classification, for any prediction of behavior may well turn on which view of the world is correct. A sociobiologist, for example, will predict that altruism is more likely to occur within groups that have some common genetic bond, while the social theorist who downplays human nature as a source of egoism would argue that altruism is possible in any community, regardless of its composition, that nurtures a respect for it.

On the empirical level, one pressing question is how altruism and egoism interact in assigning various social goods. To be sure, some relationships are based on pure exchange in spot markets, while others are based on communal sharing, hierarchy, and even a nascent sense of equality.[2] Even so, the key question remains: How does one determine which activities and which groups are governed by which pattern of behavior, and why? Surely the choice of governance form is not random. We should be genuinely surprised if families operated internally on a market system, in which any benefit had to be obtained by purchase or barter. Similarly, if we discovered that the family did operate on an explicit market model, then we would be simply astonished to learn that major social allocations among strangers took place under a system of communal sharing driven by the ostensible altruism of group members. There must be good reasons why certain forms of behavior are chosen in particular settings; and finding out these reasons requires a detailed knowledge of the dispositions of all persons, their initial endowments, and the opportunities available to them.

On the normative level, there is the question of what legal rules and social practices *should* be adopted given the insights obtained. Here the point of greatest interest is whether some form of government regulation should be used to alter the mix between self-interested and altruistic behavior. Do we subsidize activities that call on individuals to be more self-reliant? Do we restrain voluntary market exchanges in an effort to control the various forms of egoism that some people have come to deplore? Do we think that the altruistic sentiments within any society are so strong that it is possible to organize political life on communitarian principles, whereby each cares for others (almost) as much as for family and for oneself? It is also possible to ask how far we should alter our views about the desirability of certain forms of regulation if we conclude that altruism is more, or less, pervasive than previously believed. Does change in our estimation of human motivation offer any warrant to increase the size of the public sector, to reduce it, or to leave it as it is?

In this chapter I seek to address these interconnected issues. In the first section, I address the issue of how far altruism extends: Does it cover all individuals, or only those with whom an actor has some specific bond or affinity? Rarely does altruism extend to the community at large; but in most cases, it is focused on some narrower group, so that altruism toward some often exposes individuals outside the preferred group to greater political peril. In the second section, I then examine how this limited form of altruism operates both within the context of the family and in informal exchanges within larger ethnic or religious groupings. I also explain how much conduct that passes as disinterested altruism is better understood as a set of informal exchanges of self-interested parties that in constrained circumstances often outperform ordinary markets in advancing the welfare of trading partners. The rosy view of these informal exchanges can easily lead to the mistaken belief that communitarian norms can survive in larger, more impersonal settings. In the third, and last, section, I attack this conception and demonstrate how a political commitment to communitarian values often exposes the social system to the exact kinds of selfish behavior that communitarians rightly seek to avoid.

Altruism and Self-Interest

I shall begin with the theoretical question whether altruism is a form of disguised egoism or one of disinterested benevolence. The answer lies in which of two different views of the world one chooses. If one starts with the proposition that egoism is a learned social behavior that can be neutralized like any other, then there is no obvious barrier to insisting on universal altruism. In the extreme case, if we suppose that one can learn to respond to the misfortunes of others just as if they were one's own, there should be no stopping point short of the familiar (Marxist) maxim "From each according to his ability, to each according to his need." The sense of self is suppressed to the point that any individual is indifferent to how the fruits of his or her labor are dispensed. The system of production may be organized on the assumption that one responds to the net return others receive just as though they had received that return himself. There is no reason to ensure that those who sow may reap, and thereafter consume. Nor will they care whether they are able to reap what they have sown. Their turn—itself an egoistic notion—will come some future day when they will be the recipients of the altruism of others.

The practice of universal benevolence generates an ideal distribution of goods without any reduction in output. Unfortunately, that level of benevolence is unattainable in any real world setting. Although the biological influences may not dominate all others all the time, they cannot be ignored in any balanced assessment of human motivation; and these influences typically work to the advantage of the individual and his or her kin, not of humanity at large. Criminal behavior frequently involves acts not only of rational self-interest, but also of gratuitous cruelty, motivated by spite and resentment. But whether criminal conduct fits the mold of rational behavior, its control, not the advancement of altruistic conduct, constitutes the primary target for the energies of government. Even the most determined advocate of the welfare state would prefer to keep the police force intact to abandoning it while committing all tax revenues to transfer payments and social support systems. The breakdown of the socialistic economies of Eastern Europe, and the operation of politics as usual, both in Washington and at the local zoning or rent control board, are better explained by a theory that stresses rational self-interest and not one that posits widespread altruism. Government failure under all sorts of different constitutional systems should offer a clear warning to the limits of universal altruism in the organization of our public life.

This skepticism is directed only toward *universal* altruism, in which an individual actor is indifferent to the identity of the people whom his conduct benefits. But self-interest and universal altruism are not the only two choices in evaluating individual behavior. Also to be considered are forms of *selective* altruism that operate powerfully in public life. People often act altruistically toward some and egoistically toward others. Consider how various interest groups operate inside a political market, especially under majoritarian rule. Individual actors demand some preference or benefit from the system at large, but their pleas are not those of a narrow egoist. They are the pleas of a large group that wants a fair shake from the political system—a group that wants to get a school built in a preferred location, or a construction contract for a favored firm, or a voting district line drawn in a certain place, or a key political operative appointed to a special board. That person will not go forward and say that the favor in question must be granted for him alone; rather, he will say that as the representative of some larger community, he is acting with a deep and abiding concern for others in making the request. Selective altruism explains why some people will go out on a limb for others. It may, for example, offer the best explanation of the large number of votes in many elections. Rational egoists may choose to stay at home unless they think they have some real chance to alter the out-come of the election. But for selective altruists, the perceived gain from vot-ing transcends the personal gain from seeing a preferred candidate elected or initiative pass. It also embraces the gains provided to other group mem-bers with whom the voter shares a strong personal identification.

It is the negative implications, however, that are most troubling in this context: the idea of altruism for a group carries with it a far less pretty corol-lary. Individuals outside the group are likely to be disadvantaged if selective altruists are given free rein to compete in political markets where property rights are weak and political coalitions are easy to form (it was James Madison's nightmare).[3] The interdependence of utilities between the actor and other members of the favored class will reduce the cost of forging a coherent fighting force out of any interest group. As these groups become more cohesive and less costly to maintain, the struggles within the larger political entity become ever more protracted and bitter—and easily drown out individual voices, including those of restraint and reason.

Politics on this view is a refined form of warfare in which the use of force is ruled out, but the use of political pressure is regarded as par for the course and an integral part of the game as it is played. But the power of selective altruism is not limited to these restrained maneuvers. We do not need any detailed elaboration of the many massacres and bloodlettings that have taken place. To be sure, individual acts of violence often take place between individuals of the same ethnic or racial group: black-on-black (or white-on-white) crime in the United States and elsewhere offers one too familiar example. But where established political forces organize and direct conflict and bloodletting, it almost always takes place across some ethnic or racial divide. A 1993 *New York Times* story surveying the worldwide situa-tion, noted some "forty-eight ongoing and simmering ethnic conflicts that girdle the globe."[4] Bosnia, Ireland, Nigeria, Rwanda, Somalia, and surely the Nazi Holocaust were driven by these collective antagonisms. Thus, it is Serb against Croatian, Christian against Muslim, Arab against Jew, Hutu against Tutsi. The American Civil War is, of course, a counterexample, in that brother often fought against brother and prison conditions were deplorable; yet it was also a war that did *not* feature organized violence, torture, and rape against helpless men, women, and children.

The mechanism is clear. The same sense of selective altruism that leads many of us, sometimes, to perform selfless acts for the benefit of those with whom we share a common identity gives us just enough protective cover to perform acts of great cruelty against persons whom we can describe as "others": that is, those persons whose improved welfare negatively affects our individual utility. The gains selective altruism offers members of a group will be offset by the mayhem it causes to outsiders. The sharp ethnic national and racial lines that capture the struggle between clans, tribes, groups, and nations should caution us against giving unquestioning praise to altruistic behavior. The biological theories, which find in common genetic endowment and shared ancestors the source of unified behavior, loom larger than we would sometimes like to acknowledge.

THE MODEST USES OF SELECTIVE ALTRUISM

After this melancholy account, one might ask, is altruism simply a dangerous force that should be resisted whenever possible? I do not think that so pessimistic a view of altruism is necessary—at least, not if it is applied to daily voluntary interactions and kept out of the public sphere of politics. When people are situated in cohesive communities, their common biological origin and the opportunities for reciprocal assistance and support reduce the need to rely on legal sanctions to keep individuals in line. Families, closed groups, small towns, and communities can monitor at low cost the behavior of those who receive assistance and support. And they are likely to derive substantial indirect benefits and satisfaction from the assistance they render, given their personal identification with the recipient. In these restricted and local settings, selective altruism reduces the need to use formal procedures to reach decisions or to offer explicit reasons to legitimate them.

Within the Family

One simple thought experiment helps illuminate the truth of these propositions. Suppose we believe that the family offers the preferred structure for raising young children, and further that it is a mistake to allow the "luck of the draw" to determine which persons are blessed with favorable environments. Assume also that the occasional use of social services does not suffice to equalize the enormous gaps in fortune across infants born in households that occupy widely divergent economic niches. From these assumptions, and from behind a veil of ignorance, should we assign children to families by lottery, so that the "arbitrary" advantages of birth will not determine the fortunes of the individuals who comprise the next generation?

The hue and cry that would go up against so totalitarian a proposal is not the main point of this parable; nor is the enormous bureaucratic nightmare that would result from conferring on state child welfare agencies a monopoly over childrearing. Rather, anxiety would generally center on the care, attention, and upbringing that should be expected under this system. While there would surely be some affection, empathy, and the like, children will be more vulnerable and less protected under such a lottery than under the current system.

The explanation is obvious and, for that reason, compelling. The natural love and affection based on biological connection between parent and offspring is far from being a perfect protection against misconduct, and is not an inevitable spur to excellence and devotion. But the natural love and affection between parent and child—the interdependent utility functions on which all societies implicitly rely—usually offers the young and the helpless far more protection than any substitutes an impersonal bureaucratic state can devise. We take advantage of these sentiments precisely because we know, as some economists sometimes forget, that a system of market exchanges across generations is not feasible even if blessed under law. Infants cannot contract to take care of their parents in their dotage; and even if they could, the greatest care is often given by parents to those children whose unfortunate handicaps may make it impossible for them to reciprocate in the future. Parental guardianship is a low-cost system of rearing and protecting children that takes advantage of biological altruism.

Informal Exchanges

Altruism also helps to reinforce the exchange relationship within close-knit communities based on close ethnic ties. The common background, common culture, and perceived interdependence of happiness makes it easier to have transactions that are one-sided when viewed in isolation, but that balance out over time. For example, the informal lending societies within immigrant communities in the United States do not depend for their effectiveness on legal enforcement. Instead, parties make loans without the usual forms of security and at below the market rate of interest because it is understood that today's borrower, should he become established, will be tomorrow's lender to the next generation on similarly favorable terms. The limited altruism overcomes any breakdown of enforcement mechanisms over time. The same arrangements could not be undertaken with complete strangers: where the informal bonds are fragile, the risk of opportunistic rupture is too great to bear.

Of course, other kinds of reciprocal interaction occur outside close-knit ethnic communities. People lend milk to neighbors who have run out, swap babysitting chores, pick up newspapers when neighbors are out of town, watch for strangers on the street, and the like. Yet here again the activities in this domain are not chosen at random. In virtually all cases, for example, no money is exchanged between the parties; instead, there is a system of informal and unenforceable barter. Absence of a price, or of legal enforcement of promises, should not, however, be taken as proof of the absence of the forces of rational self-interest normally found in the marketplace.

The opposite interpretation is more powerful. The same impulse to economize on transaction costs that drives market behavior finds a very different form of expression in this context. It is costly to set up a market and to establish explicit cash prices. That cost is worth bearing where the goods purchased from A are then resold to B, or where the cash A receives from B is used to purchase goods in a subsequent transaction with C. But so long as there is strong reciprocity in certain confined settings, the parties can spare themselves the cost of calculating prices by exchanging services that are known to be of roughly equal value, even if they do not know the monetary value of the things they are exchanging. Thus, if I watch your children today and you watch mine tomorrow, there is no reason for either of us to pay the other, so long as we know that our services are of roughly equal value. There is a hint of this point in the Roman law: the contract of *mutuum* (goods loaned for consumption) requires only that goods be returned, not that interest be paid. If there is strict alternation, both sides are better off if no interest is required, for both sides are spared the costs of having to set interest rates and to compute and collect what is owed. Only if the loans all run only in one direction do we have to make the interest payments explicit.

In other contexts, it may well be that the return services are not identical: I may water your flowers and you may pick up my newspaper. But, again, so long as the relevant values are low (and the cost of finding market substitutes high), both sides are better off with the informal arrangement than with a large network of explicit transactions where goods or services are exchanged for cash. Any perceived imbalance in the transaction can be offset by small moves on one margin or another—margins not easily detectable by the kinds of question-and-answer data collected in most surveys. And any remaining short-term imbalance can be offset by a plate of cookies on a Saturday afternoon.

Alan P. Fiske has divided social interactions into four classes: communal sharing, authority ranking, equity matching, and market pricing.[5] In his view, equity matching and market pricing fall into different domains which are regulated according to different principles. He further insists that informal transactions are motivated by equity and not by profit. But the domains of equity and profit are not so rigidly separated. Rather, in certain limited classes of transaction, the principles of equity offer low-cost and effective means to ensure that both parties share the profit from some valued common venture. Imagine, however, a set of reciprocal practices that preserve equity but produce net *losses* for each side: If equity, independent of mutual gain, drives an arrangement where I pick up your papers when you are out of town and you do the same for me when I am out of town, what happens when both of us are in town? We do not maintain the custom because it is now easier, and makes more sense, for each of us to pick up his own paper. So, in the domain of losses, the class of customs with perfect equality will not survive. The informal custom is driven by the search for mutual gain, just as in market exchanges.

People involved in these reciprocal relationships get uneasy not only when they regard themselves as net losers (in which case they will end the pattern of cooperation) but also when they perceive themselves as big winners. If profit is the goal, then this uneasiness seems inexplicable. But if each participant wants to preserve joint gain over the *lifetime* of the interaction, A's disproportionate gain is likely to lead to a smaller gain, or even a net loss, to B. In this case, A will not perceive the relationship as "fair," and will make short-term adjustments to forestall the likelihood of B's breaking off the relationship or making new demands to keep it alive. A's security is advanced by keeping B away from the brink. Any reduction in the imbalance should not be chalked up to some inarticulate form of fairness. It has the clear function of allowing A to purchase stability over the long haul. A's responsible behavior also increases his chances of forming other informal arrangements with C, D, and E, whose willingness to do business with A depends on their perception that he will not take advantage of them over the life of the relationship. The great financier Bernard Baruch said that he became rich by selling too soon. In many relationships, both business and social, people become rich by taking too little.

More generally, it is dangerous to assume that intuitions about fairness have no relationship to utility. Quite the opposite: a keen sense of fairness may be the best way to preserve these informal arrangements. While fairness may provide the perceived basis for informal adjustments, there is usually a strong correlation between fair practices and norms conducive to long-term mutual gain. Scratch the surface of a claim of fairness, and you will find, not that it is misguided, but that it rests on hidden assumptions of social efficiency. The theory of rational behavior has a huge amount to say about the forms of reciprocal altruism in everyday life.

The theory of reciprocal altruism, which explains many informal transactions between neighbors, is also sufficiently powerful to identify the circumstances in which these mechanisms will be abandoned in favor of working markets. The key advantage of informal markets is that they avoid the costs of setting prices. Yet the lack of explicit price becomes more costly as the number of transactions between the same trading partner decreases, thereby increasing the possibility that one side will be left a net loser over the full life of the relationship. Similarly, as the amount at stake in each transaction increases, there is a smaller probability that the gains will even out. As the transactions decrease, and the value per transaction increases, a tipping point is reached: the cost of establishing prices is now worth incurring because it allows accounts to be squared transaction by transaction. Many different persons may enter the market to engage in spot transactions, so that the cost of creating explicit price information can be spread over multiple transactions. Trying to even things out in business, with its size and erratic nature, is no longer possible with a plate of cookies; and even giving someone a Jaguar is far less efficient than paying substantial debts with cash.

Altruism also clearly plays an explanatory role in many commercial transactions—as has been tested by a number of survey experiments seeking to demonstrate a wedge between ordinary conceptions of fairness and profit-seeking behavior in the marketplace. One such set of experiments was analyzed in detail by Daniel Kahneman, Jack Knetsch, and Richard Thaler, with a view to showing the pervasive interjection of nonmarket norms derived from a sense of community fairness.[6] In one set of questions, they asked whether it is appropriate for the owner of a hardware store to raise the price of his existing supply of shovels after a snowstorm, given that his costs have not increased. Strong popular sentiment disapproves the practice, even if price increases are permissible as a matter of law. Yet here the instinct is perfectly consistent with the behavior we should expect to find in well-functioning markets. Breach of contract is not the only risk market participants face: opportunism, or the exploitation of short-term monopoly positions, is yet another. The local merchant who raises prices in response to these short-term fluctuations in demand is a person not to be trusted. His customers will have to take additional precautions, not reflected in the price of goods sold, to prevent their being taken advantage of: they will have more need to purchase a shovel before they know whether they will have to dig out of a blizzard. With trust shattered, they have no incentive to return to this original merchant, who suffers a loss in good will as he reaps the short-term monopoly profit. Yet the situation will be quite different if the hardware store raises its price immediately after the storm because its own supplier has raised its prices on the new shipment. Now everyone understands that the lower price is not sustainable since it will force the hardware store to sell at a loss. Since there is no short-term monopoly gain to exploit, qualms about unfairness disappear.

This pattern of behavior makes good sense for the merchant who gains customer loyalty by forsaking price increases despite his monopoly opportunities. If the merchant knows his customers, he can use nonprice methods to ration the shovels when demand is acute. The greater stability in the customer base thus provides a greater ability to plan for the future as well. Because, however, the cost of working out a specific legal protection against advantage taking is normally too expensive to undertake, an informal obligation not to gouge governs ongoing relationships with regular customers. Yet if a steady customer, who purchased the shovel at the pre-storm price, *resells* it at a tidy profit to someone else, then he becomes the object of moral condemnation and may be cut off without further ado.

To push matters further, strip away any past relationship, and ask whether it is appropriate for the hardware store to charge a higher price to strangers in town. Now, with no implicit long-term contract to buffer the relationships, the ethical intuitions become blurrier. The outsider is not someone who stuck by the merchant when times were hard, and refused to buy at the large supermarket when it held a year-end sale. In this case, the local customers may well desire a form of price discrimination in order to reduce the likelihood of outsiders purchasing goods found in short supply, and may fault the merchant who gives strangers the same deal as he gives loyal customers. Indeed, the local customers will be even more uneasy should that outsider offer a premium over the stated price if the local merchant appears reluctant.

Ordinary norms of fairness will tend to fray as the perceived advantage taking is relieved; but for present purposes, these doubtful cases hardly matter. Such informal social understandings clearly do not amount to a binding legal promise by the local proprietor to keep his prices low for established customers. The kinds of fairness questions raised do not translate well into legal discourse, and the same people who think that some conduct is unfair may well be reluctant to make it illegal. The obstacles blocking legal action are greater than those preventing social criticism or resentment—and so it should be. The legal system is a cumbersome engine to fire up, and informal social interactions can often restrain misguided behavior.

A similar analysis applies to a second example offered by Kahneman, Knetsch, and Thaler. They posit a business that has employed a worker in the shop for six months at $9 per hour. When the standard market wage moves down to $7 per hour, the question is whether the employer should lower that worker's wage in response. Most responses (83 percent) stated that any such reduction was unfair even if the employee would not quit if the wages were reduced. But nearly as large a majority thought that it would be fair for the same business to hire an equally competent *replacement* worker at the lower wage.

Once again, the past relationship places an ethical constraint on the employer's behavior; the fairness norm is not, however, necessarily at war with market understandings. The current employee may well have entered into an implicit understanding that the employer had assumed the risk of wage fluctuations. Such risk could well work for the employer's benefit if the interim wage levels moved slightly up, for the employee might be unable to bear the cost of quitting. But what is sauce for the goose is also sauce for the gander: when wages trend down, the employer is subject to the same social obligation—at least in the short run; but only so long as the higher wage package does not threaten the survival of the firm, at which point the stickiness in wages is disastrous for both parties.

The gist of the argument is that we should not regard the network of informal exchanges as evidence either of altruism or of market failure. Two further considerations fortify this conclusion. First, no one who is in favor of the use of market mechanisms to allocate goods and services in an economy would place any limitations on these informal transfers and the correlative set of informal sanctions. Allowing the legal enforcement of contracts does not impose a *duty* to sue. Informal mechanisms may be pressed into service first, using legal force as a backstop to bolster their effectiveness.

The power of reciprocity often holds even when there is no threat of loss of reputation or of legal sanction. The theory of self-enforcing contracts holds that persons will continue to exchange goods and services sequentially so long as each party believes that the future value of the relationship is worth more than any short-term gains either can obtain by deliberate breach.[7] Thus, in the silent trading that took place between Europeans who picked up goods that African natives left along the beach, only to leave in their place European goods, the two sides (if only to avoid violence or capture) did not meet face to face. Such exchanges endure over time because the party that holds only limited quantities of the other's goods will reciprocate with payment because it values the trading relationship more than the goods that it has left at risk. The system is not perfectly stable, for an unanticipated radical shift in values or expectations—brought on by war or famine, or the introduction of some new trading partner—could induce one side to take the goods and leave nothing in exchange. But if markets and external conditions are relatively stable, then the informal reciprocal relationship can continue for a long time, even in the absence of explicit prices or legal enforcement.

The glue that holds these informal exchanges together is the long-term average reciprocity of advantage. That theme helps, in turn, to explain not only bilateral trading arrangements but also the law of eminent domain. The Fifth Amendment to the U.S. Constitution states that private property may not be taken for public use without just compensation. In this context, the question often arises whether some comprehensive form of regulation (for example, wage and price controls) should be regarded as a taking, compensable by the state, or as a mere regulation, for which the current orthodoxy says no compensation is needed.[8] For many regulations, it is often difficult to measure directly the gains and losses suffered by individual members of society, just as it is for some informal reciprocal relationships. Nonetheless, the inability to attach precise values to gains and losses does not make it impossible to establish some rough equivalence between them. Thus, if all persons are similarly situated under a particular regulation, then there is good reason to believe that it provides them with an "average reciprocity of advantage," and so prevents the forced redistribution of property through the political process that the takings clause forbids.[9] The line between proportionate and disproportionate impact helps sort out mutually advantageous legislative forms from those that are not, even when direct measurement of gains and losses from government action is not possible. In the eminent domain context, reciprocity is regarded as evidence of equality and joint gain, not of equality and altruism. Reciprocity should be viewed the same way in informal exchanges. In both settings some systems of exchanges work better without explicit prices.

Altruism and Communitarianism

The approach taken in the previous paragraphs hews to the reductionist view of human nature and social organization that lies at the heart of my methodological approach. The alternative approach seeks to find the origins of altruism in a communitarian approach that emphasizes the bonds that empathy and concern have in forging social relationships even in large social contexts, especially on such matters as Social Security and health care.[10] This communitarian approach is flatly inconsistent with my alternative approach which analyzes most social relationships within the framework of egoism, subject to two key caveats: first, biological connectedness within families and ethnic groups does matter; and second, the methods of informal exchange, commonly seen as falling outside the market, are really forms of mutually advantageous conduct consistent with individual rationality.

With the alternative positions stated, I turn finally to the question of what follows if altruism is a significant factor in our social organizations. Here the analysis has to be broken down into its two components. First, what institutions are appropriate when we believe that universal altruism (that is, care for all persons) dominates? Second, what institutions are appropriate when we believe that selective altruism (that is, care for persons like the actor, but not everyone else) dominates?

Universal Altruism

Any political system works better when people are universally altruistic than when they are not. But the critical question is one of *relative efficiency* of the alternative arrangements. Markets work better when (or if) all persons are universal altruists than when they are egoists. The same is true for the government provision of essential services, since there is far less reason to monitor for fraud and misbehavior. But the harder question is what happens to the *relative* efficiency of market and government institutions when altruism is not universal? Can we say anything in general that might incline us to a larger or a smaller state? The inferences are difficult indeed to draw. Consider two forms of activity: intervention in the marketplace to protect against ostensible cases of exploitation, such as rent control, price control, or minimum wage; and systems of redistribution through state-run social services.

In the first case, it seems obvious that the altruist landlord, seller, or employer will be less resistant to legal regulation of social issues than his egoist counterpart. But this likelihood hardly settles the case in favor of government intervention. If the phenomenon is universal, then tenants, buyers, and employees should also be more willing to take into account the interests of their trading partners, thereby lessening any need for these legal protections. Accordingly, if one believes, as I do, that all these forms of regulation are seriously misguided in competitive settings, then a healthy dose of altruism is not going to lead to a major revision of that antiregulatory stance. Similarly, it is doubtful that anyone who supports these forms of government regulation in competitive settings will abandon that support if persuaded that universal altruism abounds in the general population. Universal altruism makes both markets and regulation work better, but it does not change their relative efficiency.

Social welfare programs can be analyzed in similar fashion. With universal altruism, there should be greater popular support for redistribution of wealth to the poor and, hence, less resistance to social welfare programs driven by a concern with need. By the same token, there should also be more private charitable activity. Again, the increase in altruism makes both systems easier to operate, but does little to alter the the their relative desirability—at least, in ways that are predictable and well understood. Administrative costs, for example, are always the bane of public systems of redistribution, but these should diminish markedly if the likelihood of official abuse and recipient misconduct is far lower than we now suspect them to be. If the fear is that private charity simply cannot carry the load, then there is some reason to increase the size of the state to offset any shortfall in private contributions. But the rigidity of public bureaucracies cuts in the opposite direction, causing some social loss. The overall effects are simply too complex to allow for any confident prediction.

Selective Altruism

About the second scenario, selective altruism, more confident conclusions can be drawn. The case for government intervention is *weakened*, not strengthened, by the influence of this form of altruism. In modern political discourse, the danger signs are ignored as politicians love to carry over, to the larger, and more impersonal, decisions within the political order, the vision of family sharing and caring. That vision is, of course, appealing: we are all traveling in a stagecoach, dependent upon each other for our welfare and our defense against a common enemy in an alien and hostile territory, bound to help each other in our period of adversity. In that setting, the clear lesson is that we all have to pull together to survive. The unmistakable implication is that coordinated behavior cannot take place through the selfish mechanisms of the market, but requires an expensive state-run social service establishment, supported by general tax revenues and run by professional bureaucrats.

This fashionable argument ignores the key structural differences between states and families, and thus assigns to the former a role largely appropriate to the latter. Taken together, the overlap of affinities, the obvious opportunities for repeat transactions, and the ability to observe the behavior of other family members support, within limits, the degree of solidarity that the altruist presupposes. But none of those conditions holds in the modern political state, where the exercise of altruism is effectively stymied by the *diversity* of individuals camping together in one territory. The forces of migration, both internal and international, will not be denied within a nation or world whose disparities of wealth and opportunity are so manifest. Individuals in search of personal improvement are not wedded to hearth and home, but will travel great distances and endure risks for personal freedom and economic advancement. New entry into any community should be welcomed for the economic and political vigor it brings. But from the time of the first zoning ordinance, economic mobility has always been in tension with political stability, for once new individuals move into a community, ballots as well as dollars are at issue. Old political coalitions can be displaced by new arrivals from a nearby city or from across the seas.

One key question is the success of integrating new arrivals with established residents. On this score the diversity essential for market competition and social creativity is at risk in any legal order that places community altruism at central stage. In melding old with new cultures, much depends on the choice of legal rules and institutions. A commitment to public altruism entails a large redistributive state, which in turn leaves more running room for political coalitions to exert an influence. The existence of different ethnic and racial groups with their different agendas makes it unlikely that in an age of identity politics anyone can tease out some fancy political solution that will help one group without harming a second. If the functions of the state were confined more closely to those of the nightwatchman, if public power and persuasion were directed more toward diffusing aggression between political groups, then state energy would be directed to problems for which win/win solutions are more probable: all people gain from the enforcement of contracts, the control of violence, and the maintenance of a court system.

Of course, our present political constitution celebrates—or, at least, tolerates—interest group politics on legislative matters, all supposedly in the interests of the larger community. The upshot is a rise of win/lose transactions, outcomes that can only polarize a society marked by much racial and ethnic diversity. The rise in political struggles in the contemporary United States on matters of race—of which the current titanic nationwide battle over affirmative action is only one conspicuous illustration—is a function not only of the constant increase in the number of different groups that hold power inside this country, but also of the key constitutional doctrines that have expanded the number of issues left to the mercies of the political process. The forces of selective altruism translate into a group cohesion that intensifies and focuses political struggle. We choose in the name of benevolence the political form that aggravates the dark side of selective altruism. What starts out life as a warm embrace for the community of mankind ends up in explicit barriers and exclusion. So long as redistribution remains the internal norm, it is just too costly to allow outsiders in to share the benefits. The price of a strong program of domestic welfare places unnecessary obstacles in the path of free immigration.

Markets do better than governments in responding to the pressures of selective altruism, because they diffuse the political pressures of collective decision making. Markets usually operate through bilateral exchange in a system in which constitutional limitations protect the parties from state expropriation. These exchanges are often impersonal, but need not be, for a contract can cover everything from a spot transaction with the friendly corner grocer to a public limited partnership or stock fund. In a diverse population, one prediction is that spot transactions will be more common across different groups than long-term relational contracts will be. People get to pick their partners, and it is easier for me to buy my groceries from a Korean grocer than to become his partner. The element of trust and altruism may well be missing between us, and most people would recoil at the prospect of turning over their material wealth and personal happiness to a person whom they do not trust. Yet, by the same token, trade across ethnic and racial groups opens up opportunities of gain for middlemen who can straddle both sides (say, because of intermarriage, language skills, or exceptional tolerance, charm, and good will).[11] Within a market system, these persons are most likely to self-select the role of broker between groups, a welcome result because they are most likely to succeed and, by example, to lower the costs of similar actions for others. The reduction in the scope of politics, and an effort to contain or eliminate the state's role in redistribution, could do a great deal to ease some of the tensions that are now part of the political order.

THE PRETENSE OF ALTRUISM

The greatest danger with altruism stems not from its presence, but from its *presumed* presence—that is, from the false belief that it plays a robust role in many political contexts. Much modern communitarian rhetoric presupposes that individuals will go along with activities that satisfy some greater public good even at the cost of some personal dislocation. It is further bolstered by the deep conviction that most government officials are well-trained, well-intentioned guardians of the public good, whose technical expertise and disinterested compassion command our trust and enable them to use their power to make sensible decisions on sensitive issues. Unlike the market models that presuppose narrow and selfish individuals, "this public interest model depends," as Frank Michelman has written,

> at bottom on a belief in the reality—or at least the possibility—of public objective values and ends for human action. In this public interest model the legislature is regarded as a forum for identifying or defining and acting towards those ends. The process is one of mutual search through joint deliberation relying on the use of reason supposed to have persuasive force. Majority rule is experienced as the natural way of taking action as and for a group—or as a device for filtering the reasonable from the unreasonable, the persuasive from the unpersuasive, the right from the wrong, and the good from the bad. Moral insight, sociological understanding, and goodwill are all legislative virtues.[12]

The strong system of individual property rights is dismantled; and in its place is substituted a collective structure whose bywords are public participation and disinterested deliberation. While it would be silly and ungracious to insist that intelligent deliberation on public issues is nowhere found in modern communities, it would be naive to imagine that wise deliberation can survive the constant pounding from self-interested political behavior. Benevolence in public institutions has a short half-life no matter how noble its original intentions.

The life cycle runs this course: The individuals who launch a new program, board, or commission may be filled with idealism about its operation and dedicated to making the program work. With time the excitement ebbs, the problems become mundane and technical; public attention wanders as new challenges leap into view. The original deliberations only established the desirability of the major program, but did little to articulate its scope or the details of its operations. Once the program is in place, its day-to-day administration falls into the hands of a professional cadre beseiged by powerful interest groups whose influence grows as public interest wanes. Small "technical" changes in the rate of payout, in the form of investment, in the findings needed to sustain an administrative ruling, or in the time of filing a permit can exert—far removed from the public scrutiny that gave birth to the program in the first place—enormous subterranean influences over its size and direction.

Over time, a slow process of disintegration and reconfiguration sets in, transforming and expanding a program from within. With the program established, its pampered beneficiaries can take defensive positions on the political high ground. It takes much more firepower to overrun an established program than it does to set it up in the first place, especially when the benighted rhetoric of high public ideals tends to anesthetize courts and legislatures to the dangers of a program's actual operations. It is seductively easy to praise deliberation as self-executing; but all too often its champions are unable to make the sober judgments needed to pinpoint and prevent future abuses. From all this, one proposition stands tall: *the more altruism that is built into a system at the front end, the greater the opportunities for factional discord at the back end.* On this score at least, the reconciliation of liberty and property with social welfare seems clear: a strong system of property rights at the front end reduces the likelihood of communitarian faction and discord. The following sections provide some thumbnail sketches of how the pattern has unfolded in Social Security, organ transplantation, zoning, and rent control.

Social Security

In some ways the centerpiece of the modern welfare state is its system of Social Security. Introduced with great fanfare in 1935, Social Security was trumpeted as the method by which to guarantee the security in retirement—and, thereafter, from disability—of all workers who contributed to the fund. Operating in large measure on the model of the family, the fatal choice of the system was to place all its contributions into a single trust fund, invested in government bonds and administered by the United States. By law and unlike ordinary pension funds, no individual worker had any vested right to any particular share based on individual contributions. That system was devised in part to ensure that the then-first generation of workers, who contributed little or nothing to the program, would nonetheless be entitled to share equally in its benefits, without delay. Over time, the program continued to generate high payouts that could be sustained only by successively higher rates of Social Security taxes on workers. Today for a majority of American workers, the Social Security tax takes about as much money out of a paycheck (including, of course, the employer's hidden share) as does the income tax itself. Yet the ostensible trust fund surpluses— which represent only a promise from the United States to collect future taxes—are insufficient to fund the promised payouts to the younger generation that will retire after present recipients have died. At some point, yields from the fund must be increased, benefits cut, taxes raised, or some combination of the above.

Naturally, there is much argument on how this should be done, and the adversaries square off along interest group lines. Thus, the Federal Advisory Panel on Social Security Reform, unanimously rejecting further tax increases, opted instead for a program to invest some Social Security taxes in private stocks and bonds to increase the real growth of the fund.[13] But the panel's members were sharply divided on whether the federal government should hold directly these shares (and, hence, exercise the votes attached to them) or place the stock in the hands of individual recipients, a move strongly opposed by the AFL-CIO, with its attachment to collective solutions. There were further differences over the percentage of funds to be invested in private programs and in the adjustments that might be made in eligibility age, benefit levels, and taxation to keep the program in balance.

Every alternative is fraught with uncertainty. To raise the eligibility age for the program places greater demands on private pension programs whose design assumes that Social Security payouts might expand, but never contract. To invest some portion of the proceeds into the stock market is to eliminate the political risks of the current system, but to substitute some economic risk in its place; yet who makes the decision which risk is greater, and for what portion of the population? Reducing the cost-of-living increases to compensate for the defects in the current index could also improve fund viability over the long haul, but also faces obvious political opposition. Moving the government out of Social Security is surely the best of the options, but the transitional questions admit of no easy solution.

All the proposals for change leave untouched the communitarian defense of the established system to the effect "that the nation as a whole is responsible for assuring a decent retirement income for all workers."[14] This bedrock faith illustrates how altruistic motivations can blind us to the consequences of major social choices. Arguments of this sort are seriously incomplete. They ignore how the present program of transfer payments reduces social growth, and how it imposes large loss on younger families forced to contribute today large sums to Social Security, from which they will never get a decent return tomorrow. The political transformation is plain. What started out as a system of public sharing has ended up as an intergenerational struggle in which the joys of altruism are experienced only by those fortunate enough to be picking the pockets of the next generation.

This confrontation was made unavoidable by the initial decision to place all contributions in a common pool. Yet all of these results could have been avoided if any initial shortfall had been made up out of general revenues, leaving individuals to contribute to their own retirement plans, adopting whatever formula they saw fit. If some measure of government compulsion is deemed necessary to guard citizens against their own improvidence, the law need only require them to set aside some fraction of their wages in personal retirement accounts that one could, as one saw fit, invest in stocks or bonds. Ordinary pension plans do not require all employees to follow the same investment strategies. There is no reason Social Security has to lock everyone into investment strategies they don't want. Less altruism leads to less political conflict, and to more responsible individual behavior.

Organ Transplants

The question of organ transplantation is dominated root and branch by the belief that any acceptable system of organ allocation must reaffirm communitarian values of sharing.[15] The quasi-government agency that supervises the rules whereby organs are collected and distributed is called the United Network for Organ Sharing (UNOS)—as if it were possible to "share" organs as opposed to giving them exclusively to one person. The insistence that community values be served nixes any semblance of a private market for either the collection or the distribution of organs. Only gifts of organs from either the dead or the living are tolerated, and payment to any organ donor—the term is consciously chosen—to cover more than out-of-pocket costs is strictly forbidden.

Unfortunately, the shortcomings of this appeal to community norms is measured in human lives. Organ shortages grow apace as the techniques for transplantation become better, and the supply of cadaveric organs declines. Neither organ donor cards nor ad campaigns have increased the supply of organs or eased the overall shortages in supply. Needy individuals are free to pay thousands of dollars to transplant surgeons and hospitals, but nothing to organ donors. Yet beneath the veneer of altruism lie highly contested methods for doling out the available organs on a neutral basis.

One noted controversy asks whether purely technical criteria should allocate these organs so as to maximize the number of lives saved.[16] A byproduct of that approach is to increase the chances that white patients will receive organs before equally needy black ones. There are a proportionately large number of white donors and black recipients, and transfers within a race generate a better match, making survival more likely. Within a market system, this differential success rate would influence, but not determine, who gets an organ. Bidders could still take into account other items, such as their own general health and personal habits. Within our political system, however, the pressures of racial politics are so strong, and our stated commitment to altruism so great, that UNOS uses a "neutral" allocation system designed to increase the percentage of black recipients, arguably at the cost of reducing the expected number of lives saved—an odd deviation from the equal dignity of persons that lies behind any altruistic standard. At the same time, little is done to alleviate organ shortages. Once again, the belief in liberty does not work for any systematic conception of the common good; and precisely where communitarian rationales are pushed the hardest, they turn out to be the weakest. A rule allowing individuals the liberty to dispose of their organs as they see fit would not preclude gifts, but just might induce an increase in the supply of organs that might save human lives.

ZONING

Local land-use politics also illustrates how a strong communitarian logic backfires in its application. A zoning board may use its power to grant or deny permits in ways that bear scant relationship to the lofty public justifications that ushered in a permit's adoption. Owing to their political origins, zoning boards labor under an intrinsic territorial bias that tends to short-circuit attempts of unidentified outsiders to secure good housing in safe neighborhoods: clout resides with those who vote. The history of exclusion on grounds of race, wealth, and religion has been well documented; indeed, it was a concern in 1926 when the Supreme Court gave its judicial blessing to zoning in *Euclid v. Ambler Realty Co.*[17] But from the outset, the courts have never neutralized the power of zoning boards to decide who builds on one's own property and who does not. At most, the courts sought to keep these abuses at bay by imposing a second layer of judicial review to ensure that local powers are exercised only for legitimate ends. And even here courts are often unwilling to intervene to prevent arbitrary denials of building permits even when "town officials are motivated by parochial views of local interests"[18] or make decisions that are "at worst . . . mistaken and protectionist."[19]

Courts rarely intervene in zoning simply because economic values are lost to arbitrary restrictions. Rather, their intervention is typically pegged to some special claim, most notably one of racial discrimination. Here is no place to chronicle in detail the New Jersey litigation over the Township of Mount Laurel, which began in the early 1970s. The township's initial plan zoned 70 percent of its land for large-lot single homes, 29 percent for manufacturing, and 1 percent for commercial—when the land itself was 65 percent vacant.[20] The township's effort to keep out poor people and racial minorities is evident even from this skeletal description of the facts. The simple approach, especially for large parcels of vacant land, would be to strike down the zoning restrictions and allow development to follow market instincts, thereby defeating the politics of exclusion. But, instead, the New Jersey Supreme Court boldly tried to counteract one regulatory system with another, by imposing affirmative obligations on the township to facilitate the development of minority housing within its borders. The ensuing political struggle has lurched inconclusively for a generation, consumed by local political crosscurrents that no court can control from afar.[21] The basic lesson was forgotten: key players can hijack any communitarian system.

Rent Control

The same tale has been played out with rent control, the conscious antithesis of private markets. Rent control allows a present tenant to remain in possession of a landlord's apartment unit after the expiration of a lease at a rent fixed by the state, below market value. The system received its initial constitutional blessing in the early 1920s as a temporary measure to counter the housing shortages in Washington, D.C., brought on by the influx of personnel during the First World War.[22] Over the next eighty years, it kept in different guises a foothold in certain communities—New York City, Cambridge, Berkeley, Santa Monica. Yet once again the familiar disconnect arises between the lofty communitarian arguments used to justify the system and the dubious special pleading that keeps it firmly entrenched.[23]

Ironically, the traditional systems of property rights that give owners the right to exclude or invite at will are attacked for their relentless individualism, and for inhibiting the discourse necessary for concerned citizens to reach common ground on the issues of the moment. Such is the stated theme of Mary Ann Glendon's 1991 book, *Rights Talk: The Impoverishment of Political Discourse*. Alas, rent control offers a powerful counterexample to her thesis, in graphically illustrating how the abandonment of strong property rights leads to an *unwanted* decline in public discourse. Rent control, after all, does not simply set the maximum rent at which a unit can be rented out to *anyone*. Rather, the regime emphatically denies the landlord any right to evict any present tenant at the expiration of a lease. As with zoning, the raison d'être of rent control is to protect sitting tenants (that is, current voters) and their bargain leases for as long as they, their spouses, and perhaps their descendants wish to remain. The political coalition propping up rent control would crumble instantly if landlords could displace current tenants with new tenants while keeping the controlled price. What sitting tenant is so altruistic as to prefer the welfare of an anonymous potential tenant to his own?

Rent control is more than an economic misadventure. It also invites fierce partisan struggles which make a mockery of any conception of disinterested deliberation for the common good. Glendon (like Michelman) is a Harvard law professor who works in Cambridge, Massachusetts, and has witnessed the ongoing hostility between those bitter rivals, landlords and tenants, as the wise city parents for years fixed rents at a fraction of open-market rates and pummeled any landlord with the temerity to remove his premises from the rental market. Even before his belated conversion from libertarian thought, Robert Nozick used small technical violations in the labyrinthine regulations to extract a favorable settlement from Erich Segal.[24] Given these ground rules, how can this dialogue be anything other than shrill and impoverished? Under rent control, First Amendment rights of freedom of speech do not curb these partisan tendencies. They are not exercised to promote informed public debate, but are used to help organize the political coalitions given their running room by the appalling judicial abdication of judges in the protection of property rights. The Cambridge political sideshow does not take place in Chicago (a town certainly known for its divisive politics on other issues), where leases turn over frequently and uneventfully. Only when property rights are secure against confiscation does public discourse get the chance to move political action toward the common good.

To see why, compare the public dialogues in a community faced with two competing schemes. The first calls for all community members to chip in for rent subsidies for 10 percent of the population. The second scheme allows for a political majority to command 10 percent of the community to fund that entire subsidy out of its own pockets. Both schemes may be passed by majority vote. What kind of dialogue will take place in these two cases? In the latter case, a majority can gang up on isolated individuals, in order to organize a winning coalition. Not so in the former case, where each member of the majority has to contribute as much to the common project as does its ardent opponent. Now he will vote with greater caution. The same dynamic works for expenditures for other public goods: parks, buildings, and wetlands. One makes a more dispassionate assessment of alternatives when one pays and receives instead of just receiving. The incentive structure shapes public discourse in both cases: in the first, it facilitates exploration of the common good; in the second, it becomes the handmaiden to confiscation. Deliberation as such is neither good nor bad. Its merits are determined not only by the constitutional framework protecting freedom of speech, but also by the protection afforded to property rights. In a deliberative democracy, the strong protection of private property does more for common discourse than does any celebration of altruism. Individual liberty and protection of property are not in tension with democracy; they are broadly supportive of it.

CHAPTER 6

❖ ❖ ❖

Forfeiture: The Flip Side of Rights

The debates over altruism bring to center stage a protracted conflict between two conceptions of rights. The older system of negative rights—an inexact and somewhat misleading term—rests on two principles. The first recognizes the civil capacity that all individuals have in their own labor and property: the right to contract, to make wills, to sue and be sued, to give evidence, and the like. The second—from which the term *negative rights* derives—protects all persons from others' interference, either by force or by fraud, in the conduct of their own affairs. The two principles combined make for a short, snappy, and knowable set of rights, one that it is internally consistent and easily universalizable, and sets the stage for productive human behavior (exchange) while limiting destructive forms of behavior (theft).

The modern vision of positive rights does not overtly reject this set of negative rights; nor does it explicitly cut back on the correlative duties of noninterference the older system created. Instead, it optimistically supplements those rights by a fresh set of entitlements that runs against a political entity, the state, and not against other persons as such. Thus, individual citizens no longer have merely the right to buy food, clothing, shelter, and, increasingly, health care, so long as they can find a willing seller; now citizens also have a (limited) claim against the state, one that requires it to provide them directly these key goods and services without their having to purchase them. These positive entitlements come with correlative obligations that impose covert redistribution through various forms of taxation.

These two theories of entitlement envision very different roles for government: the latter contemplates the use of government power for the redistribution of wealth in a manner the former flatly precludes. Having covered the merits of this dispute in large measure in the earlier discussion of natural rights and their utilitarian foundations, in this chapter I focus on the flip side of the fundamental question: What behavior should be expected from the *recipients* of various forms of legal and social assistance? More concretely, how should our conception of individual responsibility for *self*-protection be modified given the fundamental shift from a regime of negative rights to a regime, such as our own, in which positive rights occupy an ever larger fraction of the social space?

I aim to examine not how legal rights against others are created, but how they are lost: What forms of conduct, if any, will be regarded as sufficiently wrongful to require citizens to *forfeit* their rights in whole or in part? The issue can arise in ordinary private disputes governed by the law of tort or of contract. Will one speeding motorist be allowed to recover from a second? Will a plaintiff who has missed a deadline be able to recover something for work supplied? The same issue can carry over to charitable gifts or state welfare programs: Can a welfare recipient receive benefits if he or she uses drugs in violation of a program's rules? The differences in orientation matter. The nineteenth-century tendency was to hold both plaintiffs in tort and contract disputes and recipients of welfare or charity to higher standards of conduct than has been the case in the twentieth century. The expansion of individual rights has been accentuated by a contraction of the available defenses to these claims.

These twin changes cannot be chalked up to simple coincidence, for the principles of forfeiture are established by the same world view that influences the creation of legal rights. More specifically, the risk of forfeiture looms larger in a world of negative rights and limited government than it does in the modern world of positive rights, and does so over the full range of voluntary exchanges, forced interactions, and charitable transactions. In one sense, this result might appear unexpected, for the broader the set of original entitlements, the more pressing the need for some counterweight to limit the scope of the rights so created. But so bald a conclusion would overlook the vast change in attitudes toward individual responsibility that has fueled the rise of the welfare state. The basic assumption behind many of today's legal and social innovations is that ordinary individuals are incapable of protecting themselves by contract from being exploited by the large institutions with which they routinely must deal. That perceived inequality is then used, first, to justify the creation of new rights; and, then, to narrow the types of recipient behavior that preclude, or limit, these otherwise valid claims: the recipients of positive rights also need protection against their own foolish and perhaps even willful actions which in an earlier day led to a forfeiture of rights. Yet protecting people against the consequences of their own folly, mistake, or incompetence is not costless. The release of pressure in one location only builds up pressures elsewhere; as the losses are pushed onto individuals who have managed their own affairs well, these burdens could easily drag down their economic level, thus increasing the fraction of the population in need of support. The watchword of modern political programs is often *social security*. The effect of these programs is to increase the insecurity of some people as it reduces it for others. Price protection for farmers heavily burdens consumers, so that efforts targeted to reduce insecurity for some can easily increase insecurity for the system as a whole.* It is instructive to examine the nineteenth- and twentieth-century patterns in two major common-law areas, tort and contract, before turning to the treatment of charitable obligations and welfare rights in both periods.

The Common Law of Forfeiture in the Nineteenth Century

Contract

During the nineteenth century, individual misconduct typically precluded—or, at least, reduced the amount of—damages a plaintiff could recover.[2] The diversity of views on when and how such forfeiture took hold in employment cases reveals the subtlety of the underlying problem. One constantly litigated question involved employment contracts between farmers and field hands. The typical agreement stipulated that a field hand was to work on a farm for a year for room and board and a cash payment (often set at $120 per annum), payable at the end of a year of service. Sometimes

---

* Hayek says: "[T]he politics which are now followed everywhere, which hand out the privilege of security, now to this group and now to that, are nevertheless rapidly creating conditions in which the striving for security tends to become stronger than the love of freedom. The reason for this is that with every grant of complete security to one group the insecurity of the rest necessarily increases. If you guarantee to some a fixed part of a variable cake, the share left to the rest is bound to fluctuate proportionally more than the size of the whole. And the essential element of security which the competitive system offers, the great variety of opportunities, is more and more reduced."[1]

a farm hand quit before the end of the year, and then sued for back wages prorated for months served; thus, if he worked for nine months, his claim would be for $90. Could that payment be recovered even when the worker cut short the term of service?

The temptation to allow some recovery for back wages was surely substantial. Suppose the farm hand worked for 364 days of the year and quit the day before the expiration of the contract. Denying any compensation for the 364 days worked would make the allocated payment for the last day's employment seem to be the last day's room and board plus $120—that is, the benefits forgone if the farm hand quit the day before. In addition, the farm hand could argue that the farmer was left *better off* by the farm hand's breach of this contract than he would have been by the hand's faithful contractual performance. After all, most farmers would prefer to receive 364 days' work without having to pay $120 for receiving a single additional day of labor. If any inconvenience arose from losing a day's labor, with crops left at risk before harvesting, a wage of $5 or $10 per day surely would have attracted a queue of otherwise reluctant substitutes to fill the gap.

Yet the dominant judicial view denied all cash compensation for the early departure. One reason was that nonpayment followed the custom of the community. In 1824, in *Stark v. Parker*, a Massachusetts farm hand, who was entitled to $120 at the end of the year, had quit after nine and one-half months, claiming $95 for his labors. Judge Levi Lincoln noted pointedly:

> [T]he usages of the country and common opinion upon subjects of this description are especially to be regarded, and we are bound judicially to take notice of that of which no one is in fact ignorant. It may be safe to affirm that in no case has a contract in the terms of the one under consideration, been construed by practical men to give a right to demand the agreed compensation, before the performance of the labor, and that the employer and the employed alike universally so understand it.[3]

Here two common themes of the nineteenth-century world view surge to the fore. First, the court was confident that it could identify the custom; and equally so that the custom generated a sound rule of decision, consistent with the dominant natural law view. Nor did the court think this case fell into any exception to the general rule: both employer and employee alike had equal knowledge of the custom and had contracted in reliance on it. The passage just quoted does not even hint that inequality of bargaining position or some imagined source of imperfect information could upset the contractual relationship between the parties.

The second theme concerns the sanctity of the basic contract. Judge Lincoln proceeded to note that the plaintiff's demand for proration led to the creation of a contract very different from the "entire" arrangement (the bonus to be paid only if the farm hand performed the contract in its entirety) agreed to by the parties: "The plaintiff might as well claim his wages by the month as by the year, by the week as by the month, and by the day or hour as by either."[4] The judge's point is not without intellectual force. The plaintiff is in effect claiming the right to redo the arrangement to read that he is to get $85 in cash if he leaves after eight and one-half months. Adopting that division would recast the original agreement into a novel series of options, some of which could prove disadvantageous to the farmer. Thus, the proration would work a real injustice if agricultural hiring were concentrated at the beginning of the growing season: if a farm hand departed even several weeks later, good farm hands to take his place for the rest of the year would have already taken jobs elsewhere. Once courts start to rewrite a contract, how do they decide what temporal divisions are unique or even desirable?

Nor was it clear whether the farmer could turn the tables. If the farm hand could depart early and still claim the proportionate share of the bonus, could the employer then with impunity cast the farm hand out of a job by paying proportionate wages when the hiring season was over, forcing the farm hand on short notice to find suitable employment for the remainder of the term? The strong legal obligation on the employee thus bolstered the farmer's contractual obligations. The greater security—that the employer's return promise to the worker meant just what it said, and no less—was a powerful inducement for farm hands to enter into these contracts in the first place.

Both of these sound utilitarian considerations were buttressed by the judge's old-fashioned moral condemnation of an employee's misbehavior. Over and over again, the court stressed the same theme: "Nothing can be more unreasonable than that a man, who deliberately and wantonly violates an engagement, should be permitted to seek in a court of justice an indemnity from the consequences of his voluntary act; and we are satisfied that the law will not allow it."[5] The court harbored a real sense of outrage that *any person*, regardless of social status or position, would dare to sue on a contract he had deliberately breached. If anything, the only person who should have an action on the contract was the farmer whose rights had been violated. If he did not sue, the sole explanation was that the unpaid bonus on the contract offered him a security in excess of his actual damages. Self-help by keeping all the unpaid wages removed the need of a lawsuit to control the breach of an agreement by a farm hand.

The basic approach was not confined to employment. In *Smith v. Brady* (1858), the same sentiment was echoed in New York in the rebuff of a plaintiff builder's effort to recover for benefits conferred after his completion of a building that did not comply in all relevant respects with contract specifications: "Indeed, in this state the sanctity of contracts in this respect at least, has been steadily maintained, and no encouragement has ever been given to that loose and dangerous doctrine which allows a person to violate his most solemn engagements and then to draw the injured into a controversy concerning the amount and value of the benefits received."[6]

The law did not lift a single finger to soften the plight of those who break their promises. Fortunately, it was also, forcefully, alert to advantage taking on the other side. Note the relevant rule in employment cases:

> Any apprehension that this rule may be abused to the purposes of oppression, by holding out an inducement to the employer, by unkind treatment near the close of a term of service, to drive the laborer from his engagement, to the sacrifice of his wages, is wholly groundless. It is only in cases where the desertion is voluntary and without cause on the part of the laborer, or fault or consent on the part of the employer, that the principle applies.[7]

A judge who never learned modern economic theory had an instinctive sense of the risk of these problems arising in everyday life: an employer is just that much more likely to engage in misconduct if he is allowed to profit from his own wrong. Once alerted to that danger, the court must fashion a defense against employer misconduct. An employee who quits within term does not forfeit his wages if driven from the job by the misconduct of a rapacious employer. Once again, as in other formative periods of the law, legal intuitions and practices often outpaced formal knowledge. The whole system had an intellectual simplicity and structural integrity that might lead us to assume that it commanded universal respect.

Nonetheless, every legal proposition dissolves into a majority and a minority rule. While *Stark* represented the majority,[8] *Britton v. Turner*, a New Hampshire case of 1834,[9] was the leading authority for the minority legal position. Rather than dwelling on custom and common understanding, Judge Parker* allowed the plaintiff's action (again for $95 for nine and one-half months of service) for two reasons. First, thinking it very odd that the defendant should be left better off from the plaintiff's breach than from his performance, Parker feared that the astute farmer might provoke the breach to obtain an undeserved windfall. But Parker also believed that no plaintiff in breach of contract could sue on the very contract he had breached. To avoid that conceptual puzzle, he argued that a theory of unjust enrichment entitled the worker to recover his proportionate share of wages, subject to a setoff by the employer for any loss from the early quitting:

> The rule, by binding the employer to pay the value of the service he actually receives, and the laborer to answer in damages where he does not complete the entire contract, will leave no temptation to the former to drive the laborer from his service, near the close of his term, by ill treatment, in order to escape from payment; nor to the latter to desert his service before the stipulated time, without a sufficient reason; and it will in most instances settle the whole controversy in one action, and prevent a multiplicity of suits.
>
> There may be instances, however, where the damage occasioned is much greater than the value of the labor performed, and if the party elects to permit himself to be charged for the value of the labor, without interposing the damages in defense, he is entitled to do so, and may have an action to recover his damages for nonperformance. [10]

This passage reveals only a narrow gap between the majority and the minority rules, for both judges were alert to the risk of bilateral opportunism: that is, that each party would try to weasel out of his obligations while holding the other side to his. Thus, Judge Parker celebrated his benevolent rule for precisely the same reason that Judge Lincoln celebrated the opposite one: to prevent employer provocation to induce breach before the end of term. The only difference is that Judge Lincoln sought to prevent abuse by reinstating the farm hand's action for employer misbehavior, while Judge Parker was prepared to allow the farm hand's action in all cases, knowing that the employer would have little reason to induce the farm hand to quit if he had to pay for the labor previously expended, *quantum meruit*—that is, for whatever it was worth.

---

* So much weight did this judge attach to the decision that he had its citation etched onto his gravestone.

Parker also realized that misbehavior is a two-way street, and thus armed the farmer with two weapons to combat abuse by the hired hand. The first allowed the farmer to set off against the farm hand's damage suit any loss sustained from the latter's breach of contract. If the farmer had to pay $30 in wages to hire a new laborer for the remaining two and one-half months, and incurred $10 additional search costs, then a $95 recovery got reduced by $15 to $80, to compensate the farmer for the $5 wage hike and the $10 search cost. Second, Parker avoided multiple lawsuits by allowing the setoff against wages in the employee's lawsuit to reduce litigation costs. Nineteenth-century procedure is often attacked as archaic, but how many cases make it into court today for $25, even adjusted fortyfold (at a guess) for inflation? Modern legal systems, with more complex rules, cannot process many disputes under $1,000.

Placed side by side, *Stark* and *Britton*'s similarities dominate their differences. Both respond to the same incentive questions and take the same view of the danger self-interest poses to contractual stability. If Judge Lincoln in *Stark* correctly reported the custom and usages of the country, then presumably he had the better of the argument in giving the employer the dominant hand: no reason appears why this custom would be inefficient (see chapter 2). Nonetheless, by treating worker and employer on conditions of rough parity—including their equal ability to commit abuse—both contractual regimes should be equal to the task of policing these employment contracts. And in both cases, the two parties could negotiate a cash settlement in the event of early departure to further narrow the difference. Nothing in *Britton* smacks of the protective rules of modern labor law that have developed in the twentieth century, both at common law and by statute. Forfeiture plays a central role not only for what it does, but as a powerful marker for the individual responsibility that underlies both the majority and the minority approaches to labor contracts.

Tort

At a formal level, the issue in tort follows a parallel course to the contractual one: first, a plaintiff says what the defendant did wrong; then the defendant says what the plaintiff did wrong. The question of forfeiture arises when the defendant admits his wrong and then claims that the plaintiff's own conduct blocks or reduces the amount of recovery. In this situation, one recurrent dispute is whether the same substantive standards should apply to the conduct of both parties, or whether a plaintiff should receive some special dispensation that will improve either his chances for or the amount of recovery.

The answer to this question depends on the nature of the relationship between the parties. When the parties have no direct contractual connection to each other, evenhanded treatment seems preferable. Thus, when two drivers collide on a public highway, neither is the guardian of the other, and both have equal obligation to obey the rules of the road. That view largely survives today: the standard common-law response in highway accidents holds the plaintiff to the same basic negligence standard as the defendant, and teenagers to the same standards as their elders.[11]

Highway accidents, which are often caused by individuals acting in their private capacity, do not supply a good benchmark to gauge the transformation of tort law in the twentieth century. The havoc wreaked by trucks and other commercial vehicles is tied to their size (and speed), not to their market power. To some extent, it is a matter of luck who is hurt in a collision, and the overall tendency is to curb accidents by making improvements in road construction, vehicular safety, and traffic enforcement.

Strong class conflicts did surface, however, in the industrial accident cases, which pitted employees against their employers. The standard accounts often claim that the role of the law is to counterbalance the natural differences in economic strength and, thus, to impose new and additional duties on the employers. But within this contractual setting, the objective of the parties is to maximize the size of the gain to be divided between them.[12] That in turn requires them to adopt rules that minimize the cost of both accidents and their prevention. We need not appeal to a theory of exploitation to explain why employers often assumed greater obligations than those found in the hired-hand cases of earlier times. Identical precautions between the parties no longer make sense when the parties have differential capacity to avoid accidents. In many workplace situations, however, workers can take only those individual precautions that affect their own safety. They cannot institute changes either in the basic structure of industrial operations or in the deployment and maintenance of capital equipment. In addition, unlike the wage cases discussed above, the employee labors under a powerful incentive to take care that operates independent of the liability rule: be careless in the conduct of your affairs, and *your* life and limb are at risk. Employers for their part had greater institutional capacity to avoid harm. But as they did not work side by side with their employees, they were not so frequently exposed to a direct threat of injury, and thus had less built-in incentive for survival, apart from liability, to do so.

The legal system, even in the nineteenth century, responded to these differences in position. The basic forfeiture doctrine was still in place, for a negligent plaintiff could not recover from a culpable defendant. Even so, the standard of care expected of an employee was usually reduced, in recognition of his instinct of self-preservation. Some effort has been made to demonstrate how the law systematically favored the employer defendant: thus, Lawrence Friedman has denounced contributory negligence as one of "the traps for unwary plaintiffs," along with the fellow-servant rule and its fellow traveler, the doctrine of assumption of risk.[13] But Gary Schwartz's closer examination of the relevant cases undercuts that claim.[14] The cases followed the sensible economic theory of accident avoidance: an employer able to take systematic precautions was usually bound to protect a plaintiff employee against momentary confusion or mistake.

Some further evidence of the asymmetrical risk positions of employers and employees can be gleaned from the workers' compensation systems that arose in the second half of the nineteenth century. These systems began as *voluntary* contractual responses to industrial accidents, not as mandatory state programs,[15] and all operated around a basic bargain that altered both sides of the common-law equation of negligence and contributory negligence. The injured worker no longer had to prove the employer's negligence as at common law. Instead, from the earliest time, the employer's liability covered by time-honored formula all "personal injuries by accident arising out of and in the course of employment"—that is, all work-related injuries.[16]

All things have their price. The employee's quid pro quo for expanded coverage was to assent to a sharp limitation on damages. By design, full recovery under the plan did not leave the injured party (if alive) as well off as if the injury had never occurred in the first place. Yet that limitation on recovery had its own social function. The worker who knew about the limited level of recovery would stay away from certain dangerous work if his chances of injury were great, or his own risk of loss unusually large—say, because of some pre-existing health condition. Those workers who did take the job still had important incentives to avoid injury precisely because their recovery was systematically limited. Since the damage awards were set low, it followed that the common-law contributory negligence defenses were no longer necessary to curb misconduct by plaintiffs. The upshot was that the cases where recovery was forfeited were limited to those of a worker's reckless behavior or willful misconduct.

This overall situation thus seems to satisfy the two tests of social efficiency: first, its voluntary nature suggests that it marks a systematic improvement over the common-law regimes it displaced; second, its incentive properties suggest that it developed an explicit set of asymmetrical rules to handle the asymmetrical incentives of the two parties. This delicate contractual balance could not emerge in a world driven by employer exploitation. Rather, the great lesson that comes from the development of workers' compensation is the interconnection of all parts of a system: it is not wise to impose ideal incentives on employers while ignoring incentive effects on employees. As both remain part of the accident-reduction picture, some forfeiture ingredient is thus an essential part of the overall scheme.

Charitable Obligations

The forfeiture question has special urgency in cases of charity. During the nineteenth century, an extensive network of mutual-aid societies were a cross between market insurance and social-support networks. Premiums or dues could be charged for membership, but these were not necessarily calibrated to match the expected payouts; rather, they rested on an uneasy mix between mutual support, self-sufficiency, and a desire to help those in need.[17] Yet as with contract and tort cases, those who dispensed charitable assistance took into account the potential foibles of a recipient's conduct. Unlike contract and tort disputes, charitable organizations were not subject to legal sanctions, but extensive social norms guided their day-to-day operations. Within this environment, their scope increased. Precise numbers are hard to come by, but these movements were neither evanescent in duration nor trivial in scope. And the cash payments were only part of the network of support services they provided. For example, the New York Children's Aid Society helped 91,000 people between 1854 and 1872.[18]

Following earlier natural-law thinkers, charitable conduct was regarded as a species of imperfect obligation: the moral duty to assist the poor was not directed to any particular person; in consequence, the enforcement of this duty was left to an uneasy amalgam of moral and social sanctions or to individual conscience and expressions of social disapproval. The legal system had no role in deciding which individuals had access to charity and which did not. Accordingly, charities were entitled to deny services to anyone as of right, no matter how great the need.[19] The position stemmed from the common-law view that ordinary persons had the right to exclude others from the use of their property and to withhold services from whomsoever they saw fit: exclusion from property, absolute choice of contracting partners, and choice of donees all went together. (For the common carrier exception to the basic rule, see chapter 10.)

Hand in hand with the right to exclude was immunity from liability for ordinary negligence in the routine provision of charitable services.* This doctrine typically barred malpractice suits against providers of medical services, first to indigent patients and then to paying patients as well.[21] The position was sensibly qualified in two different ways. First, the legal immunity did not extend to wrongs a charity committed against outsiders: a charity could not hide behind its immunity when the waste discharged from its facilities contaminated a neighbor's well, or when its delivery trucks struck and injured a pedestrian; the only persons who waived the right to sue were those who came to the charity for medical care. Second, the charity could waive by contract all or some of its legal immunity: for example, it could purchase malpractice insurance for the protection of its patients.[22]

At first look, these doctrines seem distinctly unlovely and wholly inhospitable to poor people in need of medical care: they were being asked to run the risk either of being totally excluded from that care or of receiving inferior care. Paradoxically, however, the risks of exclusion and of uncompensated injury considerably spurred the growth of charitable institutions during the last third of the nineteenth century owing to the tie-in of these stony doctrines with the broader social and moral sanctions used to encourage charitable care. Since no one was obligated to set up charitable institutions, there were no undue legal impediments in the path of such initiatives. Although it is now easy to bemoan individual miscarriages of justice caused by charitable institutions left to their own devices, it is more important to focus on what evoked that great burst of charitable activity in the first place. That powerful inducement was the freedom of action preserved by the common-law approach. Against the few individuals who suffered the sting of exclusion or malpractice, we must consider the tens and hundreds of persons whose access to care was promoted precisely because charitable institutions were untouched by any onerous regulation or liability.

Since charitable budgets were—as they are today—limited, if not fixed, a primary concern was how to maximize the benefits over all the indigent: that is, how to prevent scarce resources from being drained off by those who

---

* "If, in their dealings with their property appropriated to charity, they [members of the hospital board] create a nuisance by themselves or by their servants, if they dig pitfalls in their grounds and the like, there are strong reasons for holding them liable to outsiders, like any other individual or corporation. The purity of their aims may not justify their torts; but, if a suffering man avails himself of their charity, he takes the risks of malpractice, if their charitable agents have been carefully selected."[20]

were not really needy or who had, in fact, resources of their own; and then to channel those resources to those who were most in need. Since rationing by price was not possible, this goal was achieved in the classical system by the creation of a strong division between "deserving" and "nondeserving" poor, with the latter receiving less care than the former. Marvin Olasky has well described the historical operation of this system.[23] From colonial times through the early twentieth century, a powerful moral ambivalence surrounded the dispensation of charitable care. The religious underpinnings for charity posited an unquestionable moral obligation to assist the poor in their time of need, but that obligation was consciously tempered by a genuine distrust of many of the poor and their motives. To be sure, many people need help because of genuine misfortune beyond their control—accident, disease, a death in the family. But over the broad run of cases, need in and of itself did not guarantee assistance. It was important to know *why* a person was in need of care, and how that condition related to issues of character and moral worth. To speak, as was commonly done, of the "idle" or the "slothful poor," to berate the poor who were "dissolute," or "stubborn, disorderly and disobedient," was perceived as commendable realism, not moral smugness or gratutitous character assassination. The prevailing ethos of the time was to be on constant guard against the sentimental idealism that could lead charitable efforts astray.

Although the term *moral hazard* had not yet been coined, the early writers on charity, driven in large measure by their religious conception of human sin (original or otherwise), wrote and acted as if they lived under its spell. If sloth and idleness were the enemy, then work at the direction of the master of the poorhouse was the antidote. Thus, Charles Chauncy wrote to the society for Encouraging Industry and Employing the Poor in 1752: "It would be an evident Breach of the Law of the Gospel, as well as of Nature, to bestow upon those the Bread of Charity, who might earn and eat their own Bread, if they did not shamefully idle away their Time."[24] Note the pointed irony here: where the law of Nature has often been treated as the source of the obligation to provide charitable care, now appeals to that elusive doctrine cut in the opposite direction, it being a *breach* of that law to bestow charity on those who do not deserve it. Social institutions, such as the poorhouse, were established to force the idle to make do with bread and water while others who labored received a more substantial meal.

The traditional accounts of charity were also careful to specify sources of loss whose individual victims and their families merited full assistance. These sources correlated with the common-law conception of an act of God or a *vis maior*, and included the victims of storm, fire, earthquake, or other calamity.[25] At the time, no person could be held legally responsible for harms sustained from these sources. Charitable care filled the yawning gap occupied by worthy persons without hope of legal redress. While individuals who were injured or made ill through drinking or cavorting were also in need of help, aiding them was to run the risk of underwriting socially destructive forms of conduct. It was no coincidence that in the nineteenth century the temperance movement was flourishing, and that potential recipients of charitable assistance were routinely checked for alcoholism.[26] In all cases, the fundamental operating principle was that the origin of a recipient's loss offered reliable evidence about character, and aid was provided for those whose primary conduct that assistance was least likely to alter for the worse.

Then, as now, it took a good deal of ingenuity to structure aid so that as much as possible went to its intended beneficiaries: to give aid to the wife and the children, while denying it to the husband and father known to be a drunkard.[27] Aid was a tied good, for it was impossible to aid the drunkard's wife and children without some benefit spilling over to the drunkard himself. But whatever the embarrassments in the marginal case, charitable institutions in the nineteenth century placed this distinction center stage: they understood that if they were to raise the resources needed to discharge their function, they would fail ultimately if they spent those resources in ways that coincidentally aggravated the same practices they condemned. The threat of forfeiture of benefit was the best way to constrain misbehavior and stretch out scarce resources in a nonprice environment.

The setting and form in which aid was supplied was critical as well. Religious groups provided direct assistance in religious environments, where they could monitor the behavior of their recipients, a prospect that leaves many well-intentioned people uneasy today. Similarly, charity was never given as a simple cash grant.[28] No one received chits or coupons to be spent as he or she saw fit, lest they be bartered away, or used to purchase useful goods which could then be exchanged in side transactions for prohibited items, such as alcohol or tobacco. In order to avoid the illicit subversion of charitable assistance, the recipient had to consume the food and service provided in plain view of the charitable provider. And always there were strings attached to these gifts in-kind: material support was paired with instruction in one comprehensive package, especially for children. In particular, religious orders made it a point to work with (and thereby monitor and guide the conduct of) the recipient so as to prevent any untoward behavior on his or her part.[29] For the most stubborn recipients, aid was often dependent on the person's actually moving into a poorhouse, a totally controlled environment whose master had the power to dispense favors to those who followed the rules and to impose sanctions on those who did not.[30]

Finally, the consensus view was that charitable work had to be done at a very local and immediate level, one recipient at a time. Olasky quotes a wonderful dialogue from *McGuffey's Reader*—the standard nineteenth-century elementary text—that stresses the importance of modest ambitions properly executed. Mr. Fantom (McGuffey's names, like Shakespeare's, often make their own point) protests that charity can relieve the miseries *of the whole world*: "It is provinces, empires, continents, that the benevolence of the philosopher embraces; every one can do a little paltry good to his next neighbor." Mr. Goodman responds, "Every one *can*, but I do not see that every one *does*. . . . [You] have such a noble zeal for the *millions*, [yet] feel so little compassion for the units."[31] Compassion is thus regarded here not as a social ideal played out on some large political stage, but rather as a gritty virtue, played one case at a time. Grand pronouncements count for little; particular actions, for a great deal.

At every juncture, then, the nineteenth-century approach walked a fine line between the toughness needed to contain asocial behavior and guarded compassion for those who have fallen victim to it. Deciding exactly how this dilemma should be resolved is no easy business, even for those with the best of intentions, and requires hands-on knowledge and long experience. It also requires a cadre of unpaid workers whose dominant motivation is often religious and always charitable.

No one could claim that this patchwork system of charitable interventions was able to remove all the poverty in its midst. But a defense of that system does not require a dramatic transformation in the social landscape. The question is not, Was the system perfect?—but, Was it better than the next best alternative? Overall material wealth—far lower then than it is now—effectively limited the support that could be given no matter what the legal regime. No one is clever enough to redistribute wealth that has not been produced, and the nineteenth-century approach was sensitive to concerns of wealth creation as well as to those of wealth distribution. We should commend the earlier system for its qualified successes, and not condemn it for shortcomings that no system of legislation or regulation is, in fact, able to eliminate.

THE TWENTIETH CENTURY WELFARE STATE

The rise of the welfare state in the twentieth century has led to an erosion of our expectations of individual responsibility. In contract, tort, and charitable activities, this transformation was expressed in two dimensions: an expansion of the basic case for liability or entitlement was coupled with a narrowing of the permissible grounds of forfeiture for individual misconduct. And in all activities the desire to secure compensation in the individual case has undone many of the safeguards against wasteful activity built into the earlier legal regime. The old maxim "Hard cases make bad law" was a pointed reminder of how compassion in the individual case can undermine the fabric of sound legal rules—as has happened in varying degrees in these three domains.

Contract

The older regime stressed the parity of position of contracting parties and sought to counter opportunistic behavior in both sides so that a healthy wariness applied to both sides of all bilateral relationships—employer-employee, landlord-tenant, producer-consumer, owner-builder, and the like. Too often the modern rules start from the presupposition that one side to a relationship wields great economic power and is capable of serious misconduct, while its trading partner is both vulnerable to exploitation and largely incapable of wrongdoing. In addition, the modern view commonly presupposes that mere social sanctions—for example, the loss of reputation, will not curb the perceived excesses of the dominant party, even those firms that spend millions to promote brand names and protect good will, knowing all can be lost in the twinkling of an eye.

These twin assumptions largely dictate the form of the modern law. Once again, it is instructive to focus on the employment contract. So long as employers, and not employees, commit abuse, the law should direct all its firepower against the former, not the latter. If reputation no longer constrains misbehavior, then the law has to redouble its efforts to protect the weaker party against exploitation. Indeed, the very use of the term *exploitation* signals a rejection of the older view of contract as a source of mutual gain, as exemplified in the farmer/laborer cases, and thrusts to the fore a rival principle that treats the outcome of ordinary contracts as akin to the outcome from theft: the employer gains from contract only because the employee loses.

Now we cannot have a law that bans all employment contracts, so the newer approach exacts its toll in indirect fashion. One target of attack is employment-at-will, a common arrangement that allowed the employer to fire and the worker to quit for good reason, bad reason, or no reason at all.[32] Notwithstanding the frequent use and evident simplicity of employment-at-will contracts, as a matter of public policy many courts have insisted that wrongful dismissals be sanctioned by heavy damage awards.[33] The same attitude carries over in the creation of statutory overlays on the employment contract, all of which are driven by the vision of contractual exploitation: the National Labor Relations Act (NLRA) of 1935[34] uses a system of collective bargaining that utterly displaces individual contracts between management and workers. An industrial strike results when the two sides cannot agree, and consequently disrupts the affairs of third parties. The NLRA does not apply to the transportation industries, which (including the airlines) are governed by the Railway Labor Act (RLA). The RLA also accepts the institution of collective bargaining but seeks to make it difficult for workers to strike, to avoid the immediate and massive disruptions that can be caused by the shutdown of a major national carrier.[35] Yet even here the classifications can be quirky: the United Parcel Service strike of 1997 was governed by the NLRA, not the RLA. The difference is crucial: by insisting that the status quo ante, no matter how antiquated, be kept until some new agreement is reached, the RLA consciously deprives management of its ordinary power to hire and fire. The net effect is that workers are part owners of the firm. Lost in the shuffle is the ability of competitive firms to supply uninterrupted service without the creation of a union stranglehold on the economy.*

The constant theme of exploitation also spawns minimum-wage laws that hamper the operation of employment markets, especially for young and unskilled workers. Fear of exploitation gives rise to the vast proliferation of antidiscrimination laws, which often work at cross-purposes with each other: the strong protection against age discrimination makes for a major redistribution from younger to older workers and tends to protect senior employees, heavily white male, against the newer claims of younger employees, many of whom are women and members of minority groups.

---

* In 1997, Adam Bryant, for example, noted the powerful position of American Airlines' pilot union just before President Clinton intervened under the Railway Labor Act to authorize a sixty-day "cooling off" period. No such intervention took place, later that year, under the UPS strike, which inconvenienced many small firms dependent upon UPS for receiving supplies and filling orders.[36]

The refusal to permit the orderly turnover of labor must in the long term reduce needed investments in human capital.*

For these purposes, however, my concern is not with the unwise decisions that introduce government control over the employment relation, but with the transformation that the law necessarily effects in dealing with cases of employee misconduct. Once an antidiscrimination law or a collective bargaining statute is put into place, it is no longer possible for employees to be legally dismissed at will. In each and every contested case, it is necessary to decide whether the dismissal was made for the reason prohibited by statute. In principle, an employer need not show that incompetence was the reason: it could be sheer caprice unrelated to union membership, or to race, sex, age, or disability. It is, for example, permissible to fire someone from an accounting job because he or she has had the temerity to apply to law school. But in most cases an employer's pious claims that it has engaged in permissible irrational behavior will be met with genuine and deserved judicial skepticism. In practice, therefore, the employer will usually claim worker incompetence as the grounds for dismissal. To this claim, the employee responds with the cry of "Pretext!" Every dismissal or demotion is a potential target for litigation after the fact before a jury that has multiple explanations to choose from: Was there really a planned reduction-in-force, or did the plant manager say that the sixty-two-year-old incumbent was "slowing down"? The range of excuses is often extraordinary.[38]

In addition, the permissible grounds of dismissal have shrunk even in areas that relate to competence. The Americans with Disabilities Act of 1990,[39] which prevents discrimination in employment against a current or prospective disabled worker, does not treat alcoholism as a condition warranting swift retribution. Today alcoholism (or, at least, the condition of recovering from past alcoholism) counts as a disability, which the employer is prohibited from taking into account in dealing with individual workers who have relapsed. The fuzziness of the basic conceptions is a breeding ground for litigation.

More than one commentator has lamented the relative stagnation of wages in the United States (not to mention elsewhere) in the past twenty

---

* This theme has now been picked up by writers on the other side of the political spectrum. Lester Thurow, for example, has noted that today the elderly have far outstripped their children in both net worth and current income. The shift constitutes a major reversal from the situation as recently as twenty-five years ago. In the 1960s, Thurow reports, the average seventy-year-old spent only 60 percent of the average thirty-year-old; today he spends 20 percent more.[37]

years, especially in the ranks of blue-collar workers. As the economic journalist John Cassidy has observed, the rate of wage stagnation has affected all classes in the post–1973 period, with only persons in the top quintile eking out small gains.[40] The gains in the 1945–73 period were both larger and more evenly distributed across all groups. Faulty inflation measures (such as those that ignore improvements in product quality) might conceal some advancement in real wages in the post–1973 period. But if so, then the gains of the pre–1973 period are also likely to be understated for the same reason. Either way, therefore, the slowdown in wages seems undeniable. Unfortunately, in the overall story, the shift in attitude toward contractual freedom is not treated as important. The shift in the legal environment has generated powerful, but perverse, incentives. The broad expansion of basic employee rights has sharply narrowed the grounds for permissible dismissal. A relationship once governed by informal sanctions and sensible contractual rules has been largely taken over by the state, whose own rules tend to conflict with the requirements of the workplace. Unfortunately, however, the constant effort to limit unjustified termination works its way back into the system, making job formation ever more perilous for the employer. And once again, more money is taken from the system to resolve disputes that turn on delicate questions of motivation with long and tortured histories. These costs are taxes paid, in part, by employers and employees alike.

Tort

As noted earlier, the traditional tort law adopted an even-handed standard on the question of whether a plaintiff's conduct resulted in his forfeiture of recovery. Where the nineteenth-century system could be criticized for allowing that misconduct to block all recovery, even in cases where the defendant was as much responsible as the plaintiff for a loss, the response to that criticism is a system of comparative negligence that divides the losses between the parties.* Although this shift does not by itself mark a disintegration of the appropriate standards of plaintiff conduct; once again the erosion in standards is unmistakable.

---

* The comparative negligence rule says that when both plaintiff and defendant are at fault, the loss will be divided between them. There are many different schemes for division, some of which require a case-by-case determination of the percentages of fault allocated to each party, while others posit some automatic division. The complications become more manifest when allocations are required among three or more parties.[41]

The tort system today has limited relevance for workplace accidents, which usually fall within the province of workers' compensation statutes. The decline of responsibility each individual has for his or her own safety is more evident in the law of product liability which governs the relationships between manufacturers of goods and consumers who use these goods in their daily lives. The traditional view of this subject allowed the consumer to recover only to the extent that he or she made "normal and proper" use of the goods in question[42]—a rule that rightfully protects anyone injured by a product's latent defects. Yet modern product liability law allows— although here the tide is mercifully ebbing—the injured party to recover so long as the product use or misuse is regarded as foreseeable, which, to an institutional defendant possessed of wide experience of its customers' foibles, it normally is.[43] More than one drunken plaintiff who has rammed his speeding car into a telephone pole has recovered from the car's manu- facturer.[44] The older view understood these events as misbehavior by the plaintiff, and thus as something he could prevent, rather than as errors by firms that built or serviced vehicles months before an accident. Where the instinct to respond to the moral hazard question led earlier courts to require such an injured plaintiff to forfeit recovery for the harm in question, today the courts remain too willing to treat such individual misconduct as a neu- tral or natural event (like lightning) against which the manufacturer must guard the consumer. It is no coincidence that the judicial attitude found in the wrongful dismissal cases has carried over to personal injury actions. In both settings, ordinary individuals escape responsibility for the conse- quences of their own actions.

Charitable Organizations

The switch in attitude toward charitable organizations is similar in many ways to that in contract and tort. It occurred in, roughly, two stages: First, by 1950, judges by common-law decision had systematically completed undoing the earlier immunity from liability for negligence in the provision of medical care. At that time, many hospitals and physicians started to resort to contractual devices to limit their liability for medical malpractice in both paying and charitable cases. These contractual protections themselves were judicially invalidated following the 1963 watershed decision of *Tunkl v. Regents of University of California*,[45] which announced that the party with "superior bargaining strength" could not exempt itself from malpractice lia- bility by contract. Paying little attention to the norms of institutional autonomy, *Tunkl* adopted the same world view as a well-known pair of contemporary product liability cases, *Henningsen v. Bloomfield Motors* (1960)[46] and *Greenman v. Yuba Power* (1962),[47] which explicitly rejected all contractual defenses in personal injury cases brought by consumers against manufacturers.[48] The shift in judicial approach meant that both the commercial and the charitable areas were henceforth organized under judicial norms that explicitly rejected the validity of private contractual arrangements. Large portions of the medical malpractice and the product liability crises of the next generation may be traced to the inability of private institutions to vary the standard terms of doing business from the norms prescribed by state judges. And as these judges paid ever less attention to the risks of a plaintiff's misconduct, the gap between the ideal legal rules and the actual legal rules grew ever wider, precipitating the well-known dislocations in both product liability and medical malpractice law.

The second half of the attack on the older legal regime was directed against the ability of private institutions to control their charitable business.[49] In the 1960s and 1970s, several legal decisions hinted at the obligation of charitable institutions to take in all comers so long as they advertised themselves as so doing.[50] A charitable institution could avoid any supposed obligation if it clarified the terms and conditions on which it was prepared to offer service. Even so, the movement to give all persons a strong right to medical care in times of necessity quickly gained speed and resulted in the 1986 passage of the Emergency Medical Treatment and Active Labor Act (EMTALA), which in its simplest form requires a hospital to admit, regardless of ability to pay, all persons who arrive in its emergency room in active labor or in need of emergency medical treatment.[51] For such cases, a hospital has lost its power to decide whom to admit. Instead, it must treat a patient at institutional expense until he or she is stabilized so long as it has the necessary facilities. The stiff sanctions include, in addition to potential malpractice liability, suspension from Medicare and Medicaid programs which, for urban hospitals, constitute a substantial portion of total patient revenues.

Part and parcel with a covered institution's expanded basic obligation is that it no longer has any right to refuse treatment because of a patient's misconduct. It does not matter whether a patient has been treated on numerous occasions before, or at what expense or with what success; nor does it matter if the patient has voluntarily consumed drugs or alcohol; or misused or refused to take medications; or disregarded medical instructions about diet, exercise, or self-treatment.* The central feature of EMTALA is that the expanded right is treated as categorical and absolute: as totally non-forfeitable.

The repeated justification for so stringent a duty is that men and women in dire need will die if hospitals are allowed not to treat them.[53] The implicit assumption is that the only change EMTALA has made is to ensure treatment, as a matter of right, for persons who once could have been denied it. But that misses all sorts of destructive side effects of EMTALA. One major consequence is that the number of available facilities will diminish, as institutions close down or limit the intake from emergency rooms.[54]

Under the old common-law system, a hospital did not have to shrink the size of its emergency facilities to reduce its potential legal liability. Under the modern legal rules, it will do just that, even though that will result in less care for all. Hospitals are forced to cut out care to the deserving poor and their paying customers (not all of whom are rich) in order to fence out the high-risk cases that could spell their financial doom. No longer can a hospital ration care as it sees fit; now it must take patients in off the queue, regardless of their relative needs. In response, the other side tends to game playing. Nothing in the current law says that a needy patient must choose the hospital nearest to his or her home, and I have heard more than one hospital administrator state (with obvious discomfort and off the record) that pregnant women often wait, in cars or cabs, near a hospital with excellent high-risk obstetrical facilities until they go into active labor—with the delayed admission leading to increased medical complications.

In the absence of public reimbursement, this regime necessarily creates long-term financial trouble. Oftentimes the prenatal care has been spotty, and the medical records incomplete, in part because public coverage frequently offers only limited medical services before a patient finds herself in emergency straits. A pregnant woman thus maximizes her situation according to the discontinuous coverage available. In some cases, the discontinuous incentives could be broken by offering comprehensive free health care across the board, a decision likely to increase the demands for those services. Or alternatively, the level of subsidy offered in active labor is

---

* For example, in 1992 one federal appellate court held that the duty was owed to an agitated, nauseated, and confused patient, who was intoxicated from heavy drinking and failed to take her antipsychosis medication. The hospital escaped liability only because it conducted appropriate screening techniques.[52]

constrained, so as to increase a mother's incentive to take prenatal care at her own expense. As a system of mandatory public assistance struggles to find the right mix between routine and emergency care, it is hard to fault any public provider for failing to reach the ideal trade-off. But imposing on hospitals chosen by individual recipients the obligation for emergency care in active labor without compensation has long-term effects on these institutions everyone wishes to avoid: namely, driving them into insolvency; or forcing them to reduce or eliminate their emergency care facilities for paying and nonpaying patients alike.

Nor can a hospital withhold care in cases that it regards as futile or perverse. One notorious case under EMTALA, *Matter of Baby K* (1994),[55] required the hospital to provide extensive care on four separate occasions when a mother brought in her anencephalic infant for emergency care. The great tragedy of the statute lies not in the individual case that illustrates its absurdity, but in the long-term consequences of transferring operational control from the hospital, which pays the cost, to the government, which, as might be expected, refuses to pick up the tab for the care it mandates. The dramatic episodes that propelled the statute's passage have nothing to do with its operation. The current legal regime is a far cry indeed from the nineteenth-century one.

Welfare Rights

The modern system of welfare rights relies far more on state bureaucracy than on private initiative. The shift was made in large measure because it was thought that the uncoordinated activities of private organizations could not be counted on to guarantee support for those who need it. But the disadvantages of public institutions were easily overlooked. Unlike private organizations, state bureaucracies cannot draw on an army of volunteers, often motivated by a sense of religious zeal, to administer their programs. Governments must hire staff and contend with a complex matrix of hiring rules and union regulations that impede staff members' effective mobilization. And impersonal bureaucratic structures find it difficult to police the full range of substantive issues that caught the attention of the nineteenth-century charitable workers who operated closer to the ground. Yet state agencies also fear that large grants of discretion to individual field workers could easily lead to abuse in the administration of the laws: self-interested workers are harder to monitor than well-motivated volunteers. A public welfare system, struggling to find the right mix between predictability and flexibility, is likely to miss both. Matters of informal adjustment have, for example, led to judicial innovations that may well undercut the responsiveness of the system as a whole. For example, the Supreme Court's 1970 decision in *Goldberg v. Kelly*[56] imposed a constitutional requirement that all welfare recipients receive a hearing prior to the termination of their benefits. However fortunate for this individual recipient, the Court's decision is open to the powerful objection that it allows the wrong people to milk the system for too long, while needy applicants wait in line to receive necessary aid.[57]

This dubious expansion of constitutional rights is symptomatic of the mistaken world view that ignores the adverse incentive effects of legal programs on their intended beneficiaries. It is easy to establish the point that potential welfare recipients do not respond to changes in incentives with the rapidity found in financial markets. But it is a greater mistake to leap to the opposite conclusion that people down on their luck are oblivious to the set of rewards and punishments they face.

The literature on this subject is vast, but two general bodies of data establish the general point. The first measures the changes in the number of individuals below the poverty line in response to the upsurge in welfare support that began with the adoption of Lyndon Johnson's Great Society programs starting around 1965. The second looks at the changes in the size of the welfare rolls in response to (and in anticipation of) the 1996 welfare reform package, passed by a Republican Congress and signed into law by a Democratic President.

The basic figures on the size of the American welfare effort defy easy and comprehensive summary, but there are some baseline statistics.[58] Support increased slowly during the period between 1949 and 1965 (from around $20 billion to $40 billion in constant dollars). But during that period of relatively low growth, the poverty rate plummeted from nearly 35 percent of the population to around 15 percent. In the years since 1965, the annual spending has increased around eightfold (representing around $5.5 trillion cumulative expenditure);[59] yet the number of people below the poverty line, after another small initial drop in the late 1960s, increased: by the early 1990s, roughly the same percentage of persons remained below the poverty line as had in 1965.[60] Likewise, increases in welfare have been matched by increases in unwanted forms of individual behavior. From 1960 to 1994, a twelvefold increase in welfare support has been matched by a sixfold increase in illegitimate births, from just over 5 percent to around 32 percent.[61] The fears of the nineteenth-century moralists have come home to roost.

Perhaps these correlations can be explained away in part by the introduction of some magic third variable. But if so, it is very hard both to identify just what that variable is, and to explain why it should have such great influence on the observed patterns of behavior. Surely changes in social attitudes matter, but have they moved anywhere as fast as the changes in federal and state funding? Patterns of migration within the United States matter as well; but once again, they tell no consistent story. The greatest migrations from South to North took place just before and after the Second World War, but any resulting instability did not reflect itself in either poverty or illegitimacy rates. Perhaps these estimates overstate the present poverty or understate the systematic benefits of the welfare program, but the sheer magnitude of the gross shifts make it highly unlikely that any clever explanation can undercut these powerful, if depressing, correlations.

Redistribution of wealth is not the major consequence of the present transfer system: if it were, then the payments in question should have been sufficient to lift bodily above the poverty line most of those now below it. But the fact that the percentages of persons below the poverty line failed to fall, as the support has increased, has only one explanation: the persons in receipt of aid have found it less necessary to work in ways that generate income (at least, income that can be reported). As public support increased, private effort decreased, making for no movement in the overall rates of poverty. So even ignoring the negative effect that higher taxation rates have on the formation of wealth, clearly the expansion in welfare support strongly altered for the worse the behavioral incentives of the targeted population.

In the middle 1990s, the long-simmering political response to this overall deterioration resulted in an extensive set of reforms that sent the control of welfare back to the states.[62] The early returns from this program show how the poor do respond to incentives. A 1997 Jason DeParle story in the *New York Times* on the effects of the reform starts with this headline: "A Sharp Decrease in Welfare Cases Is Gathering Speed."[63] The contents confirm the headlines: The aggregate decline in the welfare rolls from March, 1994, to October, 1996, was around 18 percent, going from around 14,398,000 to 11,864,000. The three states that have been most "energetic" in insisting that welfare recipients take work—Indiana, Oregon, and Wisconsin—have all witnessed declines in welfare of more than 40 percent. Sixteen other states had drops of more than 25 percent, and only Hawaii (whose local economy is reeling from a self-induced depression) has shown any increase in welfare recipients. But perhaps the most revealing statement in the story is the speculation (borne out by the numbers) that "the prominence of last year's debate had already prompted people to look for work," *before* the passage of the Personal Responsibility and Work Opportunity Act.

Nor can the decline in the welfare rolls be explained away as a one-time response to the change in legal rules. According to a January 1998 report of the Department of Health and Human Services (HHS), the decline has accelerated: "In August 1997, the most recent month for which we have figures available, there were 9,995,000 people on welfare. That's a drop of more than 2.2 million since the welfare law was signed in August 1996. The number is at its lowest since February 1971, when it was 9,952,000,"[64] when the population base was smaller than today. That 10,000,000 person figure also represents a decline of 1.4 million people to August of 1997. From March 1994 to August 1997, there has been a 30-percent decline in welfare rolls, from 14.4 million to just under 10 million.

The current orthodox accounts of poverty cannot explain these swift and sustained responses. The quick private responses prior to the implementation of the 1996 reforms shows how incentives work on all individuals regardless of wealth; the consistent follow-through in the program reinforces that same conclusion. To be sure, some credit for the decline in welfare rolls goes to an improved economy; but the large variation in state-by-state responses suggests that most of the gain stems from the internal reforms of the welfare system. HHS attributes 40 percent of the 1997 reductions to a better economy, 30 percent to changes in federal and state welfare policies, and the rest to other factors.[65] But it seems odd to explain so much of the recent 12 percent drop in welfare rolls to a 3-percent growth in the gross domestic product. The observed data dovetail comfortably with the plain-vanilla economic view that most people, most of the time, respond to incentives. Tougher rules on eligibility by both private and public agencies do more to reduce dependence on welfare than do public exhortations.

The initial program remains subject to the political winds: one year later, the "workfare" component of the new welfare reform program was, after bitter controversy, made subject to the minimum-wage requirements of the Fair Labor Standards Act.[66] President Clinton achieved his goal of having all workfare recipients classified as "employees" entitled to receive at least the minimum wage, as well as other protections afforded under this act. Key Republican senators and state governors had balked, claiming that they could not create a sufficient number of jobs if constrained to pay the minimum wage. The debate, and its unhappy resolution, highlights the close linkage between minimum-wage and welfare laws. By far, the best solution is to eliminate the minimum-wage laws altogether, so as to remove the need to create some special exception to them. However, in a second-best world, the soundness of the exemption rests on the simple view that minimum-wage laws block the formation of new jobs and thus exacerbate the welfare problem. In dealing with these contentious issues, no one should be ashamed to argue that all individuals respond to these incentives. The source of shame lies in having to argue for a point that should be accepted as an accurate description of human affairs.

The traditional attitudes of forfeiture are justified today because they recognize that no individual, whatever his or her station in life, is immune to the forces of self-interest. The ideal of the legal system is not to cut individuals off from legal protection or social support because they have deviated from the basic rules of the system. It is to create a set of incentives that induces high compliance with the norms, and thus enables everyone to receive the full legal and social protections a modern society should be to able to supply to most, but never all, its members. The greatest danger to progress on this frontier is the comforting, but false, illusion that no one need ever be left behind. On forfeiture, as on so many other issues, the best should never become the enemy of the good.

CHAPTER 7

❖ ❖ ❖

Boundaries: Firm and Fuzzy

The right of an owner of property to exclude all others from his property is one of the most prized—and most feared—rights any civilization can confer on its members. From one point of view, a system that creates this right also allows individuals to harness their talents and to develop natural resources under their control, both to their maximum extent. But from another vantage point, the right to exclude is condemned as snobbish or nettlesome behavior that inconveniences or harms people left on the outside looking in. Standard libertarian theory tends to resolve this conflict in an all-or-nothing fashion—in favor of the principle of exclusion. Robert Nozick, the most famous modern philosophical defender of libertarian principles (at least, before his recent conversion), has stressed the centrality of boundaries, noting that duties of rectification are triggered by "boundary crossings," whereby one person invades the space of another.[1]

Nozick shrewdly recognized that uncertainty often makes it difficult in practice to grant boundary lines the pride of place they receive in theory. All sorts of actions may result in some boundary crossing; and for them, sometimes the best that can be done is to pay compensation after the fact.[2] But any preoccupation with explicit compensation misses how boundaries are often not rigid, but semipermeable. As becomes clear in dealing with the protection both of the person and of property, compensation for boundary crossings often comes not in cash or its equivalents, but rather *in kind*, as in the right to commit *like* invasions of the person or property of another.

So understood, the problem of choosing and using boundaries arises in all areas of human interaction. This chapter thus begins with a discussion of the role of boundaries in the separation of persons. It then moves on to consider the role of boundaries in organizing a system of property rights in land as this relates to both trespass cases (featuring direct entry into the property of another) and nuisance cases (featuring nontrespassory disturbances and annoyances that fall short of entry). Thereafter, the story branches out to explore how boundaries operate with new resources, such as the spectrum. While, in all these settings, the sharpness of boundaries may become fuzzy, the boundaries themselves never disappear.

BOUNDARIES OF SELF

For human beings, the boundary starts and ends with the body, and that boundary is crossed by the least touching of another person. But the sanctity of this boundary is not as absolute as libertarian theory sometimes suggests. As often happens in the law, a legal rule invites exceptions, which here are clustered under the general doctrine of "privilege." Accidental contact in crowded places and friendly touchings are protected by a general privilege which, while akin to consent, is somewhat separate from it. These interactions are so frequent, and so minor, that it is to the mutual advantage of all to allow them to proceed without hindrance. Since the number of persons involved in these comprehensive exchanges is too large for voluntary transactions, customary practices fill the gap. It is only when conduct becomes malicious or the damages become severe that the privilege ebbs away, and we start to think in terms of tort remedies for physical invasion. The boundaries that set the line between persons are presumptive. The exceptions to the rule are not arbitrarily chosen but are consistent with the basic object of the rule itself, which is to ensure the maximum level of freedom of action consistent with the like freedom of others. The conventions here are strong; and regardless of background and circumstance, we all understand the rule that requires us to respect the "space" of others, even though no visible fences do, or could, mark the boundary between persons.

BOUNDARIES OF LAND

The question of boundaries, and of fences, arises in more conventional terms with land, where once again the social response is more nuanced than a stout libertarian approach might suggest. Robert Frost's famous line from "Mending Wall"—"Good fences make good neighbors"—makes for an ironic twist. The narrator (who reports, but does not endorse, this flinty observation) does not doubt the importance of boundaries; he only suggests that sometimes it is both costly and unnecessary to mark them with a fence. Yet at the same time the idea of neighbors is possible only if we accept the idea of having boundaries between separate plots of land. To insist otherwise is to demand that we all live in one large commons where everyone is forced to become partners with everyone else.

The disadvantages of such an all-inclusive commons seem evident enough: no amount of deliberation or participation could allow everyone, or even large groups of strangers thrown together, to live happily under a single roof. The variation in temperaments and tastes is just too great. A little community and a little participation might be a good thing; and the same is true with a little bit of common property (as discussed further in chapter 9). But too much of a good thing turns out to be a bad thing, and the simple and most profound sentiment that drives us in the direction of private property is that we would all prefer to have more neighbors and fewer partners in this world.

This basic preference in favor of private property does not necessarily mean that everyone wants to live in a private fortress, or that we ignore the communitarian values of participation and deliberation about the common good. The use of privately created common areas—lobbies, elevators, hallways, gardens, play areas—in condominiums and apartment houses shows that the desired equilibrium position does not make all space private for single persons. Rather, by separating individuals into smaller groups, private property introduces a greater measure of agreement into the deliberations that remain: it is easier for each family or group to make decisions on its side of the boundary than to have common property for all families and groups together. The simple act of division reduces the stress on the decision-making procedures internal to both groups. It is in this felt need to break down the tyranny and clumsiness of vast collective decisions that private property has its origins.

Only by drawing boundaries and creating separate spaces is it possible to organize a system of private property. The creation of boundaries confers benefits on those who are given some exclusivity, and imposes costs on those who are excluded. To simply tally these gains and losses from any individual trespass, however, is quite beside the point. The question is whether we can find some systematic advantage to a rule that treats the boundary as irrelevant in all cases, and we cannot. The ability to plan and to plant depends on secure property rights that allow those who sow to reap. Good relations between neighbors thus requires guarding these boundaries lest one person be overrun by another. But, by the same token, good relations between neighbors are easily thwarted when boundaries are made rigid and inflexible in any and all circumstances. The best way to approach a boundary is to endow it with a certain presumptive validity, and then to identify the circumstances in which its strictness can be relaxed to the mutual advantage of the parties on both sides of the line. Paradoxically, a world with semipermeable boundaries can strengthen the institution of private property.

To show how this problem sorts itself out, I shall focus first on conflicts between neighboring landowners, and identify some of the diverse situations where the limited relaxation of the boundary works in general to the benefit of both neighbors: agricultural boundaries, nuisance rules, lateral support, spite fences, and solar easements. Afterward I shall turn to the role of boundaries in other, more modern contexts.

Agricultural Boundaries

The first example comes from a simple agricultural practice. In medieval times, when fields were plowed, a nonproductive space at the end of a field was needed to allow the plow to turn around. The simple solution was to plant in long thin strips, so as to reduce the ratio of unusable to usable land. But such a solution depends neither in whole nor in part on cooperation between neighbors, and the question was whether neighbors could do better by agreement (or by custom) if they deviated from a pure system of private property to a system that contained elements of common property. And it turned out that, at the boundary, they could. If the two parties shared a common area (just for two) for turning the plow at the end of each strip of land, they could reduce the amount of wasted space by 50 percent. It still had to be determined where that common strip should be situated. At first blush, there seemed no reason not to place it all on the land of one party and have both use it. But the burdens would not be distributed quite evenly between the parties, and the designated loser might ask, Why put up with the inconvenience with nothing to show for it? In circumstances like these, the tendency is to split the turning strip equally between the two neighbors, so that each gains half of the surplus. Or if the situation does not quite permit that, some possible side payment between the parties might equalize the financial burdens from an uneven physical division.

Nor is only simple equity at stake. Like many homespun conventions, this one also reveals a deeper economic logic that explains why it (like other rules that "split the difference") tends to endure, as noted in chapter 5 in the practice of reciprocal giving. To the extent that this settled rule divides the surplus, it reduces the possibility that one side or the other will defect unilaterally from a solution that serves both well. And to the extent that you have a clear point of reference—an even division at the boundary—a broad custom in agricultural regions is more likely to emerge if no one has to figure out time and time again why sharing at the border advances their joint welfare. To be sure, this solution will not work everywhere: fences are needed when cattle and other animals are the source of both value and conflict—unless the parties think that one large meadow is better than two small ones, as they often do. And then the common area will work only if the two neighbors admit cattle into the commons in rough proportion to their respective shares of usable land.

The limited commons in open fields, moreover, has its direct parallel in the law of takings and eminent domain. Often a critical issue for a farming community was the location of a road to take goods to market. Place it anywhere along the boundary line between two neighbors and each can have access to it from his own land. A rule that says that they contribute the land evenly, without compensation, leaves both net winners when the value of the lands retained by each is increased by the greater access to markets. So a legal principle that calls for both neighbors to contribute a like amount of land (or make side payments when their contribution is less than half) has the same virtues of stabilization found in the old farming custom: it reduces the incentive for parties to push the road over to the neighbor's land.

Nuisance Cases

Deviation from strict boundaries is not confined to situations where land is used in common. It is evident to all observers that the law of trespass has a harder edge (at the boundary) than the law of nuisance,[3] which, roughly speaking, governs those invasions that do not involve actual entry onto the land of another person. In dealing with these physical invasions that fall short of actual entry, we can identify a number of situations (and not only in specifically agricultural settings) where the relaxation of the strict boundary crossing rules can generate substantial gains to both sides.[4]

The most famous illustration of this principle is the so-called rule of "live and let live," which says that all individuals have to put up with a certain amount of noise and interference from their neighbors, on condition that the neighbors reciprocate in kind. This was the fact pattern that Nozick missed, and the explanation for this result was put forward in unmistakable terms in 1863 by Baron George Bramwell in *Bamford v. Turnley:*

There is an obvious necessity for such a principle as I have mentioned. It is as much for the advantage of one owner as of another for the very nuisance the one complains of, as the result of the ordinary use of his neighbour's land, he himself will create in the ordinary use of his own, and the reciprocal nuisances are of a comparatively trifling character. The convenience of such a rule may be indicated by calling it a rule of give and take, live and let live. . . .

The public consists of all the individuals of it, and a thing is only for the public benefit when it is productive of good to those individuals on the balance of loss and gain to all. So that if all the loss and all the gain were borne and received by one individual, he on the whole would be the gainer. But whenever this is the case,—whenever a thing is for the public benefit, properly understood,—the loss to the individuals of the public who lose will bear compensation out of the gains of those who gain. It is for the public benefit there should be railways, but it would not be unless the gain of having the railway was sufficient to compensate the loss occasioned by the use of the land required for its site; and accordingly no one thinks it would be right to take an individual's land without compensation to make a railway.[5]

This obscure nuisance decision provides considerable insight into reciprocal injuries at the boundary.[6] First, Bramwell makes a clear and powerful statement of the central analytical role of methodological individualism: there is no disembodied public interest as such, but only a large and complex set of private interests held by each individual in accordance with a set of values and preferences that others might not share. Owing to that diversity of views, there is no shortcut for determining the public interest by appealing to some attractive moral alternative that only a minority of the population might embrace, or to some unsavory proposal that regrettably commands the assent of a majority of the population. Only by netting out the private gains and losses is it possible (if it is possible at all) to locate that elusive public interest. The proposed change is welcome if one person who owns all the relevant resources will be satisfied by the change in position— that is, would pronounce himself a gainer.

Second, Bramwell emphasizes the importance of the Paretian criterion of social welfare, based on the simultaneous improvement of all individuals in the relevant group. Indeed, this opinion is prescient in that it identifies the most rigorous definition of economic efficiency well before the economists were able to formulate the same test.

Third, Bramwell's opinion is noteworthy for its articulation of the intimate connection between the private law of nuisance and the public law of eminent domain. Where some parties win and others lose, the payment of compensation is one method that allows the transaction to go forward while equalizing the burden among parties. Yet by the same token, no compensation is needed in cash when it is supplied *in kind* under some general rule, such as "live and let live," which by and large benefits and burdens all alike. But that result flips over when the damage by way of invasion runs all in one direction, as when sparks from a train destroy the crops of a nearby farmer. Compensation is now required, both to equalize the burdens, and to give the railroad an incentive for efficient behavior.

Within this general framework, Baron Bramwell identified those situations between neighbors where the relaxation of the strict boundary conditions is likely to work to mutual advantage without the payment of compensation. These imitate, in a more complex setting, the same kinds of deviations from strict boundary conditions that have proved critical in dealing with physical invasions of the person, where accidental touchings were excised from the legal system as a matter of law. Minor invasions done without malice are removed en masse from the legal system. Stated otherwise, there is little sense in suspending the ordinary legal rules when malice is involved: almost by definition, malicious conduct is intended to cause harm that is valued for its own sake, and not for any collateral benefit it might generate. There would be no sense in creating a privilege for the person who bangs pots on a party wall in order to keep his neighbor up late at night. It is, as the common legal definition states, harm inflicted "without any just cause or excuse," thereby ruling out such moderating elements as self-defense or honest mistake. In cases of physical injury, the presence of malice ordinarily solidifies a case for recovering compensatory damages, and opens up the possibility of punitive damages. Malice gives a good reason for not relaxing liability for boundary crossings. Likewise, since substantial harms are not likely to cancel out each other over the long run, the usual presumption requiring one party to take into account the costs inflicted on another applies without skipping a beat.

The most common cases of physical interaction between neighbors are low-level interactions that are the inevitable byproducts of routine human activities. And, once again, a set of customary practices paves the way to grasping a sensible legal rule. Yet unlike the cases of plowing at the boundary lines, we cannot be confident that the parties will be able to generate the best solutions consensually if left to their own devices. Huge numbers of landowners live in close proximity to one another; none of these can simply pick up stakes in order to avoid nasty interactions at the boundary. Some neighbors, at least, will yield to the temptation to act strategically if boundary lines are given absolute respect. They are in a position to demand compensation—or, worse, to seek injunctions of useful activities—for trivial invasions of their space. Even in the best of all worlds, it would cost money, and impose impediments and encumbrances on legal title, to negotiate thousands of transactions to reach the position where "live and let live" places us from the outset. In this setting, relaxing the sharp boundary makes perfectly good sense; and the relaxation should come in the only way possible, as matter of law.

To be sure, the rule in question may not be perfect for all individuals; but on this question at least the aggregation of individual preferences should not pose any undue difficulty. It can be taken as given that most individuals will experience some differences in tastes, but only to the extent that they value quiet over noise and clean air over fumes. Since the levels of intrusion are low, their differences in sensitivity are likely to be low as well. The reciprocal nature of the gains and losses make it likely that most individuals will benefit from the increased liberty of action more than they will suffer from the additional disruption in their daily lives, perhaps not with each individual interaction, but surely when we take an expansive view of the subject over the long haul. Some extrasensitive individuals might find themselves in neighborhoods with levels of pollution higher than they can comfortably tolerate. Although we might wish to lower those average levels of air pollution, we should not make our targets so ambitious as to spend millions of dollars to abolish noise or smells altogether. At some point, it is easier for sensitive individuals to move away from certain locales than to remove the last bit of air or water pollution for their benefit. Their compensation comes in the higher prices they can obtain by selling their holdings to some newcomer who stands to profit on net from the adjusted baseline that permits higher pollution levels in a particular neighborhood. The basic locality rule at common law, applied to certain industrial districts, has just that effect.[7] More reciprocal harm is tolerated, and those individuals who lose from these interactions can sell their properties (with the regional benefits intact) and move to other neighborhoods where the background noise or pollution is less. Some degree of population sorting works better than the hopeless task of abandoning useful activity for a blissful but unattainable quiet and solitude.

We need both bustling cities and quiet countrysides, and no legal policy should seek to convert either one into the other.

Although the relaxation of boundary conditions in these live-and-let-live cases could be mistaken for a preference of tort arrangements over contract, or for public regulation over private ordering, it is neither. The rules here are designed to allow strangers to live in peace and harmony with each other. They are not designed to force any association between individuals: The rules that keep unwanted strangers from the doorstep remain utterly untouched. Nor does this approach preclude any correction by voluntary arrangement between private parties if they think that relaxation of the boundary condition is too great or, for that matter, not great enough. Thus, in the effort to set boundaries between strangers, we should not forget that many individuals come together by agreement, if not with each other, then indirectly, through the intervention of a common landlord or developer. By inserting covenants into leases and deeds, that developer could set the boundary conditions in whatever ways are thought fit for a new community of tenants or buyers, as the case may be. Certain individuals may desire high levels of peace and quiet; and, if so, a landlord or developer is able to cater to their tastes. Or in some cases, a more articulated social convention could grow within a community: considerable noise could be tolerated during the daylight and evening hours, and relatively strict standards of silence demanded during the sleeping hours.

These rules have staying power; for example, even when the planned communities have the opportunity to back off the live-and-let-live rules, they don't. Their persistence in subdivisions furnishes a strong clue to why they function as good public default rules when transaction costs block voluntary transactions between neighbors: they provide reliable evidence about what other persons would have agreed to if they could have voluntarily transacted. But live-and-let-live operates only as a *default* rule. The state has little reason to impose this norm of reasonableness (or, indeed, any other) on groups that have fashioned other standards for themselves. After all, those individuals who do not like the rules of one association are free to move to any other. So long as that exit right is intact, dissenters should not be allowed unilaterally to impose the reciprocal interferences they prefer on others who disagree with them. This sorting of individuals into smaller and more homogenous groups reduces internal disagreements and thus the stress that bitter disputes might otherwise place on their common governance structures. Explicit agreements should displace background legal or social norms no matter what their content.

Lateral Support

The live-and-let-live rule relaxes boundary conditions by refusing to impose liability for certain low-level boundary crossings. Those boundary conditions may also be relaxed in reverse, so as to make wrongful *non*invasive conduct adjacent to the boundary line. Once again, a nineteenth-century English judge—George Jessel—stated the rule clearly and forcefully:[8] each landowner owes a duty of lateral support for the land of his neighbor. In effect, the rule creates by operation of law a reciprocal negative easement: reciprocal, because it works in favor of all against all; and negative, because the easement does not involve any invasion of another person's land.

The logic of the basic rule again stresses mutual advantage to all neighbors. The obvious danger is that if each neighbor digs out his land to the boundary, then the neighboring land will subside. As a rough empirical generalization, each is better off with the protection against disruption than with the right to disrupt. By operation of law, the right of lateral support makes that the default position for all. This situation becomes more complicated, for it would be a mistake to allow people to build close by the boundary and then claim the easement of support for structures added on. That rule would give a strong incentive to build first in order to perfect support rights against one's neighbor. It is always dangerous to create rights on a "use it or lose it basis," since that rule encourages premature development solely to gain rights against neighbors when a single owner of both plots would choose to defer construction until both projects were intrinsically profitable. To counter that risk, the unconditional obligation of lateral support was wisely confined to land in its original state. For the support of pre-existing structures, however, a lesser obligation was imposed: the builder had to give *notice* to the other owner in time to allow him either to shore up his own support before the first neighbor began construction, or to negotiate the purchase of rights of support. Taken together, these rules create a set of incentives that facilitate the orderly development of land by denying both sides any chance for gain by building too soon or, for that matter, too late. Since each party is allowed to choose the time at which it starts development, the lateral support rules are designed to make each party's return from investment independent of the time that construction begins.

The system, moreover, only operates in a presumptive fashion. The owner of a single plot of land can alter these reciprocal obligations at the time of subdivision. Between strangers, contracts binding both plots of land can be created that alter the rules in one direction or another before anyone begins construction. The builder of a large skyscraper can therefore obtain by contract the right to lateral support if that proves convenient or desirable, a negotiation done much more easily before construction commences than once the building is in place. But in those cases where the support for a single parcel of land comes from land owned by many different parties, the legal creation of rights of lateral support mercifully dispenses with at least one round of complex negotiation. The rule itself may not be perfect, but that is hardly the point: it works on average better than the strict boundary conditions sometimes associated with the law of property.

Spite Fences

Other forms of noninvasive conduct also alter the hard-and-fast nature of boundaries at common law. Thus, the element of malice that proves important under the live-and-let-live rule also comes back to deal with a hardy perennial of the common law: the spite fence. The situation is easy to envision. Two neighbors get into a squabble with each other. Their deepening animosity leads one, or perhaps both, to take steps from which their only gain stems from the ability to inflict inconvenience on the hapless neighbor. Various forms of physical invasion are already prohibited, and, for these malice aforethought only magnifies the recoverable damages from trespass. But individuals routinely build fences for privacy at the boundary line, even if they interfere with the view and light of their neighbor. Why, it might be asked, does that conduct become wrongful when the same fence, with the same consequences, is built solely out of malice? Stated more generally, why does malice make unlawful an action (building a high fence) that does not constitute a boundary crossing?

The answer to that question can be found only by examining the situation from the ex-ante perspective (before the dispute unfolds). Ex-ante each neighbor would be better off if he could find a way to stop those tactics of mutually assured destruction before they began. In response, the rule about spite fences allows one neighbor to enjoin the construction of a neighbor's fence if it is being constructed only for reasons of spite. As with the live-and-let-live cases, the compensation each party receives comes not in cash, but from the like restrictions imposed on neighbors. But, as with the live-and-let-live cases, certain key limitations have to be observed in order to have the rule make sense. Thus, the general rule is not applicable to persons who build what might be called "spite houses," which are buildings with some intrinsic use of their own. The basic intuition is that no one would spend large sums of money on a spite house. So rather than risk formulating a rule that cuts too deeply, it is better to settle for one that might not cut quite deep enough.

As with so many common-law rules, the legal dispute over spite fences spilled over into the law of takings through the important 1889 decision of Justice Holmes in *Rideout v. Knox*.[9] That case upheld a Massachusetts statute that declared "any fence unnecessarily exceeding six feet in height, maliciously erected or maintained for the purpose of annoying the owners of adjoining property" to be a private nuisance, even though it did not constitute a physical invasion. Although Holmes's instincts were sound, his reasoning left something to be desired. Initially, he noted that a universal rule that treated all buildings erected with malice as private nuisances cut far too broadly, and put virtually all construction at the whim of a jury. But he did not allow the same objection to carry the day against a fence even though the difference between the two cases was in his view "only one of degree," as "[m]ost differences are, when nicely analyzed."[10]

Curiously, the Massachusetts statute does a better job than Holmes's resigned validation of it might suggest. The right question asks what happens to the *sum* of the value of the two parcels under different legal regimes. Use the malice rule for spite houses, and, ex ante, the value of both parcels plummets; confine that rule to fences over six feet high, and the combined value of both plots increases. The six-foot safe harbor zone under the statute is not just a matter of degree or the choice of an arbitrary number. Rather, it conforms to the height of the ordinary solid fence, which good neighbors choose for two reasons. First, to secure privacy from neighbors and passers-by, who cannot see over the fence unless they jump or climb to do so—both actions in conscious violation of privacy, on which more later. Second, to allow a maximum amount of light and air to enter the premises. That consensually chosen baseline is thus used to create a statutory safe harbor sufficient to protect the perceived interests of most landowners in both privacy and light.

The risky inquiry is therefore only undertaken with respect to fences that deviate from the ordinary where the owner can still give reasons why the higher fence is necessary, putting on him the burden of explaining away the increased height. The constrained nature of this inquiry thus helps ensure the reciprocal nature of the advantage. The rule meets constitutional standards because we can advance specific reasons to show why this deviation from the sharp common-law boundaries helps maximize the joint value of the neighboring plots of land. Simply dismissing these fine differences as matters of degree ignores the role of common practice in evaluating the economic impact of other enactments, including some that cut more deeply, and more mischievously, into the traditional prerogatives of ownership. Indeed, thirty-two years later opinion in *Pennsylvania Coal v. Mahon*,[11] addressed the limits of the state power to regulate the use of land Holmes relied on *Rideout*. Unfortunately, the best test he could devise announced that when state action goes "too far," it crosses some magical constitutional line. His confusion on private law matters reduced points of high constitutional principle to matters of degree.

Easements for Light and Air

Yet in all this confusion, one might want to ask, why the preoccupation with malice at all? Suppose that the rule in question simply prohibited the construction of all fences over six feet in height—period. Now the law would cut deeper into the ordinary prerogatives of ownership, but that restriction just might be justified, given that it increases the light and air received by other landowners. Of course, owners who wish to build higher might still enter into agreements with their neighbors. But their efforts to coordinate with many separate owners could well prove costly and unsuccessful. After all, the earlier English common law offers some evidence that easements of light and air were part and parcel of the ordinary bundle of property rights that each neighbor enjoyed against the others. Although that rule would cause relatively little inconvenience in rural settings where buildings were placed far apart, it would place an impossible crimp on building within cities. Let one individual build his house, and all others will now be prevented from making like use of their land. If this argument is accepted, then easements of light and air could achieve the very result that was forestalled in dealing with lateral support: one neighbor could acquire additional rights against his fellows by prompt construction that cuts off their like rights.

In a society where the rights of neighbors are equal, this result will quickly prove untenable. Let this sequence start even once, and the next landowner who tries to build will be greeted with a suit demanding injunctive relief: your building is a nuisance because it prevents me from building a similar structure given the protection you seek for light and air. Any response that the injunction should be denied because no physical invasion has occurred is sadly misplaced in this peculiar intellectual universe: after all, the incipient builder is poised to block other new construction even though it does not constitute a physical invasion of his own property. So parity can be maintained between landowners only when *neither* builds at all—an outcome hardly calculated to maximize the joint value of both plots of land.

Historically, therefore, the English doctrine of "ancient lights" developed in a fashion that provided for the first owner to build protection against new construction that blocked his light, but only if his air and light remained undisturbed for a long period of time. Unfortunately, that rule encourages neighbors to build fences that block the light and air of their neighbors, not out of malice but to preserve valuable rights of construction for future use. This self-help remedy requires the neighbor to pay for an unneeded fence that gratuitously and prematurely blocks the neighbor's light and air. It is no wonder that the doctrine of ancient lights rarely, if ever, surfaced in the United States and has generally disappeared in England.

The dominant rule, then, confers an easement of light or air against a neighbor on no landowner. That rule received its most dramatic confirmation in a 1959 Florida case, *Fontainebleau Hotel Corp. v. Forty-Five Twenty-Five, Inc.*[12] The owners of the Fontainebleau Hotel on Miami Beach were allowed to construct a four-story addition that cast a giant shadow in the afternoon over the swimming area of the Eden Roc Hotel immediately to its north. While the court's decision may look odd after the fact, four points help place it in context. First, the location of the Eden Roc's pool was not chosen by chance: it was constructed on the southern portion of its own lot so as to escape the shadow of its own hotel. Second, the Eden Roc, which sought protection from the south, was quite willing for its shadow to be cast over lands to its north, come what may. Third, the relative values were such that the revenue gains (and customer satisfaction) from the Fontainebleau addition probably far outweighed any loss of afternoon amenities at the Eden Roc, given that the loss of sunlight was at most partial. Why try to tailor a special rule for beachfront hotels without powerful justification? And, fourth, the Eden Roc was still in a position to purchase protection from the Fontainebleau for a price. To be sure, the transaction costs could be tricky, but no trickier than those that would require the Fontainebleau to purchase the rights needed for construction if this case had come out the other way. Why encourage a lawsuit to set the stage for renegotiation, when negotiation is already possible?

In urban settings, courts from time to time have been asked to re-create the easement of light and air for the benefit of an incumbent landowner *after* his construction was completed. Even those courts that reject the hard-line approach of *Fontainebleau*—one that categorically denies any easements for light and air—have usually resisted any departure from its principles in urban settings. Thus, in 1985, in one New Hampshire case, *Tenn v. 889 Associates, Ltd.,*[13] the court recognized the possibility of creating an easement of light and air, but refused to do so for the benefit of the urban plaintiff who had built his six-story office building up to the property line and sought to use his conduct to deny the defendant the same privilege. The parity of use between neighbors should be preserved regardless of who builds first. The landowner who wants to preserve light and air can build back from the line to preserve that open space.

Nor do changes in technology justify a change in the underlying structure of property rights in this context. The static conception of property rights does quite well in dealing with claims to easements of light that allow the operator of solar collectors to gain southern light from over a neighbor's land. In *Prah v. Maretti* in 1982,[14] the Wisconsin Supreme Court held that in light of this technology an "unreasonable obstruction of access to sunlight might be a private nuisance." Unfortunately, its reasons for so doing were remarkably unpersuasive. It first noted the general trend of increased land-use regulation in the name of the general welfare, but did not demonstrate why or how such regulation achieved that stated end. Second, it argued that solar easements are entitled to greater respect when created to gather solar energy than to advance aesthetic interests, as though there were some abstract lexical ordering between the two: but surely some aesthetic easements are worth far more than many solar ones. Third, it noted that society has an interest in the development of alternative sources of energy, which is fair enough, but hardly explains why that interest requires the creation of any implicit subsidy instead of, say, a removal of regulatory barriers on the production or distribution of other energy sources.

Most important, the Wisconsin court misperceived the type of situation it was in. It thought that the case had to be resolved as one between strangers, and so failed to appreciate the ability of the subdivision developer to make rules to resolve boundary disputes for prospective purchasers in advance. The preservation of light required the owner of a southern lot to abandon construction on the northern half of his lot. If the value of the easement were sufficiently great, then the developer could do better financially by imposing a covenant on each lot for the benefit of the lot to the immediate north. The developer's failure to take that step was strong evidence of a considered initial judgment that the construction rights were worth more than any competing claim to light. Even if this prospect were overlooked at the time of separation, or became realistic only after the subdivision was complete, a better solution would be to correct—on a case-by-case basis, if needed—the original allocation by a private covenant that runs with the land. The rarity of these arrangements is reasonably good evidence that the value sacrificed by the subservient landowner is greater than the value received by the dominant one. As that is the case, the hard-and-fast rule at the boundary on matters of light and air remains the appropriate line of division.

COMING TO THE NUISANCE

The next relaxation of the boundary conditions is more complex because it rolls the dimensions of time and space into a single legal problem. When the Nobel-laureate Ronald Coase wrote about the problem of social cost in his classic 1960 essay,[15] he illustrated it with the celebrated 1879 case of *Sturges v. Bridgman*,[16] which involved a dispute at the boundary between a physician and a druggist. The druggist had long made up his compounds in the back of his shop without inconveniencing anyone. But when the physician, who had recently moved next door, decided to construct a new examining room at the rear of his premises, the noise the druggist made at work, long harmlessly dissipated, now became a substantial nuisance to his new neighbor. The question was whether the physician could recover damages for his inconvenience and obtain, in addition, an injunction against a continuation of the druggist's long-established practice.

Coase used this case chiefly to show that no matter which way the original right was assigned, the party who valued its use more highly would end up having it. If the druggist had the right and valued it more, he would keep it; if not, he could sell it to the physician. The same result worked in reverse. If the physician had the right and valued it more, then he could keep it; if not, then he could sell it to the druggist. To Coase, the basic point was that the initial distribution of rights did not determine the ultimate use of property—at least, if transaction costs were low enough to permit voluntary exchanges.

The case has continued to exert a hold over the legal imagination. Recently Brian Simpson wrote an extended essay on the social history of the case,[17] which provoked a tart reply from Coase himself on some of the broader implications of the case.[18] Simpson's research revealed a pattern of broken negotiations and disappointed maneuvers that dogged this unhappy lawsuit to its bumpy conclusion. Here the easiest way to understand the case is to ask simply: Has the plaintiff made out a prima-facie case of nuisance? Recall that for better peace between neighbors the presumptive definition of a nuisance is a nontrespassory invasion (that is, no personal entry into a neighbor's land) that results in visible inconvenience to the affairs of a neighbor. If the question of time does not enter into the equation at this level, it seems clear that the physician thus far has the whip hand in the negotiations, since the noise came from the druggist's operations and not from his. But every good prima-facie case opens up the possibility of some suitable justification or excuse. The defense that seems ideally tailored for this occasion is for the plaintiff to assume the risk of the injury by, as is customarily said, "coming to the nuisance." That defense would be easily established if for some reason the physician had built his examining room on the defendant's land. But fortunately for the world of legal paradoxes, this entire case gains its difficulty and notoriety precisely because the plaintiff had remained a good neighbor by not crossing over the boundary line. A second defense that could be raised in this context is the statute of limitations, which the defendant would claim started to run from the time that he began his own activities. The defendant in *Sturges* pleaded it—but to no avail, for reasons that will become clear.

The usual judicial resolution of this drama allows the plaintiff to win, and thus puts on the defendant the obligation to purchase any needed property interest in order to continue with his business. But why should this be the case given the twin defenses of assumption of risk and the statute of limitations? In order to answer this question, recall from the discussion on easements, both of lateral support and of light and air that one objective of the legal system is to prevent one party from making a pre-emptive strike by developing his own land to gain some permanent legal advantage over his more dilatory neighbor. Stated otherwise, the objective is to try to imagine how the case would be decided if both parties changed their patterns of land use simultaneously, even when it is manifest that they did not.

In order to execute that program in this context, think back to assess what options were open to the physician the moment the druggist began to operate his noisy business. If the physician knew that subsequently the druggist's original activities could end up creating an easement to make noise indefinitely, then the physician would be worse off by doing nothing than by immediately bringing suit to protect his legal position. After all, by hypothesis, if the two activities started at the same time, he could have prevailed in his action for injunction and damages. So the only way he could stop the creation by prescription of an easement to cause damages would be to sue the druggist promptly.

The prospect of that lawsuit raises the query: to whose benefit? It hardly would have helped the physician to have to act early to protect his rights. And it certainly would not have helped the druggist to be shut down.

Why precipitate a conflict over future legal rights when there is no present inconvenience to daily activities, notwithstanding the admitted transmission of noises across the boundary line? So it is clearly desirable to avoid the early suit.

One way to do so is to have the two parties negotiate some sort of stand-still agreement. That option, however, is costly and holds open the possibility that the physician might demand in payment for his release of rights a good deal more than his anticipated harm. These negotiation problems become still more intractable if a defendant's activity extends noise and vibration across the unoccupied lands of many individuals. So the law uses its own devices to create an all-purpose bargain of its own. The plaintiff is instructed, firmly but politely, that he cannot sue today; and the defendant is told that he cannot plead the statute of limitations tomorrow by claiming in retrospect that the harm "really" started when he, the defendant, commenced his operations. It thus becomes clear why Judge Jessel held that the statute of limitations only began to run when the plaintiff suffered actual interference with his use of the property: to make sure that the suit could not begin too early or be barred for coming too late. The resulting bargain does not have the easy symmetry found in the simultaneous activities subject to the live-and-let-live rule; nor does it contemplate the parity of position found in the rule on lateral support. But its basic logic is the same: the law forces an exchange between the parties for the benefit of both.

The success of this engineered deal yields immediate dividends: the druggist can use the land as he pleases right now. As time progresses, this judicial accommodation could prove doubly successful if the potential conflict between neighbors never ripens into an actual one. (The physician never builds the examining room close to the party wall, or the druggist sells to a new owner who abandons the older noisy practice when the neighborhood becomes more fashionable.) Under this scenario, the postponement of the legal dispute works its magic at both the front and the back ends; and one would guess that for either or both of the reasons just mentioned, just this outcome is likely.

Alas, some cases do not sort themselves out so neatly: sometimes the postponed conflict cannot be avoided altogether. Now we have the physician who exercises the right to examine close to the boundary. If we took a snapshot of the transaction—or, as economists like to say, treated it as a one-period problem—we might be tempted to say that the party who is last to arrive is the one who stirs up the dust. The temptation would be to create a kind of prescriptive right for the druggist based on unopposed long use. But once we recall the structure of the legal agreement imposed at an earlier time, we cannot adopt so limited a perspective on the problem. Now we are in payback time: the physician can exercise his right, and the druggist has to give way. The only help the druggist receives from the court is a bit of time to get his belongings in order, so as to minimize the risk of any sudden disruption. But since the physician will usually know his plans in advance, he can, before his facilities are completed, give notice to the druggist so that adjustments can be made before any conflict arises.

This result is found in most of the case law,[19] and for reasons that extend beyond exotic boundary line disputes between druggists and physicians. The typical example involves an established piggery or mining operation that was set up far removed from thickly populated areas. When new neighbors move in, as they so often do, the courts have rebelled against the prospect of an entire region's being held hostage to the activities of a single landowner: it "would preclude development and fix a city forever in its primitive conditions."[20] The judicial solution has been to carry over the approach in boundary disputes to large social contexts.

Characteristically perhaps, academic commentators have been uneasy with the result. A 1972 article proposed the following liability rule: "of two incompatible land uses the one which had but did not take the opportunity to avoid creating costs of incompatibility should bear the costs."[21] This rule does not, however, pinpoint the time when this measurement should be made, and thus overlooks the key dynamic element. For its part, the Restatement of Torts equivocates on this issue, by offering this evaluation of the assumption of risk defense: "The fact that the plaintiff has acquired or improved his land after a nuisance interfering with it has come into existence is not in itself sufficient to bar his action, but is a factor to be considered in determining whether the nuisance is actionable."[22] Unfortunately, the statement gives no idea as to the form of the analysis, much less any explanation why it is apparently nodding in favor of the first to build and improve. Taking the middle course is not always a sign of wisdom or compromise; in this case, moderation makes the Restatement look like some rudderless collective enterprise. Given what has been said, the overall sense of the legal deal should be clear enough after it is set out. It is possible to reconcile the conflicting time and space in land-use disputes by focusing on the fundamentals of a dispute.

That reconciliation, moreover, is not good solely for localized private disputes. As is the case in many areas of the law, an accurate ability to resolve private disputes is a precondition for negotiating analogous public issues. In

Hadacheck v. Sebastian,[23] the question before the Supreme Court was whether the City of Los Angeles was within its rights to order the shutdown of a brickyard that lay in the path of urban development. If it turned out that none of the neighbors were in a practical position to enjoin the development, then the state should just be allowed to step into their shoes and do the dirty work for them. The powers of the agent do not normally exceed those of the principal, and here the government took its action for the benefit of these neighbors who were protected by the ordinary law of nuisance.

Once the conceptual underbrush of the coming-to-the-nuisance cases is cleared away, the constitutional path becomes clear. The case falls within the traditional scope of the police power, which allows the state to enjoin a nuisance as it might any other ordinary wrong. The only accommodation that need be afforded the owner of the brickyard is a chance to close down its operations in an orderly fashion, which at most should require some short delay. More important, the correct analysis of the case also explains why the scope of government power is *limited* in other contexts, typically those that involve no private nuisance at all, such as the large-lot zoning enactments regularly and regrettably sustained without difficulty.[24] But an expansion of state power will come inevitably from some loose analysis that throws all the activities of both parties into a blender and lets a legislature resolve the local conflicts as it chooses. It is, therefore, not surprising that *Hadacheck* has often been cited for the far broader proposition that the government can choose its legal approach whenever there is an incompatibility between neighboring land uses.[25] From there it is but a small step to the near plenary power of the zoning laws.

SUCCESSIVE HOLDERS OF THE SAME PROPERTY

The integration of space and time in boundary disputes affords a convenient transition to a related issue: how do boundaries operate between successive owners of the same parcel? This problem is ordinarily obscured to common understanding because ownership of land and chattels is normally regarded as permanent—at least, in the sense that one person is subject to no definite limitations over the period of ownership, and can consume, sell, or dispose of property just as if he or she were to live forever. But on some occasions private parties have thought it wise to create temporal boundaries between successive owners of the same parcel. In family situations, this could be done by creating an interest for life in one person and a remainder interest (of indefinite duration) in a second that falls into possession at the death of the tenant for life. The common family settlement, "to A for life, remainder in fee simple (that is, forever) to B (A's child)" is the simplest illustration of this arrangement. Of far greater importance, the common commercial lease allows a tenant the use of the premises for some definite period, after which they revert to the original owner. The division in the family setting is by lives, and that in the commercial setting by years; either way, the law has to police the boundaries between two successive generations of holders.

One key point about these temporal divisions is that they contain no trace of the reciprocity found in the live-and-let-live cases. Nor can we talk about the sharing of common spaces or about reciprocal easements of support. Here one party holds possession of the property today, and the second stands ready to take it at the appointed time. Typically, the party who is out of possession can do little to harm the party who is in possession, but the converse proposition is surely false: the party in possession can do grave harm to the next holder. Just as an owner is tempted to consume his own seed corn, so he is more tempted to consume the seed corn of another.

In this setting, the creation of a temporal boundary provides a regrettable opportunity for another forbidden boundary crossing. Ideally, the tenant in possession acts as though he were also the holder of the future interest, and thus should set off against his short-term gain the associated long-term cost that will be borne by another. In practical terms, this means that the ideal tenant for life will not overplant the soil if the consequence is a greater loss of productivity in the future; nor should the tenant for life cut down timber, or exhaust mines at a rapid rate, or ignore the maintenance of buildings that will crumble and grounds that will go to seed after he is gone. The risk is that the tenant for life will reduce the property to rubble in order to maximize his own separate return. The common-law counterweight to this danger came through an action for waste that covered (clearly) those cases where the tenant in possession "affirmatively" laid waste to the land, and (less clearly) those cases of "permissive" waste where he failed to prevent the deterioration of the property by steps that a prudent landowner would entertain.

But exactly what conduct is expected of the tenant in possession? It is hard to give any categorical answer, since so much depends on the nature of the resource in question. It will not do for the tenant in possession to cut down an entire forest, but why not cut down trees when they are ripe for harvesting, especially if a sole owner would do the same? Similarly, if a mine is already open it is far from clear that the tenant should stop extraction altogether and thus make a gift, of sorts, to the remainderman. The best that one can say in the abstract is that the patterns of use followed in earlier periods should be roughly those followed by individuals with successive interests in the property—that is, they should act in the same manner as the prudent owner of the entire estate.

Accomplishing this task, however, is more easily said than done: in a sense, that is precisely the point. While the time boundaries are clear, the use boundaries are not. Varying circumstances and idiosyncratic owners stymie any purely legal effort to fashion an ideal set of rules to guide the property through its successive possessors. Since any legal norm is prone to error, the case for consensual solutions rises in importance—the inverse pattern from the live-and-let-live situation, where regularities between neighbors are more easily observed. But who designs the overall plan? Judge Posner observes that agreements of this sort are hard to come by, because the tenant and the remainderman have to square off in a bilateral monopoly situation and face the temptation to hold for the greater gain.[26]

Posner's observation, however, misses the key point, which is that the best way to handle a bilateral monopoly is to cut off that potential before it arises. And in common practice, that is just what is done. Thus, if a single party creates both interests—as happens when a testator (or grantor) creates both the life estate in A and the remainder interest in B—then the will (or deed) can (and usually does) specify exactly what can be done with the property and by whom and at what time. Likewise, when two unrelated parties negotiate a lease, they can at the outset include provisions that assure a smooth transition of interests at the end of the term. Thus, the tenant should be given an opportunity to remove his equipment; and, if leasehold improvements are constructed, some formula could be adopted to make the landlord pay something—say, an assessed valuation or some arbitrated figure—for their residual value at the end of the lease, lest the landlord, as holder of the future interest, take advantage of the position of the tenant. And those terms commonly included in these arrangements can be made default provisions either at common law or, for greater precision, by statute.[27]

Most critically, the rules on divided interests need not be confined to real estate at all. Few people create divided interests in land for personal reasons, as these are awkward to maintain. The common vehicle for divided interests in property is the trust. A trust typically contains stocks, bonds, and other liquid assets and, if well drafted, may well authorize a trustee to invade the corpus of the trust for the benefit of the tenant for life (commonly a widow) at the expense of her children, who may well have independent means of support. Successive divisions of interest also arise in financial instruments, as when the interest-only portion of a bond is sold to one part, and the principal-only portion is sold to another; the separation between the two financial interests is rigidly preserved, given the arm's length position of the respective parties. So across the broad array of consequences, the legal rules are default rules, but typically they are not as robust as are rules between neighbors. The fit between law and intentions is not strong enough to cover the immense variation often found in transactions of this sort. Hence the rise of contractual solutions.

INVASIONS OF PRIVACY

Boundary disputes may not be confined to purely physical interactions between neighbors; social issues can be at stake as well. To be sure, it might seem a long march from the law of nuisance and lateral support to the law of privacy as it relates to eavesdropping and spying, both in the public and the private context; but, in fact, the journey between these two points is short—a welcome result in my aim to articulate a unified approach to legal problems.

Let us assume that we have a rule that allows all individuals to eavesdrop at their pleasure so long as they do not trespass on the land of another. In preserving privacy, the traditional law of trespass will, of course, offer landowners some assistance. They can hide behind their walls or congregate in the center of their property in order to reduce the chances of being overheard. Or they can use various devices—walls and fans—to prevent neighbors from listening in to what they have to say. But these cost money and interfere with both light and air, as well as peace and quiet.

Fortunately, it is possible to design better arrangements that free up land for more useful pursuits. If each person values privacy (the defensive posture) over snooping (the offensive posture, in more ways than one), then a social norm that blocks overhearing works to the mutual advantage of all neighbors. How can we determine whether that norm commands social respect or is just the product of idle speculation? As before, the trick is to look for guidance in some voluntary setting, which in this instance is the applicable social rule governing the conduct of patrons in restaurants or clubs. It is bad form to stop in the middle of a conversation at one table and lean over, ever so slightly, to hear what is being said at a nearby table. This "no-overhearing rule" is widely observed, and its infrequent violations are sanctioned informally by a swift stare or sharp word. That these rules flourish in a consensual setting is a good reason to apply them to analogous nonconsensual settings, where the values attached to the various activities do not differ markedly from those found in restaurants and clubs. Now hosts and waiters are not available as intermediaries, and modern electronics has made possible types of snooping that cannot be achieved by the ordinary ear.

In the private law, the question is whether these nontrespassory invasions should be made actionable; the uniform response is that they should be.[28] The creation of a uniform legal prohibition against the use of hearing devices of all kinds is far cheaper than any self-help strategy that owners could adopt. The imposition of reciprocal prohibitions on snooping works, on average, to the ex ante advantage of parties on both sides of the boundary. As in other settings, what starts out as a private-law response to casual, low-level interactions ends up as a constitutional norm capable of ordering relationships between the individual and the state. The once-insistent government position that snooping by electronic devices is not wrongful, because it is not trespassory, has been effectively falsified by prior developments in the common law of privacy. Electronic wiretapping, an unreasonable search and seizure in violation of the Fourth Amendment safeguard, receives a clear answer. The practice is presumptively allowed no more to governments than it is to private parties, but must be justified on the same grounds as other searches.

In 1967, after much hesitation, the Supreme Court reached that position in *Katz v. United States*.[29] But, as is its habit, its reasoning placed far too great a reliance on some undifferentiated notion of reasonable expectations.[30] It is all too easy to say that one is entitled to privacy because one has the expectation of getting it. But the focus on the subjective expectations of one party to a transaction does not explain or justify any legal rule, given the evident danger of circularity in reasoning. More specifically, the legal result should not change because states have habitually practiced snooping, so that no one has any reasonable (read, predictive) expectation that their conversations will go undetected. It is dangerous to allow a succession of government wrongs to ripen into a prescriptive right against its weary citizens, whose expectations have been dashed by repeated instances of government misbehavior. That misplaced argument can be avoided by stressing the social optimality that comes if we adopt a rule that extends protection against certain forms of nontrespassory conduct, as can be done in ordinary invasion-of-privacy cases. Once the desirability of a rule is established, then its frequent violation by government is no longer viewed as framing expectations but as violating rights.

BOUNDARIES IN THE AIR WAVES

In ordinary land-use disputes, the best legal rules have proved relatively stable over time. But there are, of course, movements at the edges. The reciprocal harms tolerated under the live-and-let-live rule need not be constant over time. To the contrary, we should expect that as standards of living rise, the permissible level of reciprocal harms will diminish. In the other direction, however, as the value of land increases, so that people are pushed ever closer together, reciprocal toleration may increase, leaving uncertain the direction of the overall change.

Those shifts are driven by the single desire to maximize the net gain from these reciprocal easements. But the shift in property rights assumes a much more powerful role when technology opens up resources that were simply unavailable for human use in the formative stages of the common law. In particular, technology has had a profound role to play in telecommunications, where over-the-air broadcast of radio and television signals requires the disregard of one established set of boundaries and the creation of a second set in its stead. It takes little reflection and no learned citation to realize that in the long haul no one would benefit from a rule permitting all landowners to jam broadcast signals at their boundary line unless they are paid to allow them through. The ensuing private obstacle course could defeat a valuable technology before it ever got off the ground. Here the usual counterrule to boundary conditions is satisfied: all parties are made better off if the traditional boundaries on land are relaxed.

Manifestly, broadcast signals require a new system of boundaries lest competing users of the spectrum broadcast over the same frequencies, allowing none to be heard. Although it was realized in the first quarter of this century that highways had to be created in the sky for broadcast signals as well as for airplanes, it hardly follows that some centralized system is always required to make the needed allocations. Indeed, historically, the original device for assigning frequencies imitated the patterns that had long been used for determining the ownership of unowned land:[31] the first person who used a frequency was entitled to keep it in perpetuity. The test itself has some small wrinkles, for just as one person passing over land does not occupy it, so a person who uses a frequency once and no more does not occupy it either. Rather, one must use a frequency consistently and regularly over a period of time, with the intention to exclude others. Nor should these boundaries be more rigid than those in law: since broadcasts over nearby frequencies always interfere with each other to some degree, the live-and-let-live rule for land had to be carried over to the new medium. Some low-level interference between users of neighboring frequencies had to be tolerated, and was.

The historical evidence suggests that this system for allocating broadcasting frequencies, once established, would have proved stable in the long run. The basic rights could have been protected by trespass analogies. The frequencies could be used, sold, leased, or mortgaged like any other physical asset. Control over the system is decentralized so the competitive markets that arise from the practice of occupation can be maintained, if needed, by an application of the same antitrust rules applicable to other product and service markets. Small users could gain air time, not by buying an entire frequency, but by leasing it for limited periods from owners who act more like owners of rails and freight cars and less like owners of cargo. As demand shifts across areas, frequencies once devoted to radio could switch to television or telecommunications. The parties also have an incentive to narrow their broadcast bandwidths because they can devote the excess to new uses. And the government can purchase what frequencies it needs in an open market or, if necessary, condemn certain frequencies under its eminent domain power. The entire field could be thus assimilated into the traditional fabric of the common law as old rules carry over to new technologies.

But this ideal was not to be. Instead, the need to police boundaries became the opening wedge for an extensive system of regulation, starting with the Federal Radio Act of 1927,[32] which shortly became the Federal Communications Act of 1934.[33] The intervention began under the leadership of the then-secretary of commerce, Herbert Hoover, who worked a massive conversion of the spectrum into a mixed-system, in which the spectrum became public property and was in turn licensed to private users.[34] This profound change in ownership patterns was not needed to handle the boundary disputes, for which the applicable common-law principles had already evolved. Alternatively, the Federal Radio Commission (FRC) could have simply auctioned off frequencies for private use. Unfortunately, both these approaches were rejected when the rhetoric of the time confused private property with anarchy and assumed that only federal intervention could constrain the "chaos" in spectrum use.[35] The Federal Radio Act thus pre-empted the private rights created by occupation and effectively nationalized an entire system.

Next, the Federal Communications Commission (FCC) developed regulations to discharge its statutory mission of assigning licenses in accordance with its understanding of its statutory mandate to serve "the public interest, convenience and necessity." In 1943, Justice Felix Frankfurter wrote a learned but misguided opinion that upheld the statutory standard against charges of vagueness.[36] To be sure, Frankfurter recognized the government had to make sure, as it were, that broadcasters followed the rules of the road. But he thought this task rather too modest for the FCC, which should also set standards to determine the "composition of the traffic." Yet the FCC has been unable to give cogent reasons why any applicant should receive a new license or the renewal of an old one.[37] Apart from some prohibitions against hate speech and the like, the Commission has never found a way to distinguish between worthy recipients and less deserving pretenders.[38] The entire process quickly becomes much of a sham when a successful licensee is routinely allowed to resell his interest to a new broadcaster who is then, under current rules, virtually certain to have his license renewed. In effect, the auction of frequencies is conducted with a year's delay by the lucky applicant for the original FCC license.

Nor should the license be regarded as a form of de facto ownership just because it is almost invariably renewed. The FCC determines in large measure how it can be used. In one famous case, the FCC stripped a license from a radio station that simply leased space to a large number of foreign language shows.[39] The licensee's failure to supervise the content of its shows was in violation of its statutory obligations. It is as though the owner of a parcel of land would not let his lessees determine what use to make of his property; or as though the government chose to nationalize the ownership of all land in order to eliminate the need to resolve boundary disputes under the law of nuisance. But the discussion of boundary conditions is still not over. The critical question that remains is to determine the proper remedy for any boundary crossing or, indeed, any private wrong. That is the subject of the next chapter.

CHAPTER 8

❖ ❖ ❖

From Rights to Remedies

Ubi ius, ibi remedium. Loosely translated, this Latin maxim means: where there is a right, there is a remedy. This principle has long been recognized as one of the staples of every legal regime: to deny it is to rely exclusively on social sanctions to contain admitted violations of legal rights. Recognition of this simple truth carries with it a wealth of complications of inescapable importance to lawyers, but which rarely attract the systematic public attention they deserve. Unfortunately, that general neglect leaves unrealized a deeper understanding of both the uses and the limitations of law.

The range of remedial choices does much to define the shape of the law. In some cases, the remedy chosen eliminates any reason to resort to the courts at all. Self-defense and defense of property are both self-help remedies, as are the recapture of goods and the abatement of a nuisance. When these self-help remedies are allowed, they may be abused: what legal safeguards can ensure that self-help does not become a thin cloak for aggression? In other cases, the remedies come from within the legal system. Damages are the most obvious remedy. But how are they to be calculated? And what other types of remedy will be ordered, either as supplement or substitute? The remedy of injunction may require a defendant to refrain from performing some given act. The remedy of specific performance may require the performance of some other act. These private remedies can be absolute or conditional, and they can be combined with one another. In addition, in many cases, the state will provide a set of close substitutes for private remedies: fines, licenses, and bans. The way people behave is determined not only by the conduct that is defined as right or wrong, but also by the sanctions they face once some wrong has been committed. This chapter addresses the full range of remedial practices of both the private and the public law.

The problem of remedies can introduce complexity into the simplest of situations. Take the boundary question examined in the last chapter. Suppose a boundary crossing has taken place. Everyone admits that it is a trespass, and hence a wrong. What next? Is the proper remedy solely an award of damages for the past entry; and, if so, how is it to be measured? But if the trespasser turns into a squatter, is forcible eviction an acceptable self-help remedy? Alternatively, must the owner accept the wrong and be content with damages, or can a court issue an order removing the defendant from the land? Now suppose that the intrusion is relatively minor, as when the owner of one plot of land constructs a tall building that encroaches on a neighbor's land by a few inches. Is it still obvious that the building must come down because the boundary line has been crossed and a small bridgehead established? If it is not, then what principles can be used to separate the two cases?

The law of contract offers similar examples. A seller promises to convey land to a buyer in a week's time, but then announces that he is unwilling or unable to perform that obligation when it falls due. Is the innocent party entitled to damages as of the moment of the announced breach? Or is he entitled to a remedy of specific performance—in this instance a court order to convey the property as promised?

What principles determine how to choose among self-help, damages, injunctions, and specific performance? Most people's moral instincts extend to recognizing that trespass, encroachment, or breach of contract is wrong. But in the day-to-day operation of the system, the more pressing question involves the choice of remedy. That topic became the source of intensive economic analysis with the publication in 1972 by Guido Calabresi and his then student A. Douglas Melamed of their now-classic article, "Property Rules, Liability Rules and Inalienability Rules: One View of the Cathedral."[1] In that article, Calabresi and Melamed sought to capture this fundamental remedial divide by introducing the now standard distinction between property rules and liability rules. A property rule gives an individual the right to keep an entitlement unless and until he chooses to part with it voluntarily. Thus, Calabresi and Melamed wrote: "An entitlement is protected by a property rule to the extent that someone who wishes to remove the entitlement from the holder must buy it from him in a voluntary transaction in which the value of the entitlement is agreed upon by the seller."[2] Property rights are, in this sense, made absolute because the ownership of some asset confers, in language reminiscent of Blackstone (see pages 254–55), on a given individual the sole and exclusive power of dominion to determine whether to retain an asset or to part with it on whatever terms he sees fit.

In contrast, a liability rule denies the holder of the asset the power to exclude others or indeed to keep the asset for himself. The standard definition goes as follows: "Whenever someone may destroy the initial entitlement if he is willing to pay an objectively determined value for it, an entitlement is protected by a liability rule."[3] Now the owner is helpless to resist the efforts of some other individual to take that thing upon payment of its fair value as objectively determined by some neutral party. The property rule confers on the holder of an asset a holdout advantage—an advantage that, under a liability rule, that holder loses. As older lawyers would say, the specific protection of a thing ceases when the law provides in its place protection only for the wealth it represents.

The main task is to decide which remedy ought to be conferred on which individuals in which settings, and why? In a world in which transaction costs were zero, with all disputes able to be costlessly resolved, the choice between liability rules and property rules would be of little or no importance—in yet another application of the ubiquitous Coase theorem, which holds that, regardless of their initial allocation, resources will end up at their highest and best use so long as there are no impediments to trade.[4] On the one hand, the holdout danger from a property rule would be of no consequence because the two parties could entertain an infinite number of offers and counteroffers within an infinitesimal period of time, for that in essence is what zero-transaction costs entail. Alternatively, a liability rule would have no serious downside either: armed with our zero-transaction costs assumption, any dispute on valuation could be resolved both accurately and instantly. In both cases, each asset would end up in the hands of the party who valued it most: the choice of institutional arrangements would be of little or no consequence to the final outcome or to the overall operation of the system.

It is, however, an open question whether one can even understand what a world of zero-transaction costs means, given the violence it does to our ordinary understanding of the importance of time: an infinite number of transactions cannot be completed instantly. In any event, in our world transactions costs are far from zero. Rather, they are positive, and large, so that the choice between the two rules is certain to have major consequences for the operation of any legal system. In one sense, the risks of property rules and liability rules are the mirror images of each other. The holdout risk of a property rule arises when one party resists a voluntary transaction because he thinks he can hold out for a sum in excess of what the property is otherwise worth to him. That risk can be obviated by allowing the person in need of the property to take it for a sum that represents the fair value of the property to its holder, stripped of his distinctive holdout advantage. But to achieve that result, it is necessary to force one person to surrender his entitlement for a price set by a third party, and thus to expose him to the risk of being forced to part with his entitlement at a price lower than he would be prepared to accept voluntarily under the worst of all circumstances. These two risks—the *holdout risk* and the *expropriation risk*—stand in an inverse relationship one to the other. It is not possible to eliminate both risks simultaneously, and any effort to reduce the former will require forced exchanges that will increase the risk of the latter and vice-versa. In these circumstances, we cannot take any refuge in absolutes, but must search for a legal regime that minimizes the sum of these two persistent inconveniences.

For those who come from an absolutist tradition, the dilemma here creates no real difficulty in choice. Property rights are absolute, almost by definition, for it makes no linguistic sense to say that *A* owns property when *B* has an option to purchase at a price to be determined by some third party. "It is surely odd to claim that an individual's right is protected when another individual is permitted to force a transfer at a price set by third parties. Isn't the very idea of a forced transfer contrary to the autonomy or liberty thought constitutive of rights?"[5] That heroic stance fails, however, in functional terms because it assumes, without contextual examination, that an absolute rule of property protection will always outperform the more nuanced protection of a liability rule. So if it could be shown that in some contexts the holdout risk is very large, then this absolute judgment stands in ever stronger opposition to the common good. Natural law theorists, every bit as much as utilitarians, must make peace with the point.

Since we must be aware at the outset of the dangers of overclaiming, we have to replace the language of absolutes with the language of presumptions. A presumption here is basically a legal method to get at some uncertain truth through a series of successive approximations, each one of which is designed to edge us closer to the ideal answer.[6] We start with one rule and keep to it unless some good reason intervenes. On that score, the standard legal response in virtually all legal systems presumes the dominance of property rules over liability rules. The key exception to that response arises where conditions of *necessity*—that is, cases where external circumstances limit both sides to a single trading partner—create a major holdout problem. Matters are somewhat different in the public law, where liability rules, chiefly in connection with takings under the eminent-domain power, are more commonly found. Yet even in public law contexts, the attractiveness of property rules translates itself into an uneasiness about forced exchanges under a liability rule. The upshot is that these transactions usually go forward only in *constrained* institutional settings that limit the occasions in which it is permissible simply to take and pay.

The reason for this pattern of reliance on the two types of rules is as follows. In most situations, the owner of a particular asset may choose from a large number of potential trading partners. In those settings, the holdout advantage conferred by a property rule is relatively small, for a potential seller can play one buyer off against another until a competitive price is reached. At that point, the exchange will usually go through without explicit legal intervention on terms that leave both parties satisfied with the outcome. To inject liability rules into this setting, however, would require some state intervention to set the appropriate value for the parties in *each and every* transaction.

Worse still, the intervention has to take place in circumstances where the risk of undercompensation is pervasive. The losses that flow from a given transaction are often difficult to determine with accuracy: remote and speculative contingencies can be involved; and the issues of valuation are not confined to matters that admit of easy economic calculation, but cover all sorts of other personal and business dislocations. Just how does one value the inconvenience of not being able to move into a new home at the start of the school year or an office at the height of the business season? What personal aggravation follows when an entire construction project is slowed down because someone has plucked away key equipment that is needed to lay a foundation or to install needed wiring? Do we allow one business to take some key equipment from another in the dark of night if that business is willing to pay full compensation? What happens when customers can no longer gain easy access to a business because its street has been torn up or rerouted? Can that process be expanded indefinitely, where the last taking becomes the justification for doing the next one? The inability of one person to receive what has been expected compromises his ability to perform his own promises. The buyer who is unable to take possession of a new home is that much more likely not to leave his present home, thereby bringing some third party into the fray.

These effects accumulate. Over time, the inefficiencies of a liability system multiply, seriously eroding the security of possession and the security of exchange needed for a complex commercial life and a satisfying personal one. A system that encourages people not to cross boundaries and not to breach promises minimizes the mushrooming of legal disputes. Only when the holdout risks become large are these dangers worth running, and then the presumptions should be reversed.

This pattern replicates itself over many distinct areas of law. In this chapter, I deal with the question of sanctity of contract, or the question of when and under what circumstances damages are an acceptable substitute for specific performance of an obligation. I then address the question of when the absolute and exclusive rights of property should properly yield to the necessity of another. Thereafter, a discussion of specialized situations, including the cases of encroachment and the utilization of caves, leads back to a more general one of the relationship of damage actions to both private injunctions and public permits, as both private law and constitutional issue. The last section of this chapter completes the circle by showing how an undue plasticity in the selection of remedies can lead to the destruction of the very rights that legal institutions should protect.

THE SANCTITY OF CONTRACT

The choice of remedy plays an important role in shaping the basic understanding of contractual commitments. One of the most common forms of exchange is the ordinary sale, commonly defined as a voluntary transaction in which the seller transfers ownership of property in exchange for cash. This definition leaves no gaps in the basic delineation of rights. Before the transaction, the owner has clear title to the property, and the buyer title to the cash. The two sides then enter into an exchange that leaves each happier than before. What makes this system work is the stability of possession that David Hume recognized as one of the dominant rules of a sound society.[7] A transaction takes place only if both sides agree to it: all individuals keep their initial holdings until they have agreed to part with them.

A liability rule would dash those expectations. Instead of sale, any individual could take anything owned by any other person and leave on the table its equivalent in cash—assuming he knew what that amount was. But the dangers are not confined to takings between strangers. Sometimes a party who enters into a contract chooses to breach as a matter of course, subject to the obligation to pay damages for the breach. Thus, Holmes's famous aphorism, "The only universal consequence of a legally binding promise is, that the law makes the promisor pay damages if the promised event does not come to pass."[8] This same thought is captured in the modern idea that a contract does nothing more than create in the promisor the *option* to perform *or* pay damages, where the ideal, or "expectation," measure of damages is designed to leave the innocent party just as well off as he would have been if the original promise had been performed.[9] If the breaching party is left better off, and the innocent party is no worse off, who should complain?

Under this view, the law of contracts is dominated by liability rules, not by property rules. In some cases, this view captures the dominant business morality. With pure financial transactions, as with stocks and bonds, the damage remedies dominate, and for good reason. The parties themselves care only about the evident cash equivalence of these perfectly fungible assets, and can easily buy and sell any set of specific instruments they desire. So it is easier on all sides to pay cash to settle up the transaction and to eliminate the bother. But it is not the law that sets the parties' expectations; rather, social expectations drive the legal rule.

These social expectations run the opposite way, however, in most standard business contexts. The sanctity of contract, it has been repeatedly said, is not intended to allow *A* to change his obligations to *B* simply by paying some additional damages: "Where parties have made an agreement for themselves, the courts ought not to make another one for them."[10] Why, after all, should someone ever be allowed to profit from what both sides regard as his own breach? If *A* and *B* agree to the sale of *A*'s house to *B* for $100,000, then *B* normally bargains to get the house and not a damage remedy. That remedy looks as though it were a unilateral revision of the original deal. Thus if *B* collects $10,000 in damages for nonperformance, it is as though the house were first sold by *A* to *B* for $100,000 and then, against *B*'s will, retaken by *A* for $110,000. Of course, *A* might want to reserve an option to buy his way out of a contract. But, if so, the usual practice is to write that option into the agreement and to specify in advance the amount of money that must be paid to *B* in order to undo the sale. The options are made explicit and are not dependent on concealed provisions for unstated prices determined only after the fact. It is difficult to conceive of a more inconvenient system. The holdout potential is effectively negated by the availability of alternative suppliers, so the case for using a liability regime is at its low ebb. For routine transactions in land and chattels, strong property rights and voluntary transactions offer the only hope for a stable and productive institutional environment.

That general preference carries over to particular cases. In closed business communities, the customary norm is clear. As Lisa Bernstein reports in her detailed study of the grain and feed industry, the merchant who chooses to dishonor a contract of sale by paying expectation damages is normally drummed out of the trade.[11] In her terminology, the deliberate breach of a contract for a higher price amounts to the violation of a relationship-preserving norm, which leads to dissolution of the business relationship. The obvious realities drive the business practices: cash damages are rarely sufficient to cover the dislocations brought on by the nonperformance of the promise. The breach itself then creates further ripple effects by destabilizing relations between the innocent buyer and his own customers (who now are protected, at most, by a liability rule if their seller finds it impossible to perform). Commercial parties are almost always willing to deal when external circumstances call for modifications in price or delivery, but they wish to have the strong property rights so as to make sure that the renegotiations follow a sensible course that does not prejudice their own obligations to third parties. Expectation damages are not the norm when a seller finds it convenient to breach. They kick in when some external event—a fire, a strike, a government order—blocks sale. These *impossibility* defenses are the mirror image of the necessity doctrine: they explain not why something had to happen, but why it could not happen. But in both cases, only exceptional circumstances lead to the suspension of the ordinary expectation of performance first. Typically, a contract is not viewed as an option to deliver or pay damages, as Holmes insisted in *The Common Law*. It is viewed as an obligation to deliver—period.

PROPERTY AND NECESSITY

In property settings, the prior "sanctity of contract" is replaced by the "absolute rights of property." Impossibility of performance is now paralleled by the necessity of physical invasion. The parallel to the deliberate breach of contract occurs when *A* takes and keeps the property of *B*. Consistent with the general preference for strong property protection, the common remedy in all legal systems allows the owner to recover the thing so taken, thus restoring his original balance against the rest of the world. But that rule is reversed when one person takes or uses the property of another in order to avoid the imminent danger of injury, death, or destruction, as the case may be. It is therefore permissible to cross over private land that abuts a public highway if the road itself becomes impassable. The necessities have to be those of the moment and brought about by sudden and unexpected changes in external conditions for which no advance adaptation has been possible. Similarly, the duration of the intrusion is limited to the necessity that created it. A sailor can take refuge at someone else's dock only for the duration of a storm; a passerby can walk over land to escape danger, but cannot stake it out as his own. Once the necessity has passed, the owner can again assert his full panoply of rights, including exclusive possession, without having to bargain further with the intruder. Finally, in most cases, the destruction and damage of property, although perhaps not its mere use, gave rise to a correlative obligation to pay for the harm so caused. Cases of necessity are real, and cannot be eliminated from any accurate summary of the common-law rules or, indeed, from any systematic philosophical study of property rights.[12]

This view of necessity cases has been challenged, mistakenly in my view, by Ian Ayres and J. M. Balkin.[13] In their view, the necessity cases are really governed by an extended set of liability rules which establish a kind of continuous internal auction. In the first round, one party can take property from the other, and thus use, without revealing, the private information he has about the value of the property to him relative to the price that the legal system calls on him to pay. This one-sided ability to take and pay ignores, Ayres and Balkin note, the private information of the other party which in turn might not be captured in the valuation rule. Yet that information can be harnessed, we are told, by reversing the roles of the parties. The original owner can now *retake* what has been taken from him so long as he pays the higher price that represents the value of the thing to the other side. In principle that cycle can repeat itself indefinitely until one party ceases to take the thing.

Ayres and Balkin use the familiar duo of *Vincent v. Lake Erie Transportation Co.*[14] and *Ploof v. Putnam*[15] to illustrate how their system operates. *Ploof* makes it clear that the outsider has a right to enter private lands under conditions of necessity. *Vincent* then establishes the correlative duty to pay compensation for any damage so caused. The first part of their analysis is easy: under the rule in *Vincent*, the owner of the boat can gain access to the dock to preserve his life, so that property rights are protected only by a liability rule in conditions of necessity. But Ayres and Balkin go astray when they write: "The dock owner has a second-stage option to unmoor the ship, but at a cost: The dock owner gives up a cause of action against the shipowner for damages and exposes himself to tort liability for any resulting damages to the ship and its crew."[16]

That conclusion misstates the legal position. The shipowner is not simply given a right of action for personal damages. If circumstances permit, the shipowner is entitled *to use force* to regain the dock from its true owner. It is as though the property rights flipped over by virtue of necessity. So long as that necessity lasts, the shipowner has all the prerogatives of owner against the ostensible owner of the land. The legal system does not create an indefinite series of options between the two parties to reveal some information that is supposedly known to one side but not the other—as if they had time to bid one against another. Rather, it creates in the short run temporary property rights in the outsider—rights that nip any auction in the bud. The only way the original owner could reclaim the dock is to show that he, too, labored under like necessity, for, although authority is scant, it seems that if *both* parties face a common necessity, the tie goes to the original owner—at least, on the assumption that only one party can be saved. As the great seventeenth-century Dutch legal thinker Samuel Pufendorf put the point: "A man ought not to be stripped of his possessions against his will, if it be clear that he will at once fall under the same necessity, if the possession passes to another."[17] Necessity, then, removes from the owner the protection of the original property rule and places in its stead a liability rule, for the duration of the necessity only.

Encroachment

The law of encroachment also illustrates the perennial tension between the holdout and the expropriation risks. Although trespasses between neighbors all presuppose wrongful boundary crossings, there are, so to speak, entrances and entrances. In the simple case, the wrongdoer does not remain on the premises, so that damages per force are the plaintiff's only possible remedy. The choice of remedy, however, becomes more critical when the defendant erects a permanent improvement on a tiny portion of the plaintiff's land, where the improvement can be removed, typically at enormous cost to the owner of the improvement. Suppose a large building extends a few inches on the wrong side of a boundary line, or a sewer or a drain pipe runs underneath the land of a neighbor, where it causes no damage or inconvenience. What remedies should be available to an aggrieved landowner?

The law of encroachment typically requires removal of the offending structure so that the land can be restored to its original state. The decision in 1935 in the Massachusetts case *Garagosian v. Union Realty Co.* reveals the full stringency of the dominant rule.

> The fact that the aggrieved owner suffers from little or no damage from the trespass, that the wrongdoer acted in good faith and would be put to disproportionate expense by removal of the trespassing structures, and that neighborly conduct as well as business judgment would require acceptance of compensation in money for the land appropriated are ordinarily no reasons for denying an injunction. Rights in real property cannot ordinarily be taken from the owner at a valuation, except under the power of eminent domain.[18]

This unyielding and dogmatic solution has given rise to a good deal of anxiety because of the holdout problem it fosters. No one doubts that a single owner of both plots of land would not bother to remove the building once it was constructed, so why allow one landowner to impose that enormous cost on the other? To be sure, the encroacher could seek to buy his way out of his legal duties. In principle, a wide number of outcomes could improve the position of both sides: the cost to the innocent landowner in most cases is low, while the gains to the offending landowner from receiving cash could be enormous. But that attempt surely raises the prospect of a serious holdout problem if the innocent landowner insists on asking for far more than the tiny sliver of land is worth in any alternative use. Indeed, the huge bargaining range may actually block a negotiated solution. Each party may possess some private information that leads it to believe that it can do better than divide the surplus equally; or there may be some bad blood between the parties that leads one or the other side to take an especially aggressive stance, as appeared to be the case in *Garagosian*. Garagosian made his purchase at the request of his wife's wily stepbrother after Union Realty had shut down his concession shop in its theater.[19] Given the dominance of the holdout issue, the encroachment cases bear a close resemblance to the necessity cases just considered.

What then might justify the creation of this bilateral monopoly and its attendant dislocations? The Massachusetts court in *Garagosian* noted first that the removal remedy was justified because it combatted the danger that "a continuance of the wrong may ripen into title by adverse possession or prescription." It then concluded that

> the basic reason lies deeper. It is the same reason which lies at the foundation of the jurisdiction for decreeing specific performance of contracts for the sale of real estate. A particular piece of real estate cannot be replaced by any sum of money, however large, and one who wants a particular estate for a specific use, if deprived of his rights, cannot be said to receive an exact equivalent or complete indemnity by the payment of a sum of money which represents its value. Leaving an aggrieved owner to remove a trespassing structure at his own expense and risk, would amount in practice to a denial of all remedy, except damages, in most cases. If the landowner should attempt to right his own wrongs, a breach of the peace would be likely to result.[20]

The argument here hints at, but misses, the strongest case for the removal remedy. The basic contention is that removal is to encroachment as specific performance is to the conveyance of real estate. At one level, the parallel is surely correct: in each case, the use of the strong legal remedy means that no party is allowed to obtain any legal advantage by the commission of a wrong. Both removal and specific performance thus deny the power of the wrongdoer to force an exchange in the same fashion as the state. At this point, the puzzle becomes somewhat deeper. The basic structure of the eminent domain remedy—at least, when matters of valuation are not corrupted[21]—allows for social gains: the individual who receives perfect compensation is in theory left (at least) indifferent between the compensation that is received and the property that has been surrendered. The state (assuming that its collective decisions are well made) benefits from the exchange, and through it do all its citizens, including the person whose property has been taken—so long as he remains a member of the community, which need not be the case. Where the method of forced exchanges leaves somebody better off and nobody worse off, who can protest the outcome? Why should this appealing analogy not be followed in either the conveyancing or the encroachment cases?

One customary explanation is that real estate is unique, and this feature has been held to account for the dominance of specific performance, at the instance of the buyer with some special attachment to the land whose intensity cannot be accurately measured by any damage calculation.[22] With encroachment, however, the argument that there is distinct subjective value in the encroached strip rings hollow. In most of these cases, the land is barren, often with little or no value. If a negotiation for the purchase of that same land were undertaken before the encroachment, its price would be minimal—at least, if the purchaser faced no antecedent holdout problem. And no one thinks that the price at which the unhappy encroacher settles with the aggrieved landowner after the encroachment represents no more than the subjective value of the property in its original condition. The uniqueness argument thus offers scant justification for incurring the holdout risk.

What, then, does? The explanation comes into focus when one considers the expropriation risk that must be created to obviate the holdout problem. Thus, suppose that the encroachment is not ordered to be removed. If no legal remedy is provided, then there will be no limitation against the practice; the optimal strategy for all landowners will be to launch a preemptive strike by taking first and apologizing later. So the damage remedy has to counter that threat. Unfortunately, the encroacher will have slender incentive to curb the wrong if he has to pay only for the losses so inflicted: that penalty allows the encroacher to come out clearly ahead by unilateral action. Still, it may be asked, Why worry if the damage remedy leaves the original owner as well off as before: someone is better off, and no one is worse off, so who should complain?

One response is simply that it seems deeply unfair to give all the gain to the party who just barges in. But matters do not rest solely on that intuition. Some elements of loss are difficult to quantify and compensate and may be ignored as speculative, but litigation costs are always positive and may well render unprofitable the suit for recovery for small damages. The damage remedy will often be no remedy at all. Therefore, the *frequency* of violations will be high unless something is done to wrest profits away from the encroacher—as, of course, the removal remedy does.

The explanation for the strict remedy in encroachment cases thus lies in its ability to reduce the probability of the initial invasion. Usually the removal remedy will drive the rate of encroachment close to zero, because it is normally so easy to determine what the boundaries are before construction begins, by reference to either a landmark or a survey. If the removal remedy reduces the number of encroachments to zero, then an efficient solution is reached by preventing any holdout problems from arising. That condition could never be satisfied in the necessity cases, where sudden circumstances might always disrupt property rights. To be sure, in practice, errors will lead from time to time to encroachments and their holdout embarrassments. But this ostensible inefficiency is overcome by giving due weight to the number of potential encroachments the strict rule itself prevents. Occasionally, the evidence will establish that the encroacher had nothing to gain from the action. The invasion could be *de minimis* and innocent. Fortunately, it is in just those few cases that the removal remedy is normally not applied. But the moment there is bad faith or nontrivial invasion, then the stricter rule kicks in. So in the broad run of cases, the system looks more efficient. As with the coming-to-the-nuisance cases, the soundness of the legal system is not measured solely, or even primarily, by those sorry cases that end up in litigation (see chapter 7, pages 202–06).

We are now, moreover, in a position to explain why the rules for encroachment differ from the eminent-domain rules with which they are often compared. With the state, there is normally no reason to deter the initial taking in the first place. The possession of sovereign power usually carries with it the power of condemnation, typically to prevent holdouts by individual owners when, say, the government wishes to construct a road or a highway. Indeed, it is just this logic that led to the rulings during the 1930s holding that no individual landowner was entitled to prevent overflights, even though these were traditionally regarded as trespasses on real property.[23] It was well understood that no air traffic at all could develop if each landowner could exact a toll from every airplane. By the same token, the damages caused to any individual parcel of property were smaller than the gains privately obtained when airplanes flew over neighboring lands, thereby reducing the transportation costs for both persons and services. So unlike the usual encroachment case, the externality risk was small, but the holdout risk was large: thus, the law developed in a fashion that stopped the latter and not the former. Only in those cases with real danger of physical damage is the externality problem both large and disproportionate: there, the law of eminent domain allows compensation at least in the direct overflight cases.[24] In principle, that rule should be extended to nontrespassory invasions, but the extraordinary partiality for government endeavors has led some courts to deny compensation to landowners who suffer a nuisance that is not the result of a direct overflight.[25]

Caves

Most caves are places to get lost, but some contain underground scenery of great beauty and hence substantial commercial value. Occasionally, therefore, the question arises of who owns a cave whose mouth is on the land of one owner but whose interior is largely below the land of another. That simple issue once again brings to the fore the trade-off between holdout and expropriation risks. As usual, these determinations are of little consequence in a zero-transaction cost world, since any mistake in delineating the bundles of rights can be corrected by a set of costless trades until the proper person obtains the unified rights. But in a positive-transaction cost world, subsequent correction of initial mistakes presents a more daunting task, for high transaction costs could block the potential gains from trade. The rules of individual ownership therefore should be, and largely are, organized in a fashion that minimizes these correction costs. The usual articulation of the common-law rules—that ownership entails possession, use, and disposition—represents an effort to simplify future transactions by endowing a single person with control over all relevant aspects of a single thing. Uniting these three rights in a single person thus prevents the routine bargaining breakdown that could ensue if one person held exclusive possession of land or chattels that only a second person could use and a third person could sell.

In dealing with caves, the remedial questions are tightly enmeshed with matters of basic ownership: Does the ownership of the surface of land also carry with it the ownership of the subsoil? After all, if the surface owner has not physically taken possession of the underground minerals, why give him ownership over potentially valuable mineral rights? The correct answer is that the single ownership of surface and minerals minimizes the holdout and externality problems that would otherwise exist. If the two estates were separate in their initial conception, then holdout problems would arise because the owner of the mineral estate would have to bargain with the owner of the surface in order to gain access to what exists below. At the same time, externality problems would arise because the working of the minerals could easily lead to subsidence of the soil above. The rule that unites both estates under the hands of the surface owner facilitates both the voluntary transactions that permit the extraction of minerals and the creation of the necessary easements for the mining to go forward, even when (as is usually the case) the owner of the surface interest is not the party best able to exploit the minerals below ground.

Yet in some cases the tradeoffs between holdouts and expropriation are far trickier in disputes over the ownership of caves discovered underground. On this point, Ronald Coase showed great insight into the nature of the basic problem but then (oddly enough) understated the importance of transaction costs in framing the correct solution:

Whether a newly discovered cave belongs to the man who discovered it, the man on whose land the entrance to the cave is
located, or the man who owns the surface under which the cave
is situated is no doubt dependent on the law of property. But the
law merely determines the person with whom it is necessary to
make a contract to obtain the use of the cave. Whether the cave
is used for storing bank records, as a natural gas reservoir, or for
growing mushrooms depends, not on the law of property, but on
whether the bank, the natural gas corporation, or the mushroom
concern will pay the most in order to be able to use the cave.[26]

Coase did not include tourist attractions on his list, and that omission
is not insignificant. Prospective users can find close substitutes for keeping
records, storing natural gas, or growing mushrooms. Tourists have little
interest in visiting bank vaults, gas tanks, or mushroom farms, but they do
want to see the natural wonders of the caves. Ironically, the difficulty with
this passage stems from Coase's failure to take into account the serious
transaction costs problem when two persons stand in a stark bilateral
monopoly relationship to each other.

To see why the ultimate use is sensitive to the theory of acquisition,
consider the three possibilities set out by Coase himself. The first assigns the
interest in the cave to the surface owner. Frequently, however, the cave in
question will lie beneath the land of two or more surface owners, while its
entrance lies under the land of only one: indeed, for a ticklish problem to
arise, this *has* to be the case; otherwise, the same person who owns the cave's
mouth would also own its interior.

The fears of divided ownership under the rule assigning the cave to the
surface owner are confirmed in *Edwards v. Sims,*[27] a 1929 case that grew out
of a bitter dispute between Edwards and Lee over the ownership of
Kentucky's Great Onyx Cave. (Sims was the judge who ordered the survey
of the cave, which Edwards challenged in a higher court.) The appellate
court upheld the order for the survey: it adopted the conventional view that
assigns (or recognizes, depending on your jurisprudence) ownership rights
to a cave so that each person owns that portion of a cave that lies beneath
his portion of the surface. The separate ownership meant that a survey was
needed to establish the underground boundaries between unhappy neighbors. The upshot was a fierce, protracted, and intractable holdout problem
over the division of the spoils from the possible use of Lee's land, to which
access could be gained only through Edwards's entry way. To make matters

worse, prior to the suit, Edwards had conducted guided tours over the entire cave, including Lee's portion. Once Lee was declared owner of a portion of the cave, the court had to craft a remedial formula to divide the tour proceeds previously earned—a formula that took account not only of the respective value of the two portions of the cave but also Edwards's expenses (advertising and cave improvements, for example) used to generate the gross revenues. The lawsuit dragged on for about a dozen years, to no one's edification. [28]

A similar set of disputes could happen under the second of Coase's rules, which would award the cave to the nonowner who discovered its mouth. The holdout problem would arise if the landowner blocked the cave owner from reaching the cave that the landowner was unable to use. Once again, blockade is the likely outcome, only this time of the entire cave.

The enormous holdout problems from the first two of Coase's three proposed solutions coalesces support around his third one—that assigning complete ownership and use of the cave to the landowner who owns its mouth, regardless of under whose land the cave lies or of who has discovered it. [29] Now the entire cave would be subject to a single owner, obviating the need to forge that single (but unattainable) transaction that would allow the efficient exploitation of the underground space. As an added bonus, the entire financial imbroglio over proceeds generated by the Great Onyx Cave would have been averted if sole ownership of the cave had been vested in that party.

Coase's three solutions do not exhaust the range of permutations. A fourth possibility treats the cave as jointly owned by the two surface owners in accordance with the percentage of land lying under each, perhaps with some additional share given to the person on whose land the cave mouth was found. [30] But the scheme differs from the first in that each party would have a proportionate share of the whole cave instead of exclusive ownership of the determinate fraction lying beneath his land. This fourth solution overcomes the holdout problem by allowing the party with control over the cave mouth to use the whole cave without the consent of the other owner, who then would receive a pro-rata share of the net profits to the other party. The holdout problem is thus replaced by the serious accounting problem created by divided ownership. Indeed, since the owner of the interior space would have no control over the utilization of the cave, a simple rental arrangement seems preferable to a share of the profits, based on the maxim that residual ownership claims should follow effective control.

A fifth solution uses a liability rule that would allow the owner of the mouth to occupy the remainder of the cave by paying the other owner just compensation. Here the necessity in question is not sudden and unexpected, as in ordinary necessity cases. But since nature, not human contrivance, has determined the location of the cave, there would be little reason to fear that one side would use its power to bypass feasible voluntary transactions, which is the great fear in the encroachment cases. Indeed, once the merger of the two interests is done by force, a sixth solution emerges after private litigation: in 1936, the state condemned the interests of both Edwards and Lee for $396,000, in order to own and operate the cave itself.[31] Yet how much compensation was properly required? If the two parties had agreed on a division of control and proceeds, then the state would have to pay an amount at least equal to the value of their respective interests. But here the two parties could not agree, so why should the state pay either more than the value of his interest, given the impasse that limited its value? The state, having supplied a service to overcome the reluctance of the two sides, need not pay them the value that it had added to their combined interests.[32]

Whatever the tortuous turns of this one case, the general point remains clear: the reallocation of property rights, with or without compensation, should not rest on a priori grounds. The preferred solution—let ownership of the cave go to the person who owns its mouth—has, alas, costs that could manifest themselves in other contexts. Thus, let another surface owner mine his own land and he could well destroy the integrity of the cave below, thereby creating an external harm that could have been averted under the standard *ad inferos* rule. The superiority of assigning ownership of the cave to the owner of its (single) mouth thus rests upon an *empirical* estimation that it is worth trading in a huge holdout problem for what in this context seems to be a far smaller externality problem. The concern with transaction costs, which bests explains the *ad inferos* rule, also explains any desired exception.

DAMAGES, INJUNCTIONS, AND PERMITS

A similar set of tradeoffs arises in the choice of remedies for physical harms to other individuals or their property. Once liability for past physical injuries is established, the remedy must be damages. The precise amount of damages has important consequences in individual cases, but an improper measure normally has limited consequences. Most physical harms are caused by accident; and in that context, there is little to fear from damage cascades. The ordinary driver, for example, runs the risk of injuring himself in any collision, so even if he does not fear liability for damages, he still cannot afford to be utterly indifferent to his own behavior. The fear of harm to oneself induces some caution, even if it be less than ideal.

In the context of deliberate harm, criminal sanctions are often introduced if only to punish insolvent defendants who have committed real offenses. But even if we confine ourselves to private law approaches, the choice of remedy makes a far greater difference: people who contrive to hurt others usually find ways to stay out of the line of fire, and to run and hide after the commission of a wrong. Since deliberate wrongdoers are not held hostage to their own misconduct, few among us rest content upon learning that the law stands ready to compensate after the infliction of physical harm, but will do nothing to enjoin them before they have occurred. Only in a perfect world could we hide behind the armament of tort damages, for the compensation, there always collectible, could be set high enough to ward off all deliberate wrongdoers. But so long as valuation and collection problems remain the norm, it is critical to look to some remedy that operates before an injury and not after it: thus, the need for injunctive relief.

In order to gauge the importance of the remedial issue, let us compare the stakes inherent in two related questions. The first of these is the familiar battle over the basic theory of liability for accidental harms: Do we adopt a strict liability rule which holds the defendant liable for accidental harms no matter how many precautions he took, or do we hold him liable only if he was negligent because he failed to take some measure of reasonable (that is, cost-justified) or customary precautions?[33] The second question asks, assuming the threat of some violation, do we give the strong property rule protection of an injunction before the fact, or the weaker damage remedy after the fact?

The relationship between these two rules was brought to a head in Texas in 1936 in the tort classic of *Turner v. Big Lake Oil Company*.[34] At issue in *Turner* was whether the defendant was strictly liable in tort, when water leaked out of a cistern it operated in the Texas desert to store the runoff from its drilling operations. The Texas court recoiled from the prospect of allowing damages under a strict liability system, fearing this remedy would be sufficient to shut down a necessary and profitable industry for the state—no small charge. An earlier New Hampshire case, *Brown v. Collins*,[35] had rejected the strict liability rule in tort—there when a horse bucked on a public way when frightened by a railroad whistle. Chief Justice Charles Doe went so far as to say that the rejection of a strict liability rule in tort was necessary for the preservation and advancement of civilization itself—again no modest claim.*

Today the strict liability rule is in the ascendancy in disputes between landowners, because of an increased concern with the preservation of the environment. The key point, however, is how utterly exaggerated are the effects the choice of either tort liability rule is supposed to have on social well-being.[37] Strict liability has the advantage of using clear liability rules to police the boundaries between neighbors, at the cost of somewhat greater frequency of litigation. A negligence standard carries with it the mirror image of advantages and disadvantages: it can eliminate suits for accidents that were unavoidable at some reasonable cost, but only by introducing fuzziness near the due-care line. The dominant feature of *both* systems, however, is that they induce actors to take only cost-justified precautions. The difference between the two systems in terms of the total cost to certain activities is relatively minor, and clearly civilization at any era of industrial development can do quite nicely under either rule. It is not as though the *injured* party were required to compensate the *injurer.*

The stakes get a lot higher when the choice is between damages under a strict liability rule and injunctive relief. In the *Turner* scenario, relative to negligence, a strict liability rule means that a defendant pays somewhat more in tort damages and somewhat less in legal fees: precaution levels remain about the same. In contrast, the injunction, especially an unconditional injunction, shuts down operations altogether unless the defendant can bribe the plaintiff to release the injunction, a holdout problem *par excellence.* Given this profound shift in the balance of power, injunctions are usually confined to situations in which there is actual recurrent damage or an imminent threat of damage. Furthermore, even when issued, injunctions are normally structured to minimize interference with the defendant's activities, while protecting the plaintiff's land from any harm those activi-

---

* "Even if the arbitrary [strict liability] test were applied only to things which a man brings on his land, it would still recognize the peculiar rights of savage life in a wilderness, ignore the rights growing out of a civilized state of society, and make a distinction not warranted by the enlightened spirit of the common law: it would impose a penalty upon efforts, made in a reasonable, skillful, and careful manner, to rise above a condition of barbarism. It is impossible that legal principle can throw so serious an obstacle in the way of progress and improvement."[36]

ties are likely to cause. One can always protect a plaintiff by shutting down a defendant's operations (or, for that matter, by closing down all the oil fields in Texas). The wholesale injunction thus moves far beyond the strict liability tort action. The tort action is a somewhat higher tax on activities; the injunction shuts down the activity. With strict liability, industry profits may drop by one percent or two percent, if that. With an industrywide injunction, profits drop off to zero. That difference is worth worrying about.

In most cases, the presumption lies with granting injunctive relief. Even so, courts generally worry about going too far. Frequently, injunctions are issued to the point where damage is sharply reduced but not necessarily eliminated.[38] Productive activities are allowed to continue so long as the defendant complies with certain stipulated conditions related to the risk of continued harm. Thus, a well-drafted injunction may instruct the defendant to keep waste within his land, but will then allow him to figure out whether it is cheaper not to generate waste at all or to capture it before it runs onto the plaintiff's land.

Indeed, the presumption in favor of the injunction is overridden when even the most modest dollop of property protection is thought to give an innocent party an undue holdout advantage. In 1904, in *Madison v. Ducktown Sulphur, Copper & Iron Co.*, the Tennessee court denied any injunctive relief to plaintiffs who were owners of "thin mountain lands, of little agricultural value."[39] The estimated value of the plaintiffs' land was in the order of $1,000 and that of the defendant's mining and manufacturing operations over $2,000,000. It does not take a Ph.D. in economics to see the holdout danger implicit in the case. So the court denied the injunction, which it viewed as a de facto confiscation of the defendant's interests in their own extensive holdings. One need not go that far to indicate that the most sensible solution is to allow injunctive relief when the relative balance of convenience is anything close to equal, but to deny it (in its entirety, if necessary) when the balance of convenience runs strongly in favor of the defendant. The usual presumption is that the expropriation risk is greater than the holdout risk.

However great the risk of injunctions, the social risk of choosing the wrong remedy becomes far greater when the state requires that landowners obtain one or more *permits* in advance of any real estate development. Note the contrast. In an ordinary action for injunctive relief, the injured party must prove, usually by clear and convincing evidence, that he is at risk from the defendant's activity. This simple rule means that the defendant's original activity does not need to obtain permission from any individual or group before it starts. Once started, that activity can be brought to a halt only when there is some clear and present danger of an invasion of the plaintiff's interest. In most cases, the defendant will avoid taking that risky course of action for four related reasons, all of which apply with great strength to land-use cases, where permits are most commonly required.

First, the informal restraints of neighborliness work as a powerful constraint against many forms of misbehavior. Pollution usually starts close to home and diminishes with distance. Neighbors are often friends or, in industrial cases, employers, customers, or suppliers; and even when they are not, they often move in the same local circles and thus provoke a wide array of social sanctions when they deviate too far from community standards of good behavior. These standards, moreover, vary across different communities in different settings, so that local knowledge can be brought to bear in setting appropriate levels of pollution. Typically, that level will not be zero, as the individual who complains about pollution in one case will benefit from its creation in the next. In these situations, "live-and-let-live" is a maxim not only of law but also of good social sense (see pages 191–95). No one claims these sanctions are uniformly operative or entirely obviate the need for legal restraints. A weaker proposition, however, seems worthy of support: the stronger the social sanctions in place, the weaker the case for legal ones.

Second, the informal pressures on landowners to avoid nuisances are not only social but often personal and physical. Usually harm to a neighbor can be inflicted only by persons who first inflict harm on their own property. The pollution, erosion or flooding of neighbors' land does not occur in a vacuum: frequently water or filth has to run for some length over a defendant's own land before it reaches the plaintiff's. Wholly without any legal intervention, therefore, the defendant's own land is hostage to the plaintiff's well-being. (Note the parallel to automobile accidents.) While the level of care that self-preservation commonly generates is admittedly less than optimal, the possibility of self-injury imposes an automatic loss to a defendant that no amount of legal maneuvering allows him to avoid. This physical constraint, therefore, may act as useful buffer for the benefit of neighbors.

Third, the landowner still remains at risk of tort liability for damages he causes. Typically, this threat is more potent in the land-use context than it might be with, for example, hit-and-run drivers. Land cannot move, and it is nearly impossible for a defendant whose activities are a source of pollution, erosion, or flooding to conceal those offensive activities. Happily, the land itself offers a kind of security for the right of action, so that at the margin insolvency is a less pressing risk than it is in automobile accidents.

Fourth, injunctive relief under the tort system remains a potent backstop against dangerous behavior. People will take care with their investments if they know that they will be shut down once they pose an imminent threat to the neighbors: no one wants to lose the extensive investments placed at risk by injunctive relief. The decision therefore to delay imposing legal remedies until the threat of harm is imminent does more than simplify the process of adjudication. It removes the power of the state to blockade activities that are not likely to cause any substantial harm over their expected lives.

Government permits change these relationships. Once a permit is required, the individual citizen becomes a supplicant before the government in all cases, whether or not any real threat of harm exists. Huge numbers of activities are necessarily brought into the system, only a tiny fraction of which would have resulted in direct conflicts between neighbors. Yet government at all levels is allowed to hold up operations for an indefinite period of time, often on the slenderest grounds, because the all-too-frequent presumption of state benevolence imperceptibly but inexorably eases the standards that must be met to enjoin certain forms of action. A permit may be denied by a state regulator who neither has to show that the applicant's conduct puts other persons at risk; nor, in fact, has to make any of the showings that are necessary for obtaining private injunctions.

In addition, the permit powers are strictly cumulative. The ability of the state to issue one permit with respect to one type of hazard in no way limits the power of the state to require a second permit for a different type of hazard arising from the same activity, and then a third. Permits, unlike judicial decisions, are typically issued by specialized bodies which often take strong ideological positions on the issues that come before them time after time. No longer is it possible to go before a judge who is selected not solely for his views on wetlands and environmental damages. The ostensible expertise of agency personnel is little more than a pretext for a strong one-sided commitment which skews the distribution of power within a legal system: neutral judges have only limited powers to issue injunctions, but interested program administrators have a life-or-death power to issue or deny permits. It is therefore a mystery why any court should defer to a process so rife with the possibilities of mischief. And that mischief has its clear consequences: the succession of permits required can easily consume resources that exceed the commercial value of an undertaking subjected to the permit power.

In dealing with uncertain future harms, the most that the tort law can do is strike some balance between freedom of action on the one side and risk to person and property on the other. No tort rule can reduce both risks to zero simultaneously. The best the law can do is to minimize the sum of the expected costs from both types of error, taking into account their anticipated frequency and severity. For the reasons stated, the risk of premature legal invasion is often far greater than that of tardy legal invasion. The law of remedies for nuisances seemed to be aware of both kinds of error. So why today's strong impulse to resort to multiple permit procedures?

One possible explanation relates to one inherent weakness in the private injunction, which takes the form of a familiar collective action problem: who should seek injunctive relief? In the simplest situation, conceive of a defendant whose pollution activities could injure one, some, or even all of twenty neighbors. If the pollution is discharged, the injured parties, once identified, have an incentive to bring suit for the harm suffered. But which of these parties is the obvious candidate to maintain a suit for injunctive relief before harm occurs? Acting individually, each neighbor is likely to make the familiar self-interested calculation: "Why should I incur all the costs of providing for an injunction when the probabilities are that someone else will benefit from the prevention of harm?" That selfish calculation is in general correct. If the injunction costs $100, and provides $200 worth of private benefits, and social benefits to the neighbors of $4,000, no individual neighbor whose probability of being harmed is under 50 percent would rationally seek that injunction himself. While in principle it is possible to pool expenses to obtain that injunction, the familiar litany of coordination and holdout problems will likely scuttle that enterprise before it bears fruit.

This predictable impasse opens in theory a genuine opportunity for useful government intervention. The virtuous government would tax all the neighbors their pro rata share of the cost, and then bring the suit for injunctive relief if necessary. If it is lucky, the government can recover its expenses and then use them to fund the next round of activity. In this optimistic scenario, a credible threat of legal action is likely to deter anyone from committing the harmful actions that might trigger it. I will ignore all practical complications in apportioning costs, setting tax levels, and setting a regulatory course of action. In some cases, these may prove so formidable that no sensible form of state intervention is possible. But in many cases, these problems could be overcome by, say, taxes proportionate to the market value of real property.

This argument acknowledges that the state may assume a useful role in coordinating relief from threatened harms. Yet that power justifies allowing the state only to seek injunctive relief on the same terms and conditions that would be available to a united citizenry that could coordinate its own litigation efforts. But using state power to overcome the collective action problems does not justify the next step of adopting the more stringent forms of intervention routinely used in most permit systems. Giving the government power to sue allows many diverse citizens to act as one party. But if the appropriate balance in the simplest case—that with one potential defendant and one potential plaintiff—allows the plaintiff to obtain an injunction only on some showing of imminent peril, the state when acting for all citizens should be in no better position. It, too, should have to demonstrate the same level of peril as the individual citizen does. The basic task—to minimize the sum of overenforcement and underenforcement of injunctive relief—does not disappear because the government has injected itself into substantive litigation. As currently construed, the permit power thus goes beyond the collective action rationales that called forth the use of state power in the first place.

THE CONSTITUTIONAL DIMENSIONS OF ENTITLEMENTS

The discussion of permits addresses the transformation of power as we move from private to public law. The issues relating to various forms of relief have, moreover, clear constitutional implications. How should the state deal with problems of holdout and expropriation which establish the preference for property rules in most private law contexts, subject only to the exceptions in cases of necessity or impossibility?

Private Holdouts

From this point of view, the entire law of eminent domain should be seen as standing for the proposition that no property rights are regarded as absolute against the state, when they may be taken only with the owner's consent. After all, the explicit constitutional protection of private property takes the form of a liability rule: "nor shall private property be taken for public use without just compensation."[40] So long as the government takes for a public use, individual property owners are powerless to resist its encroachment, but must accept a cash settlement when forced to surrender their property rights. Yet one great vice of liability rules is removed when that power is confined to the state: no damage cascades are possible, because *only* the state may exercise the eminent domain power. The dangers that arise from successive unilateral actions are thus eliminated.

In light of this implicit check on abuse, the use of the eminent-domain power is justified as a means to overcome or obviate serious holdout problems. Calabresi and Melamed, for example, noted that the eminent-domain power is frequently used to assemble small parcels of land into a larger unit that can be devoted to a public purpose. Land owned by a thousand people may be purchased with tax money for use as a public park.[41] Similar issues arise also with street improvements financed by special assessments on abutting landowners. Yet where the state has a choice of where to buy or to rent, it forgoes the use of its condemnation power because of the utter absence of the holdout problem.

By the same token, it is a mistake to regard the eminent-domain power merely as a pro-government liability rule writ large. An ambivalent attitude toward a "take and pay" approach led the framers of the Constitution to adopt a compromise that, at least on its face, creates a legal regime more complex than the sharp dichotomy between property rules and liability rules suggests. Although it is too easy to forget or belittle, the takings clause also contains an explicit public-use component which denies the state the automatic power to operate under a regime of "take and pay"—that is, denies it the benefit of an unconstrained liability rule.

What kinds of constraint are appropriate? Here the nineteenth-century Mill Act cases[42] are suggestive of earlier attitudes. In practice, it was possible to identify two classes of mill: grist mills, which were held open to the public at large to use on reasonable terms; and power mills, whose output was controlled privately by the mill owner without any correlative common carrier obligation (see chapter 10). Both types of mill were highly site-specific investments, and the power they generated could be obtained only by altering the flow of water within a river and often by flooding private lands. For constitutional purposes, the judges held that the flooding of lands was for a public use no matter what kind of mill was built. Constitutional language that was not perfectly adapted to its purpose used a liability rule to avert a serious holdout problem. In essence, the public-use requirement was met, not because of the public nature of the end use, but because the holdout problem required a switch from the property rule to a constrained liability rule.

At this juncture, however, it is vital to note the constrained nature of this liability rule. The Mill Acts did not contemplate action by anonymous persons bereft of institutional identities: they operated within a specific institutional framework consciously designed to limit the risks that arose from giving one party the right to take another's property for his own use. The drafters knew that the acts were needed to overcome a site-specific holdout problem that would arise if each nearby landowner could hope to hold out for a lion's share of the anticipated profits from the mill's operation. Yet it was too risky to allow people to flood their neighbor's land at will: Would the mill owner be good for the damages? Why should he be allowed to set unilaterally the extent of the flooding to another? To control these risks, the liability rule did not operate at the pleasure of the prospective mill owner. Rather, that party needed to gain approval of its location and size from independent public officials prior to flooding. Extreme wipeouts could be avoided, and the interaction of multiple dams along a single stretch of water could be coordinated. No privately generated liability rule could control these problems.

In addition, the Mill Acts called for a compensation premium, here set at 50 percent over market. The rule was a mixed blessing. On the negative side, it could block some efficient transactions whose anticipated net gain fell below the premium. On the positive side, it offered some protection of subjective elements of value that are sometimes hard to quantify in an objective setting. Indeed, the bonus seems too large for that purpose, and probably gave a landowner some portion of the overall gain from the new venture into which his land was conscripted. In so doing, it is likely that the bonus also reduced any political resistance to the taking, which could easily be galvanized if the private aggressor kept all the gain from his own action—a public-choice dimension ignored in the more static analyses of the takings law. The Hayekian principle is that the use of state power should be countenanced only where we can establish a manifest advantage from its use. The premium was a proxy for that large social net advantage.

A similar analysis applies to one of the classic takings cases, *Miller v. Schoene* (1928), which contained Justice Stone's broad pronouncements on the scope of the police power.[43] That case involved a pest that spent part of its life cycle as a harmless denizen of cedar trees, only to wreak havoc on the more valuable apple trees that grew nearby in a later stage of its development. Viewed narrowly, the case held that the owners of the cedar trees should not receive any compensation when their trees were destroyed to protect the nearby apple trees. But an institutional account of the case must abandon the passive voice and ask who chops the trees down and when? Here the simplest rule would allow the apple tree owners to act on their own accord, without having to pay compensation. But the statute rejected that initiative by requiring a state entomologist to certify the danger to nearby apple trees and to order the cutting. Once again, the intervention of the state official supplied a buffer between the owner of the cedar trees and the wrath of the apple growers. Indeed, that feature would still have been desirable even if compensation had been owing from the state (or, more likely, from the owner of the protected apple trees).

State Holdouts and Unconstitutional Conditions

The expropriation risk is not the only source of danger in government action. Just as government needs to exercise the eminent-domain power to overcome individual holdouts, so, too, the law must develop some response when the shoe is on the other foot: that is, when the government uses its monopoly position, for example, to hold up private owners seeking to improve their own lands. Just that concern has manifested itself in the courts under the doctrine of "unconstitutional conditions."[44] Ordinarily, the bargaining process works well because, in the event of impasse, the parties are able to walk away from each other. But that option is far less valuable to the citizen who, if denied a state permit, has nowhere else to turn. Hence this inversion: in the ordinary case, the right to exit carries with it the lesser right to do business on whatever terms and conditions one sees fit. But with the government monopolist, the "greater power" of denying the permit altogether does not necessarily carry with it the right to issue that permit on whatever terms and conditions the state sees fit. These bargains may be struck down even though they leave both sides better off than they would have been if no deal had been struck at all. This odd result makes, however, perfectly good economic (and constitutional) sense.

To see the danger of the government holdout, suppose that the value of a parcel of land will be increased by $2,000 dollars if a permit is issued for some new land use. The government, which knows the size of the gain, then says: "We'll grant that permit but only if you're willing to surrender for public use a lateral easement at a cost of $500 to you." If faced with the choice of either (a) having no permit and granting no easement, or (b) getting the permit and surrendering the easement, you capitulate, and accept the former, and are now $1,500 to the good. And you would do so for any condition whose burden nets out at less than $2,000.

But how do we know whether this transaction is socially beneficial over all? If the landowner's cost is $500, then the transaction does not look so bad if the public at large receives $900 in total benefits. Instead of having simply $2,000 in private gain, we now have $1,500 in private gain plus $900 in public benefits. That total gain of $2,400 is greater than the $2,000 in gain achievable simply by granting the permit. But beware: this example only shows that sometimes the best use of the property combines real estate development on one portion of the land with a lateral easement on another portion of the land. Even without bundling, the government can always bring about that happy state of affairs by condemning the lateral easement for $500. It does not have to bundle the sacrifice of the easement with the issuance of the permit.

To see why this condemnation alternative is preferable, consider an alternative scenario where the expected increase from developing the property remains at $2,000, but the exaction costs the landowner $900 and provides only $500 in public benefits. That is, we flip the relative public benefit and private loss from the creation of the easement in perfectly plausible ways. *The landowner will still surrender.* Better a $1,100 profit than the status quo ante. From a social perspective, however, we spend $900 to acquire $500, so that the overall project value dips $400 to $1,600. This onerous condition allows the local government to take property when it is worth more in private hands. The total value of the combined use of private and public holdings *declines* when the state is allowed to play the exaction game.

That undesirable outcome will never happen if the state is always forced separately to acquire the lateral easement by condemnation. Now the permit will be issued, as all other conditions are satisfied. Yet the government will not condemn the lateral easement because it is not worth its cost. Attaching conditions to permits thus leads to poor results in some cases and to good ones in others. The separation of regulation from condemnation leads to consistently good results, so long as it is difficult to persuade residents to pay $900 in taxes to obtain $500 in benefits. The just-compensation requirement imposes a much-needed price restraint on planners, and it is systematically evaded when conditions and permits are bundled together in a single transaction.

The issue of exactions has recently worked its way up to the Supreme Court in two important cases, *Nollan v. California Coastal Commission*[45] and *Dolan v. City of Tigard*.[46] *Nollan* arose out of an act of defiance. The Nollans wanted to demolished a dilapidated house on beachfront land they had contracted to buy in order to erect a more modern home in the same place. The Coastal Commission was prepared to grant the permit, but only if the Nollans ceded a public lateral easement across the front of their property. As the preceding examples indicate, in a sense the commission was offering the Nollans a good deal. They were better off taking the bitter with the sweet from the state than they were with the status quo ante. But unlike their more timid neighbors, they ripped down the old bungalow and started construction of the new house without a permit. As befits this saga, they lost in the California Court of Appeals,[47] but the United States Supreme Court upheld their temerity by finding that the state's demand for an easement amounted to outright "extortion." However, the Court did not supply any coherent explanation as to why the practice that promised short-term social gains would leave in its wake long-term dislocations. Rather, by calling the risk one of extortion, it confused the expropriation risk with the holdout risk, when the two have to be analyzed in tandem.

In *Nollan*, the California Commission offered no good reason for conditioning the permit. But in the follow-on case, *Dolan*, two such reasons for imposing conditions were advanced. In *Dolan*, the landowner wanted to expand her plumbing supply store and the adjacent parking facilities. Arguably this expansion could have two effects: first, the expansion of the impermeable parking area could increase the runoff of water into a creek, creating flooding risks for downstream neighbors; second, the access rights to the parking lot would be worth more because of the increased traffic expansion would bring. The City of Tigard, in order to pursue the objectives of its own master plan, sought to capitalize on these two features of Mrs. Dolan's proposed expansion by making her an offer she could not refuse: the city would give the permit for expansion only if Dolan would deed to the city land for a bike path and a flood easement over a nearby creek. As in *Nollan*, she would be better off with the expansion subject to the conditions than she would have been if forced to make do with the status quo. How, then, might the two cases be distinguished?

The Court's answer featured a test of "reasonable proportionality," which calls out for a close examination of the reasons invoked to justify the attached conditions and thus brings us back to the theme of harms and benefits raised in the first half of this book. The first question is whether the flood easement could be justified as a means of coping with the additional runoff from the expanded covered area; the second, whether the bike path was needed to cope with the expansion of traffic. The argument was that if the state had a good reason to impose the conditions, then the fear of holdouts and exactions were effectively neutralized. From the available record, it seems that the city should lose on both of these disputed issues.

Start with the flood easement and the parking area. Without question, if the alteration of the ground cover increased the runoff into the creek, Mrs. Dolan ran the risk of liability, perhaps under the 1868 rule of *Rylands v. Fletcher*, which imposes strict liability for the escape of things that one brings, keeps, and collects on the land.[48] This prospect of liability set up the possibility of injunctive relief, just as if the city were a private owner. On the view taken here, however, the city could not show anything like the imminent peril needed to obtain an injunction. The city was entitled to be free of excessive runoff, but choosing the method to prevent it should fall in the province of the landowner. If grading the parking lot, or adding culverts or drywells were to collect or redirect the water flow, then the city should not be concerned with how a private landowner meets its public obligations.

Indeed, the facts in *Dolan* reveal that most water that went into the creek came from all sorts of other places. The case just illustrates the importance of keeping an eye on the intertemporal relations that were important in the coming-to-the-nuisance cases (see pages 202–06). Thus, to the extent that Dolan must yield a flood easement to remove water generated by her neighbors, the city should tax those neighbors who create the externality to compensate Dolan and others who are forced to surrender land to abate the danger previously created. *Dolan* thus offers yet another textbook illustration of how planning can go awry: All the people who first pave over their land create all sorts of externalities, without cost. Next the local government subsidizes those externalities by requiring innocent landowners who come late to the scene to provide the facilities to counteract the dangers. If earlier landowners knew that they would be held accountable for escaping water, then they might have developed their land more sensibly than they did. Unfortunately, the planning process that intervenes late in the game only tries to minimize loss *given* the initial patterns of development and, therefore, subsidizes harmful activities and penalizes innocent ones. So when the dust settles, *Dolan's* reasonable proportionality test should take this form: Step 1: the planner should first determine whether the Dolans can build their parking lot without flooding. Step 2: if they can, then any demand for the flood easement counts as a compensable taking for which the city has to pay full value.

In contrast, the traffic control did not raise any issue of harm prevention at all. Rather, it involved a disguised claim to recoup the benefits the new construction confers on Mrs. Dolan. But any bike path would largely benefit people who ride past the plumbing and supply store for a day in the country. That change in traffic patterns would hardly count as a specialized benefit that inured to Dolan from the expansion. No one would make that claim that the city could just take the bike path without compensation. Why, then, treat this benefit as a reason for issuing a conditional permit given the allocative dislocations noted above? Dolan had to pay for her fair share of the new improvement, but should do so through her basic real estate taxes, rather than through any special exaction directed toward her alone. Singling out individuals for special burdens that others do not bear is pretty reliable evidence that some form of compensable taking has occurred. The Supreme

Court had little reason to remand the case for further fact finding on this point because the basic structure of the city's argument seems flawed on its face.

FROM REMEDIES BACK TO RIGHTS

Although the content of basic rights is often determined by the remedies available for their protection, sometimes what is advertised as a novel remedial pattern actually operates to nullify traditional rights. As I have discussed, the set of permissible remedies for violation of property rights is some mix of specific relief and damage protection, with the strong presumption in favor of the former. Indeed, Calabresi and Melamed address the obvious combinations in their two basic rules (property and liability) that stress either injunctive relief or damages for ordinary nuisances. That remedial debate is consistent with the time-honored conclusion that where no nuisance has occurred, a plaintiff is left without a remedy. Indeed that liability option constitutes what Calabresi and Melamed call their third rule of no liability. At this point, however, we should ask the question of why no liability should be regarded as an appropriate resolution of a nuisance case. With large-scale nuisances where filth and fumes spew over the boundary line, the only good answer to this question is that the one landowner had granted the other an easement to cause a nuisance, thereby waiving any rights of recovery. Alternatively, in those many live-and-let-live situations, the no liability outcome is justified by the reciprocal benefits that each landowner can confer on the other. Common to both cases is the reasoned elaboration of why liability is denied. And once that liability is denied, then it follows that the plaintiff is entitled to no remedy at all.

Calabresi and Melamed were, however, as much interested in articulating their typology as they were in organizing a coherent law of nuisance. That concern led them to develop their now famous rule 4, which provides: "Marshall may stop Taney from polluting, but if he does he must compensate Taney."[49] The injunction may be granted at Marshall's option but only if it is first purchased. Set into its proper context, this "startling" rule[50] has a perfectly mundane existence. If the easement to cause harm had been purchased by the defendant, then the only way in which the plaintiff could acquire his original right to quiet possession is through a purchase arrangement. Normally, we would expect that transaction to be voluntarily negotiated, in which case the usual holdout problem could arise. Rule 4 could then be justified as a way to overcome that holdout problem by requiring the plaintiff to repurchase the necessary right. And should the plaintiff's land be acquired by the state, then the rule promises nothing more startling than the exercise of the eminent domain power to buy out an easement. Similarly, if the plaintiff is in desperate straights for absolute quiet, presumably rule 4 would allow him to buy out the low-level noise that a particular defendant is normally allowed to commit.

Yet Calabresi and Melamed have a far more subversive mission at hand, for they in no way tie the use of rule 4 to these special situations in which the original property rights are shifted. Rather they take the much more aggressive position that a court or the legislature can simply decide which of these four rules it wants to adopt, and then just impose it. In that regard, Calabresi and Melamed are no longer talking about the choice of remedies for protecting entitlements. They are talking about the infinite ability of legal institutions to first define, then redefine, and redefine again the entitlements between individuals. Notwithstanding therefore their ostensible commitment to economic efficiency, their intellectual approach puts them strongly in the anti-property rights and anti-laissez-faire tradition that has exerted such great power of academic discourse.

One early manifestation of the new position is Robert L. Hale's famous book review of Thomas Nixon Carver's *Principles of National Economy* (1921). Hale's review was entitled, pointedly, "Coercion and Distribution in a Supposedly Non-Coercive State,"[51] and his basic point was that it was quite impossible to define what was meant by coercion unless we first know what is meant by property rights—and the traditional understanding that property rights include the right to exclude was a contested value judgment that everywhere propped up the system. For all we could say, an owner coerces a worker by refusing to give him a job, just as a worker coerces an owner by refusing to take a job that is offered. The world has coercion in so many places that it is pointless to limit that concept to the use or threat of force. The only question is what form of coercion we want: and that usually comes down to all sorts of state regulation of market transactions.

The same position is articulated in the more modern philosophical literature. G. A. Cohen, for example, takes the position that the right of a property owner to exclude a squatter necessarily limits the freedom of the trespasser.[52] And so it does. What Cohen's example shows, however, is only that the idea of freedom cannot possibly mean the ability to do what one wants wholly without regard to the rights of others. And those rights in property are, of course, established in order to create the appropriate incentives for investment in land and other resources. The challenge therefore is not to show that the right to exclude imposes costs on other individuals, a point that can be cheerfully acknowledged. It is to explain why some resources operate better as private resources and others as resources held in common, a task I undertake in the next two chapters.

This massive dose of philosophical indeterminacy also carries over to Calabresi and Melamed's fourfold classification of legal remedies. To see why, simply apply their logic, and that of Hale and Cohen, to violations of the person. Just the whisper that "a woman can stop a man from raping her, but if she does she must compensate him," shows how far this position deviates from our ordinary understanding of individual rights. It is with evident relief that Calabresi and Melamed recognize that the concern with "bodily integrity" precludes the application of an ordinary liability rule (take-and-pay) in these contexts: "we would not presume collectively and objectively to value the cost of a rape to the victim against the benefit to the rapist even if economic efficiency is our sole motive."[53] Obviously rule 4 would be still more grotesque: now the woman would have to pay the rapist not to rape her.

But no matter; if we are intent on rule 4, she will still be unable to purchase peace, for now she has the unhappy task of buying out the next man, and the next man after that who wants to rape her. What little plausibility is found in rule 4 depends on the implicit assumption that we have but one man, one woman, and one interaction. Introduction of multiple players over multiple periods, and any philosophical allure of these new configurations of rights and remedies should dissolve before our very eyes. No wonder no one thought of the rule until 1972.

The hint from this illustration carries back to the nuisance cases that are the primary concern of Calabresi and Melamed. Rule 4 should be peremptorily ruled out of bounds *everywhere* because of the massive destabilization of property rights it creates. Consider the connection between this rule and the coming-to-the-nuisance problem analyzed in the previous chapter. In the *only* legal case that has flirted with rule 4, *Spur Industries v. Del E. Webb Development Co.*[54] (decided coincidentally in the same year, 1972, as the Calabresi and Melamed article), the Arizona court held that a corporate developer could be obliged to pay the costs of shutdown to the owner of a cattle feedlot whose operations were intolerable to the buyers of the development's individual units.

Apart from that lonely experiment, Calabresi and Melamed's fourth alternative has largely been ignored in nuisance cases, and for good reason. The basic rule of nuisance law entitles all persons to enjoy their land free of nontrespassory invasions by their neighbors—that is, from noises, fumes, vibrations, wastes, and the like. Awarding damages or injunctions, or some combination of the two, clearly respects that basic entitlement. However, once the purchased injunction is put on the table, the discourse changes. Now individuals have the right to pollute their neighbors, who may be lucky enough to buy back their original immunity from pollution, one polluter at a time. To allow a court or a legislature to choose at will among these four alternatives confers on them the right to define, and redefine, property rights at will. The result in *Del Webb* has a surface appeal only because of the confusion surrounding the coming-to-the-nuisance issue. There is no good reason a landowner should have to buy legal protection against pollution more than once—when he first purchases the land.

An economic analysis designed to explain property rights should not be used to destroy them. Although rule 4 has little role in private law, it has of late received broader currency in the topsy-turvy world of public law. If a landowner has to buy protection against pollution, it is a short step to the converse proposition that, in the absence of pollution, an owner may be allowed to develop and use his property only if he first purchases that right from the state. Hence, we can develop a system requiring developers to "mitigate" environmental damages, even when their conduct falls far short of a common-law nuisance. Want to build a house on your own land? Then set aside at your own expense some portion of your land as a nature preserve or a wetland.[55] The choice of the word *mitigation* is no accident. The landowner becomes, by state declaration, a potential wrongdoer who can properly be asked to mitigate the damage he may create. So the modern law may come to subvert the original maxim, making the new rule, *ubi remedium, ibi ius:* wherever we can grant a remedy, we have, for better or worse, created a right.

CHAPTER 9

❖ ❖ ❖

Common Property

The importance of individual autonomy and private property for social development is undeniable. Yet too much of a good thing can often prove to be a bad thing. A fully matured legal system is not one in which all resources have passed from some primitive commons into private control. Many natural resources take a form in which their value is maximized only by leaving them, in whole or in part, in some form of social commons. Air and water cannot be uniformly and completely reduced to private ownership. Likewise, many natural resources, such as oil and gas, are most efficiently deployed under some mixed regime of property. And in respect to highways and parks, the case for private ownership has to be established, not merely presumed.

Much as one might revere John Locke, he surely misspoke in his *Second Treatise of Government*[1] when he claimed that all natural resources were given first to mankind in common, so that their transfer from common to private ownership is the major task of legal institutions. His implicit, but undefended, assumption is that common forms of property are both undesirable and unstable, while private forms of ownership are always just the opposite. Yet his preferred method for moving from a commons to a regime of private property—the unilateral decision to take by each actor—does not work for water rights which were, and are, subject to only limited rights of acquisition. His argument for private property, moreover, seems to support the privatization of all roads, parks, and open spaces, even though common practice from the earliest times has gone uniformly the other way.

Yet often the response to the Lockean view has been overreaction in the opposite direction. The socialist tradition, starting with Marx and Engels in *The Communist Manifesto,* called strongly for the abolition of all private property rights in land and for all rights of inheritance.[2] The insistence on this polar opposite is also not without its intellectual antecedents. Rousseau's *Discourse on Inequality* (1755) shows an equal hostility to the very act of fencing off private property: "The first person who, having fenced off a plot of ground, took it into his head to say *this is mine* and found people simple enough to believe him, was the true founder of civil society."[3] For Rousseau, a transition from common to private property was wholly unwelcome because "the fruits belong to all and the earth to no one."* Rousseau thus refused to understand private property as a functional system justified by long use, but viewed it as an egotistical, destructive, and impulsive arrangement which rewarded luck and unbridled greed, themes that have been restated frequently in more modern times.[5]

Sensitive to this charge of egotism, Locke sought to meet it by imposing two constraints on the system. The first is the famous proviso that insists that privatization of any thing is allowed only when "enough and as good" are left over;[6] the second, a prohibition against waste.[7] A moment's reflection shows, however, that neither of these two constraints can effectively police the transition from a regime of common to private property. The constraint against waste does not inhibit the unwelcome egotistical actions of any individual. So long as the individual who removes something from the common must pay some positive cost (whether in labor, uncertainty, or money) in making resources private, he will not commit waste, for he will be making himself better off than he would have been if he had done nothing at all. Wholly without regard to any legal side constraint on waste, he will only convert common to private property when his gains exceed his costs. By confining himself to those actions, he can beat back any charge of waste even if he simultaneously ignores the interest of others. If the commons defines the proper initial position, then Locke's constraint against waste is too weak to impose sufficient restrictions against excessive privatization: external losses may still be systematically ignored even though the constraint is satisfied.

Attacking the problem from the other side, Locke's second constraint, the insistence that "enough and as good" be left over for others, is *too* restric-

---

*   The full sentence reads: "What crimes, wars, murders, what miseries and horrors would the human race have been spared by someone who, uprooting the stakes or filling in the ditch, had shouted to his fellow-men: Beware of listening to this impostor: you are lost if you forget that the fruits belong to all and the earth to no one!"[4]

tive of private appropriation. If just as much and as good must always be left available to others, then *all* takings are prohibited no matter how large the private gains, so long as resources are in any measure scarce in a state of nature. Once the initial appropriator removes anything from the commons, how can there be as much left as before? And if one takes, as self-interest dictates, the best that one can find, how can what remains be as good as what has been taken? If Locke had weakened this condition to some balancing test—for example, take when one's private gains exceed losses to others—then often *almost* as much and as good will be left over. But in his effort to avoid this slippery slope, Locke takes a categorical position that has the virtue of clarity but the greater vice of error. His first constraint does not bind at all; his second binds too tightly. We have to start over.

A PEACEFUL COEXISTENCE OF PRIVATE AND COMMON PROPERTY

Fortunately, this "balancing" approach holds the key to satisfying Locke's sound intuition that *some* restraints should be imposed on the ability of individuals to remove property from the commons. The proper approach always requires a legal system to make, however imperfectly, the appropriate *marginal* adjustments. In deciding on removal, the proper question is whether the additional gains from privatizing the commons is greater or less than its incremental costs. If the former, then the action should be allowed; if not, then it should be prohibited. Thinking in these marginal terms was not always congenial to Locke or his contemporaries, and the formal apparatus for understanding economics at the margin only developed toward the end of the nineteenth century in Alfred Marshall's *Principles of Economics*, dating from 1890. The point here is not to criticize Locke for his failure to anticipate the future; rather, it is to understand the limitations of his position. Because of his failure to consider adjustments at the margin, Locke's two constraints pull us away from all such intermediate positions: either everything must be left behind (because of the requirement that as much and as good be left behind), or anything desired may be taken (without fear of waste).

Yet in this context, social practice often outpaced theoretical understanding. In actual fact, regimes of private and common property have coexisted, often peaceably, throughout history. Even the Roman system of property law, normally celebrated for its insistence on the absolute nature of individual *dominium* over particular assets, recognized that both common and private property were permanent and indispensable parts of the total system. A similar distribution of property rights between private and common characterizes modern legal systems, even those that operate in strong and vibrant capitalist economies. The persistent theoretical question is why a mixed solution should dominate either of the two extremes.

Analytically, the only way to define and justify a middle position is by identifying at least two divergent tendencies that must be reconciled to reach the optimal solution: otherwise, we should prefer a corner solution that banishes one form of property and relies solely on the other. Once the advantages of private and common ownership are isolated, they can be traded off against each other in individual cases. As a matter of abstract principle, either extreme position may be defended; and so, too, may any middle position; but no matter how shrill the rhetoric on either side, any responsible quest for a sound system of property rights searches for the maximum net social advantage by minimizing the sum of two rival inconveniences.

The first inconvenience is the loss imposed on strangers by any practice of exclusion. It is just this loss that Rousseau and later champions of socialism quickly spotted. The flip side of private ownership is the correlative obligation on *all others* to forbear from entry or use of the property belonging to another, or from using force or deception to block its transfer to a third party. In the eighteenth century, Blackstone spoke of the right of property "as that sole and despotic dominion which one man claims and exercises over the external things of the world, in total exclusion of the right of any other individual in the universe":[8] the unmistakable implication of the last three words is that everyone, but everyone, else is out. Since this inherent limitation necessarily imposes costs on third parties by restricting their freedom of action, it is fruitless to claim that the institution of private property represents all gain and no pain.

Thus, any satisfactory justification of private property must claim instead that some compensating advantage makes these external losses worth bearing. Sometimes, at least, they are not. Where, for example, the cooperation of a large number of individuals is necessary in order for any one to obtain private gain, private property can often create problems of mutual blockade that prevent all persons from achieving their desired ends. Just think of what would happen if the law required the consent of all underlying landowners before airplanes could fly high in the skies or broadcasters transmit their signals.[9] The problems of negotiation are large if rights of exclusion are allowed; yet by the same token, routine overflights and transmissions do not interfere significantly with productive use of the land. On the other side, the existence of private rights *between broadcasters* (which are confined to specific frequencies), and *between airplanes* (which must travel in designated lanes) shows that the principle of exclusion has a newer use even though landowners must tolerate some invasion of their airspace. This different configuration of private rights is chosen to be congenial to the nature of the resource in question.

Any complete analysis of property rights cannot overlook, moreover, the substantial costs of implementing stable systems of common property. In some instances, the problems are few because plenty of food is available for the taking. Rousseau's image of the "fruits of the earth" makes it appear that the major function of a system of property is to divide the spoils nature provides. Yet even where fruit just grows on trees, someone has to decide who gets the fruits from the lower branches, and who must climb somewhat higher. A system that allows the first taker to keep the fruit is as egotistical with respect to fruit as a system of private property in land is with respect to the earth and the trees that grow on it. In temperate climates, moreover, crops do not just grow on trees; cultivation is also required.

Given that constraint, a system of common ownership may well create major obstacles to the effective use of the land. Someone (it is never clear who) has to coordinate the activities of the various claimants to the common asset. Where use of the resource is open to all, coordination may be frustrated by the arrival of a single willful latecomer. In addition, incentives for productive labor must be created when the natural fruits of the earth are not naturally there for the taking. The older writers on private property were fond of saying that no one should be allowed "to reap where he has not sown." Coming from temperate regions, they knew whereof they spoke. Crops from the earth were not the result of natural abundance, but depended on large amounts of human labor. If Y could gather the crops X planted, then X came out worse off than if he had done nothing at all.* Protecting

---

*   Thus, Blackstone: "And the art of agriculture, by a regular connexion and consequence, introduced and established the idea of a more permanent property in the soil, than had hitherto been received or adopted. It was clear that the earth would not produce her fruits in sufficient quantities, without the assistance of tillage: but who would be at the pains of tilling it, if another might watch an opportunity to seise upon and enjoy the product of his industry, art, and labour?"

He had similar views with respect to chattels and construction: "But no man would be at the trouble to provide either [habitations or raiments], so long as he had only a usufructuary property in them, which was to cease the instant that he quitted possession;—if, as soon as he walked out of his tent, or pulled off his garment, the next stranger who came by would have a right to inhabit the one, and to wear the other."[10]

the harvest induced the original planting, and outsiders could gain from a strong system of property rights that allowed the harvested fruits to be bartered or sold.[11] In their concern with the negative externalities resulting from exclusion, the opponents of private property forgot, as Locke did not,[12] the *positive externalities* that are the unintended but welcome side effects once voluntary trade is allowed: the increased wealth creates additional opportunities for third persons to enter into win/win contracts of their own. Institutions of common property impose costs of coordination and may dull the incentives for production and trade that a system of private property nurtures.

The question, then, is which of the two sets of costs—coordination or exclusion—is likely to prove larger. This cannot be answered in the abstract, but depends heavily on the nature of the resource in question and the technology available to exploit it—as the examples of the broadcast spectrum and overflight should demonstrate. It follows that the constant trade-offs of the gains and losses of exclusion will vary across different settings, leading ideally to different social arrangements. Indeed, this is not a matter of a simple choice between property open to all and property closed to all but a single owner: in practice and in theory, it is possible to articulate a wide range of workable intermediate solutions.

Indeed, no single regime of property rights will be good for all times and all occasions. The paradigmatic case of private property involves ownership by one person—*private* itself coming from the Latin meaning "single" or "sole." But the system of private property also allows the creation of concurrent ownership (the joint tenancies and tenancies in common of the common law) among small groups of individuals by means of voluntary agreement. Not all forms of common ownership have to be created through a voluntary recombination of strong private rights: it is also possible to have *closed* systems of communal rights, such as common fields or grazing areas. Blackstone noted that the appendant commons (those created as of right) allowed "the owners or occupiers of arable land, to put common beasts upon the lord's waste, and upon the lands of other persons within the same manor.* Finally, there are systems that fall between, as with medieval villages where access to the commons was allowed uniformly to village members, but outsiders were excluded.[14] Locke understood the point, noting that enclosure of land cannot be made when the land is held in common by compact—that is, by a small group of individuals who have agreed to keep

---

*   "Commonable beasts are either beasts of the plough, or such as manure the ground."[13]

it open by contract.[15] Finally, many systems of water rights are partly open, partly closed: access to a navigable river was open to the public at large, but the right to withdraw water from that river was limited to riparians—that is, to persons who owned land along the banks of the river.[16]

The variety of possible property arrangements shows that the superiority of private property, relative to some system of common property, cannot be established by a priori argument. In some contexts, the recognition and protection of certain public rights does a far better job of adjusting the conflicts of interest between the claimants of exclusive property rights and their opponents. It is important, therefore, to set out with some particularity the boundaries between these various regimes in order to decide whether a certain resource should be held privately or in common.

The choice of one system of property rights in preference to another is *not* simply a matter of social convention or arbitrary preference such that, so long as the rules of the game are clear at the outset, their content is of no concern. To follow David Hume, these rights may be artificial, in that they are set by human convention, but they are not arbitrary, for one set need not be as good as another.[17]

A detailed examination of the property rights rules in primitive societies—loosely speaking, those that have not mastered the art of writing[18]—strikingly confirms this general thesis. These societies have developed complex rules of property rights under the most stringent of imperatives: the sheer necessity of survival. These legal regimes had incentives for efficient behavior and strong elements of both private and common property. The overall situation is well summarized by Martin J. Bailey:

> Looking at a [comprehensive] set of cases, one discovers a striking set of regularities in aboriginal rights structures. Typically, the rights in each tribe vary among types of property; but in the case of land, the rights vary with the use or resources involved. Families often had private property in land (with clear boundaries) for one food resource but not another. As the norm, groups hunted across the entire tribal (or village) territory without regard to property lines that might exist for other purposes. Also the norm, private property existing in food and other personal property as well as in land for horticultural use, where that use existed.[19]

Bailey goes on to say that the same property could shift from private to common with the seasons, so that some tribes, such as the Bushmen of the Kalahari desert, and the Penobscot, Montagnais, Naskapi, and adjacent tribes in Quebec and western Labrador, kept their lands private in winter and then treated these same lands as communal in summer.[20] The patterns in question are far from arbitrary. In winter, food was scarce and private property was used to allow each family to eke out a living from its own turf. Animals being small and territorial, the question of who owned what animal could be solved by territorial rules. In summer, when larger game were available, their capture often required cooperative efforts; thus common property (and cooperative hunting, with divided spoils) became the norm.

Bailey does not claim these trade-offs were made perfectly; and in many cases, the balance was sufficiently close that nearby groups could follow somewhat different regimes, and both survive. The social desirability of these mixed solutions is confirmed by a simple test: no one could see how the system of property rights could be improved by flipping over the use of private and common property regimes. Bailey found no cases of small plots of land being used for hunting large migratory animals in summer, or of large communal efforts being made for the smaller animals of winter. The basic patterns show the importance of taking into account both exclusion and coordination. Indeed, the ability to respect boundary lines for some purposes, but not for others, is not peculiar to primitive societies. Even modern advanced societies have allowed hunting across common property lines, as Forest McDonald noted with respect to land-use practices in late colonial America.[21]

The Lockean description, then, does not hold true as we move backward in time toward the state of nature. In addition, the orthodox treatment of the issue in early legal sources also found a place for both common and private property. Particularly instructive is the classification of "Things" in the Institutes of Justinian, which provides a brief and powerful statement of the conventional classification on the subject, adopted first in the Roman system and subsequently carried over quite comfortably into the English common law. Instead of aligning himself with either class of philosophical purist, Justinian in his *first* sentence on the matter divides property into public and private: "Of these, some admit of private ownership, while others, it is held, cannot belong to individuals; for some things are by natural law common to all, some are public, some belong to a society or corporation, and some belong to no one. But most things belong to individuals, being acquired by various titles as will appear from what follows."*

---

* The reference to various titles—that is, ways of acquiring ownership of private property—forms the basis for Blackstone's treatment of the subject in the Commentaries.[22]

Justinian's list thus contains three separate categories. The first, those things belonging to all, includes "the air, running water, the sea, and consequently, the sea-shore." The second, those things belonging to a society or a corporation, includes public buildings and (ominously) city walls, which are not only public but "sanctioned" by divine law, "because any sanctions against them is visited with capital punishment." Justinian was thus careful to distinguish, as we sometimes forget, between property left in the commons and that held by the state which reserves the right to exclude its own citizens. In the third, private property includes everything else, whether acquired by occupation or by transfer from other individuals.

Justinian's text lacks any rigorous justification for this tripartite division, because ancient writers were most disinclined to offer functional accounts of the foundations of property law similar to the one Bailey advanced for primitive social systems. For Justinian, "natural law" or "natural reason," terms used interchangeably, was the universal solvent by which legal truths were tested, and was chosen because of its reliance on rational processes of inference alone (see my discussion in chapter 1).[23] Natural law contained two components: First, it was the law common to all nations regardless of variations in local culture and local laws: "[T]hose rules prescribed by natural reason for all men are observed by all peoples alike, and are called the law of nations."[24] Second, it was a law that endured; it was immutable, not subject to variation and volatility across places; and it was not easily repealed or revised.* While Justinian's tripartite scheme makes good, practical sense, nowhere does he *explain* why the rules ordained by natural law should be followed. Instead, the appeal to natural law assumes that if everyone has done something for a long time, whatever has been done cannot be bad, even if we do not quite understand why it is good. Lacking in Justinian, and in the classical writers who followed him (Glanvil, Bracton, Grotius, Pufendorf, Locke, Hume, Blackstone), was any overt *justificatory* apparatus for the classification he announced or for the assignment of given forms of property to a particular class.

---

* "But the laws of nature , which are observed by all nations alike, are established, as it were, by divine providence, and remain forever fixed and immutable; but the municipal laws of each individual state are subject to frequent change, either by tacit consent of the people, or by the subsequent enactment of another statute."[25]

In order to fill that void, it is necessary, in light of the utilitarian program I set out in chapter 1, to demystify the law of property and ask how the institution in question relates to the human ends it is designed to serve. Here, clearly, long-held widely established customs should, in principle, be entitled to some respect, just as Justinian urged. The customs in question typically apply to recurrent situations in any society. The participants to an immediate dispute have strong and clashing interests in its outcome. Viewed in isolation, these interests tend to cancel each other out: what the one side gains the other side loses. But, in the long run, both parties to a particular dispute gain from choosing the ideal rule—a goal most likely to be reached if a disinterested third party, whose interest in systemwide soundness is usually stronger than any possessed by the parties, helps decide the matter. As Adam Smith was later to say:

> From the system I have already explain'd you will remember that I told you we may conceive any injury was done one when an impartial spectator would be of the opinion he was injured, and would join him in his concern and go along with him when he defended the subject in his possession against any violent attack, or used force to recover what had been thus wrongfully wrested out of his hands. [26]

Real-world approximations to Smith's impartial spectator work best in certain trades or businesses, where there is considerable repeat play within a closed community, where technological innovation is low or unimportant, and where the same persons are likely to assume all the roles in a given set of transactions, as by being the buyer in one case and the seller in the next. It is something of a leap, however, to extrapolate from those customs of close-knit groups to the general rules of humankind, where the same mechanisms of repeat interaction are likely to prove less effective.* To understand why Justinian's tripartite division works as well as it does, we must take a systematic look at the costs and benefits of these various rules, as applied to different settings. What would the world look like if the different resources were shuffled about in Justinian's three categories of property: common, publicly owned, and private?

---

* Robert C. Ellickson stresses just this contrast in defending the efficiency thesis, which "asserts that *land rules within a close-knit group evolve so as to minimize its members' costs.*" (Italics in original.)[27]

Common Property

Suppose the law allowed anyone to take possession of the high seas or to rip down his or her proportionate share of the city walls. While consequential-ist systems of most stripes are frequently attacked on the ground that they yield indeterminate outcomes, that objection will not work for the funda-mental categories at issue here. The discussion of primitive systems holds true even in modern times. Separate ownership of land makes little sense in a hunter-gatherer community where no one makes specific investments in real estate: it is cheaper and easier to allow all to move through a common territory. But that same conclusion does not hold when outsiders wish to come in—for what is a commons within the tribe or group is private prop-erty against outsiders. And even within the group, strong systems of private property are likely to develop in respect to movables, especially those that required labor to create. The choice of rules cannot reflect some hidden preference for private or common property when both arrangements exist side by side. Rather, it reflects efficient patterns of allocation, just as stan-dard economic theory predicts.

The same analysis applies to water rights in the high seas and rivers. These are generally held in nondivisible commons. For Blackstone, the issue was an imperative of the natural law: "For water is a moveable, wandering thing, and must of necessity continue common by the law of nature; so that I can only have a temporary, transient, usufructuary property therein."[28] Drop the natural law imperative, and ask why this distribution of rights makes sense. What would the system of water rights look like if made whol-ly private? The initial question of who is entitled to assume the preferred position as private owner is not easily answered, for it is hard to know who was the first user of an ocean or river, or any part thereof; and metes and bounds are not easily established over a body of water. But the key inquiry here is not whether exclusive possession can be implemented in practice if allowed in theory: it is whether exclusive possession should be allowed in the first instance.

Consider the relative costs and benefits of exclusion as against those of coordination: exclusive possession in the first taker is likely to impose high costs on all nonowners relative to the gains obtained by the holder of prop-erty. Today, the oceans and rivers may be used for transportation, recre-ation, fishing, and trade. The thought that one nation or person could block all these activities on the high seas or impose tolls for such use is an unpleas-ant specter. And for what purpose? No one has to build or maintain the

Mediterranean Sea. The privatization is not justified as a means to create value that others can share.

In a regime of common waterways, the costs of coordination are in general low: it is possible to develop—as were, in fact, developed—rules of the road that allow ships to pass each other by in peace and safety even as they ply common waters on separate missions. It was, and is, possible to organize these rules without supervising the composition of the traffic, a lesson largely ignored by the Federal Communications Commission (see chapter 7, pages 211–13). To be sure, these commons may turn out to be complex: some form of public enforcement might be needed to prevent their pollution or degradation of the commons; hence public nuisances have long been subject to state sanctions.[29] In advanced systems, some maintenance of public waterways may be necessary, but even that new complication does not justify closing the commons and knocking out the ease of communication and transportation facilitated by the open system: some nondiscriminatory tax on traffic could be imposed for maintenance of the common areas. In addition, any private parties charged with maintaining the commons could (as I develop in chapter 10) do so not as private owners, but as common carriers, required to serve all comers at reasonable rates.

Yet even here the analysis is not at an end, for while the primary values in the use of seas and rivers are preserved when they are held in common, further improvement is possible if some *limited* conversion of water to private use is tolerated. The underlying practice confirms the importance of making marginal adjustments to fundamental institutions. In principle, the formal problem to be solved (though Justinian and the Romans would have scarcely put it this way) is how to devise a system of rights in a body of water, which has value in multiple uses simultaneously, to maximize the combined return from its common *and* private uses. Any solution that keeps all water in rivers and seas claims implicitly that the first drop of water diverted from the river produces losses to the common that are greater than the corresponding private gains. Where water is plentiful, and rivers and seas are high, this extreme position looks wrong on its face, even though, contra Locke, "enough and as good" does not remain. But in marginal terms, an initial low-level set of diversions should, at least under some circumstances, produce private gains that exceed the losses to the commons.

The Romans had an intuitive sense of the relative values at stake because they in fact adopted an intermediate solution that left the commons dominant, but allowed some diversion from it—an approach not significantly different from keeping land private for some uses and common for others. Thus, within the classical systems of water law, it was routinely held that each of the riparians had a "usufructuary" interest—the same term picked up by Blackstone in the passage quoted above—in the water. That interest in the "use and fruits" of the water allowed them to make limited diversions for domestic uses: some damage to the commons was tolerated, but unlimited use was prohibited.[30] The interest, moreover, was not defined in terms of any strict percentage of total flow. When the waters in the common were low, then the amount that could be taken from it was reduced in proportion as well—as we should expect if the purpose of the system is to maximize the value from the sum of private and collective uses.

However functional this system may have been, the doctrinal solution was conceptually tricky for the Romans. The model for the usufructuary interest in water was the usufruct in land—an interest analogous to the life estate under English law, except that it was not transferable without the consent of the owner of the underlying property.[31] With land, the usufruct was created by grant from the owner of the underlying property; it allowed the usufructuary to use the land and to gather the fruits. There was typically a single usufructuary and a single owner of the land, so typically *all* the fruits could be gathered and consumed. In contrast, the usufruct in water was not created by a single owner of the commons. And water does not generate any fruit capable of collection. Nor does the language of tilling the land have any obvious analogy with water. Finally, there was no obvious explanation why someone who did not have title to the water could make some portion of it his own by unilateral act: Why wasn't his conduct an illegal conversion?

If the gap between the usufruct in land and that in water cannot be bridged in doctrinal terms, why does it survive? The only answer is that the large social gains from the practice made its survival inevitable. The Romans borrowed private law conceptions applicable to land and, with some tugging here and hauling there, invoked them to establish a mixed regime in water that proved stable not only in Roman times, but also for long periods of English law, where riparians likewise were said to have a usufructuary interest in water. And we keep that solution today. The fact that our major legal systems have simultaneously entertained such different property rights regimes for land and water is a tribute both to their good common sense and to their avoidance of dangerous philosophical generalizations. It is not a sign of any fatal intellectual ambivalence or inconsistency.

The proof here is in the pudding. Locke himself resorted to just this body of law in justifying his rule of acquisition: "Though the water running the fountain be every ones, yet who can doubt, but that in the pitcher is his only who drew it out? His *labour* hath taken it out of the hands of Nature, where it was in common, and belong'd equally to all her Children, and *hath* thereby *appropriated* it to himself."[32] Clearly, something serious is amiss here. Locke used the labor theory of value to account for property rights in both land and water, but was helpless to explain how two so divergent sets of property rights can be accounted for by one single variable—the extent of labor added. With water, systems of unlimited acquisition by private act work very badly, yet the labor theory of value gives no clue to what intermediate measure could determine how much water can be removed or why: if one pitcher of water can be taken out, why not an entire swimming pool? Locke's view suggests that the rules of acquisition suitable for fountains will work for rivers as well, and will do so for all time.[33] An ounce of labor gets a river full of water: no wonder socialists and communitarians have had a field day chasing after Locke for his cavalier attitude toward the unearned increment!*

The alternative account I have urged here stresses the contingent nature of social judgments about property. The strength of that position is revealed by the subsequent evolution of water law. Technology—specifically, the use of mills for power—changed the relative value of various water uses during the early nineteenth century.[35] Not without pain, the system of property rights changed with it: the dominantly defensive position of the older system of water rights gave way to alternative systems that allowed more extensive private use of the river. While the relative proportions of private and common uses had changed, the legal system evolved, if only by fits and starts, to a new position that had the same generic feature as the older system of common law: it maximized the value of the sum of all relevant uses, at least to the extent that human institutions can do so.

As the exploitation of water moved west in the United States, the instream uses were perceived to have scarcely any value at all. The rough waters were ill suited for either transportation or fishing, and riparians located on mountain bluffs had little claim that their proximity to the water gave them ease of its use. In response to these different conditions, a new system of water rights evolved: that of prior appropriation whereby the first person along a river to make productive use of a given quantity of water received a priority for the use of the like amount of flow in future years. In effect, the rules of capture for land were modified to facilitate the private use

---

* Or, for that matter, with efforts to justify the acquisition of property on a theory of desert. Although John Christman mistakenly argues that his elegant analysis destroys the Lockean theory by undermining the theory of individual desert, his view fails to meet the full range of efficiency arguments on its behalf.[34]

of water by nearby landowners. The first appropriator—the first party who was prepared to make extensive private investments in the water—was given the dominant right. If this evolution in water rights was merely fortuitous, then one must explain why prior appropriation did not arise on gentle English rivers or riparianism on the Colorado. And if the structure of water rights was immutable, then why any variation at all?

Yet the contingent nature of property rights in water hardly implies that prior appropriation is ideal even if it makes more productive use of water. Large sections of the Colorado River were reduced to barren salt flats by the aggressive removal of water under a prior-appropriation system. As with other systems of property rights, increased intensity of use could easily call for a variation in the overall legal system. The government could continue to rely on the prior-appropriation system to determine the order of private use, but subject it (much like bag limits for ducks) to some overall limits that define the amount of water that must be left in the river for other purposes. Once again, the fluid nature of the resource invites some principled adjustments in the rules governing its use.

The soundness of the Roman and English views on water rights, as just explicated, is only reinforced within the transaction cost framework, first made central to the analysis of property rights by Ronald Coase.[36] Coase's central insight was that for efficiency purposes, any initial allocation of property rights will do so long as it costs nothing to correct initial allocative mistakes made by the positive law. But once transactions costs are high, then the initial allocation stands a good chance of becoming the final one: thus, the legal system should, through custom or positive law, seek to make initial assignments that approximate the ideal end state. If one were to allow waters to be taken by first possession, everyone else in the world could presumably band together and purchase those waters for the public domain. But such reassignment would require vast efforts to coordinate thousands of separate individuals, many not yet in being, so that it could not happen, even with good fortune. Sometimes where you start is where you end; and for water, it is wise to keep the rights in common in the first place.

Publicly Owned Property

Justinian's second form of public property included public structures—most notably, the city walls—built and maintained by the state. One could conceive of these as jointly owned by citizens and capable of partition, like a family farm or other ordinary forms of joint property: one owner could take his share or insist that the whole be sold and the proceeds divided. But however sensible a partition might prove for a family farm, it would be disastrous for fortifications, whose value depends on their integrity; for them, the external costs of partition and alienation would dwarf any private gain.

Although the stakes are lower, public highways exhibit many of the same characteristics: their value comes from their being kept open for the use of all in common, subject neither to partition by citizens nor to privatization by anyone. The standard legal doctrines for highways on land are similar to those for navigation on the high seas. And in those cases where some permanent use is made of public highways, as with the placement of telegraph poles on public lands, the state is allowed to exact compensation for the permanent dispossession of the public from its general use of the lands.[37]

Private Property

Most lawyers attach pride of place to property that can be reduced to private ownership. It is there where their work is concentrated: just this property can be acquired, used, and disposed in transactions that generate legal consequences. The sheer volume of transactions has tended to overshadow the equally critical commons components of the legal system.

Justinian's system of ownership has had enormous staying power in the law, and set the framework for Blackstone's treatment of private property in his *Commentaries.** First on the list are the modes by which private property is acquired, which are so critical because land and animals are regarded as owned by no one in the initial position.[39] The legal system, however, abhors any gap in the world of rights. There are latent sources of instability when things capable of private ownership are left unowned. In order to close this gap, standard legal principles encourage simple, unilateral private actions to give certain kinds of resources a unique owner: occupation of land and capture of animals, for example. Thereafter, the rules of voluntary transfer—sale, gift, bequest, and perhaps inheritance—allow for the consensual transfer of rights.[†] Thus, if A has rights over some thing, then

---

* Of the titles he discusses—Title by Descent, Title by Purchase, Title by Escheat, Title by Occupancy, Title by Prescription, Title by Forfeiture, and Title by Alienation—only two have to do with consensual arrangements.[38]

† The word *perhaps* before inheritance is deliberate. Blackstone believed that inheritance was not a natural right of property but a privilege that could be given or withheld by the state.[40] From my point of view, his concession seems mistaken, for it leaves open two possibilities of which neither is conducive to the overall creation of wealth: first, the property reverts back to its unowned state, so that the first occupier after death can control it; and second, the state acquires ownership of the property, which is not conducive to its productive use.

the transfer of those rights to B should work to the mutual benefit of both parties. In ordinary cases, these transfers create few or no disadvantages to third parties, who have the option of trading with either A or B, depending on who owns the thing.

The rules of initial acquisition that allow for capture of wild animals do not, however, appear nearly so immutable or so sound as the natural law tradition has it. Even in ancient times, the common-pool problems of over-exploitation were serious: there are many records of mass extinction brought on by overhunting, especially in Hawaii, Australia, and New Zealand, where the local creatures had no built-in defenses against human predators. But in most cases, a set of shadowy, implicit customs probably limited the dangers to the common stock.

Yet the costs of an occupation rule need not be constant across time. Harold Demsetz's powerful 1967 analysis of the capture rule for wild animals rings true today.[41] Where hunting and fishing are done solely for the local consumption of a tribe or community, their yields are likely to be sustainable. But the moment that the catch is coveted for sale to some large external market, the new demand can threaten extinction if the "immutable rule" of capture remains in force. At this point, the capture rule will usually give way to some alternative regime that creates (when nonmigratory animals cooperate by remaining in territories throughout their lives) exclusive hunting territories for specific groups. Now that one party owns both the stock and the yield, as is the case for animals with fixed territories, incentives for long-term conservation of resources create gains that justify the increased costs of defining and policing the territorial boundaries. The new set of property rights does a better job of balancing external costs with internal gains. To be sure, the political transition may be neither painless nor equitable, if the new system of enclosures shuts out some individuals who once had enjoyed rights to commons. Although the creation of hunting territories surely will produce some uncompensated losers, it substantially diminishes the risk of wholesale destruction of valuable forms of game and fish.

Unfortunately, Locke missed the full complexity of the relationship between capture and exchange. In his view the possibility of exchange—as marked by the introduction of *"that little piece of yellow metal"*[42]—obviated the need to place any limitations on what could be withdrawn from the commons: "he who appropriates land to himself by his labour, does not lessen, but increases the common stock of mankind; for the provisions serving to the support of human life, produced by one acre of inclosed and cultivated land, are (to speak much within compass) ten times more than those which are yielded by an acre of land of equal richness lying in waste in common."[43] The clear implication of this proposition is that outsiders are amply compensated—through the enhanced possibility of their gaining through trade—for what they have lost by way of acquisition. Using territories for hunting has the same result, but sticking with the rule of capture of individual animals (which Locke himself had endorsed)[44] invites the risk of systematic overhunting, which calls in turn for direct regulations limiting capture.[45]

Water rights are subject to the same analysis, for any ability to resell water gives additional reasons to limit a riparian's right of capture. The free resale of water is likely to result in everyone's taking out of the river as much as he or she can. In order to prevent the excessive depletion of the common pool, standard rules of English property law refused to allow the riparian to alienate water as a commodity separate from the land.[46] The effect of that tie-in arrangement was to limit the amount of water that could be consumed privately in order to preserve the amount needed to maintain the "going concern" value of the river.

The theoretical implication should be clear. The labor theory of acquisition supplies no answer to the question of whether private property should be alienable. On that question, the key issue is whether the acquisition of private property leads to the destruction of some valuable common. If it does, then the case to prohibit disposition is strong, for any short-term gains from trade are likely to be dwarfed by the permanent degradation and exhaustion of the common pool. If it does not, then the gains from trade are *added* to the gains from increased production that a system of property rights yields. The ultimate empirical judgment does not generate any immutable system of property rights. Rather, it depends on the relative force of two inconsistent tendencies. In all cases, the objective is to fashion legal rules that maximize the sum of value attributable to both the common stock and private use.

So long as the results of this inquiry are contingent, it follows that transitions between legal regimes will be appropriate when the relative values of a rival use shift in dramatic ways. Although the cost of transition from one property rights regime to another has been insufficiently studied, such transition rarely takes place without genuine disruption or injustice. Recall the effect that banning the Hearst newspapers from the German front in the First World War had on the well-established system of property rights in news (see chapter 1, page 36). Often the stakes were still greater. While the

English enclosure movement, which converted common lands to private ones between the sixteenth and eighteenth centuries, may well have provided some overall efficiency gains, the customary claims of poor and marginal groups to the commons were destroyed because they were not documented in writing.[47] In its historical context, Locke's famous chapter on property could easily be read as a limited defense of the enclosure movement. Similarly, the shift from a system of riparian rights (the limited rights held by landowners adjacent to rivers and lakes to remove water) to prior-appropriation rights (great rights of removal to the first appropriator, even if not a riparian) in the Western states during the nineteenth century was often accompanied by political turmoil and private violence.[48] Finally, the rules that allowed for first possession of minerals, whales, and fish from the public seas have proved increasingly unsatisfactory over time, and the international effort to rework them by comprehensive treaty has been a prolonged exercise in global frustration.[49]

The difficulties of fashioning suitable rules for the acquisition of water or wild animals need not, however, carry over to labor or to unowned land. For labor, the traditional rule of "acquisition" was Locke's: from birth every person has property rights in his own person ("every man has a property in his own person; this nobody has any right to but himself").[50] Similarly, since land does not breed, the common-pool problems evident with wildlife are far less of a concern. Accordingly, the case for altering the traditional first-possession rule is far weaker, especially since suitable rules can, as noted earlier, be used to police the boundaries between private individuals. Recall that the occurrence of boundary disputes is the price paid to avoid the governance problems that arise from forced associations. It is far easier to keep a neighbor off your land than it is to prevent a co-owner from using more than his pro-rata share of common property or to force him to contribute a pro-rata share of labor to the joint venture.[51]

THE CONSTITUTIONAL COMPLICATIONS

In the modern era, the imperfect appreciation of the distinctive position of common property in any complete system of property rights has led to a serious incompleteness in the basic American constitutional structure. While the U.S. Constitution explicitly protects private property ("nor shall private property be taken for public use, without just compensation"[52]), it is silent about what should be done with property held in common. Must it be left in the original position? Can it be sold or given away? Who should have access to it? In order to answer these questions, a wide range of constitutional doctrines has been proposed, none of which has any sure constitutional moorings. Consider how these problems play out in four substantial areas of constitutional dispute: privileges and immunities, the dormant commerce clause, oil and gas, and the navigation servitude.

Privileges and Immunities

The first of the important cases is *Corfield v. Coryell,** which construed the privileges and immunities clause of Article IV of the Constitution: "The Citizens of each State shall be entitled to all Privileges and Immunities of Citizens in the several States." *Corfield* is best known for its impressive enumeration of the individual rights that fell under this clause,† but the case itself involved the more mundane issue of whether the state of New Jersey could prevent citizens of other states from collecting oysters in its territorial waters. Notwithstanding Justice Washington's famous list, New Jersey was allowed to use its sovereign power to keep the outsiders from sharing in the harvest. But why? If, as under the Roman law, the oysters were unowned, then why shouldn't outsiders be in a position to claim them, for privileges and immunities include the right "to take, hold and dispose of property, either real or personal"? If one begins with Justinian's view that the oysters are not owned until reduced to private possession, then outsiders can collect oysters on the same terms as the good citizens of New Jersey.

---

* The decision was handed down by Justice Bushrod Washington while riding circuit between Supreme Court terms.[53]

† "What these fundamental principles are, it would perhaps be more tedious than difficult to enumerate. They may, however, be all comprehended under the following general heads: Protection by the government; the enjoyment of life and liberty, with the right to acquire and possess property of every kind, and to pursue and obtain happiness and safety; subject nevertheless to such restraints as the government may justly prescribe for the general good of the whole. The right of a citizen of one state to pass through, or to reside in any other state, for purposes of trade, agriculture, professional pursuits, or otherwise; to claim the benefit of the writ of habeas corpus; to institute and maintain actions of any kind in courts of the state; to take, hold and dispose of property, either real or personal; and an exemption from higher taxes or impositions than are paid by the other citizens of the state; may be mentioned as some of the particular privileges and immunities of citizens, which are clearly embraced by the general description of privileges deemed to be fundamental: to which may be added, the elective franchise, as regulated and established by the laws or constitution of the state in which it is to be exercised."[54]

The analysis takes a very different turn if oysters are regarded as common property, as Justice Washington concluded:

> Where those private rights do not exist to the exclusion of the common right, that of fishing belongs to all the citizens or subjects of the state. It is the property of all; to be enjoyed by them in subordination to the laws which regulate its use. They may be considered as tenants in common of this property; and they are so exclusively entitled to the use of it, that it cannot be enjoyed by others without the tacit consent, or the express permission of the sovereign who has the power to regulate its use.[55]

What was once an abstract philosophical dispute has been transformed into an intensely practical issue. Justice Washington started from a Lockean position that all oysters were owned in common. He then accepted that taking possession of the oysters reduced them to private ownership; but his commoners included only the citizens of New Jersey, not the citizens of the world. An issue that all the learned authors had skirted—just who has access to the commons?—was now settled by referring to the federal structure of the U.S. Constitution. Yet if Justice Washington had followed the classical Roman view that treated wild animals as unowned in a state of nature, then the case would have had to come out the other way: anyone could take anything.

The Dormant Commerce Clause

In 1896, *Geer v. Connecticut*[56] addressed Connecticut's passage of a statute forbidding any person from killing "any woodcock, ruffled grouse or quail for the purpose of conveying the same beyond the limits of the state." Because the statute applied to citizens and noncitizens alike, it could not be challenged under the privileges and immunities clause of Article IV. But it was challenged as an impermissible exercise of state power under the commerce clause: "Congress shall have Power . . . to regulate commerce with foreign Nations, and among the several States, and with the Indian Tribes."[57] The clause reads as though it only confers powers on Congress over commerce, yet imposes no limitations on the states, except where state law is in direct conflict with federal legislation. But the clause has long been read as containing a "negative" or "dormant" power to preclude state regulation that interferes with trade and transportation across state lines even in the absence of congressional legislation.[58]

In rejecting the challenge to the statute, Justice Edward Douglass White began with a dutiful citation of the Roman texts, which he promptly misread: "Among other subdivisions, things were classified by the Roman law into public and common. The latter embrace animals *ferae naturae* [wild animals], which, having no owner, were considered as belonging in common to all the citizens of the State."[59] This passage is followed by a quotation from Justinian's *Digest* which stands for exactly the opposite proposition from what White was asserting: namely, that to be unowned is *not* to be held in common, so that all might take.* Even though the doctrinal playing field has shifted far from its ancient form, Justinian's *Digest* and the long list of subsequent classical writings were said to resolve a delicate point of federal jurisdiction. Because the Supreme Court held that the birds were the common property of the state, the preference for its citizens was justified. Because White held to the earlier classical vision of the topic, Justice Stephen Field dissented on the ground that the state's power could not be invoked: *"Here the State has never had the game in its possession or under its control or use"*[61] In the fullness of time, Justice Field's dissent became law. In 1977, in *Douglas v. Seacoast Products, Inc.*[62] the Supreme Court struck down a Virginia statute that limited the rights of both nonresidents and aliens to catch fish within its territorial waters. Virginia sought to justify this explicit discrimination by appealing to its ownership of the fish in question, but was sharply rebuffed: "A state does not stand in the same position as the owner of a private game preserve, and it is pure fantasy to talk of 'owning' wild fish, birds or animals. Neither the States nor the Federal government, any more than a hopeful fisherman or hunter, has title to these creatures until they are reduced to possession by skillful capture."[63] Two years later, the Court used the above language explicitly to overrule *Geer* in striking down an Oklahoma statute that made it illegal to sell or transport minnows outside the state that were caught within it.[64] So it was back to Justinian's traditional categories, and states cannot discriminate against outsiders in any effort to limit the capture of unowned wildlife.

Oil and Gas

Government regulation of the commons has also proved of importance in critical constitutional issues in the law of oil and gas. Before overdrilling was perceived as a problem, the dominant common-law rule used capture to

---

* He quotes from Justinian's *Digest,* "Thus all the animals which can be taken upon the earth, in the sea, or in the air, that is to say, wild animals, belong to those who take them. . . . Because that which belongs to *nobody* is acquired by the natural law by the person who first possesses it."[60] (Emphasis added.)

establish ownership of subterranean oil and gas. The rule differed from that governing wild animals in that only surface owners were entitled to drill for the oil and gas located beneath their respective lands. Even so, the lucky landowner who brought the oil or gas to the surface could claim it as his own no matter what disruption took place to the commons, that is, the pool of oil and gas beneath the surface. Where all owners of the land were similarly situated, it quickly became apparent that limitations on the right to drill, if imposed uniformly on them all, could leave them all better off than they were before. Just this conclusion was reached, or so it appeared, in 1899 in *Ohio Oil Co. v. Indiana (No. 1)*,[65] decided shortly after *Geer* and in reliance upon it. Oil and gas was a *res commune* subject to regulation for the benefit of all concerned.

Unlike *Geer*, *Ohio Oil* did not raise the commerce clause issue of explicit preference for local citizens; rather the statute applied to all persons who held surface rights over a common pool of resources, whose correlative rights and duties needed sharper definition. But the case has a peculiar twist that I overlooked in my 1985 book *Takings*.[66] The complexities here lie in the details. The challenged statute required any holder of land over the common pool to restrict the flow of natural gas from the pool within the two days "next after gas or oil shall have been struck in such well."[67] This sounds even-handed; and at most it looks to be a minor curiosity that the suit was brought by the Ohio Oil Company against the state of Indiana.

Unfortunately Justice White glossed over key facts to find harmony where, in fact, none existed. The statute was not directed at obstinate holders of land over oil and gas fields who refused to cooperate with their neighbors, but at two classes of producers who were pitted in sharp opposition to each other. The small Indiana firms drilled solely for natural gas. Opposite them was the Ohio Oil Company, a large producer from out of state which collected solely oil, not natural gas. The Indiana gas producers resented Ohio Oil's use of the gas as a vehicle to propel collection of the oil. That practice reduced both the amount of gas in the common field and the pressure available for its collection. The statute therefore hurt Ohio Oil by increasing its costs of production, while it helped the gas companies by reducing their costs and increasing their supplies. The burdens and benefits are hardly reciprocal. The statute works as a one-sided effort that lets local producers get the better of their out-of-state rivals—the commerce clause comes home to roost, after all.

Justice White's learned opinion treats the regulation as though it advanced the interests of all producers equally—as would have been the case if all the affected parties produced oil and gas in equal proportions. But the opinion dissolves into intellectual goo when the issue of disparate impact finally surfaces: these "contentions but state in a different form matters already disposed of. They really go not to the power to make the regulations, but to their wisdom. But with the lawful discretion of the legislature of the State we may not interfere."[68] So the flaccid language of deference sent the law into full retreat by a Court that saw no difference between reciprocal and asymmetrical restrictions on land use. A statute that thus takes from one company and gives to the other is treated like one that overcomes a coordination problem that afflicts both equally.

So how should the statute be analyzed under the Constitution? One obvious question is, What does passage of the statute do to the total output of natural gas and crude oil, and the profits thereby generated? Here monetary values offer a pretty good proxy for social values, for no delicate environmental issues complicate this statute, which was never justified as an antipollution measure. One approach is to ask whether the gas companies could compensate Ohio Oil and other oil producers, and still benefit from the restriction in place. If they could, then the statute would make sense. But another approach is to ask whether the oil companies could compensate the gas companies and stay in business. Same test, but a different baseline.

So which baseline do we choose? The first question is whether the property interest has been taken. At this point, the common-law rules on first possession make it pretty clear that they were, for no surface owner could be excluded from drilling for oil. So both parties have rights to drill into this common which the other cannot block. We now have the baseline against which to make calculations of gain and loss. The gas companies have to compensate the oil company for its increased cost of production because they demand the surrender of common-law rights. The arguments here are perfectly general and apply to any loss of property rights for which compensation is required. If all parties bear proportionate benefits and losses, then the political process will surely see that the benefit for each, and hence for all, is greater than its correlative burdens. The only way one can vote to advance one's own interest is to advance that of one's rivals. But that condition does not hold when the impact is disparate.

In 1922, Justice Holmes captured something of the dominant sense when he said that, in many takings cases, the question is whether the regulation in question is one that works for the "average reciprocity of advantage" of all parties who fall under the regulatory umbrella.[69] That condition is, as I have discussed, satisfied in the cases of lateral support, where each landowner has a parallel duty to his neighbor. But up and down do not raise the same physical questions, or legal issues, as do left and right. So Justice Holmes did the sensible thing in striking down the Pennsylvania statute which required coalmine owners, who had purchased the support rights held by surface owners, to restrict their operations just as though those support obligations were still in place. The surface owners had no parallel obligations to the coal companies. To be sure, it was in the interest of the coal companies to be cautious in asserting these rights, given that their reputations were at stake (see chapter 2, pages 63–64). But the legal conclusion reached in *Pennsylvania Coal* also held in *Ohio Oil*, which fails as an opinion because of its inability to distinguish one-sided transfers that offend the takings clause from reciprocal provisions that do not.

The Navigation Servitude

The delicate relationship between private property and the commons also comes to the fore in the context of water rights cases. To start with the simplest case, consider *Kaiser Aetna v. United States* (1979),[70] Kaiser Aetna at its own expense had dredged and improved Kuapa Pond into a navigable body of water which it used and maintained for its own members. The owners then cut the barrier that separated the marina from the navigable waters of the United States. The United States took the position that Kuapa Pond thus became part of the navigable waters of the United States; and that, as such, all members of the public were free to use the waters without being interfered with or charged by its owners. Waters that were once private and exclusive became public waters by federal decree. When Kaiser Aetna sought compensation for its loss, it was met with the government assertion that its *navigation servitude* swept all private rights aside. Since no property rights were infringed, the United States owed no compensation.

The bold claim in this case is that the federal navigation servitude operates as a trump card notwithstanding that water is an area normally dominated by systems of correlative rights. Thus in describing the navigation servitude, the Supreme Court wrote in 1956:

> The interest of the United States in the flow of a navigable stream originates in the Commerce Clause. That Clause speaks in terms of power, not of property. But the power is a dominant one which can be asserted to the exclusion of any competing or conflicting one. The power is a privilege which we have called 'a dominant servitude' or 'a superior navigation easement.'[71]

This argument had its origins in 1824 in *Gibbons v. Ogden*,[72] the first of the great commerce clause cases that held (correctly) that commerce among the several states included navigation, which thus fell within the power of Congress to regulate. The leap from the power to regulate to the navigation servitude is, however, far more controversial than the issue of congressional power faced in *Gibbons*, but it was made with stunning rapidity and little reflection. Many areas are subject to state regulation, of which land use is but one. Fortunately, no one has claimed that state power to regulate land use necessarily creates some paramount interest in land that sweeps all private claims aside.

Similarly, why should the government be allowed to run roughshod over ordinary rights of access to public water that have always been regarded as incident to riparian lands? The navigation servitude may be sufficient to prevent individuals from blocking the flow of a river (for example, by letting runoff silt up navigable passages), but it hardly justifies converting private rights into public ones. Yet that position has become the received legal wisdom about water rights: the state need never compensate riparians it has driven from the river.

To be sure, the government should not be required to accede to every private demand. It may improve one portion of the river without improving another, just as it may upgrade one road without upgrading the whole network. Similarly, the highway cases make it clear that the owner of land near a highway cannot sue the government for the loss of traffic because a new turnpike has been built in a neighboring town. Only access to the highway system is protected, not the flow of traffic that runs along it. But challenges to the government's navigation easement do not involve such grandiose claims. They protest locks and walls that make it impossible to reach the river from the shoreline. The improved public access shows that the taking is one for public use, but it hardly justifies the uncompensated loss of access rights: one might as well say that landowners need not be compensated for their losses because the government builds a much-needed highway on the taken land.

To be sure, *Kaiser Aetna* involves the somewhat novel set of circumstances of a private body of water that was said to become public only after its owner sought access to public waterways. The Supreme Court, however, did not find any occasion to revisit its earlier decisions on the navigation servitude, but contented itself with protecting the right to exclude: "In this case, we hold that the 'right to exclude,' so universally held to be a fundamental element of the property right, falls within the category of interests that the Government cannot take without compensation."[73] Private property owners do not lose their essential right to exclude because their private waters are linked up to a navigable body of water. Access to land and water are governed by the same principles. Just as ordinary landowners have an unconditional right of access to public highways, so too, owners of private waterways have the same right of connection to public ones.

But why, one may ask, are rights of access part of the original bundle? The explanation lies in the constant need to define ownership rights to minimize the bargaining breakdowns that come from erecting monopoly blockades. Here the common-law recognition of a right of access to public property constrains the monopoly power of the government. That same logic should carry over to rights on public waterways generally. As noted earlier, the common law from before the time of Blackstone developed a system of correlative rights in water that denied any single actor the whip hand over the system. How ironic it is, therefore, that the Supreme Court's decisions on water rights have tended to crush all competing private interests beneath its expansive reading of the navigation servitude.

In *United States v. Chandler-Dunbar Water Power Co.* (1913),[74] the construction of a government dam raised the water level in a navigable river so high as to render Chandler-Dunbar's power plant inoperative: no matter, compensation was denied. The same result was reached some thirty years later in *United States v. Willow River Power Co.* (1945),[75] where once again the United States constructed a dam that denied the power company its generating power from a headwater. Justice Robert Jackson dutifully held that the head of water may have had economic value to the power company, but concluded only that "not all economic interests are 'property rights,'"[76] where the quotation marks were thought to clinch the issue. The result seems indefensible: had any private user of the water so altered its flow, an injunction and damages would have been allowed as a matter of course.

The cases are not limited to the removal of height differentials in water levels needed for power mills, but have also allowed the government to destroy, by both flooding and orders of removal, private improvements constructed between the low- and high-water marks, even though once again, no private party could escape liability for such actions.[77] The navigation servitude has also proved powerful enough to allow the United States to destroy without compensation all riparian rights of access to navigable waters, by holding that the value of land as a "port site" can also be wiped out by the navigable easement.[78] How ironic. The standard attacks on Blackstone's view of property criticize its dogmatic assertion of the absolute right to exclude. Yet in water rights, where no common-law court has ever held this position to be appropriate, it now becomes, on dubious grounds, the lodestar of constitutional interpretation. The commons has not proved resistant to sovereign attack.

CHAPTER 10

❖ ❖ ❖

Common Carriers

Common property embraces not only water, highways, and some undeveloped land, but also the so-called common carriers, a hybrid institution which is at once more comprehensive and more important than its dullish nomenclature suggests: railroads, gas and power companies; telegraphs, telephones, and all modern forms of telecommunications are charter members of the list. Unlike oceans, rivers, and beaches, these common carriers do not get up and running as simple gifts of nature; all require substantial investment, which must be recovered somehow from some public or private source. The area is shot through with "second-best" considerations. It is always possible to add public subsidies to the mix, but only at the risk of constructing monumental white elephants. So it seems best to cover the costs of construction and operation from revenues collected from these carriers' customers. But how much can these customers be charged? And who decides the rates? Unregulated rates open up the prospect of monopoly exploitation; regulated rates open up the converse risk of confiscation of the capital invested in the new improvement. Formulating the right technical rules in this high-stakes arena occupied the energies of the legal profession from the end of the Civil War through the Second World War.[1] The topic never disappeared thereafter, and has received renewed attention in recent years with the major initiatives to restructure the electrical power and telecommunications industries. Indeed, issues developed historically with common carriers often are discussed today under the heading of regulated industries. How should the law regulate these industries to reconcile private ownership with the common good?

All regimes of private property start by conferring on an owner the right to exclude the rest of the world. That right sets the stage for deciding who thereafter is kept out and who is let in. Private property ushers in a regime of private contract. Anyone with the power to exclude also has the right "to select and determine with whom he will contract, and cannot have another person thrust upon him without his consent."[2] This categorical right is not a celebration of the human capacity to rely on bad reasons in accepting or declining contract opportunities. The greatest utility of the categorical rule lies in its dispensation of the need for an owner to demonstrate the good reasons for exclusion, which are frequently available but difficult to articulate and explain. Where the refusal is arbitrary and capricious, the availability of some eager competitor removes its sting.

In most contexts, the soundness of this world view is untouched by technological advance. As I have argued on other occasions, a multitude of choices provides far better protection against malice, exploitation, and prejudice than does any antidiscrimination law.[3] The world of contractual choice allows everyone to select those individuals most inclined in his favor and to ignore those who are least so. Contractual freedom thus allows minorities to progress without having to kowtow to majority will, which is why ostracism typically fails when new entrants are allowed to set up shop. This world of free entry is a far cry from one that tolerates unbridled force and fraud, where people cannot profit from friends but must continually ward off enemies. The correct background rule, then, grants each person the right to exclude and to choose, but none to coerce any transfer or exchange.

The relative weight of the competing considerations changes radically, however, when legal or practical restraints block new entry into a market. In the strongest case, the law grants a single person a franchise (read: local monopoly) over a given service for reasons, real or imagined, of public policy or necessity. Historically, one common situation called for the franchisee to construct a bridge or a road for which tolls might be recovered, usually in accordance with some prespecified schedule, calculated to assure the franchisee a reasonable rate of return on its investment. Often maintenance costs for bridges and roads were low, so that the initial agreement could set out the toll schedule for the useful life of the improvement, a luxury not available with the more complex operations of railroads and telecommunications.[4]

The wisdom of that initial franchise arrangement may be sharply challenged in many contexts. My concern here is not with the justification for this arrangement, but with its consequences for a general regime of freedom of contract. Once new entry is prohibited, consumers lose their ability to play one potential trading partner off against another. No longer is everyone able to seek out that person who offers the most favorable deal. The party who controls the market is in a position to make "take it or leave it" offers that do sting. If that party harbors hostile intentions, or is aware of the particular needs of some of its customers, or of their wealth, then it can deny service or demand supracompetitive prices that soak up the gains consumers ordinarily garner in competitive markets. The dangers of extraction are evident. The question is what, if anything, the law should do about it.

Now definitions matter. If we treat laissez-faire as a paean to individualism and contractual freedom, then any loss in opportunities attributable to change in market structure plays no role in the overall assessment of a sound legal structure. Legal rights fall into rigid and formal categories. But if, as Aaron Director wrote, "[l]aissez faire has never been more than a slogan in defense of the proposition that every extension of state activity should be examined under a presumption of error,"[5] then it is not only fair, but imperative, to ask what evidence is needed to overcome the presumption. Now the threat of monopoly power offers a principled social reason for limiting the scope of contractual freedom, one long acknowledged in the academic literature,[6] and accepted by both English and American judges. Speaking of the United States Supreme Court in the period between 1890 and 1910, Professor James Ely wrote: "Copious evidence suggests that the Supreme Court under [Chief Justice Melville] Fuller was not a bastion of formalism."[7] Then, after noting the *lack* of influence that Herbert Spencer and Social Darwinism had on the social attitudes of Supreme Court justices,[8] he concluded: "Their defense of economic individualism was tempered by a commitment to federalism and antagonism to monopoly"[9]—especially monopolies that were created pursuant to state franchise or license.[10]

The legal treatment of common carriers in England and the United States confirms the basic point. During the height of laissez-faire, the judges invoked strong countermeasures against monopoly power. The scholars who stress the abuses of laissez-faire and freedom of contract provide a very inaccurate portrait of the overall picture by overlooking the distinctive rules covering roads, rails, waterways, custom houses, and, later, public utilities.[11] Since that history, both English and American, bears heavily on the modern issues of take-all-comers, interconnections, and rate regulations, I turn to it first.

THE ENGLISH BACKGROUND

The early common law regulated a diffuse set of common callings, broad enough to include, in addition to many common trades, the early forms of common carriers, and the operators of inns and (horse-drawn) carriages.[12] Often an operator of one of these facilities was the sole party engaged in the recognized line of business in a given location or along a particular route: there was only one inn on a highway, which in turn was served by one carrier. In many cases, the monopoly in question was not contingent on its factual circumstances, but derived directly from some exclusive state grant. At this point, the fact of monopoly power has been crystallized in law. What type of legal response should it induce?

A clear answer to that challenge is found in the pivotal decision in the 1810 case of *Allnut v. Inglis*.[13] The plaintiff was a wine importer. The defendant was treasurer of the London Dock Company, which had received by statute the exclusive right to warehouse wines shipped into England from overseas, without first having to pay any import duties upon them. The defendant's company published a list of its prices for accepting wine for storage. When the plaintiff refused to meet the price demanded, the defendant refused to store his wine, which was then subject to avoidable duties of £500, for which recovery was sought. The court had to decide whether the company, in virtue of its statutory monopoly, was required to sacrifice its common-law right to sell or rent its facilities for the best price it could fetch, and accept instead only a reasonable price for its services. If the right were absolute, then the duties could not be recovered; if it were conditional, then recovery could be allowed.

Tracing the argument in detail demonstrates the principled limitations that laissez-faire judges placed on freedom of contract. Richardson, for the plaintiff, relied explicitly on Lord Matthew Hale's posthumous volume* *de portibus mari* (loosely translated, "concerning the gates to the sea"):

> A man for his own private advantage may in a port town set up
> a wharf or crane, and may take what rates he and his customers
> may agree for cranage, wharfage, &c; for he doth no more than
> is lawful for any man to do, vis. make the most of his own, &c—
> If the kind or subject have a *public* wharf, unto which all persons
> that come to that port must come and unlade or lade their

---

* Hale, who lived from 1609 to 1676, was a distinguished legal historian and author. This treatise was published posthumously in the 1780s.[14]

goods, as for the purpose, because they are the wharfs only licensed by the queen, according to the st. 1 Eliz. c. 11., or because there is no other wharf in that port, as may fall out where the port is newly erected; in that case there cannot be taken arbitrary and excessive duties for cranage, wharfage, &c, neither can they be enhanced to immoderate rates; but the duties must be reasonable and moderate, though settled by the king's licence or charter; for now the wharf and crane and other conveniences are affected with the public interest, and they cease to be juris privati only. As if a man set out a street in a new building on his own land, it is now no longer bare private interest but it is affected with the public interest.[15]

Bosanquet, for the defendant, countered by saying that while the defendant must open his facilities to all comers, "he may limit his engagement with the public, and then he is not bound to admit travellers in the one case [a public house], or to carry goods [a public carrier] in the other, upon any other terms than those upon which he engaged."[16] Lord Edward Ellenborough, the chief justice, promptly interrupted by referring to the prospect of free entry by others: "It must be recollected that in those cases there is a power in the public of increasing the number of public houses or of carriers indefinitely."[17] So he was aware of the role of both free entry and the different levels of market dominance within the broad class of common callings. His opinion hones in on the fundamental theme:

> The question on this record is whether the *London* Dock Company have a right to insist upon receiving wines into their warehouse for hire and reward arbitrary to their will and pleasure, or whether they were bound to receive them for a reasonable reward only. There is no doubt that the general principle is favored in both law and justice, that every man may fix what price he pleases upon his own property or the use of it; but if, for a particular purpose, the public have a right to resort to his premises and make use of them, and he have a monopoly in them for that purpose, if he will take the benefit of the monopoly, he must as an equivalent perform the duty attached to it on reasonable terms.[18]

This passage limits the role of freedom of contract for common carriers, while avoiding any tendency to construe the common-carrier exception narrower than its logic required. The passage cited from Lord Hale made it clear that the obligation could attach to de-facto as well as to statutory monopolies (as with the wharf in the new harbor); those obligations could shift with changes in market structure. The extension is not without its own conceptual and practical difficulties. Where monopolies are created by law, the recipients are bound by consent, through conditions contained within the original grant, as a quid pro quo for the market power. The legitimization of public controls is relatively straightforward. Where the monopoly position is obtained simply by early entry into a new market, the recipient does not consent to rate regulation as a condition of his grant. Regulation must come, if at all, by a sheer assertion of state power, not by consent. Unless that power is unlimited, the regulation must be justified on the ground that any monopolist charges too much and sells too little relative to the social—that is, competitive—optimum. But even when true, the case for regulation is hardly ironclad. The situational monopoly may confer only limited pricing power, and its durability could be cut short by new entry, or by technical innovation. Regulation could easily cost more than it is worth, especially if the regulation entrenches present forms of production against the innovation needed to undermine its economic dominance. On the one hand, the rates charged may be set so low that the firm cannot cover its costs. Alternatively, regulation could give the regulated party protection against new entrants whose presence eliminates the need for rate regulation in the first place.

The regulation of state monopolies presents these same pitfalls, but usually the case for imposing some regulation is stronger. To be sure, there is no necessity that any legal grant confer substantial monopoly power, but the correlation between the legal franchise and the risk of private abuse is likely to be great. Why bother to obtain a state monopoly if it confers no advantage on its holder? Statutory monopolies have great durability, and, as with the customs monopoly in *Allnut*, may have no close substitutes. So setting the terms on which they operate should make a difference in the prices ultimately charged.

Allnut shows that nineteenth century judges were alert to the dangers of the state monopoly, without suffering from the intellectual rigidity or textual formalism of which they are so often falsely accused. In *Allnut*, the governing statute was passed with the intention of expanding overseas trade, which was facilitated by allowing goods to be shipped outside the country without paying the customs duties for goods bound to domestic markets. Perhaps competitive warehouses could have served this function. But at a guess, the defendant's monopoly might have been created because the state could not supervise multiple warehouses to prevent export goods from being smuggled into the domestic market free of the required duties. But the cure to one problem raises a second: expanded export trade could hardly be achieved if the defendant's monopoly position created an operational bottleneck. To avoid that outcome, the judges stretched the statute to firm up the defendant's correlative obligations, even though Bosanquet pointed to the similar restrictions on tobacco, which explicitly limited the rents that could be charged.[19] The argument from silence was rejected by looking to the larger purpose of the act.

In keeping with the basic theme, Lord Ellenborough also alluded to the difficult issue that would arise if other warehouses were licensed to receive the imports before the duties were levied. The resourceful Bosanquet had suggested that the power to charge arbitrary rates should be allowed because it lay within the power of Parliament to authorize the establishment of additional warehouses to receive imported goods.[20] Ellenborough's answer came in two parts: first, if those new facilities were under the control of the defendant, the expansion in capacity would do nothing to moderate the monopoly problem; second, the extension of the license to a few competitors would not do the trick "if the right of the public were still narrowed and restricted."[21] It seems clear that he understood, at least intuitively, the distinction between a fully competitive market and a cartel, and perhaps even an oligopolistic market with price leadership. The former surely poses many of the risks of a monopoly; the latter less so, because the equilibrium price drops as the number of noncooperating firms increases.

The decision in *Allnut,* thus securely anchored in the past, was the point of departure for all subsequent judicial decisions, English and American, on the obligations of common carriers for the remainder of the nineteenth century and beyond. Nor were these obligations taken lightly. In fact, the designation of common carrier—or (as it was sometimes called) "affected with the public interest"[22]—led to a complete and conscious inversion of the individualistic model of private property that applied elsewhere in the common law. Ordinary individuals could choose with whom to deal and why. In contrast, the common carrier could not refuse to take customers unless they showed cause, narrowly confined: for example, rowdy behavior, inability to pay. The ordinary individual was under no obligation to offer the same deal to one customer that he gave to another; the common carrier had to discharge its service obligation without discrimination among customers who presented the carrier with similar costs—a prohibition designed to control the rent-extraction threat posed by a price-discriminating monopolist.

The ordinary individual could set prices as he pleased, constrained only by the prices his competitors quoted; the common carrier, who had no competition, could charge only reasonable rates for its services: otherwise even the nondiscriminating monopolist could extract some supracompetitive return (in fact, the precise situation in *Allnut*).[23] The ordinary party could limit its tort liability by contract; the common carrier, as a general matter, could not. The courts feared that limited liability operated like a de facto price increase.

Although the terminology of the nineteenth-century cases is not quite modern, their feel is: the courts fashioned rules that forced common carriers to provide their service at prices that allowed them to cover their costs, plus a reasonable economic profit. But at no point did they invoke the notions of "affected with the public interest" to force carriers to provide their services to customers below their true costs. Efficiency was one thing; welfare, quite another. Nineteenth-century law suggests that Patrick Atiyah, a prominent critic of laissez-faire, was clearly wrong in claiming: "The old rules holding that a man who exercised a common calling was obliged to serve anyone who wanted to deal with him, came to seem more and more anomalous."[24] In fact those rules enjoyed great vitality throughout the period.

The real challenge was to put flesh on the basic bones. There are any number of combinations of prices for various classes of customers and services that allow a firm to cover its costs and to receive a reasonable rate of return on its investments. The hard question was not to acknowledge some need to respond to the problem of monopoly, but to figure out what response was best. And it was just that set of problems that preoccupied American courts who self-consciously inherited the tradition of Hale and *Allnut* in the late nineteenth century.

LATE NINETEENTH-CENTURY AMERICAN DEVELOPMENTS

The basic conception of the English law that businesses "affected with the public interest" were subject to various forms of price and rate regulation was carried over lock, stock, and barrel into American constitutional law. In 1876, the question in *Munn v. Illinois*[25] was whether the state could impose rate regulation on the grain elevators in Chicago. The passage I have quoted previously from Hale's treatise was adopted by the Supreme Court in a decision that denied any constitutional impediment to reasonable rate regulation of these firms, given that their critical position in the transshipment of goods was enough to affect them with the public interest. The decision created an enormous dissonance in constitutional law, because it did not clearly adopt Hale's equation of "affected with the public interest" with the possession of (statutory) monopoly power. The ambiguity was further aggravated because it was unclear whether the regulated grain elevators held "a virtual monopoly" (as by cartelization) or simply represented a number of competitors necessarily located in close physical proximity to each other and to the railroad lines.

As a general economic matter, it seems clear that an interpretation of "affected with the public interest" that focuses on monopoly is the better one. Many identical firms operating in close physical proximity may indicate a competitive industry in which price regulation serves no useful purpose. Even so, in the ensuing years, many cases read *Munn* to allow, for example, for the regulation of the intensely competitive insurance industry.[26] The mischief of that position should be evident enough: rate regulation of competitive industries both reduces revenues and increases costs, vastly increasing the risks of confiscation or bankruptcy. The normative case against those forms of regulation seems strong enough to direct our attention elsewhere. For these purposes, the common carriers examined in this chapter usually fall within the class of monopoly service that lacks any close alternatives. Although the class of industry does not (or, at least, should not) include butchers and bakers, it clearly extended far beyond the customs monopoly in *Allnut*. The nineteenth-century cases never resisted that implication.

> It [the status of common carrier] is as old as the common law itself. It has arisen in a multitude of cases affecting railroad, navigation, telegraph, telephone, water, gas and other like companies, . . . [N]o statute has been deemed necessary to aid the courts in holding that, when a person or company has undertaken to supply a demand which is affected with the public interest, it must supply all alike who are like situated and not discriminate in favor of nor against any.[27]

The judicial treatment of the common carriers focused on two separate topics: liability and rates. The first determined when common carriers could be held liable for personal injury and property loss arising out of their course of business. The second established the rates they were allowed to charge their customers for the services rendered.

Liability

As the law evolved during the seventeenth century, common carriers were held to a high standard of care to the public at large. That duty could not be waived by private agreement with its customers.[28] Why? One explanation is that contractual exemptions are disallowed to prevent carriers from raising de facto rates above some state-mandated level. But this rationale could not apply to common carriers subject only to common-law tests of reasonableness and nondiscrimination. Even in regulated industries, the firm could be asked to announce its choice of liability rules before receiving its rate schedule. In principle, the monopolist has no reason to seek waivers if it can recoup its expenses, and more, by giving customers exactly the same terms they would receive in a competitive industry.

Once the standard of liability—wisely or not—becomes a judicial function, it is then necessary to define the content of the relevant rules. Although some cases held that common carriers owed their passengers only the standard tort duty of reasonable care under the circumstances,[29] the bulk of the legal authority embraced a higher standard that held the carrier liable for the safekeeping of the goods (*custodia*), excusable only by an act of God, or an act of violence, perhaps only by the king's enemies.[30] This was summarized by one early twentieth-century writer: "Certain things undoubtedly will excuse one engaged in a public calling from full performance of his usual duties. The familiar examples given in all the text books are 'acts of God and of the public enemy.'"[31] In practice, a carrier's liability was strict unless one of those two conditions were established. And even after either was established, a defendant was not automatically excused: now liability turned on negligence—that is, the failure to anticipate and avoid the identified perils.

Like all elaborate compromises, this one had its strengths and weaknesses. The basic strict liability rule was intended to make it more difficult for carriers, or their employees, to collude with third parties to rob their passengers. Yet, by the same token, the rule did not hold them responsible for crushing losses in the event of widespread loss brought on by external forces or public enemies. For those, the individual shippers had to bear the residual risk. But even here they could free-ride on a carrier's own self-interest in protecting its personnel and property from these same perils. With the risks so large, any rule was bound to create either bitter disappointment or financial dislocation. The source of relief lay not in refining these rules of liability, but in technical improvements that increased the speed and efficiency of common-carrier operations. Lawyers often worry too much about the allocation of loss between litigants. In business, it is often better to use technology to reduce the frequency and severity of loss so that the liability question recedes in importance.

This higher standard did, however, make a big difference, not so much in cases of loss, but in those concerned with interruption in service attributable to labor strikes. Court after court uniformly held these obligations to be strict. The employer whose workers were out on strike had the clear duty to hire substitute workers to continue its service, and could raise a defense only if the incumbent workers did more than leave their positions, by engaging in active violence against the firm.[32] The head note of one case bluntly states the point in 1859: "A railroad corporation is responsible for damages resulting from a delay to transport freight in the usual time, which was caused by a great number of its servants suddenly and wrongfully refusing to work."[33] Another case, in 1888, was equally blunt: "Now, the question is, what shall be obeyed,—the law of the land, or the order of the chiefs of the locomotive engineers?"[34] The question has but one answer. And the Court quickly added that the carrier had to meet its obligations to its passengers even if other carriers would refuse connections with the struck line. Over and over courts insisted that the carrier's obligation to the public could not be defeated by union pressures, whether on the struck carrier or on the other firms that did business with it. Only violence would allow it to discontinue service. These obligations were never imposed on an ordinary firm. The legal or de facto monopoly created a litmus test for service obligations.

Employees

In invoking this higher standard of liability, the nineteenth-century cases drew a sharp, and correct, distinction between the obligations a carrier had to the public at large and those it owed to its employees. Thus it was clear from the outset that the tort defense of common employment applied only to fellow servants—that is, co-workers—whose position was explicitly contrasted both with that of customers to whom the nonwaivable duty was owed, and with that of innocent bystanders. For example, in 1897, in *Fletcher v. Baltimore & Potomac Railroad*, it was held that the liability to a pedestrian for railroad ties thrown off the train was "not to be gauged by the law applicable to fellow-servants, where the negligence of one fellow-servant by which another is injured imposes no liability upon the common employer," but by a higher standard used to protect strangers.[35] However, in the employment cases—as with porters who served on Pullman cars—explicit waivers were held routinely valid not only against the Pullman Company as employer, but also against the railroad line that carried Pullman's cars.[36] Nor was the explanation lost on the courts: the monopoly position that carriers exerted in their service markets did not extend to their relations with their employees, who were free to return to their previous employment—as a stationary engineer or electrician, in one case.[37]

For employees, the usual principles of freedom of contract applied, and these often yielded not blanket releases from liability but complex arrangements that anticipated by more than a generation the workers' compensation arrangements that were adopted by statute from the 1880s to the beginning of the First World War.[38] In light of this general background, the courts were happy to recite, verbatim,[39] the highly influential defense of freedom of contract Judge Jessel wrote in 1875, in *Printing and Numerical Registering Co. v. Sampson*:

> It must not be forgotten that you are not to extend arbitrarily those rules which say that a given contract is void as being against public policy, because if there is one thing which more than another public policy requires it is that men of full age and competent understanding shall have the utmost liberty of contracting, and that their contracts when entered into freely and voluntarily shall be held sacred and shall be enforced by Courts of justice. Therefore, you have this paramount public policy to consider—that you are not lightly to interfere with this freedom of contract.[40]

Since these contracts were not regulated by public policy, it followed that the exemption clause was valid so long as it covered the situation at hand. There was no hint of the modern, destructive doctrine of *contra proferentem*, under which the words of an agreement are sometimes tortured in order to grant an after-the-fact victory to the weaker party, even at the price of introducing excessive opacity into agreements initially clear on their face. Since no artificial presumptions were created in favor of either side, in the end we have the blandest and most accurate view of statutory or contractual interpretation: "the same rule of construction should apply to them as to ordinary, valid stipulations."[41] Because the common carriers occupied no distinctive position toward their employees, no distinctive legal rules applied to the latter's treatment.

Customers

The relationship of a common carrier to its customers proceeded along different lines, in light of its monopoly power. In 1896, in *Coy v. The Indianapolis Gas Co.*,[42] the plaintiff brought a wrongful death action when his child died from a cold after the defendant had failed to complete the required hookups of the plaintiff's home to its natural gas system. At one level the issue in the case was whether this complaint sounded in contract or tort: that is, whether the duty arose by agreement or by operation of law. The consequences of this choice were substantive, not formal. The defendant urged that the contract it had entered into with the plaintiff should determine the scope of the former's liability: contract damage rules would therefore apply, and these narrow rules on the recovery of damages typically would have precluded any recovery for the child's wrongful death.[43] In an ordinary consensual setting, explicit contracts should override legal commands: industrial accident, medical malpractice, and occupier liability actions fall under the principle, although trespass and nuisance cases do not. But common carriers do not fall neatly into either category: since their service obligation predates any contract with its customers, so the Indiana court in *Coy* treated the duty as one arising as a matter of law: accordingly, tort principles bound the common carrier not only for failing to supply a hookup but also for badly managing the one it had, in fact, supplied.

Classifying the common carrier's liability in tort did not, of course, comport with the usual requirements of a stranger case. The defendant had not used force against the plaintiff, and had not created some trap or other dangerous condition; the case concerned only the failure to provide services. In ordinary cases, the usual common-law rule denied any legal obligation to rescue (or provide services to) a stranger. In 1901, shortly after *Coy*, the Indiana court applied that rule in *Hurley v. Eddingfield*.[44] Even though physicians were subject to general licensure, they were under no duty to supply services to their own patients unless they agreed to do so: "Counsel's analogies, drawn from the obligations to the public on the part of innkeepers, common carriers, and the like, are beside the mark."[45] The words were not some idle brush-off, for if the defendant had been subject to a common-carrier obligation, precedents like *Coy* would have doomed his defense. The difference between an autonomous individual and a regulated monopoly could not have been more clearly expressed. The licensing power may well have reduced the number of physicians allowed to practice within the state, but it did not create anything close to the level of monopoly power possessed by any common carrier.

The outcome in *Hurley* should not be lamented, even today. The case arose only on the pleadings, and we have no indication of the actual circumstances that led the defendant to refuse to come to the aid of the plaintiff. Nor do we have any indication as to how frequent such occurrences are—at least, in cases of genuine need. Yet we should be aware of the risks that run in the opposite direction.[46] Is it really wise, even in cases of necessity, to allow one person to use payment to commandeer the labor of another? It is one thing to impose strong obligations of service on an institution that from its inception is organized to supply standardized services to all comers. It is quite another to impose similar obligations on ordinary individuals. Modern courts and legislatures are eager to condition the grant of a license on the willingness of individuals to comply with new and additional state-imposed service obligations. In so doing, they use their own monopoly power not to maintain a competitive economy, but to extract special favors from the licensed class for the benefit of others who are not prepared to pay compensation. One great achievement of the nineteenth-century judges was their willingness to search for a proper balance: they used state power to counteract private monopolies, while they were fully aware that government power was on balance more dangerous than the autonomous choices of private individuals.

Service Obligations

Common carriers were also distinctive in their service obligations. In 1901, in *State ex rel. Wood v. Consumers' Gas Trust Co.,*[47] a natural gas company was placed under a strict obligation to supply service to a new customer along its route notwithstanding unavoidable shortfalls in its supply. The Indiana court's basic position (which tracks the parallel rule on riparian rights [see pages 261–65]) is that "there can be no such thing as priority or superiority of right among those who possess the right in common."[48] The public utility used contributions collected from all abutting owners to construct its power lines across public streets. Since all the owners provided the company with its opportunity to do business, none could be excluded from service. In the face of shortages, the correct solution cut back, pro rata, the gas allocated to existing customers so that a latecomer could share on equal terms with prior users, in conformity with the traditional nondiscrimination principle. Once again, the court had no difficulty in adopting a sharing rule for this commons, in sound opposition to the general rule that uses priority of possession to establish ownership of land and wild animals.

The duty to serve, then, has the correlative duty of universal service. But in other contexts, the pricing question is more difficult than the outcome in *Wood* suggests. To be sure, on its facts, the plaintiff, who was the new customer, presented an attractive case, since he had already outfitted his house with the furnace and equipment to use the gas and had no obvious alternative source of supply: burning firewood doesn't quite cut it. But the use of the nondiscrimination principle in various monopoly settings deserves closer attention. On the positive side, the test goes a long way toward preventing political favoritism and intrigue. It also reduces the pressures on individuals to hasten construction, file permits, or do whatever else will get them in under the wire in order to establish priority over their neighbors. The need to control against that risk is critical in the fevered world of subdivision development. The time when new construction starts or ends should not decide whether someone freezes in wintertime. Most voluntary private subdivision arrangements contain detailed contractual provisions on appearance, assessments, and use limitations; and these are drafted so that the benefits and burdens of the system are the same for early entrants as they are for latecomers: the developer does not want customers to think that a delay in purchase could transform itself into an improvement or a deterioration in the correlative rights against neighbors. The antidiscrimination norm helps to control that behavior.

In addition, the rule also gives the gas company an incentive both to set its initial design specifications large enough to cover any future use, and to lock in supplies to cover any anticipated shortfall. These are not costless options, but dangers lurk if present owners can reduce the level of common infrastructure so as to hamper the ability of other landowners to make like use of their own future lands—a problem that happens when street parking is limited, and later developing landowners are told that only they are required to have off-street parking for new units. During a brownout today, the most recent customers are not cut off before power is reduced to established customers: the pro-rata rule applies. The strict priority found in ordinary property relations (prior in time is higher in right) neatly flips over in the shift between ordinary individuals and common carriers, for exclusion yields to equal access when voluntary agreements become regulated industries.

Finally, in *Wood*, the nondiscrimination rule should work well from the point of overall consumer satisfaction. The first units of heat keep pipes and babies from freezing; the latter units allow owners to take off their sweaters indoors. The working hunch is that the first increment to the last takers will be larger than the losses to the present customers. By way of numerical example, let 100 customers each enjoy 200 units of benefits from the current service, for a total value of 20,000. The new person comes in and at the reduced rate gets 199 units of benefit, while all others are reduced to that level, so that total utility increases by 99 to ($101 \times 199 = 20,099$, or the 199 gained for the new entrant less the 1 lost for each of the 100 incumbents).

These numbers are, of course, just that—numbers; and the equations could easily be stated to reverse the inequality if the present incumbents lost 3 units of benefit and the new incumbent received 197 units of benefit from the new service. Now the net loss equals 103 to 19,897 (or 3×100 lost, offset by 197 gained). For the reasons stated, that scenario seems unlikely in *Wood*, but it could easily occur in other settings. Thus, the outlook clearly changes if the established network within a city covers all existing subdivision developments, with a new unrelated subdivision proposed some distance away that requires separate servicing of its own. In that case, a compound strategy requires the members of the new development to pay the incremental cost of extending the system (which provides no benefits for the incumbents), but uses a nondiscrimination rule to allocate that cost among the purchasers within the new development, regardless of the time of their arrival. The older legal system could surely accommodate that result by defining members of the new subdivision as a different *class* of consumer with its own separate cost structure. The favoritism question is combated at least in part by requiring newcomers to pay their incremental costs, as is often done today with pipeline extensions into new communities.[49]

The last example points to some key theoretical distinctions with using the nondiscrimination principle. First, the application of the principle *requires* that distinctions be made for consumers for whom there are different costs of service; otherwise, the expensive consumers receive an implicit subsidy for the inexpensive ones. Second, a powerful theoretical argument suggests that even when costs are identical across classes, different pricing rules should apply to different classes of consumer. More specifically, the principles of Ramsay pricing offer a formula to determine prices that should be charged in regulated settings when a firm makes a large initial investment that cannot be recovered by charging all of its users the marginal costs of production.[50]

The simple nondiscrimination principle suggests that the prices for all classes of consumer be raised the same percentage, reducing the net consumer surplus (that is, the highest price they would be willing to pay less the actual price) but allowing the firm to remain in business without subsidy for the long run. It can be shown, however, that this simple use of the nondiscrimination principle generates in theory a smaller level of consumer surplus than a rule that imposes higher additional costs on those consumers whose demand for the product is inelastic—that is, those who are least able to reduce consumption when the price increases. The fewer the options, the higher the regulated rates—a result that often does not square with political intuitions that, for example, offer residential users of telephone services (with fewer options) lower rates than commercial telephone markets (with more options). In practice, this system is difficult to apply because the relative demands of different customer groups are hard to identify. In addition, the improvement in accuracy it generates is often small relative to the costs of its identification, often below 5 percent, well beneath the radar screen in any complex administrative environment.[51]

In principle, the discriminations involved could be made at the individual level; but in practice, the most that can be claimed for this system allows for differences only between groups, and not within groups, just as the above analysis indicates. Any sensible system of pricing therefore must incorporate the initial nondiscrimination principle, although complex fact patterns, such as those that exist with incremental pricing, could require the regulator to go beyond it. In practice, therefore, this demand-side qualification of the nondiscrimination principle has less salience than the cost-differences outlined above. But no matter how one resolves the particular disputes, the broad theme remains true. It is difficult to find either in theory or in practice anyone who just ignores the monopoly problem in the stark form presented in the common-carrier situation.

INTERCONNECTIONS

"*Must carriers carry other carriers?*"[52] The issue of the obligations of common carriers has elicited either statutory or common-law replies. "The Post Roads Act of 1866, which allowed telegraph companies to run their lines freely along post roads and to fell public owned trees for telegraph poles, had required the telegraph companies in turn, to interconnect and accept each other's traffic."[53] At common law, many cases held that the basic nondiscrimination obligation required a local telephone network to supply the same connection services to small telegraph companies as it offered to the then-industry leader, Western Union.[54]

The major dispute involved the operation of the rails, which was before the Supreme Court in the *Express Cases* of 1885.[55] At issue was the right of the railroads as common carriers to refuse to make special arrangements with certain express carriers that used the railroad's lines to transport packages to their customers. Prior to the suit, the railroads had leased space in bulk—one-half a freight car to a carrier was common—to the express carriers, which then staffed the cars with their own personnel. (For what it was worth, the express companies divided territories among themselves, a clear cartel arrangement.) Once the leases broke down, the railroads denied that they were under a customary or common-law duty to recognize the special status of the express services. They took the position that they had to offer these companies only the same piecemeal rates made available to their ordinary retail customers.

The Supreme Court, over dissent, held that the railroads were entitled to stand their ground. The choice is one of exquisite delicacy. It is evident that standard track dimensions were designed to facilitate the shipment of cars from one railroad company along tracks owned and operated by another. Given their mutual dependence, railroad companies had all sorts of complex reciprocal shipping arrangements among themselves, on which the value of the nationwide railroad network depended. The need for reciprocal arrangements kept the lines of transportation open for other carriers. The key question was whether the railroads had to make these interconnections available to the express couriers, which lacked a dagger to compel the railroads to act.

That decision is close on the merits, but was reached for reasons that, while not decisive, are surely powerful. The Court noted that all business arrangements between the railroads and the express carriers had been by voluntary agreement, not by legal compulsion. In light of that history, the Court declined to get into the business of forcing interconnections precisely because it did not want to establish any interconnection prices or otherwise make and supervise contracts between unwilling partners. The Court noted that the express business "implies access to the train for loading at the latest, and for unloading at the earliest, convenient moment."[56] Yet the interest of the express companies "is in a degree subordinate to the passenger business," so that the appropriate business connections have to service the one with as little inconvenience to the other as possible.[57] The Court did not think that it could force agreements on the railroads that could require them to take steps inconsistent with their other common-carrier obligations. Even though the breakdown of negotiations with the express companies could be substantial, nothing prevented any railroad from introducing a duplicate service on its own line, without relying on the express companies. So perhaps the price of forcing coercive interconnections was too high in light of the other available alternatives.

What was true for one industry was not necessarily true for another. The outcome in the *Express Cases* did not carry over to the law of telephone/telegraph communications, where by far the greater peril lay in the breakdown of network interconnections. It was just not thinkable that a phone call placed with one company could not reach a customer anywhere else on the system. To avoid the nightmare of balkanization, the Bell System was organized as an integrated end-to-end carrier that operated under a comprehensively regulated monopoly. Under the Federal Communications Act of 1934,[58] the three basic systemwide principles were a protected franchise, quarantine, and cradle-to-grave service.[59] The first gave the Bell System its monopoly; the second prevented the Bell System's entry into other areas (such as broadcasting), and the third provided for comprehensive regulation of prices, terms, classes of service, conditions, and the like. The breakup of the Bell System into seven regional operating companies in 1982 required detailed institutional arrangements whereby all long-distance carriers, operating in a competitive market, could have guaranteed access to local exchanges.[60]

The same insights drive the current legislative reforms. The fundamental revisions of the 1996 Telecommunications Act represent a complicated effort to introduce competition into both local exchanges and the long-distance market. To achieve both systemwide integration and competition, the 1996 act authorizes extensive interconnection proceedings between the local exchange carriers and the long-distance carriers.[61] The entire act is organized on the principle that the holdout dangers in communications are so costly that interconnections between competitive carriers must be established as a matter of right. The actual proceedings are incredibly complex, because of the difficulties of working out standards and pricing arrangements that facilitate new entry on the one hand, but protect (and there is a dispute as to how much) the previous investment of the local exchange carriers from expropriation on the other. Indeed, the FCC's exhaustive Interconnection Report of 1996[62] was heavily gutted when successfully challenged by the local telephone companies in federal court.[63] Throughout it all, the basic logic comes from the nineteenth century rules that governed relations between common carriers: "the primary *sine qua non* of common carrier status is a quasi-public character, which arises out of the undertaking to carry for all people indifferently."[64] The carrier provides the service, and the customer provides the content. Any modern success in this area is largely attributable to the soundness of the nineteenth-century systems of common-carrier definition and regulation, to which the modern cases typically defer.

Rate Regulation

The Interstate Commerce Act

The original impulse behind the Interstate Commerce Act of 1887 (ICA) was the regulation of railroad rates, an issue that arose in acute form in response to the operational design of the great railroad networks of the late nineteenth century.[65] From Chicago to San Francisco, a shipper might have the choice of several carriers and could, therefore, gain the advantage of competitive rates. In this context, the distinctive nature of the common carrier recedes in importance, the presence of viable alternatives being the best antidote to monopoly power. But the competitive situation did not apply on the short-haul routes outside the large cities. The cattleman near Amarillo or the farmer near Topeka might have only one line on which to ship his goods. State regulation was inadequate to deal with this question after (and perhaps even before) 1886 when the Supreme Court held that a state could not regulate journeys that began or terminated outside its borders.[66]

To respond to this challenge, the Interstate Commerce Act in section 4 provided that the common carrier could not charge "under substantially similar circumstances" more for a short-haul rate than it charged for the longer haul of which it was a part.* This section should be understood as an effort to extend the nondiscrimination provision to provide that unlike cases should be treated differently, but only in the proper fashion. The solution of the original ICA was ingenious because it sought to prevent the use of monopoly power by railroads without getting the federal government into the business of rate regulation, which it in fact undertook in later years.

The complexities of the railroad business made the ICA's rickety solution of uncertain duration, and showed the difficulty of carrying over the nondiscrimination principle to complex regulatory contexts. From the out-

---

* "That it shall be unlawful for any common carrier subject to the provisions of this act to charge or receive any greater compensation in the aggregate for the transportation of passengers or of like kind of property, under substantially similar circumstances and conditions, for shorter than for a longer distance over the same line, in the same direction, the shorter being included within the longer distance; but this shall not be construed as authorizing any common carrier within the terms of this act to charge and receive as great compensation for a shorter as for a longer distance."[67]

set, the Supreme Court faced problems in interpreting the ICA's statutory mandate. In 1897, in one pivotal set of decisions, the Supreme Court upheld the statutory requirement that all rates "be reasonable and just"; or, conversely, that "every unjust and unreasonable charge for such service is prohibited and declared to be unlawful." But in its next breath the Court denied the Interstate Commerce Commission (ICC) the power to set rates directly, and refused to allow it to skirt that prohibition by setting rates after invalidating the rates the railroads had set for their own services.[68]

In the same year, in *ICC v. Alabama Midland Ry Co.*, the Court grappled with the key long-haul/short-haul provisions of section 4 of the ICA.[69] The gist of the case was that the defendant railroads charged more for shipments from Troy, Alabama to certain Atlantic seaports than to similar shipments from Montgomery, Alabama, which—fifty-two miles farther away on the same line—was an apparent long-haul/short-haul inversion. The defense in the case was that competition for the business between Montgomery and the Atlantic seaports counted as substantially different circumstances that justified the rate differential. The Court accepted the contention by noting that volume discounts were proper for shippers of large quantities of goods or for large groups of travelers within a single party.[70] Both those cases are illustrations of *cost-based* discrimination: the lower costs for the carrier justified the lower rates.

Furthermore, the railroad in this case sought to meet long-haul competition without sacrificing short-haul profits. The question whether this tactic should be allowed raises many of the questions that surround the "hub" mode of operation found in airline networks today.* One of the infuriating anomalies of modern airline service is that it often costs more to go a shorter distance. By way of illustration, assume that a given carrier does not fly direct from Chicago to Kansas City, but does run a hub in Denver through which it can route passengers from Chicago to Kansas City. If it charges $100 for the Chicago/Denver run, should it be obligated to charge more for the Chicago/Kansas City run even if a rival line flies direct from Chicago to Kansas for $75? To require the price for the long haul to be greater than that of the short haul may do little to protect the passengers on the Chicago-to-Denver route, but it will surely discourage competition on the Chicago-to-Kansas route, where volume is likely to be low, given the

---

* My thanks to Andrew Kull for his help on these knotty questions.

longer route structure. So long as Alabama Midland had to meet competition from other carriers that did not go through Troy, but took shorter routes, then it could stay in that market, if at all, only by meeting their prices for the longer routes. To add to the complexity, the additional cost of providing service at Troy (which slows up the through trains) could further discourage the direct service from Troy. So it is hard to make any categorical judgment about whether Alabama Midland would discontinue its Troy service if forced to reduce those rates. So while the run is shorter, the total costs may not be lower, after all, because of the overall network effects.

In one sense, this railroad case is not quite parallel to the airline case. A more precise parallel would be one where the flight from Chicago to San Francisco stops in Cheyenne to pick up and discharge passengers. Setting the rates for the Cheyenne flight is far from simple, since the stop reduces the airline's ability to compete on the Chicago/San Francisco run, and thus indirectly increases the total cost of operation. So long as one is uncertain whether the price increases respond to these pressures or to the long-haul/short-haul differences, the verdict is still out whether state intervention is good or bad. An unalloyed good is, however, to allow smaller airlines to specialize in second-tier cities as feeder airlines so as to introduce a measure of competition at each stage in the chain.

The issue under the ICA was thus a technical one, inviting cautious response. Any suggestion that the decision was right because it follows the principles of competitive markets,[71] or wrong because it follows the tenets of "liberal economics,"[72] misses the distinctive flavor of the common carrier issues involved, where the cost-based and demand-based discrimination are heavily entwined. As a political matter, the failure to place teeth in section 4 did not invite a system of unregulated rates on the network. Rather, it pushed government regulation in the opposite direction, so that it was only a matter of time before amendments to the ICA gave the ICC the power to set rates, thereby creating the risk of government cartelization of the industry.[73]

Antitrust Laws

A legal system can respond to the problem of monopoly with either rate regulation or antitrust laws. At common law, the concern with monopolies, which embraced common carriers, extended beyond them. The ancient category of "contracts in restraint of trade" retained its vigor during the nineteenth century, and sometimes supplied a more clever response than any heavy-handed direct regulation.[74] Most notably, horizontal arrangements in restraint of trade were not enforced, a prohibition that could cover clauses of noncompetition between buyers and sellers of businesses, or between present and former employees. The entire question is one of great difficulty in any age. On the one hand, the invalidation of these noncompete clauses could easily dry up the market for the sale of new businesses. On the other, their full-fledged enforcement could well keep a seller of a business out of a market, defined by product or territory, in which he had never competed in the first place. Originally the common law invalidated all such covenants as against public policy, a position subsequently relaxed in 1711 in *Mitchel v. Reynolds*,[75] which allowed partial restraints on territory and product line "such as cannot be set aside without injury to a fair contractor." The presence of monopoly power makes it difficult to leave the content of the contract solely to the appetites of the parties, and *Mitchel's* basic trade-off has held its ground in the years that followed. The famous nineteenth-century case, *Maxim v. Nordenfelt Guns and Ammunition Co.* (1894),[76] relied on *Mitchel* to sustain a portion of a worldwide restrictive covenant while invalidating the rest.*

The dangers of monopoly power arose in connection not only with noncompete provisions, but also with various arrangements for territorial division, mergers, and exclusive dealing arrangements, whose importance increased with the advancing industrialization in the post-Civil War period. It is not surprising, therefore, that 1890 saw the arrival of the antimonopoly provisions of the Sherman Antitrust Act,[78] whose initial enforcement was limited by the (sound) construction of the commerce clause, which refused to apply the act to local manufacture, but which (also correctly) eventually

---

* The covenant read: "The said Thorsten Nordenfelt shall not during the term of twenty-five years from the date of the incorporation of the company, if the company shall so long continue to carry on business, engage except on behalf of the company either directly or indirectly, in the trade or business of a manufacturer of guns, gun mountings or carriages, gunpowder explosives, or ammunition, or in *any other business competing or liable to compete in any way with that for the time being carried on by the company.*"[77]

The italicized portion was held void. The distinction makes good sense. Nordenfelt was an employee of the new company with an extensive role in its business. The italicized portion dealt with matters outside his ken or special expertise. Further restrictions could have been included as part of his severance agreement, where the greater knowledge would allow the drafting of restrictions with far greater specificity than was possible at the time of acquisition.

allowed its application to various nationwide cartels.* The railroads, as interstate common carriers, were a prime target for its application.

The application of the antitrust laws to common carriers, however, created special difficulties because of the need to forge durable interconnections among competitive rivals. One prime illustration of the limitations of the antitrust remedy is the famous *Northern Securities Case*,[82] where, in 1904, the Supreme Court sustained the United States's decision to block the merger of the Northern Pacific and Great Northern Railways—a cause célèbre of its own time. Christopher Columbus Langdell was both the dean who revitalized the Harvard Law School after the Civil War and the founder of the Socratic method of legal instruction. He has also been attacked as a barren formalist in his own chosen subject of contract law.[83] Yet, writing in the *Harvard Law Review* before the Supreme Court decision in the case,[84] he showed his understanding of the interconnection between rate regulation and antitrust laws in his harsh denunciation of the judicial decree that required the Northern Securities Company to divest itself of its shares in the Great Northern Railway. Conceding the need for some legal response to the evident risk of monopoly, he urged vainly for the Supreme Court not to apply the Sherman Act to this merger:

> Lest, however, some reader should be apprehensive that [the merger] should leave the public without protection against the 'rapacity of railway monopolists,' it seems proper to say that ... there was no call for such an act respecting them; that the only way in which railways can do an injury to the general public is by charging unreasonable rates for services which they render, and that for such an injury the state already had an incomparably better remedy than any which the Sherman Anti-Trust Act can furnish, in its unquestioned power to regulate and control railway rates.[85]

The second approach to the monopoly problem in regulating common carriers comes from the "essential facilities doctrine" which has been concisely summarized as follows: "The essential facilities doctrine requires a firm with monopoly power in one market to deal equitably with compet-

---

* The commerce clause gives power to Congress "to regulate commerce among the several states." In 1895, *United States v. E. C. Knight Co.* declined to extend the act to manufacturing.[79] In 1899, *Addyston Pipe & Steel Co. v. United States* applied it to nationwide territorial divisions.[80] *E. C. Knight* was right in its broad proposition that commerce did not include manufacture, but wrong to treat monopolization as manufacturing.[81]

ing firms operating in adjacent markets that depend on it for essential inputs."[86] The seminal case is *United States v. Terminal Railroad Association* (1912),[87] which arose out of the bottleneck position that the Terminal Railroad Association of St. Louis (which contained eighteen member railways) held over the terminal, bridge, and switching facilities in St. Louis, then a major junction point for east-west rail traffic: "Though twenty-four lines of railway converge at St. Louis, not one of them passes through."[88] The hub was organized both to facilitate the interconnection agreements, so that cars on one set of tracks could be routed to another, and to fund the cost of bridge construction over the Mississippi River, which no railroad could afford on its own.

Given these physical limitations, the railroad network would break down if connections could not be made under the supervision of the Terminal Association.[89] Since breakup was out of the question, any antitrust focus turned to making access to the facility available to all carriers on even terms, whether or not they were members of the association. From Justice Horace Lurton's opinion, it does not appear that the terminal association pursued a policy of exclusion;[90] and one careful review of the record makes it tolerably clear that the Terminal Association allowed nonmembers of the association to use the facility on equal terms with members, even if it did not give them free membership into the association.[91] Nonetheless, the Court adopted the classical common-carrier remedy of requiring the association to admit into membership any applicant on "such just and reasonable terms as shall place such applying company upon a plane of equality in respect of benefits and burdens with the present proprietary company." For those companies not seeking membership in the association, it required access to its facilities on just and reasonable terms and conditions "as will, in respect of use, character and cost of service, place every such company upon as nearly an equal plane as may be with respect to expenses and charges as that occupied by the proprietary companies."[92] In essence, the antitrust laws forged interconnections between carriers under the common-law rules of nondiscrimination.

Ironically, however, the Court's solution missed the true difficulty in the case. The Terminal Association created antitrust implications not because of some vertical arrangement between it and nonmember railroads. Rather, the source of the potential danger was the horizontal monopoly position enjoyed by members of the association. The nondiscrimination rule meant only that the outsiders had to pay the same amount as the insiders. It did not guarantee the return to any competitive equilibrium. Nor would change in membership alter this problem. If outsiders were asked to pay in advance for their share of the monopoly profits, prices to shippers, and hence to consumers, would remain unchanged. All that would be altered would be the future payment flows of the anticipated rentals. The entire episode points out the weakness of the nondiscrimination remedy in a complex setting, and helps explain why common carriers came to be treated as regulated industries subject to far more complex pricing orders. The interesting question is why the interconnection problem seemed to be solved more easily for the railroads than for the telecommunications industry: the best answer seems to lie in the idea of reciprocity. Each railroad needs to send its cars over the lines of other railroads, so that the first side needs the second as much as the second needs the first. A rule that allows parties mutually free passage on each other's tracks is similar to the common practice by which members of a single planned community subject themselves to mutually restrictive covenants on key issues of land use. The solution, which avoids any cash payments, could operate as a focal point whose fairness is hard to challenge and whose administrative simplicity is impossible to beat. The asymmetries between local exchange carriers and long-distance carriers are, however, much more pronounced. It is never possible to alter the path by which phone calls are routed to avoid that "last mile" under local-exchange control. Yet local calls may be routed through multiple long distance carriers. Sitting in the stronger position, the local telephone monopolist hence becomes the target of greater regulation, which raises deep constitutional complications with telecommunications as elsewhere.

The application of the antitrust laws to network industries has marched forward to confront another technological revolution in the continuing antitrust litigation saga that pits Microsoft against an alliance between the Department of Justice, a range of its major competitors (Sun, Netscape, Oracle), and, it appears, an eager group of senators, both Republican and Democrat, who want to join in the kill.* To see the issues at stake, make, contrary to fact, the starkest assumption, namely that Microsoft supplies the operating system on which every computer and the communications network depends. The question is what antitrust responses should be made to counteract the bottleneck position created by this admitted monopoly.

One obvious solution might be to separate the operating system from the rest of Microsoft's businesses. Microsoft could be ordered to spin off its operating system into a separate holding company which would be required

---

* To keep up on the Microsoft saga, see, http://www.ljx.com/LJXfiles/dojvms.html

to make interconnections with all potential users on reasonable and nondiscriminatory rates. In effect, one half of Microsoft becomes a common carrier, and the other continues to operate as an ordinary competitive business. This solution can be ruled out quickly, for its adoption necessarily impairs the effectiveness of the integrated systems by which Microsoft supplies its wares to its customers: no shared files leads to more costly and balky operations. It is far simpler to separate track from rolling stock (if such be desired) than to separate one computer function from another. The technology moves too quickly to make this solution tenable.

The absence of any simple structural remedy opens up the possibility of direct regulation of how Microsoft runs its business, itself a revolution in the helter-skelter computer industry. Here Microsoft has taken the consistent position that regulation is death. As a company it must innovate or die, but the need to obtain government approval for technical advances leaves it in practice with only the second of those alternatives. The position makes abundant sense in a world in which computer innovations come in six-month cycles and government approvals take at least a year. By the same token, Microsoft cannot deny (at least on the extreme assumptions set out above) that its monopoly power has long been regarded as a legitimate target for state regulation.

The issue is how to reconcile these two inconsistent imperatives. Understanding the parallel situations in railroads and communications helps sort out the relevant concerns, of which three stand out. The first of these deals with the default web browser installed on Microsoft units: should it be Microsoft's Explorer or some other system, such as Netscape's Navigator? The second concerns the minimum price that Microsoft must charge for its browser. The third probes the interconnectivity of rival systems to Microsoft's operating system.

In worrying about the configuration of Microsoft's Windows 98 system, the Department of Justice and the state attorneys general fail to distinguish among these possible points of concern. But the only issue that really matters is the last, and on that point Microsoft's competitors have already won, for nothing in the Microsoft operating system wards off a consumer choice of rival browsers, any more than it blocks the installation of America Online. Once connectivity is settled, the issues of regulation are far easier to confront than for railroad or telecommunications interconnections. The flexibility of the new technology should reduce the level of government angst, for there is no reason to worry about the volume of freight that passes over the various lines or the conditions in which the tracks are maintained.

Easy means of interconnection allow the emergence of a competitive market in web services atop Microsoft's monopoly operating system. Microsoft is wrong when it says that monopoly issues are a red herring. What it should have said is that monopoly problems are always relevant, but these have already been solved by the current technical and institutional arrangements on interconnection.

The true red herrings in this case are the default system and pricing issues. The computers sold are best equipped with some default system. So why not let Microsoft use its own? The cost of replacement is quite low, and the rival companies can easily find ways to make the substitution a simple matter of installation or to protest if Microsoft degrades or otherwise compromises the possible connections. Whatever the position of competitors, consumers (for whom of course competitors always claim to speak) have one service that they want and easy access to rival suppliers. Setting the proper default term is, as my colleague Randal Picker has stated, a "megabyte issue in a gigabyte world."

The same can be said of the pricing issues: what is wrong if Microsoft decides to give away its program for free, or even if it is willing to pay consumers to choose it? The system here does not smack of predation in the ordinary sense, because Microsoft has no intention of charging little today in the vain hope that it could raise the prices once the competition is crushed. Rather, the point simply reflects the obvious truth that money is made on the web by selling access and services to content suppliers instead of to their customers. The more customers that use the system, the higher the fees paid by content suppliers, who in turn can bill their customers for the additional convenience if they think it appropriate. The entire system thus reduces and redirects billing and collection costs, and explains why the "free goods" given to one set of customers today immediately increases the revenues that can be collected from a second set tomorrow. Netscape and other web browsers can adopt similar strategies in their effort to cater to both markets. They can give their systems away for free, by allowing them (as they now do) to be downloaded from the Internet, or they could even find ways to supply rebates or free services to pay users to adopt their system. Given that downward movement in prices, it is easy to see why Microsoft's competitors demand restrictions on its ability to reduce prices and increase distribution. But it is very hard to see any identity of interest between them and the consumers they purport to represent.

Political controversy to one side, new technology should not be allowed to obscure an old truth. The basic problem is a rerun of the issue for rails and telecommunications: can outsiders connect to the network? Once that first order problem is solved, as it has been, the issues that remain do not require the use of state coercion, which carries with it the far greater risk of stifling the innovation that the computer industry was able to achieve before its transformation into a network industry brought it on a collision course with federal and state regulation.

CONTEMPORARY CONSTITUTIONAL ISSUES

The problem of monopoly, especially in the context of network industries, is not simply the stuff of common-law adjudication, antitrust laws, and direct regulation. So long as our constitutional system protects private property, the various systems of regulation will be examined not only as a matter of economic principle, but also of constitutional policy. But making that transformation does not generate any magic set of intellectual tools that were not available on the common law and regulatory front. Indeed we often witness an odd form of inversion, for in making challenges to legislative interference, common-law principles become the staples of constitutional discourse. Just that result was achieved when the language of "affected with the public interest" was transplanted from English common law to American constitutional law in *Munn v. Illinois*.[93] *Munn* tested the limits of state regulation of common carriers under some blend of the takings and the due-process clauses. The basic dilemma with common carriers has not changed in over one hundred years.[94] The investment in wire, track, and equipment precedes the receipt of ratepayer revenue. A system that allows the carrier to recover all of its variable, but only *some* of its fixed, costs will induce the carrier to remain in operation once it has committed capital to the business. But the gimmick can work only once; thereafter, no firm will enter into a regulated business unless provided assurance that future rates will allow recovery of invested capital. The regulation that stifles monopoly extraction should not be converted into a system of covert confiscation of capital investment. These concerns received their constitutional voice in an important line of Supreme Court cases.

The issues first bubbled up to the Supreme Court during the 1890s, culminating in *Smyth v. Ames* in 1898.[95] There, the railroads sought to roll back rates set by the Nebraska legislature on local traffic, which required most carriers to operate this segment of their business at a loss. In reaching its decision, the Court steered the middle course between monopoly pricing and disguised confiscation of capital investment. It first determined the "fair value" of the property used in the business, and then calculated rates that yielded a risk-adjusted rate of return comparable to that received by a competitive firm. The Court wrote: "We hold, however, that the basis of all calculations as to the reasonableness of rates to be charged by a corporation maintaining a highway under legislative sanction must be the fair value of the property being used by it for the convenience of the public."[96]

This approach places the risk of unwise investment on the regulated railroad, as would be the case in a competitive industry, and thus limits the rate base (over which the rate of return is calculated) to the property both "used and usable" within the business. The formula sensibly gives the regulated firm a strong incentive to make the right investments in the first place. Unfortunately, it also requires, perhaps annually, an administrative recomputation of the fair value of plant and equipment, which are not sold, in whole or in part, in any active market. Indeed, even if a buyer could be found for an entire railroad, the price the road would fetch would depend on a forecast of its future rates under regulation. In the absence of any ready market, valuation is, at best, a hit-and-miss process.

To sidestep these difficulties, the Supreme Court veered in the opposite direction in 1944 in *Federal Power Commission v. Hope Natural Gas.*[97] In the post–New Deal environment, it calculated the rate of return on the actual investment of the regulated firm, wholly without regard to whether any specific asset was performing properly. This system of rate regulation makes it easy to establish a rate base, but gives the regulated firm no incentive to make the correct investment choices since it is largely insulated from the downturn brought on by specific errors along the way. So long as the "bottom line" allowed a suitable rate of return, the judicial inquiry was at an end. As Justice William O. Douglas wrote,

> It is not theory but impact of the rate order which counts. If the total effect of the rate order cannot be said to be unjust and unreasonable, judicial inquiry under the Act is at an end. The fact that the method employed to reach that result may contain infirmities is not then important.[98]

Unfortunately, *Hope* started off on the wrong foot by using this formula opportunistically. Neither the Federal Power Commission nor the Supreme Court grappled with the key transitional difficulties when Hope's pipeline rates were regulated only years after its initial capital investment, whose value had risen substantially in the interim.[99] With investment prior to regulation, the proper approach determines the value of invested capital when the regulation is imposed, so that the risk of interim depreciation or appreciation both fall on the regulated firm. It is as though the firm purchased its plant and equipment on the day regulation began for a sum equal to its then-market value. Only thereafter is it proper to make automatic rate-base adjustments that circumvent the fair value calculations of *Smyth v. Ames.*

In other cases, the courts have prevented rate regulation from being rigged to preordain an insufficient rate of return. In *AT&T v. FCC* (1988),[100] the disputed Federal Communications order "requires the carriers to refund earnings they receive in excess of the expected rate of return on capital factored into their rates." The Court struck down the order for its heads-I-win-tails-you-lose attitude. All rate calculations predict future events; these predictions could turn out either high or low. By capping rates at the level that secures the minimum permissible rate of return, over the long term the order would give the carrier at most a competitive rate of return in some years but will, to a certainty, fall below that level in other years. With time, the rule introduces a "systematic bias" that necessarily reduces the rate of return below its required constitutional threshold. Only if the caps are set above the minimum threshold is it possible for the situation to even out over time.

As *AT&T v. FCC* illustrates, regulation can spawn confiscation as well as competitive rates. Modern social practice also ordains the inclusion of implicit subsidies into the rate calculation. The firm gets its competitive rate of return, but some needy consumers pay less than their allocated cost, and the shortfall is made up by more affluent parties. This redistribution system is at odds with the initial theory of rate regulation, which was aimed at monopoly control and not covert redistribution. This newer purpose, moreover, has created major long-run difficulties in moving from one rate-making regime to another.

The telecommunications industry affords a current battleground for these recurrent issues. Historically, rate regulation is divided sharply between the state commissions and the FCC. Thus, subsection 2(b) of the Federal Communications Act provides that "nothing in this Chapter shall be construed to apply or to give the [FCC] jurisdiction with respect to . . . charges, classifications, practices, services or facilities, or regulations for or in connection with intrastate communications service."[101] That prohibition has proved so strong that the Supreme Court has refused to allow the FCC to set uniform rates of depreciation for a single piece of equipment used for both local and interstate calls.[102] Independently, the state commissions set the rate for the first fraction, and the FCC for the second.

Alas, the common practice in many state commissions has been to reduce the rates in the short-term, especially for residential customers: the depreciation expense allowed in each year is held to *less than* the actual reduction in value of the equipment. In practice, that equipment is withdrawn from actual use before the debt used to purchase it has been fully retired. The upshot is a conscious mismatch of revenue and expenditure: tomorrow's users have to pay for equipment used by today's customers. That system of deferred cost recovery unwisely makes one set of individuals pay for the benefits of another, no small consideration given normal rates of population movement and business turnover. But in a charged political environment, the system can sputter along so long as consistent practices are used continuously over time—at least if the deferred-cost recovery is not allowed to spiral out of control.

As in *Hope*, however, the legal transition wrought by the 1996 Act brought these latent difficulties to the surface.[103] That act is designed to introduce competition into the telecommunications industry in two stages: first, by opening local-exchange markets to competition by new entrants; and thereafter, by allowing the local exchange carriers (LECs), most notably regional Bell operating companies (or BOCs) to compete with AT&T, MCI, Sprint, and a host of new entrants in the long-distance market.[104]

One critical provision of the act mandates interconnection between the LECs and the long-distance carriers, "based on cost."[105] Simply mandating interconnection shows that government cannot legislate a system of pure competition in any network industry. Safeway does not need to place its groceries in Jewel markets to reach its own customers; it can compete from self-contained facilities. But the value of telephone service lies in its connection to the network. Any subscriber from any service provider must be able to reach any other subscriber from any other provider. Forging those connections raises the familiar holdout risk between the various carriers. To obviate that risk, Congress obligated all carriers to bargain with each other in good faith, and backed the system up with state-mandated arbitration in the event that parties failed to agree on rates.[106] If each period's costs had been fully recovered within that same period, then the regulators could apply either the fair-value rule of *Smyth v. Ames* or the original cost-recovery rule of *Hope Natural Gas* to establish an interconnection schedule that allows the LECs to recover their costs, without generating monopoly profits. The simplest method is to carry over pre-1996 rate-base methodology into the post-1996

Act era in order to preserve budgetary consistency over time, and limit the scope for political machinations.

The rate-base tribulations are compounded, however, because of the previous regulatory refusal to recognize depreciation losses when they were incurred. In the new regulatory regime, who has to absorb those unrecognized losses? Not us, say the long-distance and specialized carriers. These costs give us no benefit, so why should we have to pass them on to our customers? The cost increases generate rates higher than those found in some perfectly competitive markets. The FCC accepted that argument in its August 1996 *Report and Order*,[107] whose pricing approach ignored the sunk costs of the past and focused on the future—known as TELRIC, or Total Element Long Run Incremental Cost.[108]

But if interconnecting carriers are let off the hook for these unrecovered historical costs, who must bear them? Not us, say the BOCS (and here I speak as one who has worked on these matters as a legal consultant to two Bell operating companies, Bell Atlantic and SBC Communications). The counterargument starts with the observation that telephone interconnections did not first surface under the 1996 Act. Rather, today's rates reflect judgments that begin the day equipment was first put into service and continue until cost recovery was completed. As in the *AT&T* case noted above, the rules of engagement cannot systematically, over the life cycle of the equipment, preclude full recovery. Yet just that result is achieved if the original rate order postpones recovery that a later rate order disavows. If the regulators at the initial ratemaking proceedings thought it appropriate (as I do not) to make the next generation of consumers pay for present consumption, then that obligation cannot be dishonored simply because the government thereafter introduces a new system of rate regulation with the laudable objective of fostering competitive behavior.

As is always the case, the concern with fairness spills over into efficiency. One irony of the FCC's TELRIC approach is that it distorts relative prices in future markets by benefiting new competitors at the expense of the overall process of competition. The interconnecting carriers are freed from past costs that are still imposed on the local-exchange carriers, or LECs. Indeed, the distortions are still greater, for the LECs have to pick up the unrecovered historical costs for both their own operations and those of their new rivals. The only way to avoid that distortion is to require all new entrants to pick up their pro-rata share of the unrecovered historical costs which they in turn could recover (without competitive disadvantage) from their customer base.

The interconnection problem seriously threatens parity between incumbents and newcomers, even within a single time period. One objective of the 1996 Telecommunications Act is to allow alternative local-exchange carriers (ALECs) to develop their own networks in competition with the established LECs. To do so, the act allows them a choice of means to obtain as of right all or some of the pieces they need to establish their own operations. The first allows them to purchase unbundled network elements—basically, the switches, components, and other facilities and equipment that make the network run[109]—which could then be incorporated into the ALEC's own facility (which might be constituted entirely of such borrowed elements),[110] subject to an obligation that these be sold in a form that allows their incorporation into the ALEC's own system for service. The second alternative permits the ALEC to acquire retail services for resale to consumers.[111] The pricing systems for these two types of purchase differ, so that unbundled network elements are sold at cost, and retail services at wholesale prices. The differential price structure reflects the allocation of risk under the system. The ALEC that purchases the elements at retail need buy only those that can be resold, and thus does not take any residual risk in the transaction. The higher price reflects the lower risk. Purchasers of unbundled network elements run the risk that the capacity so acquired will not be resold to customers once the network is assembled, and thus pay a lower price to avoid the commensurate risk.

In October 1997, after some initial confusion about the issue, the Eighth Circuit held that the Telecommunications Act meant what it said, no more and no less.[112] The decision was itself important: otherwise, the ALECs would have been in the enviable position of enjoying both low prices and low risks. Indeed, even the consistent cost-pricing system still leaves the ALEC with one advantage. These prices are determined administratively, not in market transactions. As such, the cost of components or retail services could be either too high or too low. For those elements that are not absolutely necessary to overcome the interconnection problem, the ALEC always has the choice to buy elsewhere if the price set is too high, and to purchase large quantities of those elements that are priced too low—heads I win and tails I just don't buy at all. This asymmetry suggests that the 1996 act was misconceived insofar as it forced sales of retail services not needed to forge the connection: the state power should have been limited to the holdout problems that justify intervention in the first place.

These pricing rules resolve ongoing disputes, for the most part in favor of the LECs against their new rivals, and have been attacked on the ground that they retard the introduction of competition into the telecommunications business. Yet they obtain further support from the ongoing resolution of a similar problem in the electrical power industry—the treatment of stranded costs of facilities built before the major nationwide restructuring now taking place. The older system of electrical generation featured local monopolies whose captive customers could not purchase power from other suppliers located elsewhere on the grid. The major reforms of the industry have called for a separation of the generation from the transmission functions of the existing power suppliers. The network is to be transferred into a separate business entity that acts like a common carrier for energy from all sources, both near and far.[113]

This new network has caused many expenditures made on the strength of early regulatory commitments to lose much of their value: no doubt the more efficient operation of the overall system implies that many of those investments should not have been made in the first place. Nonetheless, the resolution of this stranded-cost problem allowed "utilities to recover their legitimate, prudent and verifiable stranded costs," on the ground that companies that made investments based on the older legal order should not have been required to foresee the transition in legal regime.[114] To be sure, that decision does not rest on any explicit constitutional text, but its logic surely has constitutional ramifications, given the decision of the FCC to go in the opposite direction.

Carried over to telecommunications, this approach on stranded cost allows the LEC to recover its investments from the new entrant. That solution, of course, creates parity between the competitors, but keeps future rates higher than they ought to be, and thus retards the spread of telecommunications services. There is, however, a solution to that problem, guaranteed to fall on deaf ears in Congress and in state legislatures. General tax revenues could be used to discharge the overhanging debt attributable to the prior low rates. The LECs receive a lump-sum compensation for the unrecovered residual costs of original investments; thereafter, all carriers provide future services at competitive rates. That solution should satisfy both the LECs and the interconnecting carriers: it eliminates competitive distortion between carriers and keeps prices tied to current costs—all positives. Yet it requires an explicit cash payout from either Congress or the states, which will prompt obvious resistance from both Congress and the states in an era of budgetary stringency. Nor is the question simply one of budgetary squeamishness. Since any general tax reduces the rate of return from investment and labor, the compensation solution has its cost. But the only alternative is a high excise tax on a specific industry, which generally creates more distortion than does a tax on general revenues. That said, pairing takings with compensation is probably the best way to control damages, given the previous regulatory decisions. But the larger lesson is that regulators generally should avoid creating these problems by avoiding short-term political solutions that have long-term adverse consequences. The fact that it is more painful to work out all subsidies within the current period is exactly why regulators should be required to operate within that restraint.

If the payments are not forthcoming, what should be done? One possibility is to block the legal transformation on the grounds that the government is unwilling to pay for the change. Don't count on that. The more likely scenario is that some carriers will end up holding the bag. In the end, the Supreme Court may have to decide whether regulation transformation allows Congress and the state commissions to play bait-and-switch in rate regulation: come in under one system, but exit under another far less favorable to you. The existing precedents on rate regulation are less favorable to government than they are in land-use disputes. In land-use cases, the prospect of physical spillovers between neighbors hands the government a large police power club on environmental issues, a weapon lacking in this regulatory setting. So it is still anyone's guess as to how this case will sort itself out under current law as it winds its way through the courts. But the fundamental fallacy of the FCC's position is to act as though it is writing on a blank slate when a ratemaking agency, state or federal, must integrate its past decisions with its future ones.

The 1996 Telecommunications Act also highlights the tension between two visions of rate regulation: monopoly control and covert income redistribution. The history of telecommunications, like that of medical care, has long given extensive credence to the idea of "universal service" for all persons, regardless of their ability to pay. Within the medical context, this has led to programs of guaranteed access to emergency and indigent medical care, and to the extensive expansion of the Medicare program, both of which have aggravated the problems of cost and access they were designed to combat.[115] The universal service subsidies embedded in telecommunications both replicate and deviate from the medical precedent. At one level, the law requires that certain forms of lifeline service be supplied at very low rates. Traditionally, the obligation has also been interpreted to mandate the subsidy of residential and rural phone service, where the latter can become quite pricey owing to the need to run extensive wires to isolated locations. Figuring out the size of these subsidies is always difficult, because many common costs must be incurred even if additional phones are not brought on line. In addition, expanding the network offers additional value to current users, giving them access to more people. (For example, the bigger network allows credit agencies to make telephone checks on more customers.) The subsidy that remains was recovered by charging supracompetitive rates to commercial and urban users, particularly the latter. That strategy worked tolerably well in a declining cost market serviced by a local monopoly carrier. Indeed, the precise cost of satisfying the universal service obligation never had to be calculated. All that mattered was that the bottom-line rate-of-return calculations met the *Hope Natural Gas* standard.

Come the 1996 act, and the local monopoly providers were slated to become an archaic institution. But the act expands the universal service obligation by stipulating thbat "[u]niversal service is an evolving level of telecommunications services that the Commission shall establish periodically under this section, taking into account advances in telecommunications and information technologies and services."[116] More concretely, the regulators are instructed to look at telecommunications services that are "essential to education, public health, public safety," and to gear universal services to cover those that have been "subscribed by a substantial majority of residential customers." The frame of reference is, moreover, expanded to cover services that are "deployed by public telecommunications networks by telecommunications carriers" and—to use that old standby—"consistent with the public interest, convenience, and necessity."[117] As might be expected, the FCC issued its own enormous Universal Service Order in May 1997, which articulated its reasons why the cost of that service should be provided from three sources: interstate access (the long-distance portion of the business), geographical averaging (for rural customers), and business customers (for residential customers).

In one sense, the key budgetary issue is not the source of funding, but the size of the funds provided. Future declines in the cost of telecommunications services no longer translate into a shrinking subsidy program. Rather, the evolving standard could easily imitate the worst features of the healthcare market by expanding the subsidy over time, without keeping net costs and benefits in line. We can string Internet wires into every school without demonstrating its educational benefit to the targeted students. The usual fatal dynamic of redistribution carries over to the new social problem without missing a beat.

Let the price of any service be reduced to zero, and demand will surge. With traditional universal service, the potential abuse from this source was limited by the nature of the service provided: basic service for individual consumers, one per customer. But in the heady world of the Internet, the sky is the limit, and, as James K. Glassman has reported,[118] the size of this program has accelerated beyond the wildest fears of its opponents. Even if schools are ignorant of the potential grants under the program, eager third-party providers are not, and they can tempt the program's beneficiaries with a list of goodies for which the federal government has committed itself. Within a 75-day period in the Spring of 1998, eligible schools and libraries applied for over $2 billion in fresh funds. These are not limited to the humdrum phone line connections to the Internet, which constitute about only 4 percent of the requests. New computers can be acquired and walls can be ripped open for new internal wiring, only to be covered with a fresh coat of paint desired for other reasons. Priorities have to be set, and a new bureaucracy of doubtful legality must sift through thousands of inflated applications. Yet the FCC's reaction has been to oppose efforts by the phone companies to separately list what is now dubbed the "Gore Tax" (in honor of the Vice President's championship of the program) on the phone bill. "Transparency" in government seems to have far greater appeal to the private firms who pay the taxes than the government agencies who administer it.

The new universal service program does, however, have one bright lining. It could well forge an alliance between the LECs and long-distance carriers who are now struggling over the jurisdictional and cost-recovery provisions contained elsewhere in the 1996 Act. All segments of the business want to minimize its total size, yet they will be at loggerheads over the division of the burdens. In the new legal regime, the universal-service obligation does not fall evenly on all companies. Instead, the system contemplates that the local-exchange carriers will be required to provide the service,[119] but will be able to count on some contribution "in an equitable and nondiscriminatory basis" from all substantial interstate long-distance carriers.[120] In principle, once the total amount of the subsidy is determined, the fraction of it to be borne by each carrier should be dependent only on the size of that carrier's revenue base.

Unfortunately, the fundamental asymmetry between the duty to supply the service and the duty to chip in for its cost will create an enduring tension between the two classes of carriers, which will only get worse as the service obligation expands. No longer can the FCC bury the subsidy in the basic rate structure. Instead, it must collect evidence on the size of the implicit subsidy, which must then be apportioned among the various firms on the network. On these matters, errors in judgment can lead to estimating the transfer payments between communications carriers, which in turn will distort the competitive dynamics of the industry, thereby undermining the major objectives of the 1996 act.

Perhaps a better way to handle universal service is to take bids from rival carriers on a determinate set of obligations that could then be funded either from general tax revenues or from an excise tax on telephone calls. But so long as most local phone service is supplied by the traditional LECs, as seems presently to be the case, it becomes difficult to see how other carriers could enter into the business. Hence the absence of any easy way to merge the competitive and subsidized portions in a single comprehensive telecommunications regime.

The lessons to be gleaned from this reform endeavor are far from clear, but it is still worthwhile to ask why there is widespread social acceptance of any of these subsidies in the first place, perhaps above that of emergency telephone service. Basic service is cheap under any circumstance; and in contrast to medical services, we can expect that technical innovation will drive costs in one direction only—down. The irony, therefore, is that universal-service obligations will increase costs and thus reduce innovation industrywide. Yet it is never explained why subsidies for access to the Internet are more appropriate than those for access to magazines or horse shows.

The frustration with universal service is just the last symptom of the unforeseen tribulations in reforming telecommunications law. The 1996 Telecommunications Act was initially oversold as a magical transformation of the tired old system of local monopolies into an industry that had entered a sleek competitive age. But that analysis overlooked the basic point that pure competition is not possible in any network industry, so the only choice is between various forms of government coercion—in this instance, between rate regulation and forced interconnection. Abstractly speaking, it is difficult to choose, although rate regulation in telecommunications is easier than in some other industries, largely because of the downward pressure on the costs of service. It is, therefore, possible to adopt a system of rate caps,[121] under which firms are allowed to price at or below the cap at their own discretion. These caps can be adjusted downward over time to take general efficiency into account. But unlike rate-of-return regulation, any savings a firm achieves while operating under the rate cap inures to its own benefit. The incentives are, therefore, to reduce costs, not to increase them, as was the case under the old rate-of-return system, where the larger the rate base, the higher the rates.

The move toward rate caps in telecommunications does not assure that the pre-1996 system was more efficient than the 1996 act. But in making that assessment, the costs of transition, always large, should never be ignored. Regulation may be necessary to counteract a natural monopoly, and the initial theme of nondiscrimination continues to flit in and out of the materials as the systems of regulation become ever more complex. But transitions are hard to control. The FCC clearly overreached its hand in its First Report and Order, and was promptly slapped down by the Eighth Circuit. But in the interim, new uncertainties were created which may not be resolved until the Supreme Court speaks, and most likely not even then. It is hard, then, to make any informed guess as to whether the 1996 act will be relegated to the class of failed structural reforms. But it is far easier to note that rate regulation of common carriers and network industries should be regarded less as a social good and more as a necessary evil. Those who go down that path will encounter difficulties that may make us pine for the simpler world of unregulated natural monopoly.

EPILOGUE

❖ ❖ ❖

A Return to Fundamentals

The march of history has been characterized by uniform advances in technology which can be used for good or for ill. These technical breakthroughs
surely require us to rethink the application of traditional legal principles to
novel situations. But it hardly follows that such re-examination should
inevitably induce us to abandon principles of legal and social organization
that have served us well in the past. Just venturing a change in legal relationships imposes heavy costs of transition, as both government officials
and private actors adjust to a novel set of principles, which may themselves
introduce new errors as they correct old ones. In addition, the transition
from old to new regime opens up new avenues for cross-subsidy and redistribution, which can undo much of the gains of a new technology.

To be sure, on many occasions the presumption against legal change
has been rightly overcome. Agriculture required permanent rights in land
that were foreign to hunter-gatherer societies. The old law of trespass could
not stand in the path of airplane overflights and broadcast frequencies. Yet,
in most cases, the old legal forms provide a safe home for new innovations.
The object and design of employment contracts and real estate leases may
change in response to new demands for labor and land, respectively; but the
voluntary introduction of new contractual terms will usually outperform
any novel, untried form of state regulation.

Any adequate legal theory must, therefore, respond as much—if not
more—to the permanent features of human conduct as to its triumphant
advances. The mundane pressures of scarcity and self-interest should not be
overlooked in fashioning our basic legal rules. Indeed, amid all of today's

technological wonders, the basic questions of political organization all fall into one of just three fundamental categories: individual rights and duties; forced exchanges for mutual gain; and forced redistributions. In setting out individual rights and duties, we must embrace principles of individual autonomy, private property, and voluntary exchanges in order to insulate these productive human activities from the ravages of force and fraud. Forced exchanges for social benefit are, however, far from an empty category, but allow us to maintain systems of common property in water and air, and embrace such important systems as public highways, common carriers, public utilities, and network industries. These first two sets of rules have one desirable feature in common: they create positive-sum games from which everyone benefits. Systems of redistribution take wealth from some and give it to others. While, at best, these are positive-sum games from which some win and others lose, all too often they are negative-sum games in which the targets of state force sacrifice far more than the winners obtain. Far from creating public goods that expand the social pie, systems of coerced redistribution usually shrink it, to the long-term detriment of us all.

Laissez-faire as a social theory has often been seen as treating force and fraud as the only problems worthy of a collective legal response, and thus has been frequently attacked as ignoring the wide range of holdout, coordination, and networking problems that arise in any complex society. So understood, its obvious intellectual failure lies in pretending that the first category of human interactions constitutes the full scope of necessary and useful state interventions. But that response fails to respond to a more complete theory of laissez-faire which acknowledges the need for legal rules that forthrightly govern both common property and forced exchanges. In those cases where voluntary exchanges cannot achieve potential widespread gains, public force may take up the slack to achieve the desired social outcome— the win/win situations not obtainable by private agreement. Accepting that principle does not clear the path for the promiscuous use of state power. Rather, it requires some clear showing that the individuals subjected to state power all benefit on net from the program that has taken or regulated their property.

Once the legitimacy of forced exchanges is acknowledged, it is no longer possible to refute laissez-faire through caricature. It is not possible, for example, to reject laissez-faire on the ground that it allows no place for taxation in funding public goods or for regulation in distributing them. Rather, the battleground switches to the question of whether the imposition of the tax or regulation makes its costs reflect benefits for all individuals so taxed or regulated. At this point, the social equation is both more complex and more sensible than it is under a strict autonomy-based theory which refuses categorically to acknowledge any forced exchanges. Under a simple autonomy regime, the only proper question is whether the legal rules minimize the use of force and fraud. Under a system with forced exchanges, the social equation is altered to ask whether legal rules minimize the sum of the risks of expropriation through force and fraud *plus* the risk of breakdown of social relations through holdout and coordination problems. At this point, laissez-faire has a decisive answer to the charges of excessive individualism that have hounded it since its birth: its object is to maximize the cooperative social gain from human behavior, and to use state force when (but only when) necessary to achieve that end.

Many common critiques of laissez-faire mistakenly assume that once we reject its narrow version, no principled objection remains to the third piece of the puzzle: income or wealth redistribution by state coercion. State programs in that direction are, of course, inconsistent with the narrow versions of laissez-faire, which do, of course, easily accommodate programs of voluntary redistribution. But once this narrow account of laissez-faire is overrun, it is easy to assume that the public interest authorizes state-mandated redistribution along with the provision of public goods. Unfortunately, this response elides the sharp distinction between forced exchanges that make everyone better off, and forced takings that benefit some at the expense of others. State redistribution is not necessary to overcome holdout and coordination problems and, far from solving either of these, aggravates both.

More concretely, even with the widespread acceptance of some state redistribution, we have scant reason to believe that, by any full reckoning, this system will work better than one that curbs all forms of redistribution, including those misguided forms of regulation and taxation that benefit the rich at the expense of the poor. All too often the rejoinder insists that we cannot abandon, or even sharply curtail, the coercive state power to redistribute income and wealth. Instead, we are soothingly reassured that the programs must be cleansed of their excesses so that they move wealth only in the right direction, with a minimum of cost, intrigue, and confusion. But in the modern state, this optimistic agenda is largely illusory. Large and powerful forces lie ready to convert state power to their private benefit. The state that grants milk subsidies for poor schoolchildren also adopts dairy price supports that negate whatever benefits that subsidy produces. We are better off with neither program than with both. Lower prices, not higher subsidies, offer the surer road to better health. Yet, at this late date, it is unlikely we shall ever rid ourselves of the price supports so long as we accept the subsidies. But a look at the aggregate data should remind us how easy it is for unintended consequences to swamp the ostensible reasons for state intervention. Overall levels of poverty do not go down as the level of public redistribution increases. Any complete theory must locate the slippage between stated intention and actual effect, and that lies chiefly in the counterproductive adaptive responses of the parties taxed, the parties benefited, and the parties who administer the overall system.

Even if we could conquer these imperfections, the case against state-coerced redistribution remains strong. It is often said that common instincts of empathy induce us to help individuals in need. And so they do. But one regrettable consequence of the use of state power is to displace the private initiatives that provide far more bang for the buck. How many doctors have continued to provide charitable services after the rise of Medicare and Medicaid? How many today are paid by a bushel of apples or a repaved driveway? The natural impulse to help others is often dulled in the face of state power that promises more than its institutions can deliver.

There is a key lesson here. The principle *primum non nocere*—"first do no harm"—works as well for legal institutions as for medical practice. It also lies at the core of any sound system of laissez-faire. That presumption survives in the world of high technology, just as it worked in ages past. We need laissez-faire to take the same vital role it took in its intellectual heyday: an enlightened reform movement, sweeping away the accumulated detritus of state regulation. In 1843, the *Edinburgh Review* hit hard on the main point: "Be assured that freedom of trade, freedom of thought, freedom of speech, and freedom of action, are but modifications of one great fundamental truth, and that all must be maintained or all risked; they stand and fall together."[1]

Too often today, we introduce complex assumptions about human nature or legal institutions to finesse the power of these words. We think that it is possible to provide powerful constitutional protections for speech and religious liberty, but only weak constitutional protections for private property against state regulation. But the expansion of state power can easily overcome these partial barricades for individual liberty. The government that holds the power to inflict or withhold its sanctions, or to grant or withhold its benefits, is a government that can limit speech and curtail religion just as it limits and curtails economic activity. Our fundamental task is to make state power strong enough to hold us together, but not so strong as to rip us apart. This deviation from sound principles of governance is unnecessary. The principles to achieve a free society are within our grasp if we only reach out to grasp them.

ENDNOTES

❖ ❖ ❖

INTRODUCTION

1. *Lochner v. New York*, 198 N.Y. 45, 75 (1905).

2. C.B. Macpherson, *The Political Theory of Possessive Individualism* (1962).

3. See Frederick Harrison, quoted (without disapproval) in Patrick Atiyah, *The Rise and Fall of Freedom of Contract* (1979), p. 587.

4. Grant Gilmore, *The Death of Contract* (1974), p. 95.

5. Ibid.

6. Lawrence Friedman, *Contract Law in America* (1965), p. 20.

7. Cass R. Sunstein, *The Partial Constitution* (1993), p. 43.

8. G.A. Cohen, most notably in his book, *Self-Ownership, Freedom, and Equality* (1995).

9. Barbara H. Fried, *The Progressive Assault on Laissez-Faire: Robert Hale and the First Law and Economics Movement* (1998).

10. See Robert L. Hale, "Coercion and Distribution in a Supposedly Non-Coercive State," 38 *Political Science Quarterly* 470 (1923). For my critique of Hale, see Richard A. Epstein, "Imitations of Libertarian Thought," 15 *Social Phil. & Pol.* 412 (1998).

11. Robert Kuttner, *Everything for Sale: The Virtues and Limits of Markets* (1997).

12. Friedrich Hayek, *The Road to Serfdom* (1944).

13. Milton Friedman, *Capitalism and Freedom* (1963).

14. Richard A. Epstein, *Simple Rules for a Complex World* (1995).

15. Edouard Calic, *Ohne Maske* (1968), p. 37, quoted in Richard Pipes, "Property and Freedom," 416 (1998).

16. See *Miller v. Schoene*, 276 U.S. 272, 279–280 (1928). For discussion, see infra p. 241.

17. Richard A. Posner, *Economic Analysis of Law* (5th ed. 1998), p. 27–29.

18. National Traffic and Motor Vehicle Safety Act, 15 U.S.C.A. §§1381–1431 (1966).

19. *Larson* v. *General Motors*, 391 F.2d 495 (8th Cir. 1968), now followed in every American jurisdiction.

CHAPTER 1

1. Ernest J. Weinrib, "The Insurance Justification and Private Law," 14 *J. Legal Stud.* (1985), pp. 681–683.

2. Quoted in Hadley Arkes, "Natural Law and the Law: An Exchange," *First Things*, May 1992, 45, 47.

3. John Locke, *Two Treatises of Government*, (1689), ch. 4.

4. Charles Murray, *What It Means to Be a Libertarian* (1997), p. 4.

5. See John Finnis, *Natural Law and Natural Rights* (1980), pp. 283–284.

6. N.E. Simmonds, *The Decline of Juridical Reason: Doctrine and Theory in the Legal Order* (1984).

7. C. Montesquieu, *The Spirit of the Laws* (1748).

8. On the rivalry, see Richard A. Posner, "Blackstone and Bentham," 19 *J. Law & Econ.* (1976), p. 569.

9. See Samuel Pufendorf, *De Officio Hominis et Civis* (F. Moore Translation, 1927), p. 19. The passage is quoted in Simmonds, *Decline of Judicial Reasoning*, p. 54, in his discussion of the same point.

10. 1 William Blackstone, *Commentaries on the Laws of England* (1765), *40–*41.

11. 2 Blackstone, *Commentaries*, *3.

12. Gaius, *Institutes* (F. de Zulueta, trans., 1946), Book I, p. 1.

13. Justinian, *Institutes* (J.B. Moyle, trans., 5th ed. 1913), Book I, Title II, pr..

14. See David Hume, *A Treatise of Human Nature* (L.A. Selby-Bigge ed. 1888), p. 495 (emphasis in original).

15. W.D. Hamilton, "The Genetical Evolution of Social Behavior," 7 *Theoretical Biology* 1 (1964).

16. Gary S. Becker, "A Theory of Social Interactions," 82 *J. Pol. Econ.* 1063 (1974).

17. Hume, *Treatise*, pp. 468–470.

18. John Rawls, *A Theory of Justice* (1971).

19. Gaius, *Institutes*, 2, 66.

20. Locke, *Second Treatise*, (1689), ¶ 28 (emphasis in original).

21. Ibid., ¶ 40.

22. Hume, *Treatise*, p. 502.

23. Locke, *Second Treatise*, ¶ 30.

24. 2 Blackstone, *Commentaries*, *8.

25. Jeremy Bentham, *A Theory of Legislation* [1931 ed.] (1864), pp. 112–113.

26. Barry Nicholas, *An Introduction to Roman Law* (1962), p. 112.

27. Rawls, *A Theory of Justice* (1971).

28. F. A. Hayek, *The Constitution of Liberty* (1960).

29. Adam Smith, *The Theory of Moral Sentiments* (1759), Part III, ch. 4.

30. Frederick Pollock & Frederic Maitland, *A History of English Law* (1968 ed.), pp. 331–32.

31. Robert C. Ellickson, "Of Coase and Cattle: Dispute Resolution Among Neighbors in Shasta County," 38 *Stan. L. Rev.* 623 (1986); Robert C. Ellickson, *Order Without Law: How Neighbors Settle Disputes* (1991). For further discussion, see chapter 2, infra.

32. See e.g., Y. B. Trin, *Tithe Case*, 21 Hen. 7, f. 27, pl. 5 (1506), translated in C. H. S. Fifoot, *History and Sources of the Common Law: Tort and Contract* (1949), p. 197.

33. See *Report of the Committee on the Law of Civil Liability for Damage Done by Animals*, CMND. (1953), § 746, para. 3. For the criticism, see Glanville Williams, *Liability for Animals* (1939), p. v.

34. For some of the variations, see Oliver Wendell Holmes, Jr., *The Common Law* (1881), p. 212.

35. 8 F. 159 (D.C. Mass. 1881).

36. 248 U.S. 215 (1918). For my more extended treatment of the case, see Richard A. Epstein, "*International News Service v. Associated Press*: Custom and Law as Sources of Property Rights in News," 78 *Va. L. Rev.* 87 (1992). For earlier discussion, see Douglas G. Baird, "Common Law Intellectual Property and the Legacy of *International News Service v. Associated Press*," 50 *U. Chi. L. Rev.* 411 (1983).

37. For a brief account, see Jesse Dukeminier & James Krier, *Property* 708-710 (1st ed. 1981).

38. See chapter 7 infra for further discussion of the appropriate boundary conditions.

39. See 1 Blackstone *Commentaries*, *75–78. For an informative recounting of the historical progression, see David Bederman, "The Curious Resurrection of Custom: Beach Access and Judicial Takings," 96 *Colum. L. Rev.* 1375, 1382–1398 (1996).

40. 1 Blackstone, *Commentaries*, *77.

41. Ibid, *78

42. Ibid, *79

43. See, e.g., *Waters* v. *Lilly*, 21 Mass. 145 (1826) (holding that the right to catch fish was not given by local custom, but had to be established in reference to a particular plot of land).

44. John Chipman Gray, *The Rule Against Perpetuities* (4th ed. 1942), § 586, p. 564.

45. *State ex rel. Thornton* v. *Hay*, 462 P.2d 671 (1969).

46. 903 P.2d 1246, 1271–1272 (Haw. 1995).

47. As proposed in Bederman, *The Curious Resurrection*, pp. 1447–1455.

48. 60 F.2d 737, 740 (2d Cir. 1932). I have critiqued the decision at length in Richard A. Epstein, "The Path to *The T.J. Hooper*: The Theory and History of Custom in the Law of Tort," 21 *J. Legal Studies* 1 (1992).

49. See *Helling v. Carey*, 519 P.2d 981 (Wash. 1974). The decision was overruled by Wash. Rev. Code § 4,.24.290. See J. Jerry Wiley, "The Impact of Judicial Decisions on Professional Conduct: An Empirical Study," 55 *So. Calif. L. Rev.* 345 (1982).

CHAPTER 2

1. John Austin, *The Province of Jurisprudence Determined* (1832) [H. L. A. Hart, ed., 1954].

2. See H. L. A. Hart, *The Concept of Law* (2d ed. 1994), ch. 5, discussing law as a union of primary and secondary rules.

3. 347 U.S. 483 (1954).

4. Austin, *Province*, p. 142.

5. Richard A. Posner, *Legal Theory in the UK and USA* (1997).

6. Robert C. Ellickson, *Order Without Law: How Neighbors Settle Disputes* (1991), pp. 4–5, 137–147.

7. Thomas Hobbes, *Leviathan* (1651), ch. 13.

8. For an exhaustive account, see James S. Coleman, *Foundations of Social Theory* (1990). A recent conference on the subject was just sponsored at the University of Pennsylvania Law Review. "Symposium: Law, Economics, & Norms," 144 *U. Penn. L. Rev.* 1643 (1996).

9. Ellickson, *Order Without Law*, p. 4.

10. See, e.g., Edna Ullmann-Margolit, *The Emergence of Norms* (1977).

11. See *Rose and Frank Co. v. J. R. Crompton, Ltd.,* [1923] 2 K.B. 261 (refusing to enforce a basic arrangement subject to an "honorable pledge" clause or to enforce action for price for specific deliveries), rev'd, [1925] A.C. 445 (refusing to enforce general clause, but enforcing action for price on specific deliveries).

12. Ellickson, *Order Without Law*, pp. 141–42.

13. See, e.g., Cass R. Sunstein, "Social Norms and Social Roles," 96 *Colum. L. Rev.* 903, 947–948 (1996) (criticizing the views of Richard Posner and me that limit the use of government action "to avoid force, fraud, and 'harm to others'").

14. Ibid, pp. 948–952.

15. See, e.g., Joseph Story, "Natural Law," his unsigned article in the *Encyclopedia Americana* (1836).

16. See, specifically, Hart, *The Concept of Law*, pp. 163–176.

17. Lon L. Fuller, *The Morality of Law* (1964).

18. *Balfour v. Balfour*, [1919] 2 K.B. 571.

19. Maintenance Agreement Act, 5 & 6 Eliz 2 Ch. 35 (1957).

20. For the older prohibition, see *Tweddle v. Atkinson*, 121 Eng. Rep. 762 (Q.B. 1861). For the opposite American response, see *Lawrence v. Fox*, 20 N.Y. 268 (Ct. App. 1859).

21. See, e.g., *Powell v. Fall*, 5 Q.B. 597 (1880).

22. For elaboration, see Richard A. Epstein, *Simple Rules for a Complex World* (1995), pp. 30–36.

23. Lisa Bernstein, "Opting out of the Legal System: Extralegal Contractual Relations in the Diamond Industry," 21 *J. Legal Stud.* 115 (1992).

24. *Toussaint v. Blue Cross*, 292 N.W.2d 880 (Mich. 1980).

25. For a summary, see Paul C. Weiler, *Governing the Workplace: The Future of Labor and Employment Law* (1990). For a more extended version of my views, see Epstein, *Simple Rules* (1995), chs. 8 & 9.

26. Sheryl Gay Stolberg, "Gray Matter: Breaks for Mental Illness: Just What

the Government Ordered," *New York Times*, May 4, 1997, Section 4, p. 1; Robert Pear, "Employers Told to Accommodate the Mentally Ill," *New York Times*, April 30, 1997, p. A1.

27. Pear, "Employers Told to Accommodate," p. A15.

28. *Gilmer v. Interstate/Johnson Lane Corp.*, 500 U.S. 20 (1991) is the principal case. For extensions into other areas, see *Cole v. Burns Int'l Security Services*, 105 F.3d 1465 (D.C. Cir. 1997); *Pryner v. Tractor Supply Co.*, 109 F.3d 354 (7th Cir. 1997).

29. See Katharine Van Wezel Stone, "Mandatory Arbitration of Individual Employment Rights: The Yellow Dog Contract of the 1990s," 73 *Denver L. Rev.* 1017 (1996). A yellow dog is an agreement whereby, as a condition for obtaining a job in a firm, an employee waives membership in a union. The clauses were upheld judicially in *Hitchman Coal & Coke Co. v. Mitchell*, 245 U.S. 229 (1917). The result was reversed in the Norris-LaGuardia Act, 47 Stat. 70 (codified 29 U.S.C. §§101–115). I have defended these yellow dog provisions in Richard A. Epstein, "A Common Law for Labor Relations: A Critique of the New Deal Labor Legislation," 92 *Yale L. J.* 1357 (1983).

30. Stewart Macaulay, "Non-Contractual Relations in Business: A Preliminary Study," 28 *Am. Soc. Rev.* (1963), pp. 55, 63.

31. 260 U.S. 393 (1922).

32. William A. Fischel, *Regulatory Takings: Law, Economics and Politics* (1995), pp. 1–47.

33. John Tierney, "Why It's So Hard To Rent an Apartment: At the Intersection of Supply and Demand," *New York Times Magazine*, May 4, 1997, p. 38.

34. Ellickson, *Order Without Law*, p. 185.

35. Ibid, p. vii.

36. *Marshall v. Welwood*, 38 N.J.L. 339 (1876).

37. H. Laurence Ross, *Settled Out of Court* (rev. ed. 1980), pp. 249–51, 275–276.

38. Sunstein, "Social Roles," p. 948, n. 166.

CHAPTER 3

1. See, e.g., *Rylands v. Fletcher*, L.R. 3 H.L. 330, 340 (1868), per Lord Cranworth. "For when one person, in managing his own affairs, causes, however innocently, damage to another, it is obviously only just that he should be the party to suffer. He is bound sic uti suo ut non laedat alienum."

2. For discussion, see George Priest, "The Government, The Market and the Problem of Catastrophic Loss," 12 *J. Risk & Uncertainty* 219, 230 (1996).

3. For a general discussion, see Richard A. Epstein, "Exit Rights Under Federalism," 55 *Law & Contemp. Prob.* 147 (Winter, 1992).

4. See, e.g., Peter McWilliams, "Ain't Nobody's Business," *Chicago Tribune Sunday Magazine*, October 17, 1993, Zone C, p. 12, excerpted from *Ain't Nobody's Business* (1993).

5. See John Stuart Mill, *On Liberty*, in *Utilitarianism, Liberty and Representative Government*. The original essay was published in 1859. [Page refer-

ences are to Everyman's Library Edition (1971).]

6. Mill, *On Liberty*, p. 72.

7. Ibid., p. 149.

8. Ibid., p. 132.

9. Ibid., p. 150.

10. Ibid., p. 74.

11. *The Mogul Steamship Co. v. McGregor, Gow & Co.*, 23 Q.B.D. 598 (1889), aff'd, [1892] A.C. 25.

12. *Fontainebleau Hotel Corp. v. Forty-Five Twenty-Five, Inc.*, 114 So. 2d 357 (Fla. App. 1959).

13. McWilliams, "Ain't Nobody's Business," p. 12.

14. Mill, *On Liberty*, p. 133.

15. See David Hume, *A Treatise of Human Nature* (1740; L. A. Selby-Bigge, ed. 1888), Bk. III, Sect. III.

16. See, e.g., *The Mogul Steamship Co. v. McGregor, Gow & Co.*, 23 Q.B.D. 598 (1889), aff'd, [1892] A.C. 25; *Allen v. Flood*, [1898] A.C. 1; *Quinn v. Leathem*, [1901] A.C. 495; *Temperton v. Russell*, [1893] 1 K.B. 715; *Bradford v. Pickles*, [1895] A.C. 587. For the American side, see, e.g., *Plant v. Woods*, 57 N.E. 1011 (Mass. 1900); *Vegelahn v. Guntner*, 44 N.E. 1077 (Mass. 1896).

17. 8 *Harv. L. Rev.* 1 (1894).

18. Ibid., p. 1.

19. Ibid., pp. 3–4.

20. Holmes, *The Common Law* (1881), pp. 139–140.

21. *Pasley v. Freeman*, 100 Eng. Rep. 450 (K.B. 1789) (Buller, J.).

22. *Gardner v. Slade*, 13 Q.B. 796 (1849).

23. *Mogul*, 23 Q.B.D. p. 613.

24. Ibid., p. 615.

25. Ibid., p. 616.

26. *Keeble v. Hickeringill*, (K.B. 1707) reported in 103 Eng. Rep. 1127 (1809). See *Tarleton v. M'Gawley*, Peake's N.P. 270, 170 Eng. Rep. 153 (K.B. 1793) for the elements of intentional interference with prospective advantage.

27. See John P. Dawson, "Economic Duress—An Essay in Perspective," 45 *Mich. L. Rev.* 253 (1947); for criticism, see Richard A. Epstein, "Unconscionability: A Critical Reappraisal," 18 *J. Law & Econ.* 293 (1975).

28. For a discussion of the relevant gyrations, see James Barr Ames, "How Far an Act May Be a Tort Because of the Wrongful Motive of the Actor," 18 *Harv. L. Rev.* 411 (1905).

29. See *Allen v. Flood*, [1898] A.C 1.

30. *Collins v. Locke*, 4 A.C. 674, 686 (1879).

31. For a strong statement of that view, see Michael Trebilcock, *The Common Law of Restraint of Trade: A Legal and Economic Analysis* (1986), pp. 25–26.

32. 148 Eng. Rep. 1201 (Ex. 1829).

33. *Mineral Water Bottle Exchange and Trade Protection Society v. Booth*, 36 Ch. 465 (C.A. 1887).

34. *Allnut v. Inglis*, 104 Eng. Rep. 206 (K.B. 1810), discussed infra ch. 10.

35. See, e.g., James Bovard, *The Fair Trade Fraud* (1991).

36. *Matsushita Electric Industrial Co. Ltd. v. Zenith Radio Corp.*, 475 U.S. 574 (1985). See also, *Brooke Group Ltd. v. Brown & Williamson Tobacco Corp.*, 509 U.S. 209 (1993) which dismissed similar charges after a jury had found for the plaintiffs.

37. For discussion, see Robert Bork, *The Antitrust Paradox*, pp. 145ff; Frank H. Easterbrook, "Predatory Strategies and Counterstrategies," 48 *U. Chi. L. Rev.* 263 (1981); John S. McGee, "Predatory Pricing Revisited," 23 *J. Law & Econ.* 289 (1980).

38. See, e.g., *Petruzzi's IGA v. Darling-Delaware*, 998 F.2d 1224 (3rd Cir. 1993); *In re Coordinated Pretrial Proceedings in the Petroleum Products Antitrust Litigation*, 906 F.2d 432 (9th Cir. 1990).

39. *Eastman Kodak v. Image Technical Services Inc.*, 504 U.S. 451 (1992).

40. *Monsanto Co. v. Spray-Rite Service Corp.*, 465 U.S. 752 (1984).

41. See, e.g., *Lovett v. General Motors Corp.*, 998 F.2d 575 (8th Cir. 1993).

42. See David Strauss, "The Law and Economics of Racial Discrimination in Employment: The Case for Numerical Standards," 79 *Geo. L. J.* 1619, 1625 (1991).

43. Guido Calabresi & A. Douglas Melamed, "Property Rules, Liability Rules, and Inalienability: One View of the Cathedral," 85 *Harv. L. Rev.* 1089, 1125 (1972).

44. See Gary S. Becker, *The Economics of Discrimination* (2d ed. 1971).

45. I push these parallels at great length in Richard A. Epstein, *Forbidden Grounds: The Case Against Employment Discrimination Laws* (1992), ch. 2 & 3.

46. Alain Enthoven, *The Theory and Practice of Managed Competition* (1988), p. 5. He begins with a long description of why social insurance differs from market insurance, and then concludes: "The element of cross-subsidy is essential."

47. Ibid., pp. 7– 8.

48. For my views at length, see Richard A. Epstein, "Corrective Justice and Its Utilitarian Constraints," 8 *J. Legal Stud.* 49 (1979) (discussing the cases that follow).

49. William L. Prosser and W. Page Keeton, *The Law of Torts* (5th ed. 1984), p. 616.

50. See *Sibson v. New Hampshire*, 336 A.2d 239, 240 (N.H. 1975) (upholding a wetland regulation while noting that filling in a marsh was "bad for the marsh, and for mankind").

51. See Joseph L. Sax, "The Constitutional Dimensions of Property: A Debate," 26 *Loyola Los Angeles L. Rev.* 23, 33 (1992).

52. For the current legal position, favoring the extensive use of government power, see *Sweet Home Chapters of Oregon v. Babbitt*, 515 U.S. 687 (1995). For a critique of the endangered species act, which generally operates through designation without compensation, see James V. DeLong, *Property Matters: How Property Rights Are Under Assault—And Why You Should Care* (1997), ch. 6.

CHAPTER 4

1. 505 U.S. 1003 (1992).

2. Ibid., 1024.

3. Sweet Home Chapter of Communities for a Great Oregon, 17 F.3d 1463, 1464 (D.C. Cir. 1994).

4. See, e.g., Cass R. Sunstein, "Lochner's Legacy," 87 *Colum. L. Rev.* 873 (1987).

5. *Doughtery v. Stepp,* 18 N.C. 371 (1835).

6. Donald Wittman, "Liability for Harm or Restitution for Benefit?," 13 *J. Legal Stud.* 57 (1984).

7. See Ronald H. Coase, *The Firm, the Market, and the Law* (1988), pp. 170–174. For the position that these are somewhat more important in understanding the choice of legal rules, see Herbert Hovenkamp, "Legal Policy and the Endowment Effect," 20 *J. Legal Stud.* 225 (1991).

8. *Garcia v. Sumrall,* 121 P.2d 640 (Ariz. 1942).

9. See Kenneth Vogel, "The Coase Theorem and California Animal Trespass Law," 16 *J. Legal Stud.* 149 (1987).

10. See Robert C. Ellickson, *Order Without Law: How Neighbors Settle Disputes* (1991), pp. 42–45.

11. Ronald Coase, "The Problem of Social Cost," 3 *J. Law & Econ.* 1 (1960).

12. A familiar theme, stressed in Guido Calabresi & A. Douglas Melamed, "Property Rights, Liability Rules, and Inalienability: One View of the Cathedral," 85 *Harv. L. Rev.* 1089 (1972); Richard A. Posner, *Economic Analysis of the Law* (5th ed. 1998), pp. 51–52.

13. Aristotle, *Nicomachean Ethics* (ed. R. McKeon, 1941), Book III, p. 964.

14. See William M. Landes & Richard A. Posner, "Salvors, Finders, Good Samaritans, and Other Rescuers: An Economic Study of Law and Altruism," 7 *J. Legal Stud.* 83 (1978); Richard A. Epstein, "Holdouts and Externalities: One More Salute to Ronald Coase," 36 *J. Law & Econ.* 553 (1993).

15. 104 S.W. 164 (Ark. 1907).

16. *Robinson v. Campbell,* 47 Iowa 625, 627 (1878).

17. 165 A.2d 82 (Pa. 1960).

18. Y. B. Trin., 21 Hen. 7, f. 26, pl. 5 (1506). A modern translation of the case is found in C.H.S. Fifoot, *History and Sources of the Common Law* (1949), p. 197.

19. Ibid., per Kingsmill, J.

20. Ibid.

21. See Restatement of Restitution §§ 115–117.

22. For discussion, see Oliver Wendell Holmes, *The Common Law* (1881), p. 97. For the rule that holds a converter liable when property is taken under an innocent and excusable mistake, see *Maye v. Tappan,* 23 Cal. 306 (1863).

23. On which generally, see Lord Goff of Chieveley & Gareth Jones, *The Law of Restitution* (3rd ed. 1986), pp. 605–623.

24. See, e.g., *Jones v. Hoar,* 22 Mass. 285 (1827).

25. See, e.g., *Braithwaite v. Akin,* 56 N.W. 133 (N.D. 1893).

26. See Gaius, *Institutes* (F. de Zulueta ed. 1945), Book III, ¶ 91.

27. See, e.g., *Mouse's Case,* 12 Co. Rep. 63, 66 Eng. Rep. 1341 (K.B. 1609). For a general account, see Grant Gilmore & Charles Black, *The Law of Admiralty* (2d ed., 1975), §§5.1–5.2. For the first formal demonstration of the basic efficiency of the structural rule, see Landes & Posner, "Salvors, Finders, Good Samaritans, and Other Rescuers," 7 *J. Legal Studies* 83, 106–108. I had stumbled on the point inde-

pendently in Richard A. Epstein, *Cases and Materials on Torts* (3rd ed. 1977), pp. 35–36.

28. Saul Levmore, "Self-Assessed Valuation Systems for Tort and Other Law," 68 *Va. L. Rev.* 771, 860, n. 214 (1982).

29. See John Rawls, *A Theory of Justice* (1971), for the most notable modern exercise in contractarian theory. See also James Buchanan, *The Limits of Liberty* (1975).

30. John Locke, *Second Treatise on Government,* ¶28.

31. 2 Blackstone, *Commentaries,* *8.

32. Ibid.

33. Locke, *Second Treatise,* ¶28.

34. Locke, *Second Treatise,* ch. 19, esp. ¶222.

35. For a discussion of taxation and the maximization of surplus, see Richard A. Epstein, *Bargaining with the State* (1993), ch. 9.

36. For my fuller defense, see Richard A. Epstein, *Takings: Private Property and the Power of Eminent Domain* (1985).

37. Stephen Diamond, "The Death and Transfiguration of Benefit Taxation: Special Assessments in the Nineteenth Century America," 12 *J. Legal Stud.* 201 (1984).

38. Thomas Cooley, *Constitutional Limitations* (5th ed. 1883), p. 613.

39. *Carmichael v. South Coal & Coke Co.,* 301 U.S. 495, 522–523 (1937).

CHAPTER 5

1. Amartya Sen, "Rational Fools," 6 *Philo. & Pub. Affairs* 317, 329 (1976).

2. See Barry Schwartz, "Why Altruism Is Impossible . . . and Ubiquitous," 67 *Social Service Review* 314 (1993).

3. James Madison, *The Federalist,* No. 10 (1787).

4. David Binder, with Barbara Crosette, "As Ethnic Wars Multiply, U.S. Strives for a Policy," *New York Times,* February 7, 1993, p. 1.

5. Alan P. Fiske, *Structures of Social Life: The Four Elementary Forms of Human Relations* (1991). For an application of these tests, see Schwartz, *Why Altruism?,* p. 692, supra at n.2.

6. Daniel Kahneman, Jack L. Knetsch, and Richard H. Thaler, "Fairness as a Constraint on Profit Seeking: Entitlements in the Market," 76 *Am. Econ. Rev.* 728–741 (1986).

7. See Benjamin Klein & Keith B. Leffler, "The Role of Market Forces in Assuring Contractual Performance," 89 *J. Pol. Econ.* 615 (1981).

8. *Lucas v. South Carolina Coastal Council,* 505 U.S. 1003 (1992); for criticism of the basic position, see Epstein, *Takings,* ch. 14.

9. The phrase is from Justice Holmes's famous decision in *Pennsylvania Coal Co. v. Mahon,* 260 U.S. 393, 415 (1922).

10. See, e.g., Michael Sandel, *Liberalism and the Limits of Justice* (1982); Robert Kuttner, *Everything for Sale: The Virtues and Limits of Markets* (1997).

11. See Janet Landa, *Trust. Ethnicity, and Identity: Beyond the New Institutional Economics of Ethnic Trading Networks, Contract Law and Gift-Exchange* (1994).

12. Frank Michelman, "Political Markets and Community Self-Determination: Competing Judicial Models of Local Government Legitimacy," 53 *Ind. L. J.* 145, 149 (1977-1978).

13. For some accounts, see Leslie Wayne, "For Interest Groups, Battle Lines Form in Debate over Social Security," *New York Times*, December 30, 1996, p. A1; Robert Pear, "Social Security: The Overview: Panel of Social Security Urges Investing in Stocks, but is Split Over Methods," *New York Times*, January 7, 1997, p. A1.

14. Michael J. Sandel, "Anti-social Security," *The New Republic*, February 3, 1997, p. 27.

15. For discussions of this issue, see Lloyd Cohen, *Increasing the Supply of Organs* (1995). For my own views on the question, see Richard A. Epstein, *Mortal Peril: Our Inalienable Right to Health Care?* (1997), ch. 9–12. For a discussion of UNOS, see James Blumstein, "Government's Role in Organ Transplantation Policy," in J. Blumstein and F. Sloan eds., *Organ Transplantation Policy: Issues and Prospects* (1989).

16. For a defense of the current rules, see Ian Ayres, Laura Dooley, and Robert S. Gaston, "Unequal Racial Access to Kidney Transplantation," 46 *Vand. L. Rev.* 805 (1993). For a criticism, see Lloyd Cohen and Melissa Michelson, "The Efficiency Equity Puzzle in Kidney Allocation: A Reply to Ayres, et al and UNOS," *Annual Review of Law and Ethics* (1996), p. 4.

17. 272 U.S. 365 (1926).

18. *Creative Environments, Inc. v. Estabrook*, 680 F.2d 822, 833 (1st Cir. 1982).

19. *Coniston Corporation v. Village of Hoffman Estates*, 844 F.2d 461, 468 (7th Cir. 1988).

20. *Southern Burlington County N.A.A.C.P. v. Township of Mount Laurel*, 336 A.2d 713 (N.J. 1975).

21. *Southern Burlington County N.A.A.C.P. v. Township of Mount Laurel*, 456 A.2d 390 (N.J. 1983) is but one benchmark of this litigation that began in the early 1970s and continues in modified form to this day.

22. *Block v. Hirsh*, 256 U.S. 135 (1921).

23. See Margaret Radin, "Residential Rent Control," 15 *Philo. & Pub. Aff.* 350 (1986).

24. See William Tucker, "Anarchy, State and Rent Control," *The New Republic*, December 22, 1986, p. 20. See also, *Gilbert v. City of Cambridge*, 932 F.2d 51 (1st Cir. 1991), sustaining the Cambridge ordinance against attack.

CHAPTER 6

1. F. A. Hayek, *The Road to Serfdom* (1944), p. 141. For a similar recognition of the risks of political guarantees, see David Schmidtz, "Guarantees," 14 (no. 1) *Social Phil. & Pol.*, 1 (1997).

2. For a useful set of materials, see Friedrich Kessler & Grant Gilmore, *Contracts: Cases and Materials* (2d ed. 1970), pp. 871–911.

3. 19 Mass. 267, 274 (1824).

4. Ibid., 273.

5. Ibid.

6. 17 N.Y. 173, 186 (1858).

7. Ibid., 275.

8. See Note in 26 *American Decisions* (1881), cited in Kessler & Gilmore, *Contracts*, p. 878.

9. 6 N.H. 481 (1834).

10. Ibid., 495.

11. See, e.g., *Daniels v. Evans*, 224 A.2d 63 (N.H. 1966), overruling an earlier twentieth century case that did allow some leeway for infants in highway accidents, see *Charbonneau v. MacRury*, 153 A. 457 (N.H. 1931).

12. For a small sample of the enormous history on industrial accident law, see *Farwell v. Boston & Worcester R.R. Corp.*, 45 Mass. 49 (1842); *Lamson v. American Axe & Tool Co.*, 58 N.E. 585 (Mass. 1900); C. Labatt, *Master and Servant* (2d. 3d. 1913), §§ 1433–1533; T.G. Shearman & A.A. Redfield, *Negligence* (5th Ed. 1898); Richard A. Posner, "A Theory of Negligence," 1 *J. Legal Stud.* 29, 67–71 (1972).

13. Lawrence Friedman, *A History of American Law* (2d ed. 1985).

14. Gary Schwartz, "Tort Law and the Economy in Nineteenth-Century America: A Reinterpretation," 90 *Yale L. J.* 1717 (1981). Schwartz's work is not analyzed in Friedman's 1985 edition.

15. For this history, see Richard A. Epstein, "The Historical Origins and Intellectual Structure of the Workers' Compensation Laws," 16 *Ga. L. Rev.* 775 (1982).

16. See *Ives v. South Buffalo Ry Co.*, 94 N.E. 4321 (N.Y. 1911) (describing and striking down New York statute on state constitutional grounds); *New York Central R.R. v. White*, 243 U.S. 188 (1916) (sustaining a revised New York statute against federal constitutional challenges).

17. For Great Britain, see Steven Davies, "Two Conceptions of Welfare: Voluntarism and Incorporationism," 14 (no. 2) *Soc. Phil. & Pol.* 39 (1997). For the analogous American experience, see David Bieto, "'This Enormous Army': The Mutual Aid Tradition of American Fraternal Societies before the Twentieth Century," 14 (no. 2) *Soc. Phil. & Pol.* 20 (1997).

18. See Marvin Olasky, *The Tragedy of American Compassion* (1992) p. 35.

19. *McDonald v. Massachusetts General Hospital*, 120 Mass. 432 (1876).

20. See, e.g., *Powers v. Massachusetts Homeopathetic Hospital*, 109 F 294, 304 (1st Cir. 1901).

21. *Schumacher v. Evangelical Deaconess Society of Wisconsin*, 260 N.W. 476 (Wis. 1935) (extending the immunity to a paying patient).

22. See, e.g., *Wendt v. Servite Fathers*, 76 N.E.2d 342 (Ill. App. 1947).

23. For detailed statement of the attitudes and practices, see Olasky, *Tragedy*, ch. 1.

24. Quoted in Olasky, *Tragedy*, p. 10.

25. Olasky, *Tragedy,* pp. 7, 12.

26. Ibid., p. 13.

27. Ibid., p. 20.

28. Ibid., p. 13.

29. Ibid., p. 14.

30. Ibid., p. 11.

31. Ibid., p. 20.

32. For a discussion of these issues, see Richard A. Epstein, *Simple Rules for a Complex World* (1995), pp. 151–193.

33. For a summary of some of the litigation in this connection, see Paul Weiler, *Governing the Workplace: The Future of Labor and Employment Law* (1990).

34. 29 U.S.C. § 141 et seq (1988).

35. See the somewhat misnamed Railway Labor Act, 29 U.S.C. § 151 et seq (1988), which since 1936 has applied to airlines. For a sympathetic account of the Railway Labor Act, see Katherine van Wezel Stone, "Labor Relations on the Airlines: The Railway Labor Act in the Era of Deregulation," 42 *Stan. L. Rev.* 1485 (1990).

36. Adam Bryant, "American Air's Pilots: Holding the Trump Card," *New York Times,* February 15, 1997, p. 23.

37. Lester Thurow, "The Birth of a Revolutionary Class," *New York Times Magazine,* May 19, 1996, p. 46.

38. For a mind-numbing collection of cases, see Walter Olson, *The Excuse Factory: How Employment Law is Paralyzing the American Workplace* (1997).

39. Americans with Disabilities Act of 1990, 42 U.S.C. § 12101 et seq.

40. John Cassidy, "Who Killed the Middle Class?" *The New Yorker* 83 (October 16, 1995).

41. For an exhaustive compilation, see Victor Schwartz, *Comparative Negligence* (3rd ed. 1994).

42. See *Escola v. Coca-Cola Bottling Co.,* 150 P.2d 436 (Cal. 1944).

43. See *Barker v. Lull Engineering,* 573 P.2d 443 (Cal. 1978) (covering use in "an intended or reasonably foreseeable manner").

44. See, e.g., *Dawson v. Chrysler Corp.,* 630 F.2d 950 (3rd. Cir. (1980); *LeBouef v. Goodyear Tire & Rubber Corp.,* 623 F.2d 985 (5th Cir. 1980).

45. 383 P.2d 441 (Cal. 1963).

46. 161 A.2d 69 (N.J. 1960).

47. 377 P.2d 897 (Cal. 1962).

48. For a similar judicial decision having to do with clauses in leases that exempted landlords from tort liability, see *Henrioulle v. Marin Ventures,* 573 P. 2d 465 (Cal. 1978).

49. For a more detailed discussion of these issues, see Richard A. Epstein, *Mortal Peril: Our Inalienable Right to Health Care?* (1997) , pp. 91–105, 369–376.

50. *Wilmington General Hospital v. Manlove,* 174 A.2d 135 (Del. 1961); *Guerrero v. Copper Queen Hospital,* 537 P.2d 1329 (Ariz. 1975).

51. 42 U.S.C. §1395dd. For applications, see, e.g., *Power v. Arlington Hospital Association,* 42 F.3d 851 (4th Cir. 1994), noting that differential treatment of unin-

sured persons triggers liability under the statute even if there is no improper motive on the part of the hospital.

52. *Baber v. Hospital Corporation of America,* 977 F.2d 872 (4th Cir. 1992).

53. See, e.g., *Equal Access to Health Care: Patient Dumping: Hearing Before the Subcommittee on Human Resources and Intergovernment Relations of the House Committee on Government Operations,* 100th Cong. 1st Sess. 14–20 (1987). The early academic commentary was generally supportive of the act, see, e.g., Karen H. Rothenberg, "Who Cares? The Evolution of the Legal Duty to Provide Emergency Care," 26 *Hous. L. Rev.* 21, 21 (1989). See also Andrew J. McClurg, "Your Money or Your Life: Interpreting the Federal Act Against Patient Dumping," 24 *Wake Forest L. Rev.* 173 (1989). For criticism, see David A. Hyman, "Lies, Damned Lies, and Narrative," 73 *Ind. L. J.* x (1998).

54. Erik J. Olson, "No Room at the Inn: A Snapshot of an American Emergency Room," 46 *Stan. L. Rev.* 449 (1994).

55. 16 F.3d 590 (4th Cir. 1994).

56. 397 U. S. 254 (1970).

57. See Jerry Mashaw, *Due Process in the Administrative State* (1985), pp. 34–35.

58. The relevant data are summarized in Michael Tanner, *The End of Welfare: Fighting Poverty in the Civil Society* (1996), ch. 3. For an earlier account that follows the story out to 1980, see Charles Murray, *Losing Ground: American Social Policy 1950–1980* (1984).

59. See generally, Robert Rector and William Lauber, *America's Failed $5.4 Trillion War on Poverty* (1995).

60. Tanner, *The End of Welfare,* p. 70, Figure 3.1.

61. Ibid., p. 77, Figure 3.4.

62. Personal Responsibility and Work Opportunity Act, Pub Law 104–193, 110 Stat. 2105 (1996).

63. *New York Times,* February 2, 1997, pp. 1, 12.

64. Robert Pear, "Number of Welfare Rolls Dips Below 10 Million," *New York Times,* January 21, 1998, Section A, p. 13, quoting Melissa T. Skolfield, HHS Spokeswoman.

65. Ibid.

66. Robert Pear, "Republican Leaders Exempt 'Workfare' From Labor Laws," *New York Times,* July 19, 1997, p. 8.

CHAPTER 7

1. Robert Nozick, *Anarchy, State, and Utopia* (1974), pp. 75–76, 152–153.

2. Ibid., p. 77.

3. See, e.g., Thomas W. Merrill, "Trespass, Nuisance, and the Costs of Determining Property Rights," 14 *J. Legal Stud.* 13 (1985).

4. For a more detailed exploration of this theme, see Richard A. Epstein, "Nuisance Law: Corrective Justice and Its Utilitarian Constraints," 8 *J. Legal Stud.* 49 (1979).

5. 122 Eng. Rep. 27, 32 (Ex. 1863).

6. For a longer analysis of this decision, see Richard A. Epstein, "For a Bramwell Revival," 38 *Am. J. Legal Hist.* 246, 269–283 (1994).

7. See, e.g., *Campbell v. Seaman*, 63 N.Y. 568 (1876).

8. *Corporation of Birmingham v. Allen*, L. R. 6 Ch.D. 284 (C.A. 1877).

9. 19 N.E. 390 (Mass. 1889).

10. Ibid., 392.

11. 260 U.S. 393, 416 (1922).

12. 114 So.2d 357 (Fla. App. 1959).

13. 500 A.2d 366 (N.H. 1985); for an earlier version of the same rule, see *Levy v. Samuel Bros.* 23 N.Y.S. 825 (Sup. Ct. 1893).

14. 321 N.W.2d 182 (Wis. 1982).

15. Ronald H. Coase, "The Problem of Social Cost," 3 *J. L & Econ.* 1 (1960).

16. [1879] 11 Ch.D. 852

17. A.W. Brian Simpson, "Coase v. Pigou Reexamined," 25 *J. Legal Stud.* 53 (1996).

18. Ronald H. Coase, "Law and Economics and A.W. Brian Simpson," 25 *J. Legal Stud.* 103 (1996); and the inevitable Simpson rejoinder, A.W. Brian Simpson, "An Addendum," 25 *J. Legal Stud.* 99 (1996).

19. See, e.g., *Ensign v. Walls*, 34 N.W.2d 549 (Mich. 1948).

20. *Hadacheck v. Sebastian*, 239 U.S. 394, 410 (1915).

21. See William Baxter & Lillian Altree, "Legal Aspects of Airport Noise," 15 *J. Law & Econ.* 1, 3 (1972).

22. *Restatement (Second) of Torts*, § 840D.

23. 239 U.S. 394 (1915).

24. See, e.g., *Agins v. City of Tiburon*, 447 U.S. 255 (1980).

25. See, e.g., *Miller v. Schoene*, 276 U.S. 272, 279–280 (1928).

26. See Richard A. Posner, *Economic Analysis of Law* (5th ed. 1998), pp. 83–84.

27. See, generally, *Restatement of the Law of Property*, §§ 137–140 (1936, main volume).

28. See, e.g., *Roach v. Harper*, 105 S.E.2d 546 (W.Va. 1958).

29. 389 U.S. 347 (1967).

30. For another illustration of the risk, see *Lucas v. South Carolina Coastal Council*, 505 U.S. 1003 (1992), discussed supra in ch. 4., pp. 88–92.

31. *Tribune Co. v. Oak Leaves Broadcasting Station*, 1926 Cook County, Illinois, reprinted in *Cong. Rec.—Senate* 215–219 (December 10, 1926). For a discussion of the early history, see Thomas W. Hazlett, "The Rationality of the U.S. Regulation of the Broadcast Spectrum," 33 *J. Law & Econ.* 133 (1990), detailing the political pressures at work in spectrum allocation.

32. Pub. L. No. 69–932, 44 Stat. 1162 (1927).

33. 48 Stat. 1064, 47 U.S.C. §§ 151 et. seq.

34. On the spectrum, see Jonathan W. Emord, *Freedom, Technology and the First Amendment* (1991), ch. 11, noting that the wrongful harm caused by use of radio frequencies was always directed to other frequency users. Landowners were not an issue.

35. For discussion of the period, see Thomas Hazlett, *Rationality*, pp. 137–148.

36. *NBC v. United States*, 319 U.S. 190, 215–216 (1943).

37. The most devastating critique is still, Ronald H. Coase, "The Federal Communications Commission," 2 *J. Law & Econ.* 1 (1959).

38. *1965 Policy Statement of Comparative Broadcast Hearings*, 1 F.C.C. 2d 393 (1965).

39. *Cosmopolitan Broadcasting Corp. v. FCC*, 581 F 2d 917 (D.C. Cir. 1978).

CHAPTER 8

1. Guido Calabresi & A. Douglas Melamed, "Property Rules, Liability Rules and Inalienability Rules: One View of the Cathedral," 85 *Harv. L. Rev.* 1089 (1972).

2. Ibid., 1092.

3. Ibid.

4. Ronald Coase, "The Problem of Social Cost," 3 *J. Law & Econ.* 1 (1960).

5. Jules L. Coleman & Jody Kraus, "Rethinking the Theory of Legal Rights," 95 *Yale L. J.* 1335, 1338–1339 (1986).

6. On the procedural side of this question, see Richard A. Epstein, "Pleadings and Presumptions," 40 *U. Chi. L. Rev.* 556 (1973).

7. Hume, *Treatise*, Book III, Section 3.

8. Oliver Wendell Holmes, Jr., *The Common Law* (1881), p. 301.

9. For articulation of efficient breach, see Richard A. Posner, *Economic Analysis of Law* (5th ed. 1998), pp. 33–34. For a powerful criticism, see Daniel Friedmann, "The Efficient Breach Fallacy," 18 *J. Legal Stud.* 1 (1988), and for partial rehabilitation, see Richard Craswell, "Contract Remedies, Renegotiation, and the Theory of Efficient Breach," 61 *S. Cal. L. Rev.* 629 (1988).

10. *Hoare v. Rennie*, 5 H & N. 19, 157 Eng. Rep. 1083 (1859).

11. Lisa Bernstein, "Merchant Law in a Merchant Court: Rethinking the Code's Search for Immanent Business Norms," 144 *U. Pa. L. Rev.* 1765, 1801–1802 (1996).

12. See, e.g., Samuel Pufendorf, *The Law of Nature and Nations* (1688), Book II, Ch. 6, "On the Right and Privilege of Necessity."

13. Ian Ayres & J. M. Balkin, "Legal Entitlements as Auctions: Property Rules, Liability Rules, and Beyond," 106 *Yale L. J.* 703 (1996).

14. 124 N.W. 221 (Minn. 1910).

15. 71 A. 188 (Vt. 1908).

16. Ayres & Balkin, "Auctions," 106 *Yale L.J.* 716.

17. See Pufendorf, *Law of Nature*, p. 305.

18. *Garagosian v. Union Realty Co.*, 193 N.E. 726 (Mass. 1935) (ordering the removal of an offending drain pipe and overhang), 728.

19. Ibid., 727.

20. Ibid., 727–728.

21. On which, see Epstein, *Takings*, pp. 51–56.

22. See, e.g., Anthony Kronman, "Specific Performance," 45 *U. Chi. L. Rev.* 351, 362 (1978) (defending the soundness of the uniqueness test for specific performance); see also Alan Schwartz, "The Myth that Promisees Prefer Supracompensatory Remedies: An Analysis of Contracting for Damage Measures," 100 *Yale L. J.* 369 (1990).

23. See, e.g., *Smith v. New England Aircraft Co., Inc.,* 170 N.E. 385 (Mass. 1930); *Swetland v. Curtiss Airports Corp.,* 41 F.2d 929 (N.D. Ohio, 1930).

24. *United States v. Causby,* 328 U.S. 256 (1946).

25. See, e.g., *Batten v. United States,* 306 F.2d 580 (10th Cir. 1962).

26. Ronald H. Coase, "The Federal Communication Commission," 2 *J. Law & Econ.* 1, 25 (1959).

27. 24 S.W.2d 619 (Ky. 1929).

28. *Edwards v. Lee's Admin.,* 96 S.W.2d 1028 (Ky. 1936).

29. See the colorful dissent of Lodge, J., in *Edwards v. Sims,* 24 S.W.2d at 621–623.

30. Advocated in the concurrence of Thomas, J. in *Edwards v. Lee's Admin.,* 96 S.W.2d at 1033–1036.

31. Ibid., at 1029. The condemnation price was fixed at $396,000.

32. For the contrary view, see Victor Goldberg, Thomas Merrill, and Daniel Unumb, "Bargaining in the Shadow of Eminent Domain: Valuing and Apportioning Condemnation Awards Between Landlord and Tenant," 34 *U.C.L.A. L. Rev.* 1083 (1987), arguing that the impasse between landlord and tenant should be ignored because the two would clearly bargain to agreement if the only question was the size of the award they could receive from the state.

33. This literature is enormous. See, e.g., Richard A. Epstein, "A Theory of Strict Liability," 2 *J. Legal Stud.* 151 (1973); Richard A. Posner, "A Theory of Negligence," 1 *J. Legal Stud.* 29 (1972); Steven Shavell, "Strict Liability versus Negligence," 9 *J. Legal Stud.* 1 (1980).

34. 96 S.W. 2d 221 (Tex. 1936).

35. 53 N.H. 442 (1873).

36. Ibid., 448.

37. For discussion, see Richard A. Epstein, "The Social Consequences of Common Law Rules," 95 *Harv. L. Rev.* 1717 (1982).

38. For representative cases, see *Quinn v. American Spiral Spring & Mfg. Co.,* 141 A. 855 (Pa. 1928); *Pritchett v. Board of Comm'rs,* 85 N.E. 32 (Ind. App. 1908).

39. 83 S.W. 658 (Tenn. 1904); cited by Calabresi & Melamed, "Cathedral," p. 1120.

40. See *Hawaiian Hous. Auth. v. Midkiff,* 467 U.S. 229 (1984); *Ruckelshaus v. Monsanto, Inc.,* 467 U.S. 986 (1984).

41. Calabresi & Melamed, "Cathedral," pp. 1106–1107.

42. See, e.g., New Hampshire Mill Act, 1868 N.H. Laws, Ch. 20 § 3, set out in *Head v. Amoskeog Mfg. Co.,* 113 U.S. 9, 10–11 (1885).

43. 276 U.S. 272 (1928). For the reference, see p. 3.

44. See Richard A. Epstein, *Bargaining with the State* (1993), esp. ch. 12.

45. 483 U.S. 825 (1987).

46. 512 U.S. 374 (1994).

47. 223 Cal. Rptr. 28 (Cal. App. 1986).

48. L.R. 3 H.L. 330 (1868).

49. Calabresi & Melamed, "Cathedral," p. 1116.

50. Levmore, "Property Rules, Liability Rules, and Startling Rules," 106 *Yale L.J.* 2149 (1997).

51. Robert L. Hale, "Coercion and Distribution in a Supposedly Non-Coercive State," 38 *Political Science Quarterly* 470 (1923). Hale's views are developed and defended at length in Barbara Fried, *The Progressive Assault on Laissez-Faire* (1998)

52. G.A. Cohen, *Self-Ownership, Freedom, and Equality* pp. 55–56 (1995).

53. Calabresi & Melamed, "Cathedral," p. 1125.

54. 494 P.2d 700 (Ariz. 1972).

55. See, e.g., *Bersani v. Robichaud*, 850 F.2d 36 (2d Cir. 1988) (effort to mitigate environmental losses from creation of shopping center by creating an artificial wetland).

CHAPTER 9

1. See John Locke, *Second Treatise of Government* (1690), ch. 5.

2. Karl Marx & Friedrich Engels, *The Communist Manifesto, Karl Marx: Selected Writings* (David McLellan ed. 1977), pp. 232, 237.

3. Jean Jacques Rousseau, "Discourse on the Origins and the Foundations of Inequality Among Men" (1755) in *The First and Second Discourses* (Roger D. Masters ed. 1964), pp. 141–42.

4. Ibid., p. 142.

5. R. B. Schlatter, *Private Property: The History of an Idea* (1951)

6. Locke, *Second Treatise*, ¶ 27.

7. Ibid., ¶ 31.

8. 2 William Blackstone, *Commentaries on the Laws of England*, *2 (1766).

9. See *Burnham v. Beverly Airways, Inc.*, 42 N.E.2d 575 (Mass. 1942).

10. 2 Blackstone, *Commentaries*, *7 and *4.

11. Locke, *Second Treatise*, ¶ 34 and ¶ 37.

12. Ibid., ¶ 50.

13. 2 Blackstone, *Commentaries*, *33.

14. Ibid.

15. Locke, *Second Treatise*, ch. 5, ¶ 35.

16. See, e.g., Glenn G. Stevenson, *Common Property Economics* (1991), ch. 3, for a discussion of the difference between unlimited open access and common property held by individuals who have agreed to keep it open by contract.

17. See David Hume, *A Treatise of Human Nature* (L. A. Selby-Bigge ed. 1888), Book III.

18. See Richard A. Posner, "A Theory of Primitive Society, with Special Reference to Law," 23 *J. Law & Econ.* 1 (1980).

19. Martin J. Bailey, "Approximate Optimality of Aboriginal Property Rights," 37 *J. Law & Econ.* 183, 184 (1992).

20. Ibid., p. 189.

21. See Forrest McDonald, *Novus Ordo Seclorum: The Intellectual History of the Constitution* (1985), pp. 32–34.

22. *The Institutes of Justinian*, Book II, Title I, pr. (J. B. Moyle ed., 5th ed. 1913) [hereinafter cited J.].

23. See, 2 Blackstone, *Commentaries*, chs. 14–19.

24. J. 1 2, 1.

25. J. 1, 2, 11.

26. Adam Smith, *Lectures on Jurisprudence* (R. L. Meek, D.D. Raphael & P.G. Stein eds. 1982), p. 17. See also Adam Smith, *Theory of Moral Sentiments* (1759).

27. Robert C. Ellickson, "Property in Land," 102 *Yale L. J.* 1315, 1320 (1993).

28. 2 Blackstone, *Commentaries*, *18.

29. *Anon.*, Y. B. Mich. 27 Hen. 8, f. 27, pl. 10 (1535).

30. See J. 2, 1, 1–6.

31. See, e.g., Gaius, *Institutes*, (F. de Zulueta ed. 1945), Bk. II, p. 30, where a purported conveyance of a usufruct to third party is ineffective, even if all forms are observed.

32. Locke, *Second Treatise*, ¶ 29.

33. For my further criticisms of the labor theory of value, see Richard A. Epstein, "Possession as the Root of Title," 13 *Ga. L. Rev.* 1221 (1979).

34. John Christman, "Entrepreneurs, Profits and Deserving Market Shares," 6 *Soc. Phil. & Pol.* 1 (1988).

35. For a splendid account of the transformation, see Carol M. Rose, "Energy and Efficiency in the Realignment of Common-Law Water Rights," 19 *J. Legal Stud.* 261 (1990).

36. Ronald H. Coase, "The Problem of Social Cost," 3 *J. Law & Econ.* 1 (1960).

37. *St. Louis v. Western Union Telegraph Co.*, 148 U.S. 92 (1893).

38. 2 Blackstone, *Commentaries*, chs. 14 to 19.

39. J. 2, 1, 12.

40. 2 Blackstone, *Commentaries*, *10–*13.

41. Harold Demsetz, "Toward a Theory of Property Rights," 57 *Am. Econ. Rev.* 347 (Pap. & Proc. 1967).

42. Locke, *Second Treatise*, ¶ 37.

43. Ibid.

44. Ibid., ¶ 30.

45. See, e.g., *Barrett v. State*, 116 N.E. 99 (NY 1917).

46. Richard A. Epstein, "Why Restrain Alienation?," 85 *Colum. L. Rev.* 970, 979–982 (1985).

47. E. P. Thompson, *Customs in Common* (1991), pp. 97–184.

48. See *Coffin v. The Left Hand Ditch Co.*, 6 Colo. 443 (1882), an action brought by a prior appropriator against a riparian who destroyed a dam used to secure the diversion of water from the river.

49. Robert Ellickson, *Order Without Law: How Neighbors Settle Disputes* (1991), pp. 191–206.

50. See John Locke, *Second Treatise*, ¶ 27. For a similar broad account of property rights in the person, see James Madison, "Property," 14 *Collected Papers* 266 (March 29, 1792), reprinted in P. Kurland & R. Lerner, eds., *The Founders' Constitution* (1987), ch. 16, no. 23.

51. See Ellickson, "Property in Land," pp. 1327–1328.

52. U.S. Const., Amend. 5.

53. 6 Fed. Case. 546 (Cir. Ct. E. D. Pa. 1823).

54. Ibid., 551–552.

55. Ibid., 552.

56. 161 U.S. 519 (1896).

57. U.S. Const. Art. 1, § 8, cl. 3.

58. See, e.g., *Southern Pacific Co. v. Arizona*, 325 U.S. 761 (1945) (judicial invalidation state law limiting length of trains); see generally, Donald H. Regan, "The Supreme Court and State Protectionism: Making Sense of the Dormant Commerce Clause," 84 *Mich. L. Rev.* 1091 (1986).

59. 161 U.S. 519, 522 (1896).

60. Justinian, *Digest*, Bk. 41, tit. 1, 1.

61. 161 U.S. 519, 539 (1896) (Field, J., dissenting).

62. 431 U.S. 265, 284 (1977).

63. Ibid., 284.

64. *Hughes v. Oklahoma*, 441 U.S. 322, 334–335 (1979).

65. 177 U.S. 190 (1899).

66. Richard A. Epstein, *Takings* (1985), pp. 219–223.

67. Acts of 1893 c. 36, § 2, reprinted in *Ohio Oil*, 177 U.S. 191.

68. *Ohio Oil*, 177 U.S. at 211.

69. *Pennsylvania Coal Co. v. Mahon*, 260 U.S. 393, 415 (1922).

70. 444 U.S. 164 (1979).

71. *United States v. Twin City Power Co.*, 350 U.S. 222, 224–225 (1956).

72. 22 U. S. 1 (1824).

73. *Kaiser Aetna*, 179–180.

74. 229 U.S. 53 (1913).

75. 324 U.S. 499 (1945).

76. Ibid., 502.

77. See *United States v. Chicago, M. & St. P. & PRR.*, 312 U.S. 592 (1941) (flooding); *Greenleaf Lumber Co. v. Garrison*, 236 U.S. 251 (1915) (removal order).

78. *Scranton v. Wheeler*, 179 U.S. 141 (1900); *United States v. Rands*, 389 U.S. 121 (1987).

CHAPTER 10

1. For one excellent overview, see Herbert Hovenkamp, *Enterprise and American Law: 1836-1937* (1991).

2. *Boston Ice Co. v. Potter*, 123 Mass. 28, 30 (1877).

3. Richard A. Epstein, *Forbidden Grounds: The Case Against Employment*

Discrimination Laws, (1992), esp. chs. 2–3.

4. Hovenkamp, *Enterprise and American Law*, p. 127.

5. Aaron Director, "The Parity of the Economic Market Place," 7 *J. Law & Econ.* 1, 2 (1964).

6. See, e.g., Joan Robinson, "A Fundamental Objection to *Laissez-Faire*," 45 *Econ. J.* 580 (1935).

7. James W. Ely, *The Chief Justiceship of Melville W. Fuller: 1888-1910* (1995), p. 73.

8. Ely, *Fuller*, p. 77. "The degree to which Darwinism and Social Darwinism *failed* to permeate the thinking of the Supreme Court in any way is most amazing."

9. Ely, *Fuller*, pp. 80–81.

10. See, e.g., William Letwin, "The English Common Law Concerning Monopolies," 21 *U. Chi. L. Rev.* 355 (1954)

11. See, e.g., Lawrence Friedman, *Contract Law in America* (1965); Grant Gilmore, *The Death of Contract* (1974); Patrick S. Atiyah, *The Rise and Fall of Freedom of Contract* (1979).

12. See A.W. Brian Simpson, *A History of the Common Law of Contract: The Rise of the Action of Assumpsit* (1975), pp. 229–233.

13. 12 East 525, 104 Eng. Rep. 206 (K.B. 1810).

14. Sir Matthew Hale, *The History of the Common Law of England* (1971), p. xiii, editorial introduction of Charles Gray.

15. 12 East 530, 104 Eng. Rep. 208.

16. Ibid. at 534.

17. Ibid. at 534, 104 Eng. Rep. at 209.

18. Ibid. at 538, 104 Eng. Rep. at 210–211.

19. Ibid at 536, 104 Eng. Rep. at 210.

20. Ibid.

21. Ibid. at 540, 104 Eng. Rep. at 211.

22. See *Munn v. Illinois*, 94 U.S. 113 (1876).

23. H.W. Chaplin, "Limitations upon the Right of Withdrawal from Public Employment," 16 *Harv. L. Rev.* 555, 556–557 (1903).

24. Atiyah, *Rise and Fall*, p. 417.

25. 94 U.S. 113 (1876).

26. *German Alliance Insurance Co. v. Kansas*, 233 U.S. 389 (1914). For a sardonic discussion of the ins-and-outs of the case law, see Walton Hamilton, "Affectation with the Public Interest," 39 *Yale L. J.* 1089 (1930). For modern validation of such rate regulation, see *State Farm Mut. Ins. Co. v. New Jersey*, 590 A.2d 191 (N.J. 1991).

27. *State ex rel. Wood v. Consumers' Gas Trust Co.*, 61 N.E. 674, 677 (Ind. 1901).

28. See, e.g., *Railroad Co. v Lockwood*, 84 U.S. 357 (1873); for an excellent summary of the earlier authorities, see *Russell v. Pittsburgh, C. C. & St. L. Ry. Co.*, 61 N.E. 678 (Ind. 1901).

29. A view taken in C. H. S. Fifoot, *History and Sources of the Common Law: Tort and Contract* (1949), pp. 158–159.

30. *Coggs v. Bernard*, 2 Ld. Raym. 909, 92 Eng. Rep. 622 (K.B. 1703). For private carriers, see *Morse v. Slue*, 1 Ventris 190, 238, 86 Eng. Rep. 129 (K.B. 1671). For a defense of strict liability, see Oliver Wendell Holmes, Jr., *The Common Law* (1881), pp. 183–198.

31. Chaplin, p. 561.

32. See, for contemporary discussion, Chaplin, supra note 20 .

33. *Blackstock v. The New York & Erie R. R. Co.*, 20 N.Y. 48 (1859).

34. *Chicago, B. &. Q. Ry. v. Burlington C. R. & N. Ry. Co.*, 34 F. 481, 484 (1888).

35. 168 U.S. 135, 138 (1897).

36. *Baltimore & Ohio &c v. Voight*, 176 U.S. 498, 505 (1899). See *Russell*, at 61 N.E. 681.

37. The facts in *Russell*, 61 N.E. 682.

38. On which, see Richard A. Epstein, "The Historical Origins and Economic Structure of the Workers' Compensation Laws," 16 *Ga. L. Rev.* 775 (1982), where I discuss the voluntary adoption of workers compensation plans during this period in many mining and railroad companies.

39. *Voight*, 176 U.S. 505–506.

40. L.R. 19 Eq. 462, 465 (1875) (itself a complex dispute over royalties from the sale of patented machine).

41. *Russell*, 61 N.E. 683.

42. 46 N.E. 17 (Ind. 1896).

43. See *Vosburg v. Putney*, 50 N.W. 403 (1891) (this remains so today).

44. 59 N.E. 1058 (Ind. 1901).

45. Ibid.

46. For a discussion of these matters in greater detail, see Richard A. Epstein, *Mortal Peril: Our Inalienable Right to Health Care?* (1997), ch. 4.

47. 61 N.E. 674, 677 (1901).

48. Ibid., 678 (1901).

49. See *Great Lakes Gas Transmission Partnership*, Op. No. 366, 57 Fed. Energy Reg. Comm'n,¶61.101, *aff'd in part and rev'd in part*, Opin. No. 368, 57 FERC ¶61, 141 (1991), defended in Daniel F. Spulber, "Pricing and the Incentive to Invest in Pipelines after *Great Lakes*," 15 *Energy L. Rev.* 377 (1994).

50. See Frank Ramsay, "A Contribution to the General Theory of Taxation," 37 *Economic Journal* 47 (1927). For a modern exposition as applied to rate regulation, see Kenneth E. Train, *Optimal Regulation: The Economic Theory of Natural Monopoly* (1991), pp. 115–145; for judicial application see *Burlington Northern Railroad Co v. Interstate Commerce Commission*, 985 F.2d 589 (D.C. Cir. 1993) (Williams J.).

51. See Train, *Optimal Regulation*, pp. 123–125.

52. Michael K. Kellogg, John Thorne, & Peter Huber, *Federal Telecommunications Law* (1992), p. 12.

53. Ibid., p. 13.

54. *Chesapeake & Potomac Tel. Co. v. Baltimore & Ohio Tel. Co.*, 7 A. 809 (Md. 1886).

55. *St. Louis, Iron Mountain, & Southern Ry. v. Southern Express Co.*, 117 U.S. 1 (1886).

56. Ibid., 23.

57. Ibid., 24.

58. Communications Act of 1934, ch. 652, 48 Stat. 1064 (1934), codified as amended at 47 U.S.C. §151. The Communications Act replaced the earlier Radio Act of 1927, 44 Stat. 1162 (1927).

59. Kellogg, Thorne & Huber, *Telecommunications*, §1.1, noting that the three "pillars" of the operation of the Bell system under the 1934 Act were a *protected franchise*, *quarantine*, and *cradle-to-grave* regulation.

60. See *United States v. American Tel. and Tel. Company* (Modification of Final Judgment), 552 F. Supp. 226 (D.D.C. 1982).

61. Telecommunications Act of 1996, Pub. L. No. 104–104, 110 Stat. 56, 47 U.S.C. §§251 & 252.

62. "FCC, In Matter of Local Competition Provisions in the Telecommunications Act of 1996: First Report and Order," 11 *FCC Rcd.* 15, 499 (August 8, 1996).

63. *Iowa Utilities Board v. FCC*, 120 F.3d 753 (8th Cir. 1997).

64. *Southwestern Bell Tel. Co. v. FCC*, 19 F.3d 1475, 1480 (D.C. Cir. 1994).

65. For further elaboration, see Hovenkamp, *Enterprise and American Law*, pp. 152–159.

66. *Wabash, St. Louis & Pacific Ry. v. Illinois*, 118 U.S. 557 (1886). I discuss this and the other commerce clause issues surrounding the ICA in Richard A. Epstein, "The Proper Scope of the Commerce Power," 73 *Va. L. Rev.* 1387, 1413–1421 (1987).

67. Ch. 104, §4, 24 Stat. 379, 380 (1887).

68. *Cincinnati, New Orleans & Tex. Pac. Ry.*, 162 U. S. 184; *Interstate Commerce Comm'n v Cincinnati, New Orleans & Texas Pacific Railway*, 167 U.S. 479 (1897).

69. 168 U.S. 144 (1897).

70. Ibid., 165.

71. See Ely, *Fuller*.

72. See Lawrence Friedman, *A History of American Law* (2d ed. 1985), p. 452.

73. See Transportation Act of 1920, ch. 91, 41 Stat. 456, upheld in *Wisconsin R. R. Comm'n v. Chicago, Burlington, & Quincy R. R.*, 257 U.S. 563 (1922).

74. See, Letwin, *English Common Law*. See also, for a more critical view of the English precedents, Michael Trebilcock, *The Common Law of Restraint of Trade: A Legal and Economic Analysis* (1986).

75. 1 P. Wms. 181, 24 Eng. Rep. 347 (HLE, 1711).

76. [1893] 1 Ch. 630, aff'd [1894] A,C, 535.

77. Ibid., 536.

78. Sherman Anti-Trust Act of 1890, c. 647, 26 Stat. 209, 15 U.S.C. §1–11.

79. *United States v. E.C. Knight Co.*, 156 U.S. 1 (1895).

80. *Addyston Pipe & Steel Co. v. United States*, 175 U.S. 211 (1899).

81. See Richard A. Epstein, "The Commerce Power," pp. 1432–1442.

82. 120 F. 721 (1903) , aff'd 193 U.S. 197 (1904).

83. See, e.g., Gilmore, *Death of Contract*, pp. 12–14.

84. Christopher Columbus Langdell, "The Northern Securities Case and the Sherman Anti-Trust Act," 16 *Harv. L. Rev.* 539, 553 (1903).

85. Ibid., p. 553.

86. Kellogg, Thorne, & Huber, *Telecommunications*, p. 139.

87. 224 U.S. 383 (1912).

88. Ibid., 395.

89. Ibid., 405–406.

90. Ibid., 401.

91. David Reifen & Andrew N. Kleit, "Terminal Railroad Revisited: Foreclosure of an Essential Facility or Simple Horizontal Monopoly?," 33 *J. Law & Econ.* 419, 435 (1990). The authors answered "horizontal monopoly."

92. Ibid., p. 411.

93. 94 U. S. 113 (1876).

94. For discussion, see *Duquesne Light Co. v. Barasch*, 488 U.S. 299 (1989); *Jersey Central Power & Light Co. v. Fed. Energy Reg. Comm'n*, 810 F.2d 1168 (D.C. Cir. 1987).

95. 169 U.S. 466 (1898).

96. Ibid., 546.

97. 320 U.S. 591 (1944).

98. Ibid., 602.

99. Ibid., 596–597.

100. 836 F.2d 1386 (D.C. Cir. 1988).

101. Federal Communications Act §2(b), 47 U.S.C. 152(b) (1996).

102. *Louisiana Pub. Serv. Comm'n v. FCC*, 476 U.S. 355 (1986), construing Section 2(b) of the Federal Communications Act, 47 U.S.C. §152(b). Section 2(b) survives unscathed under the Telecommunications Act of 1996.

103. For the new sections of the Act, and commentary thereon, see Peter W. Huber, Michael K. Kellogg & John Thorne, *The Telecommunications Act of 1996* (1996).

104. See 47 U.S.C. §271. Under the Act GTE, unlike the Bell operating companies, has the immediate right to enter long-distance markets.

105. Ibid., §252(d)(1).

106. Ibid., §§251(a)(1)&(c)(1); 252(a).

107. *First Report and Order, Implementation of local Competition Provisions in the Telecommunication Act of 1996*, FCC Docket No. 96–98 (August 8, 1996).

108. Ibid., §§51.503, 51,505. For criticism of that approach, see J. Gregory Sidak & Daniel F. Spulber, "The Tragedy of the Telecommons: Government Pricing of Unbundled Network Elements Under the Telecommunications Act of 1996," 97 *Colum. L. Rev.* 1081 (1997).

109. 47 U.S.C. §153 (45).

110. Ibid., §251(c)(3).

111. Ibid., §251(c)(4).

112. *Iowa Utilities Board v. FCC*, 120 F.3d 753, 813 (8ᵗʰ Cir. 1997), vacating FCC rule 51.315 (b)–(f) of the FCC's First Report and Order.

113. *Promoting Wholesale Competition Through Open Access Non-Discriminatory Transmission Services by Public Utilities,* Fed. Energy Comm'n Order No. 888 (April 24, 1996). See also *United Distribution Companies v. FERC,* 88 F.3d 1105 (D. C. 1996), noting that this recovery could be done by "amortization over time."

114. Ibid., Section J, Stranded Costs.

115. For my comments, see Richard A. Epstein, *Mortal Peril,* chs. 3, 4, 7.

116. 47 U.S.C. §254(c)(1).

117. Ibid., §254 (c)(1)(A–D).

118. James K. Glassman, "Gore's Internet Fiasco," *Washington Post,* June 2, 1998, p. 13.

119. Ibid., §254(e).

120. Ibid., §254(d), under rules developed at length in the Universal Service Order.

121. On which see, *National Rural Telecom Ass'n v. FCC,* 988 F.2d 174 (D. C. 1993).

EPILOGUE

1. 77 *Edinburgh Rev.* 224 (1843), quoted in Jacob Viner, "An Intellectual History of Laissez-Faire," 3 *J. Law & Econ.* 45, 55 (1960).

TABLE OF CASES

❖ ❖ ❖

INDEX

❖ ❖ ❖